CLARENDON

[signature]

Tom Beaumont James

'that delicious parke (which was accounted the best of England)'
Sir Philip Sidney, writing *Arcadia* nearby, 1577

'The habitation of Kings is levelled with dust and all the
proud revelry of a court has given way to the hooting
of the owl and the croaking of the raven ...'

John Britton, 1801

A VIEW of MAJOR GEN.[L] BATHURST'S CLARENDON PARK WILTS.

General Bathurst's house in 1791. The mansion took this form, possibly in 1717, under Peter Bathurst (d. 1748), who enlarged a pre-existing house. The mansion and the Scots pines mark this out as a post-medieval landscape, but the presence of fallow deer in the foreground provide a link to Clarendon's medieval faunal heritage. (Copyright Salisbury and South Wiltshire Museum collection)

Clarendon

Landscape of Kings

Tom Beaumont James and Christopher Gerrard

WIND*gather*
PRESS

Published by: Windgather Press Ltd, 29 Bishop Road, Bollington,
Macclesfield, Cheshire SK10 5NX

Distributed by: Central Books Ltd, 99 Wallis Road, London E9 5LN

British Library Cataloguing-in-Publication Data

A catalogue record for this book is available from the British Library

hardback	ISBN 10	1–905119–10–0
	ISBN 13	978–1–905119–10–3
paperback	ISBN 10	1–905119–11–9
	ISBN 13	978–1–905119–11–0

Designed, typeset and originated by Carnegie Publishing Ltd,
Chatsworth Road, Lancaster

Printed and bound by Cambridge Printing, Cambridge

Contents

List of Figures

We dedicate this work to Clarendon people
past, present and future

Acknowledgements

This book is jointly written by the two authors, but many institutions and individuals made substantial contributions. First we thank Andrew and Barbara Christie-Miller, who have unstintingly supported us. Our fieldwork was designed not to disrupt farming and woodland management of the estate, but on occasions we called for help which has always been willingly given. We thank all the staff of the Clarendon estate for their tolerance and good humour as students appeared in the fields and woodland, and volunteers on the palace site, sometimes for weeks on end. In particular, Felicity Rickard and Colin Marshall steered us through administration and finance, Roy Perks explained the arts of modern game-keeping, Derek and Linda Young allowed us into their home and granary, Bob Culley identified several sites described here for the first time, while Richard, Anne and Geoffrey Price helped to map coppice boundaries and looked out facts and figures while tending recalcitrant sheep and lugging fertiliser sacks of medieval roof tile hither and thither. Anne worked selflessly with the finds and has supported us throughout. Archaeology so often creates new friendships and that has certainly been the case at Clarendon.

Colleagues in the Faculty of Social Sciences at the University of Winchester (formerly King Alfred's College) shared their time and skills and we thank them warmly for their work in the field, laboratory and store. We thank Philip Marter for all aspects of the project from fieldwalking to standing remains recording with Michelle Collings, and for preparing the reconstruction drawings for the display boards; Alex Turner for leading geophysical survey; Nick Thorpe and Richard Greatorex for shovel-pit testing; Tony King and Geoff Couling for topographic survey; Keith and Myra Wilkinson for assistance with environmental queries and for facilitating volunteer effort; and to other colleagues for help with many other tasks. Richard McConnell, Ross Turle, Jane Lickman and Jane McWilliams collated much of the information for the 1996 report, for which Clive Pedlar's photographic record of buildings proved invaluable.

Volunteers, both local and from Winchester, sieved and shovelled hundreds of tons of spoil from previous excavations. They have been heroic and we thank them unreservedly. There are too many to mention here by name, but for his management of the finds processing on-site and for washing and bagging the finds in his Winchester house, we would especially like to single out Colin Anderson. Archaeology is about teamwork and never more so here.

In making the work at Clarendon possible the combination of the provision of the Clarendon landscape by Mr Christie-Miller for training of undergraduates and postgraduates in practical archaeology skills and the co-operation of the staff in the archaeology department at Winchester was of mutual benefit. Financial support for work on the palace site came from English Heritage under Section 24 of the Ancient Monuments and Archaeological Areas Act 1979. English Heritage Inspector Amanda Chadburn had the foresight to see that the work at Clarendon could be done, and the ruins removed from their *Buildings at Risk Register* through co-operation with the Estate. English Heritage and the Estate shared financial responsibility for works which overall cost towards £500,000. This enabled conservation of the surviving masonry, undertaken initially by St Blaise Ltd of Evershot (Dorset), but mainly over five years by Liam Hornsby who toiled on site, often alone, to consolidate the flint and ashlar ruins under the supervision first of John Ashurst and latterly of Martin Smith of R.J. Smith and Co., Whitchurch (Hants). Staff from R.J. Smith and Co. completed tasks in 2004–5. The Society of Antiquaries of London and the Society for Medieval Archaeology funded work such as dendrochronology, as did the King Alfred's College Research Fund. The AHRB funded a full-time doctoral research project into the medieval and early modern documentation for Clarendon Park and Forest, which was successfully completed by Amanda Richardson in 2003 and published in 2005. She advised on many points in this text, and we are most grateful to her. TBJ is indebted to the AHRB for their financial support for research leave to write up Clarendon.

For their help in marshalling such a variety of sources, we are grateful to staff at the Hampshire Record Office, Winchester; The National Archives, Kew; the Wiltshire and Swindon Record Office and the Archaeology Service at Trowbridge (especially Roy Canham, Duncan Coe and Helena Cave-Penney); the Bodleian Library; the National Register of Archives; the Wiltshire Biological Records Centre; the former Royal Commission on Historical Monuments (England), Swindon (especially Mark Corney, Jo Donachie and Dave McOmish); the British Museum; and the Salisbury and South Wiltshire Museum (especially Peter Saunders and David Algar). In particular we would also like to thank Sarah Grinsted of the Wiltshire Wildlife Trust, Casper Johnson for his help in the field, Sally Scott-White and Jean Wall of the Wiltshire Biological Records centre, Rod Stern of the British Bryological Society, Janet Forbes and Keith Alexander. Many of the ecological insights here were first made by David Clements in his contribution to the 1996 report.

Other specialists have also contributed their expertise. Ian Tyers (ARCUS) and Daniel Miles and Martin Bridge (Oxford Dendrochronology Laboratory) struggled with the Clarendon tree-ring sequences to provide exciting new insights. They worked closely with Pamela Slocombe and Dorothy Treasure of the Wiltshire Buildings Record on dating and recording Clarendon buildings. The team of archaeologists who worked on the latest finds from our fieldwork included Yvonne Beadnell (who produced the fine illustrations of recent finds); Rachel Cocks and Rebecca Conway (sorting flots); Geoff Egan

Acknowledgements and Steve Minnitt (coins); Deborah Jacques (fish bones); Marek Lewcun (clay pipes); Louisa Gidney (animal bones); Alison and the late Ian Goodall (metalwork); Alejandra Gutiérrez (medieval and post-medieval pottery, bone objects, brick and roof tile, as well as drawing many of the figures in this volume); Jan Light (molluscs); Amanda Richardson (floor tile); Becky Scott (lithics); David Stocker, Tim Tatton-Brown and Gilbert Green (stonework); Jane Timby (Roman pottery); and Hugh Willmott (glass). Further specialist advice on particular finds was provided by staff at the Zoological Museum, University of Copenhagen, who confirmed the human identity of the well-travelled 'big-toe' from Clarendon. Our thanks go also to Peter Rowley-Conwy for putting us in touch with Danish bear specialists; Keith Dobney and Umberto Albarella discussed the Clarendon eagle and the consumption of wild birds in medieval England with us; while Paul Everson contributed to the landscape study.

Several people commented on extracts of the text. Joe Bettey, Simon Draper, Sally Forwood, Anthony Harding, Colin Haselgrove, Sam Lucy, Norman Parker, Carrie Smith, Paul Stamper and John Steane all contributed valuable insights and corrections. Colin Platt inspired the beginning of the project in 1977 and has supported it throughout with wise counsel. Regrettably John Charlton died in October 2004, before our work was complete, but his support over the entire thirty-year programme cannot be underestimated. He visited the site and gave advice right up to the end of his 95-year life: his photographs are unsurpassed. He was predeceased by Clarissa Lada-Grozicka (Borenius) who also shared many insights with us. Fortunately her twin brother and sister, Peter and Ursula, were able to join the party in June 2004 when we celebrated the culmination of the Clarendon Project with a feast in the Great Hall, generously given by Andrew and Barbara Christie-Miller. Few of our closest family and friends have escaped Clarendon over the years: most have come to the Park and worked there. Clarendon has on occasions overwhelmed family life. We are deeply grateful to you all.

TBJ
CMG

Abbreviations

ARCUS	Archaeological Research and Consultancy at the University of Sheffield
AWMCM	A. W. M. Christie-Miller
BL	British Library
BLO	Bodleian Library, Oxford
CCR	*Calendar of Close Rolls*
CEA	Clarendon Estate Archive
CFR	*Calendar of Fine Rolls*
CLR	*Calendar of Liberate Rolls*
CPR	*Calendar of Patent Rolls*
CSPD	*Calendar of State Papers Domestic*
FRC	Family Record Centre
GRO	Gloucestershire Record Office
HRO	Hampshire Record Office
KACAC	King Alfred's College Archaeological Consultancy
LPFD	*Letters and papers, foreign and domestic, of the reign of Henry VIII*
NMR	National Monuments Record
NRO	Northamptonshire Record Office
OUDCE	Oxford University Department for Continuing Education
PRFD	Probate Registry Family Division
RCHME	Royal Commission on Historic Monuments (England)
SCA	Salisbury Cathedral Archive
TNA:PRO	The National Archives: Public Record Office
UW	University of Winchester
WHWANHS	Wiltshire Heritage, Wiltshire Archaeological and Natural History Society Headquarters, Devizes Museum
WRL	Wiltshire Reference Library
WSRO	Wiltshire and Swindon Record Office

Preface

This book synthesises thirty years of research on Clarendon Park in Wiltshire. It is an account of that landscape from prehistory to the present day and an investigation of the origins of the royal palace, medieval life in the royal household and the subsequent fate of the park, through the study of archaeology, architecture and documents.

Tom Beaumont James began work on Clarendon in 1977, publishing the backlog of excavations with Annie Robinson in *Clarendon Palace: the History and Archaeology of a Medieval Palace and Hunting Lodge near Salisbury, Wiltshire* (1988). Christopher Gerrard managed fieldwork on the estate for seven years, until his move to Durham in 2000. At Clarendon we found a fieldwork project within striking distance of Winchester, where teaching and research combined and where students and staff might enjoy a single, multi-disciplinary, framework of investigation. Modern teaching ideals focus on infusing teaching with live research. Here we produced research from our teaching and pushed our scope well outside the later medieval period, involving ourselves in archival, library and museum studies and new architectural survey. By June 1996 the mass of new data we had accumulated was gathered in *Clarendon Park: Archaeology, History and Ecology*, a typescript report funded by English Heritage under the terms of a 'survey grant for presentation' which listed the sites and monuments inside the Park, ranging from scatters of worked prehistoric lithics identified during fieldwalking to the remnants of a dummy airfield surviving from the Second World War.

This volume draws on that 1996 compilation together with a later *Historic Landscape Management Plan* (1998) which set out specific suggestions as to how more sympathetic land management might be encouraged for the more important sites we had identified. Among those sites was the royal palace itself, then in a perilous state of collapse, where we have since excavated and removed some of the spoil heaps left by previous excavators in an attempt to make the site more 'legible', and managed a consolidation programme of the ruins there. This work was completed in summer 2005 and the site is now open to visitors from the Clarendon Way.

With this book twentieth-century investigations at Clarendon come to a close; we could have written very much more, but we hope the story presented here may tempt others one day to enjoy, as well as to work on, this unique corner of Wessex.

TBJ (University of Winchester), CMG (University of Durham), August 2006

'... that noble and pre-eminent mansion, the king's own, from
its name and prominent position called Clarendon ...'
                    Herbert of Bosham, 1164 (Robertson 1877, 278, trans.)

'There is a noble deerpark, near Salisbury
Called Clarendon from its clear high location
Here are twenty groves, enclosed,
Each a thousand paces round, a long mile for its circuit shows.'
          Michael Maschertus (d. 1598) (Camden, trans. Gough 1806, 134)

'... the best parke in the King's dominions ... seven miles about.
Here were twenty coppices, and every one a mile round ...'
                         John Aubrey, c. 1680, writing of the 1640s

'... being fix'd by the favour of a particular friend at so
beautiful a spot of ground as this of Clarendon Park ...'
                              Daniel Defoe, c. 1700

'Chlorendon ... a sweet and beautiful place'
                         William Stukeley, 3 August 1723

'The Ruins of the Palace are large and extensive, but so truly
ruins, that it is difficult to form an idea of any single part
of it alone excepted (that) called the Parliament Hall ...'
                    James Harris, in a letter to Lord Lyttleton,
                    20 December 1769 (BM Add MSS 18729)

'... here were enacted the Constitutions of Clarendon, the
first barrier raised against the claims of secular jurisdiction
by the See of Rome. The spirit awakened within these walls
ceased not until it had vindicated the authority of the laws and
accomplished the Reformation of the Church of England ...'
From the memorial erected at Clarendon Palace in 1844

'Clarendon ... the beautiful and picturesque seat'
Salisbury Journal 1860

'... one of the toughest jobs in the history
of archaeological excavation'
Ralph Whitlock of the 1930s excavations, 1955

'... it is hardly an exaggeration to say that
deterioration can go no further'
Baillie Reynolds, Chief Inspector of Ancient Monuments,
correspondence 1957 (PRO WORKS 14/1777)

CHAPTER ONE

Themes for a Landscape

....

Discovering England's greatest deer park

The visitor to Clarendon today finds a medieval landscape still recognisable and largely intact. Ancient, gnarled oaks survive here and there, relics of medieval and early modern landscaping. If the oak takes three centuries to grow, lives on for three hundred years and takes three centuries to die, these ancient standing trees may have been placed and seen by the long-gone monarchs who have a central place in this book. Yet, until now, this remarkable landscape has kept its secrets and has remained undiscovered. This book will, we hope, bring it to the attention of a new audience of people who care about historic landscapes.

Part of Clarendon's appeal is that it is 'legible': a multi-period landscape which can be 'read'. But it also enjoys historical resonance, and this is significant for all visitors. Until the Second World War generations of children learnt of the Constitutions of Clarendon (1164) and the Assize of Clarendon (1166) in history classes: the former as a step on the road to defining liberties of state in relation to church and papacy, and the latter presented as a foundation of legal organisation and the jury system. More recently, with increasing secularisation and a narrowing of differences between Catholic and Anglican, the Constitutions are cited less often.[1] Nevertheless, the name remains familiar to many because, as royal ownership ended, the title 'Earl of Clarendon' was first taken by the locally born Edward Hyde (1609–74), who briefly owned the estate following the Restoration, when he held the office of Chancellor. Clarendon House, his London creation, was reckoned by John Evelyn to be the finest private house of that era. To the modern ear 'Clarendon' is associated with the Clarendon Press in Oxford and with businesses, schools and streets to which Hyde's title has become attached.[2] Echoes of Clarendon are found worldwide, in South Carolina and Tasmania, where one of the great Georgian houses of Australia, completed for James Cox in 1838, took its name.[3] Yet even among archaeologists and historians Clarendon, Wiltshire, is largely uncharted territory; the name is far better known than the place.

FIGURE I.
Salisbury Cathedral from the ruined palace across park and city: striking elements in a giant Gothic landscape emerging in the thirteenth century. The roof, tower and spire of the cathedral stand out clearly and the top of the spire is level with the palace on the hills above. In the eleventh and twelfth centuries this landscape was sparsely populated: no cathedral, no city of New Sarum, which then developed on the road to Clarendon Park. (Photograph by Fran Halsall)

The Clarendon story

We begin with a short narrative: a summary of Clarendon's long history. Clarendon Park, in south-east Wiltshire, was already an ancient landscape when it was favoured by the medieval kings of England as their greatest hunting park. Tools of hunter-gatherers found in the gravels at the margins of the park pre-date the earliest monuments, a cluster of Neolithic long barrows towards the north of the park (see Chapter Two). Bronze Age round barrows on Clarendon's boundaries invite speculation that what we see today were ancient parcels of land when Stonehenge was being built nearby. Scatters of stone tools and flint flakes remind us of daily life in prehistory, from the farmers of the Neolithic to their successors in the Iron Age, whose farmsteads were developed by the Romans from the first to the third centuries AD. Little of Clarendon's hidden pre-medieval landscape, with its residential, industrial and farming complexes, has been investigated through excavation, though Iron Age and Roman field systems are still readily discernible, particularly from the air. By the late sixth century AD post-Roman Clarendon seems fleetingly to have lain in a border area between the pagan Anglo-Saxon world of eastern Britain and the North Sea, and the Christian Celtic world of the west country and around the Irish Sea. At this period Clarendon gained its name, derived, perhaps, from *claefren dun*, the clover-covered hill, a name which suggests that the Anglo-Saxons had made clearances and managed the regenerated forest which had engulfed the remains left by their Roman predecessors. Later Saxon royal and ecclesiastical centres lay near Clarendon: a minster and possibly a royal centre at neighbouring Alderbury, for which Clarendon was probably developed as a hunting preserve. These discoveries, from prehistory to the Saxon period, are connected for the first time in our landscape study.

The park, then, is rich in prehistoric and Roman remains, but it is the historic period which excites the greatest archaeological attention here. Soon after the Norman Conquest, when we first find its name written down, Clarendon was already known to medieval royalty. It quickly developed from what was probably a mere hunting box set in a Saxon hunting landscape into a palace complex from which the realm could be governed; the grandest western royal residence in England, an expression of ultimate power in which deer, the kings' beasts, grazed in exceptional numbers in a giant Gothic landscape which visually encompassed the new city of Salisbury (see Chapter Three). From the twelfth century the greatest deer park in medieval England was developed at Clarendon, with a palace at its heart. Here, as well as the day-to-day business of councils and parliaments, kings enjoyed privacy in a managed, sparsely occupied landscape in which family and guests could indulge their passion for sport. Hunting and privacy were joint foci of this vast landscape, which dwarfed the retinues of those who visited. Hunting took place in open country and in woodland, with hounds and hawks and perhaps with eagles. Large areas of the park were visible from the mighty palace complex, perched on the northern scarp of the downland. Sculpture, exotic pottery, the bones of hunting dogs and hawks, and evidence of a rich diet of meat and varied deep-sea and freshwater seafood all demonstrate the highly exceptional and international quality of medieval palace life at Clarendon. In this book we chart the Norman creation of the deer park and the building of the palace, and strive for an evocative picture of the medieval hunt: of fallow bucks and does, and roe deer, and other more exotic fauna. In 1289, for example, gyr-falcons captured two cranes, whose heads were presented to Queen Eleanor at Clarendon Palace.

While medieval Clarendon was a landscape of power, a pleasure-park and palace, it was also a place of government and came to resonate in English history (see Chapter Four). Here, in 1164, Henry II framed the 'Constitutions of Clarendon' and argued with Archbishop Thomas Becket over papal power in England, outwitting Becket by thrusting upon him written documents to seal; two years later the Assize of Clarendon established jury presentment in every township and vill. Thereafter, kings visited regularly and left their mark on park and palace. King John brought his family; his son Henry III converted the Romanesque palace to Gothic splendour; Edward II summoned a parliament and Edward III and the Black Prince visited during the catastrophe of the Black Death and the contemporary English military triumphs in France; traditionally Edward III also visited with captive kings John of France and David of Scotland. Henry VI suffered his first attack of chronic mental illness at Clarendon in 1453, after which the palace was used infrequently and became derelict. Tudor and Stuart monarchs continued to exploit the park: no fewer than 340 deer were slaughtered in a day when Queen Elizabeth visited in 1574. Stripped of its deer and many trees during the Civil War and Interregnum, the park passed out of royal hands to the architects of the Restoration, George Monck and Edward Hyde. Hyde, 1st Earl of Clarendon and the famous chronicler of the English Civil War, was grandfther to queens Mary and Anne.

Post-medieval Clarendon is rich in documentary and landscape sources, including the earliest map of Clarendon Park, made c. 1650 (see Chapter Five). Buildings and structural timberwork survive from this period, dated by typology and tree-rings. Tudor, Stuart and Interregnum buildings all incorporate fragments of much older structures. The Bathurst family, owners of the estate from c. 1700 to 1900, laid out Tory and then military landscapes of regimented avenues, appropriate for a family whose heads fought in the Seven Years War (1756–63) and in the Crimea (Inkerman and Sebastopol) a century later, after which they invited volunteer troops to exercise in the park.

The mansion house, built for Peter Bathurst in the early eighteenth century, is set in its own landscape, at a distance from the Gothic ruins of the medieval palace. With the benefit of extensive and newly discovered private archives, including building accounts, sale catalogues, house and probate inventories, building campaigns at the mansion and elsewhere on the estate can be revealed and the intentions of their owners explored. Landscapes and personal histories are intimately linked. Georgian and Victorian records and surviving buildings, modern farming structures and landscape management, demonstrate how successive generations raised money against the estate, and how they developed its resources. Military men may have reigned supreme in the mansion as the Empire expanded (see Chapter Six) but when the intractable problems of the agricultural recession of the late nineteenth century took hold they brought Bathurst ownership to an end, and new owners took on the challenge of the estate in the twentieth century. This initiated new investment, which reached its apogee with the creation of the mansion's ballroom in 1926, but which was halted by the great depression, untimely death and the Second World War. Military activity in that war included a giant tank-trap ditch (the digging of which revealed more of an important Anglo-Saxon cemetery), and a dummy airfield to divert raiders from attacking nearby airforce installations.

Objectives

In writing a book with wide period interests and diverse content, our aims have been threefold. First, previous publications on Clarendon have not been able to address either prehistoric, Roman or later post-medieval developments. The publication of the excavations undertaken at the palace site between the 1930s and 1960s was intended 'to bring to life the medieval royal palace ... and show what manner of buildings once stood there, and how its royal owners used and embellished it'.[4] The broader chronological context was not addressed there for lack of archaeological fieldwork at that time and we aim to redress that here by presenting a study of the full chronology of the Clarendon landscape from the Palaeolithic to the present day. In Wessex, prehistoric archaeology has a high public and scholarly profile, so the emphasis here on the historic period is unusual. Even on the national stage few studies in British post-medieval archaeology take their work beyond 1750, as we have done here, embracing a long-term view of people and place.

Second, we aim to unite archaeological monuments with their wider landscape. Compared to castle studies, there are few books on medieval palaces written from the point of view of the archaeologist or historian. The classic compilation of historical materials, with schematic phase plans and brief narrative accounts, often based on original documentary research relating to medieval and Tudor palaces, was *The History of the King's Works*.[5] Landscape was not a feature of that great work, written by a scholar who dug at Clarendon as a teenager. Since then there have been individual architectural and art historical studies[6] and more synthetic, interdisciplinary, period-specific texts on medieval palaces.[7] There are also accounts of specific medieval landscapes such as parks, forests and woods written by historical ecologists,[8] economic historians[9] and landscape historians,[10] and some general interpretations of these landscapes' associated conceptual meanings[11] and cultural associations,[12] but there is still only a handful of case studies of high-status medieval buildings which take full account of their setting.[13] With the benefit of recent extensive fieldwork and documentary study we firmly reject the notion that the historic landscape at Clarendon was merely a blank canvas, a backdrop for affairs of State. Like artefacts and buildings, the 'natural' landscape was manipulated, not merely to illustrate social conditions but to create and sustain them, in part at least through symbolism, the hidden meaning of which requires our interpretation.[14]

Third, because so much of what has been published to date on Clarendon Park is site-based reportage, an interdisciplinary approach to landscape recommends itself and is at the core of our activities. Accordingly, this text is founded upon results from a wide range of techniques, including aerial photography, cartographic analysis, dendrochronology, documentary study, fieldwalking, hedgerow survey, geophysics, oral history, standing buildings survey, and the study of field names. What we have experienced is a dialogue between disciplines, one which combines an understanding not just of the economic and social functions of the park but also an appreciation of its conceptual environment.

There have been several recent projects which might lay claim to a similar set of goals. Other archaeological studies of 'micro-regions' in central southern England include work in the north of Wiltshire at Avebury,[15] in the parishes of Fyfield and Overton,[16] in the Vale of the White Horse[17] and on the Marlborough Downs,[18] as well projects on Salisbury Plain, nearer to Clarendon, and further south on Cranborne Chase.[19] Each takes a slightly different route through the data but in our case we believe we can offer the reader an intimate knowledge of a particular place, an understanding of the flow of change through time aided by maps and photographs (see Chapter Eight).[20] Our main purpose in doing so has been to document when moments of change occurred and ask 'why?' as well as to consider the circumstances under which prolonged periods of stasis take hold in the landscape. Is the landscape really timeless? Do political events have any effect on landscape and settlement? How do external influences have an impact? These are themes to which we will return at the end of the book.

Another theme, not peculiar to Clarendon but exemplified here, is *pleasure*. Pleasure in landscapes and vistas, flora and fauna, in buildings and furnishings, in entertainment, food and sport. All this takes place in the slowly evolving theatre of Clarendon's oaks and coppices, its gardens, farmland and sheets of water. Clarendon was, and remains, a beautiful as well as a sporting landscape. The medieval palace and its giant park were pleasure grounds on the grandest scale, dedicated to physical pursuits: élite hunting and coursing, celebrations and feasting, and private relaxation for royalty away from the public gaze. The seven or so chapels, and nearby Ivychurch Priory, which provided clergy for those chapels, are a reminder of its role as a haven for spiritual renewal. The palace provided home territory for the execution of royal business, with the pleasures of the chase near at hand. Palace and landscape provided opportunities for experimentation in décor and for acculturation of contemporary design tastes as exemplified in twelfth-century sculpture, thirteenth-century floor tiles, gypsum plasterwork with superimposed cycles of wall paintings, and images in the painted glass windows in the palace. Nor did pleasure end with the fall of the palace, as is shown in Chapters Five and Six.

A particular feature of the Clarendon story is of changing attitudes to archaeological monuments, especially medieval ones. The palace evolved from a hub of royal administration and business, as well as a home, to a ruin quarried for its building materials, becoming an antiquarian curiosity and academic project, before finally emerging as 'national heritage' under revisions to Ancient Monuments legislation in the twentieth century. Clarendon is a case study in the development of these concepts, the application of their associated management practices and the contribution and wishes of the owners who must, even today, balance questions of access against the economics of an income-generating private estate.

All landscapes are, in a sense, multi-vocal. Today they speak to owners, occupants, users and visitors in different ways, just as they have done in the past (see Chapter Seven). The park which antiquarians were happy to call 'noble', 'pre-eminent', 'delicious', 'the beste parke in the King's dominions', has in recent years attracted film directors such as Stanley Kubrick (*Barry Lyndon*, 1975), documentary-makers such as Edward Windsor and historians such as Simon Schama. Each extracted something different from the same landscape, created a different kind of narrative which they saw as novel. In that sense, this is not *the* story of Clarendon, but *a* story, which offers wider insight into the landscape history of southern England.

Decoding Clarendon's geography

Looking westwards from the palace ruins at the heart of Clarendon Park the spire of Salisbury cathedral rises from the valley below, brightly lit by the morning sun (Figures 2 and 3). Even before the cathedral was begun in 1220 the Conqueror, Henry I, Henry II and Thomas Becket, and King John stood on this very spot. Later Edward III and the Black Prince came and would have seen the cathedral spire. Many curious visitors since have braved the dense undergrowth and wandered among the collapsed buildings. But why did they come? What led them here? And what became of the landscape and the palace buildings?

At first glance the modern countryside is an arbitrary pattern of downland and woodland, of grass and trees. But Clarendon has its own private language and, once learnt, that language decodes the view. Well-travelled tracks lead here, knobbled flints protruding from white chalk paths, deeply incised and overhung with vegetation. Semi-natural and 'ancient' woodland, the remnants of medieval coppices, conceal criss-crossing banks and ditches of antiquity (Figure 4). Northwards, once barren downland pasture is now transformed by fertilisers and the arable fields there are broken up by wooded shooting belts. In the purple linseed you can make out lines and shapes, the shadows

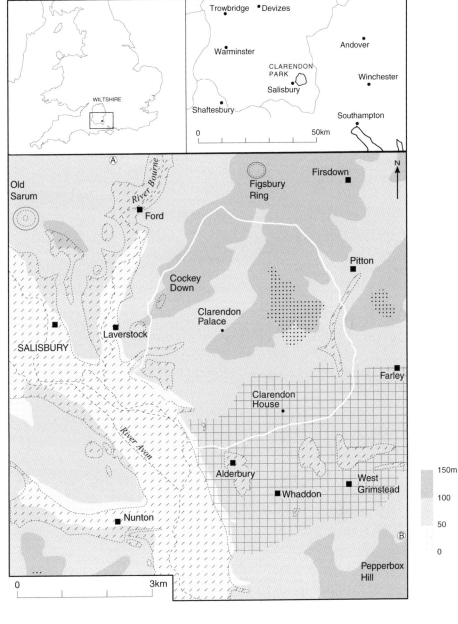

FIGURE 2.
Clarendon Park. The medieval deer park, against a background of geology and contours. Geographical determinism is no longer seen as the key to landscape development, but the downland to the north, with its thin soils, was cleared early of trees to locate Neolithic long barrows, and later served as pasture for deer and sheep. The southern clays became medieval wood pasture and were exploited from an early date for brick-making. (Drawn by Alejandra Gutiérrez)

Geology: all chalk, except for:

Chalk with flint   Alluvium and valley gravels   London and Reading clays

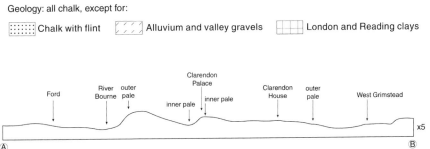

of more ancient fields. Beyond that downland, to the north and west, lie Laverstock and the Winterbournes, sheltered villages by the river Bourne which flows southwards into the Hampshire Avon. The palace which medieval royalty enjoyed exists now largely in the mind, but enough remains to fire the imagination to rebuild its walls, replace the furnishings, restore the garden and understand this lost palace and landscape.

This is a special piece of English countryside: the largest of some 150 deer parks owned by the monarchy in the Middle Ages. Overlooking Salisbury Plain to the west, Clarendon was the grandest royal residence in western England (Figure 5) and one of only three palaces which remained in royal hands throughout the Middle Ages. The medieval palace complex at Westminster was urban, its buildings on a larger scale than Clarendon, and was the main palace for the medieval kings of England, but, given subsequent development, it is hard to visualise it today. At Woodstock, the palace was levelled and much of the park drowned in eighteenth-century lake-making. Yet the plan of Clarendon palace survives and its special quality stems from the recognisable, extant medieval landscape which surrounds it (Figure 6). Clarendon Park was not broken up until the middle of the seventeenth century; most of its woodland has not been cleared and converted to arable. It survived the Civil War and the fashions of landscape grounds of the eighteenth century, adapting

FIGURE 5.
Reconstruction of the great courtyard c. 1275, at the palace's greatest extent. At that date it would have had red, brown and some green roof tiles of fired clay, over rendered white walls with ashlar corners and buttresses. The steep roofs were previously shingled with oak from the adjacent forest. (Drawn by Phil Marter)

FIGURE 6.
Vertical aerial
photograph of the
north-west sector of
Clarendon Park (a) *left*
and interpretation (b)
opposite. Archaeological
features of many
different periods are
superimposed and
remain visible in the
modern landscape.
Some elements of
earlier landscapes are
reused, for example in
the alignment of the
medieval park pale.
Presence and absence
of cropmarks depends
mostly on crop type.
(Photograph courtesy
of Simmons Aerofilms.
Neg 231.168; copyright
Wiltshire County
Council)

successfully to successive generations' demands, to emerge as a sporting estate since the nineteenth century. Only the railway, in 1846, and the upgrading of the Southampton Road (the Alderbury bypass) have cut through the park, and only towards its south-western margin.

Clarendon Park lies in the wooded border country of south-east Wiltshire. The 90-metre contour runs along the base of the northern downland scarp below the inner park which surrounds the palace. Cockey Down rises, across the valley north of the palace, to over 120 m. Exceptionally, the modern estate of Clarendon Park, which covers some 1821 ha (4500 acres), still lies very

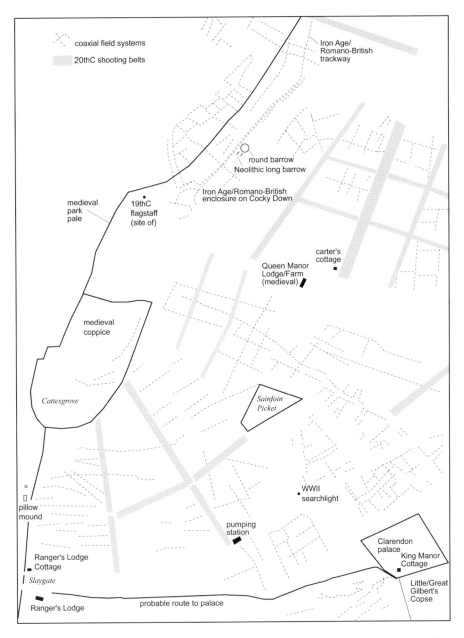

largely within the mighty earthworks of the medieval park. The park straddles a south-west/north-east divide between two zones of contrasting landscape character, upland and valley, Wiltshire in miniature. The north part of the park, as chalk downland, is an elevated, rolling landscape with light, thin, well-drained soils more recently associated with arable and sheep farming but historically called 'launds'[21] and used as grazing for deer. To the south and east, where most of the medieval and later woodland was concentrated, the chalk is capped with clay-with-flints, while the southern part of the park is on London Clays (London and Reading Beds). Here the soils and geology are better suited to a mixed economy of woodland activities and dairy farming, closer in character to the New Forest.[22] There is a long tradition of wood pasture in this part of the park and the clay has been extracted for brick-making as well as for the local fuller's earth, which the seventeenth-century antiquary Aubrey thought 'cleanseth [cloth] better than Woburne earthe in Bedfordshire'.[23] When a new mansion was developed in this south-eastern area of the estate in the eighteenth century, one of the attractions was the potential for the creation of a new lake which could take its water from a spring site there and exploit the poor drainage of the impermeable clay subsoils.

Looking at the park on a modern Ordnance Survey map, it is the lack of settlement which is striking. Dwellings and farms are widely dispersed across the landscape, with only two notable clusters of buildings at Clarendon House (south) and at the Four Cottages (east). Most people who live here work on the estate in some capacity or other; the rest rent property. About two-thirds of the land in the park is under arable, the remainder being either under commercial forestry plantations and woodland or pasture. Crudely put, these three different land uses run in bands; arable and game shooting in the north and north-west, a central sector of woodland and forestry and, in the south-east, eighteenth-century parkland and the mansion, with its lake and gardens. The combination of geology, soils and land use then creates 'windows' of varying quality on to the underlying archaeology. Thus, archaeology is best visible from the air in the north, where thin chalk soils combine with arable, but is masked by the tree canopy in the centre of the estate where surprisingly crisp earthworks often survive in the undergrowth.

Navigating across the estate is no easy matter. Members of the general public who visit walk along the Clarendon Way, a public footpath from Winchester to Salisbury which crosses the estate from Pitton, in the east, via the Palace, exiting by the Ranger's Gate towards Salisbury. Otherwise, a system of permits, for the Wild Garden near the mansion, for example, allows access. There are no public roads, but there are some 17.5 km (11 miles) of single carriageway roads and tracks. In the summer of 1951 an excursion of the Wiltshire Archaeological Society by coach and private cars to view the palace ruins began hopefully enough with a journey across the estate through 'narrow but very pleasant woodland roads', but ended with an almost impassable footpath 'through a thick undergrowth of trees and shrubs' which had been specially cleared to enable access. Following a tour with John Charlton the visitors 'extricated the numerous cars from the narrow roads – a matter of some difficulty'.[24] Frustrations like these, familiar to every visitor, help to keep Clarendon a private place.

Administratively Clarendon is also a curiosity. It has never been an ecclesiastical parish and until 1650 remained a lay, royal enclave where churchmen came by invitation only. In the post-medieval period, and with a population scattered round its margins, divided by valleys and downs, Clarendon people were affiliated to a number of surrounding parishes and some were extraparochial, affiliated to the Dean of Salisbury. In 1858 Clarendon became a

FIGURE 7.
Outer park pale. The
park was enclosed by
a massive earthwork
bank and ditch 16.5
km (10.2 miles) long,
begun in the twelfth
century and certainly
in its present form
before 1350. Parts of
this still stand today
to a height of 3.5 m.
(Photograph by Fran
Halsall)

civil parish virtually coterminous with the medieval park, the area studied here.[25]

To ease the challenge of identifying the sites mentioned in this book, four distinct zones are referred to constantly in the text. The first is the palace precinct, the formerly walled environs which immediately surrounded the palace ruins and their garden platform. Today this area, in the centre of the park and immediately adjacent to the Clarendon Way, is fenced off with access through kissing-gates. The second zone is the 'inner' park, an area partially contiguous with the palace precinct and surrounded by the banks and ditches of a pale which was designed to keep deer *out*. Third, there is the park, the area defined by its own bank and ditch dug to keep deer *in*, with the palace precinct and inner park at its heart (Figure 7). And lastly, there is Clarendon Forest, which extended well beyond the deer park, as far as the river Bourne to the west and through Bentley Wood to the east, a northern extension of the Hampshire New Forest. In the early thirteenth century, this forest was subdivided into the separate administrations of Buckholt, Clarendon and Melchet, with the chief residence at Clarendon Palace.[26] Previously, and throughout the later medieval period these areas contained a wide range of settlements, from entire villages to a single hermit 'at Bentelwode by Claryndon' in 1334.[27] They were far from continuous woodland, the term 'forest' here referring to jurisdiction rather than flora. Nor did all the land belong to the king, though the bounds described and administered by royal forest officers defined an area over which the king reserved the right to hunt certain animals.[28] Deer were regularly taken in the forest and venison carried surprising distances, as in 1245 when seventy or eighty bucks were taken by the earl of Cornwall, salted – perhaps at the palace salsary – and delivered to the sheriff of Wiltshire who was then mandated to carry it to the king at Chester.[29] In this respect, as in others, forest and park had much in common. The forest was exploited for timber: cathedral churches, local chapels, choir stalls, castle refurbishment, granaries, houses for friars; all these benefited in the thirteenth century alone. Forest trees were used to raise capital by John de Grimstede to help towards his unpaid ransom in 1330, several years after he had been taken prisoner by the Scots at Stirling,[30] while six oaks were taken in 1339 from Melchet to South-ampton 'in aid of enclosing that town against the attacks of alien enemies'.[31] Mature standards like these were mixed with coppiced underwood which was cropped for fuel and as building materials for things such as the hurdles and sluices for the mills at Old Sarum.[32] Another less intensive but equally vital feature of this local landscape was wood pasture. The 300 pigs 'of the stock of the bishopric of Winchester' sent to Clarendon forest in autumn 1244 were doubtless being fattened for slaughter.[33]

These four zones of palace, parks and forest have particular resonance for the historic periods in our study, but not exclusively so. For within these diverse habitats lay much earlier settlements, monuments and field systems which have all survived to differing degrees, depending upon later land use. It is to those more ancient landscapes that our attention turns in Chapter Two.

Clarendon before AD 1000: Beginnings

The seventeenth-century antiquarian John Aubrey was the first to publish prehistoric and Roman finds from Clarendon and among the significant excavations of the twentieth century were those of a Neolithic long barrow, a Bronze Age barrow and parts of Bronze Age and early medieval inhumation cemeteries. To these can be added numerous antiquarian observations and the results of recent fieldwork within the park. In this chapter, archaeological sites and monuments provide the basis of a comprehensive review, as we understand it, of settlement and landscape from earliest prehistory to the Norman Conquest. They reveal a dense pattern of human activity, showing how the evolution of early land use influenced medieval and later patterns and the extent to which relict and sometimes unknown features can still survive in an intensively managed landscape.

Early prehistoric Clarendon (10,000–1500 BC)

The hills and valleys of the park contain markedly fewer archaeological sites of prehistoric date than evidence from neighbouring parishes would suggest exist. This reflects the partial nature of fieldwork to date, compounded by the difficulty of differentiating worked from natural flint when fieldwalking and the presence of hill-wash, which masks lithic scatters (Figure 8). Early prehistoric Clarendon is especially elusive. Redeposited Palaeolithic material from occupation during the Ice Ages before 10,000 BC has been recorded from gravel workings and the digging of basements for mid-nineteenth-century housing to the east of Salisbury at Milford Hill, and similar geologies are found mainly on the western and eastern fringes of the park.[1] The association of prehistoric materials from the Ice Ages with gravels may arise from seasonal hunting on frozen ground, after which abandoned or lost tools found their way down into valley gravels during melt-periods. Three unprovenanced tranchet axes, labelled as 'from Clarendon Park' probably come from lower valley gravels on the east bank of the river Avon at Shute End near Dog Kennel Farm[2] but all the terrace gravels indicated in Figure 8 may be judged to have some potential for future finds, as do the areas mapped as clay-with-flints which mantle the high chalk plateaux at the centre of the park.[3] Detailed field survey elsewhere in Wessex, for example at Cranborne Chase,[4] has shown that

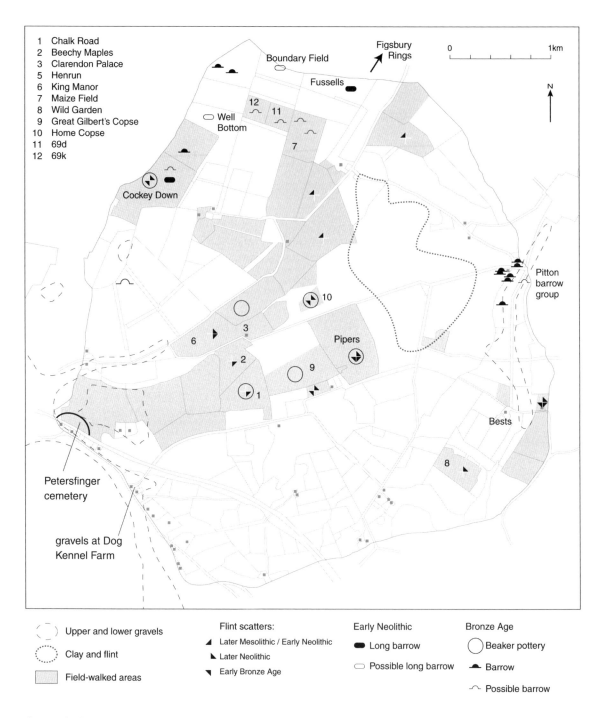

Key (numbered list):

1. Chalk Road
2. Beechy Maples
3. Clarendon Palace
5. Henrun
6. King Manor
7. Maize Field
8. Wild Garden
9. Great Gilbert's Copse
10. Home Copse
11. 69d
12. 69k

Boundary Field

Figsbury Rings

Fussells

Well Bottom

Cockey Down

Pitton barrow group

Pipers

Bests

Petersfinger cemetery

gravels at Dog Kennel Farm

0   1km

N

Legend:

Upper and lower gravels

Clay and flint

Field-walked areas

Flint scatters:
- Later Mesolithic / Early Neolithic
- Later Neolithic
- Early Bronze Age

Early Neolithic
- Long barrow
- Possible long barrow

Bronze Age
- Beaker pottery
- Barrow
- Possible barrow

forested chalk upland was attractive to later hunter-gatherer groups, but similar topographical and geological situations at Clarendon are under woodland and plantation so there has been scant opportunity for recovery of finds. Little flint of possible earlier Mesolithic date was recovered during recent fieldwork and no microliths of definite Mesolithic type have so far been collected. The expected pattern of seasonal camp sites occupied by mobile hunter groups using woodland and riverine resources in the period 9000 to 4000 BC cannot yet be confirmed.

However, Clarendon Park contains one of the best-known monuments created by Neolithic people in Britain (c. 4000–2200 BC), Fussell's Lodge long barrow. This lies near the north-east medieval pale and was excavated in 1957 – the first long barrow near Salisbury Plain to be investigated since the early nineteenth century. Importantly, the work was carried out to high, modern standards, revealing much new evidence both on Fussell's in particular and long barrows in general (Figure 9). The portion of the monument upstanding when excavated measured approximately 48 m by 15.4 m and was flanked by side ditches 40 m long. Significant physical effort, manpower and contemporary religious thought all contributed to the creation of this complex monument, to which the remains of several dozen people are known to have been carried down the valley over many years.[5] Though it survives today only as a slight earthwork, its location ensured that its visibility in the Neolithic period was deliberately restricted to the valley in which it lies. Had the intention been to provide a more conspicuous location then the higher ground immediately to the east would have been more appropriate.

This is one of about 300 long barrows now known in England.[6] Present interpretations suggest that a 'mortuary house' with a pitched roof was erected first, followed by an irregular rectangular structure 45 m long and 12 m wide, composed of upright timbers, which was associated with three pits containing human bone in their fills.[7] Later a cairn of flint nodules excavated from the flanking ditches was piled over the top of disarticulated skulls and stacked bones of about fifty-five individuals. Antler, animal bone, flint knapping debris and Neolithic pottery were all found in the ditch fills.

Recent fieldwork has assessed three further long barrow sites at Clarendon. One of these, on Cockey Down, is to be found on higher ground to the east of the Fussell's site. The ditches of this long barrow, 20 m in length, were identified from the air as early as 1924.[8] In contrast to the Fussell's barrow, this second site commands views to the north and west, though it is not intervisible with its better-known neighbour. Two other suggested examples, one near Cockey Down and another closer to Fussell's, are less certain.[9] There is no evidence at Clarendon of henges and stone circles, although there is a wide-ditched curvilinear enclosure at Figsbury Rings, prominently sited just 1.5 km north of the Fussell's barrow, beyond the outer edge of the northern park pale. Though it lacks any sign of a bank, in its earliest form this ditched enclosure with its two opposed entrances is considered to be a possible ceremonial henge monument of later Neolithic date, c. 2950–2350 BC.[10] According to this interpretation, the Clarendon long barrows appear to be part of a bigger grouping of contemporary monuments around this site, which may have been the focus for a local Neolithic community. This hints at a well-organised landscape which might be reasonably expected to include further associated sites and monuments, such as flint-mines, as yet unidentified.[11]

FIGURE 8.
Early prehistoric Clarendon. Neolithic long barrows and round barrows of Bronze Age date have long been known at Clarendon but they can now be matched by spreads of prehistoric lithics and pottery collected during recent fieldwalking. This reveals a much denser pattern of activity. (Drawn by Alejandra Gutiérrez)

Recent fieldwork shows there is now ample evidence of a Neolithic presence within the park. Many fields produced diagnostic pieces of flint; a blade and flake with laminar flake scars on the dorsal side from Chalk Road, for example, and a chipped axe or adze and an unfinished pressure-flaked projectile point, both from Beechy Maples Field. Part of a fine Neolithic polished greenstone axe was recovered from King Manor Field (west of the palace site; Figure 10), and six other areas in the central, eastern and southern parts of the park all produced Neolithic flint. Of the assemblage of 598 worked flints recovered from Best's Farm (east/south-east), a large proportion is regarded as Mesolithic or earlier Neolithic in date. The sample collected during field-walking is predominantly focused towards to the north of Best's Farm, which could reflect the proximity of the terrace gravels here, which may have been targeted as a source of raw material.[12] The largest assemblage of worked flint from Clarendon comes from gridded fieldwalking at Piper's, in the centre of the estate; a total of 675 worked flints was recovered here, mostly undiagnostic debitage, generally later Neolithic/earlier Bronze Age in date.[13] Later Neolithic pieces were also present at Best's Farm, Cockey Down, Henrun, Home Copse and Wild Garden,[14] so the whole landscape of the park was visited, exploited and far from empty.

Burial of single individuals, presumably those of rank or status, beneath round barrows began in the later Neolithic after 3000 BC and continued into the Bronze Age (c. 2000–800 BC). Among over 6000 barrows recorded in Wessex, a group of around fifteen barrows has recently been mapped at Clarendon. This group straddles the northern boundary of the park from

FIGURE 9.
Excavations under way at Fussell's Lodge long barrow in 1957. Paul Ashbee, the site director (bending nearest in the white shirt), is one of the team removing the cairn of flint nodules in the centre. This prehistoric monument was first noted from the air by O.G.S.Crawford during the inter-war period. There is another Neolithic long barrow on Cockey Down (Figure 6) and two further, more doubtful, examples have been claimed within the park perimeter. (Photographer unknown, but possibly Desmond Bonney)

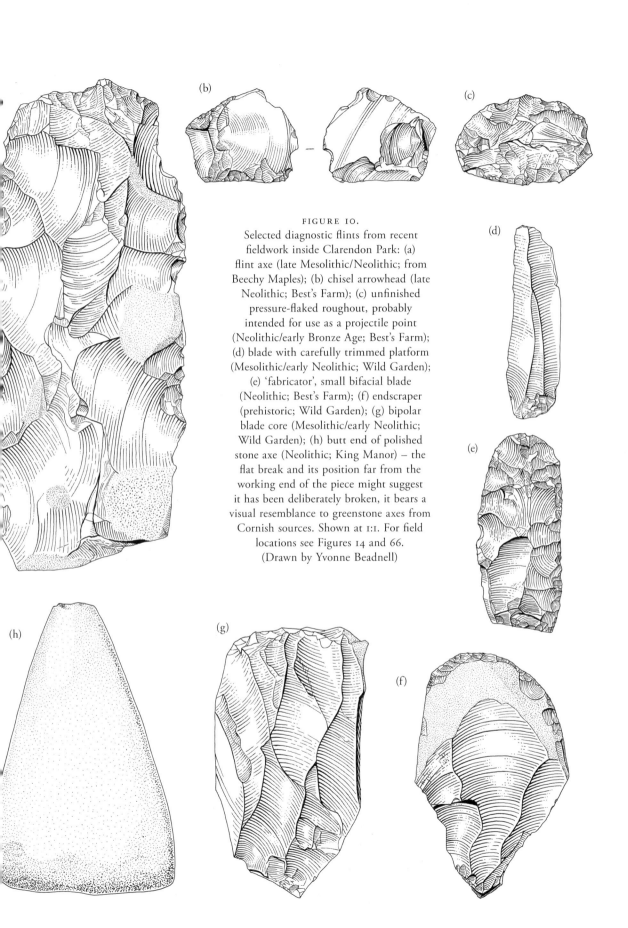

FIGURE 10.

Selected diagnostic flints from recent fieldwork inside Clarendon Park: (a) flint axe (late Mesolithic/Neolithic; from Beechy Maples); (b) chisel arrowhead (late Neolithic; Best's Farm); (c) unfinished pressure-flaked roughout, probably intended for use as a projectile point (Neolithic/early Bronze Age; Best's Farm); (d) blade with carefully trimmed platform (Mesolithic/early Neolithic; Wild Garden); (e) 'fabricator', small bifacial blade (Neolithic; Best's Farm); (f) endscraper (prehistoric; Wild Garden); (g) bipolar blade core (Mesolithic/early Neolithic; Wild Garden); (h) butt end of polished stone axe (Neolithic; King Manor) – the flat break and its position far from the working end of the piece might suggest it has been deliberately broken, it bears a visual resemblance to greenstone axes from Cornish sources. Shown at 1:1. For field locations see Figures 14 and 66.
(Drawn by Yvonne Beadnell)

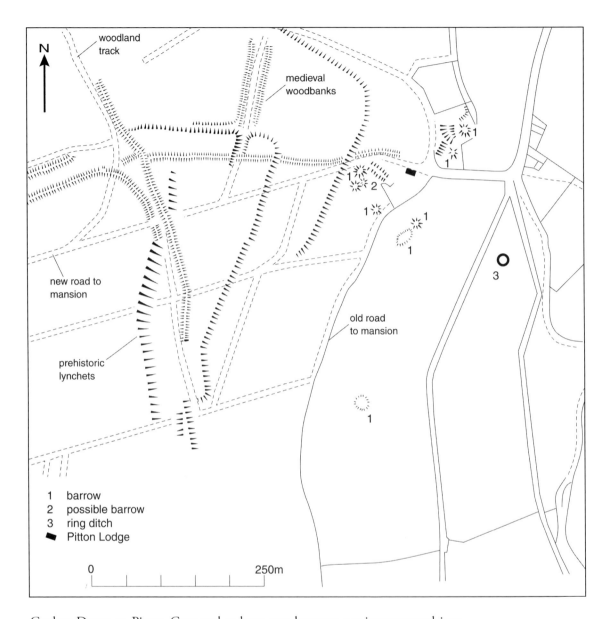

Cockey Down to Pitton Gate and at least two barrows are incorporated into the park pale. Some, located on the crest of Ford Down at the northern end of Cockey Down, were intentionally visible from the Bourne valley below: their siting is not accidental. One of only three barrows known here has been excavated. This investigation revealed an incinerated wooden mortuary structure which had left a burnt spread and traces of post holes. Thereafter a cremation was interred under a cairn of flints. It seemed there was one primary and one secondary burial, both in urns, of which just twelve body sherds were recovered. The flints were placed in a ring 8.5–9.1 m in diameter, with dumped flint filling the interior, before the outer ring was further defined by chalk and earth, possibly taken from the top of the ditch which encircled the

FIGURE 11.
A Bronze Age barrow group near the Pitton Gate on the eastern edge of the park, with prehistoric lynchets on the slope above. This group lies on the margin of the medieval deer park, a common location for other prehistoric burials at Clarendon, including the inhumation cemetery at Petersfinger. The medieval and later boundary may reflect much earlier landscape divisions. (Drawn by Alejandra Gutiérrez)

bell barrow.[15] During recent fieldwork a Beaker sherd was collected nearby[16] and, since the centre of the barrow was disturbed twice in antiquity, it is presumably associated.

Re-analysis of aerial photographs of Cockey Down suggests two further monuments: a ring ditch, and a cropmark notably penannular in shape, touching the adjacent long barrow.[17] A possible further four barrows have since been identified from sub-circular soilmarks on the ground and from aerial photography.[18] Even if verifiable, not all these burials are likely to be of the same date, though some may represent generations of kin groups. Whatever the case, the Cockey Down long barrow appears to have provided the focus for the development of the later round barrow cemetery, a spatial association seen elsewhere in Wessex.[19]

Detailed fieldwork at Pitton Gate in the east of the park has now identified a second group of nine or ten barrows, of which the most prominent are two bowl barrows north of the Gate; the larger of this pair stands 2.7 m high (Figures 11 and 12).[20] In the absence of any secure dating evidence, the only helpful suggestion to be made is that larger barrows of the Pitton type tend to be early Bronze Age, dating from the early second millennium BC. Beyond field observation it is noteworthy that the sites of most of the Pitton barrow group are on, or immediately adjacent to, the valley floor, and are close to a former watercourse. An inhumation cemetery was also discovered

FIGURE 12.
Pitton round barrow. This great Bronze Age barrow is one of a number which cluster round the Pitton (south-eastern) area of the park pale. It stands 2.7 m high and was probably reused and heightened. This may have happened from the Roman period onwards, perhaps as late as the eighteenth century. (Photograph by Tom Beaumont James)

21

by workmen digging a trench in 1941 at Petersfinger, at the western extremity of the park.[21] Two human skeletons and sherds of Bronze Age pottery were recorded there, one bowl with Beaker affinities. A bronze bangle found nearby at Ashley Hill, also in the south-western quadrant of the park, may well be associated with this cemetery.[22]

Recent fieldwork enables more to be said about the early Bronze Age at Clarendon beyond its funerary landscape. Early prehistoric pottery is not a common find from archaeological survey, as it is friable and dissolves in the ploughsoil, so the presence of two clear scatters at Clarendon is remarkable. Grog-tempered oxidised pottery of Beaker date (c. 2400–1700 BC) was recovered from shovel pits dug in Home Copse and Great Gilbert's Copse and from fieldwalking in adjacent fields.[23] A handful of similar sherds from the west end of Gilbert's Copse must represent a separate area of Bronze Age occupation. Both sites produced thick-walled fragments, suggesting urn material, but little can be deduced about the sites from which they derive. Nor should the precise grid reference of the pottery be taken to pinpoint buried prehistoric features, though the clustering of early prehistoric pottery in this one topographical zone is striking. Since they do not all appear to be from burial contexts, a string of settlements could be suggested,[24] though concentrations like this can arise from activities such as the ritual burying of midden material. Sadly, this part of the park is devoid of cropmark evidence because the geological deposits here are less responsive to aerial photography than those in other parts of the park, and much of the area is wooded, so these hypotheses cannot be confirmed. It is unusual, though, that diagnostic flint of early Bronze Age date should be rarer than pottery.[25]

By c. 2000 BC much of the woodland cover had probably already disappeared from the chalk downland, easing the digging of barrows in the north-west of the park.[26] There is no conclusive evidence for early Bronze Age fields at Clarendon, but lynchets currently under woodland, particularly those in Pitton Copse (Figure 12) and Home Copse, which are very substantial indeed, are of particular interest. These previously unrecorded lynchets clearly indicate that prehistoric agriculture was taking place off the chalk. Soils research which shows that loess soils would have extended to cover the clay-with-flints, resulting in a soil which was easy to work, supports this suggestion.[27] Their precise stratigraphical relationship with datable features, and thus their chronology, cannot be established except to note that they lie above and west of the Pitton barrow group. They are, however, quite different in character from field systems attributed to later periods and may be early Bronze Age in origin.

Later prehistoric Clarendon (1500 BC–AD 40/60)

An impressive array of rectangular 'Celtic' fields survives as cropmarks, soilmarks and earthworks which are visible on the ground as well as from the air (Figures 13 and 14). Once again, there are no associations with securely dated prehistoric earthworks or excavated sites to provide a relative date, but recent work on Salisbury Plain and elsewhere on the Wessex chalk suggests a middle Bronze Age date for their layout (1500–1000 BC).[28] The overall pattern at Clarendon is typically regular with fields laid out on a prevailing axis (mostly north-east–south-west; north-west–south-east). Axial boundaries, which are up to 2 km long, lie parallel with each other at distances of up to 100 m apart. Transverse boundaries, lying approximately at right angles, are adjusted to the slopes to subdivide the landscape into regular rectangular fields, presumably marked by hedges and ditches in prehistory. By the later Bronze Age (1000–800 BC) this must have given a distinctive and ordered look to the terrain west of Fussell's Lodge Farm almost in the same way that the modern shooting belts do today, albeit on a slightly different alignment. On slopes where soil built up behind former boundaries, scarps or lynchets formed which were subsequently reused as field boundaries. Some still represent significant topographical features today[29] and although most former field boundaries have been ploughed flat, looking northwards from the southern side of the valley it is still possible to see gaps in the lynchets, entrances leading from one field up into the next, and tracks connecting the prehistoric fields.

At around 0.6 ha in area these Clarendon fields are slightly larger than has been reported elsewhere and they are also more widespread than had been anticipated. Their survival in woodland is particularly good – in Home Copse and Great Gilbert's Copse, for example – where the trees mask these impressive earthworks from aerial survey. The very top of the downs was apparently not cultivated; it is below the watershed that the fields are found. As elsewhere, they are rare on heavier clay-with-flint soils, though neither north-facing slopes nor soils in dry valley bottoms appear to be devoid of early field systems. On the contrary, rectilinear field systems in the Savage's valley extend to the very bottom of the valley profile; even the slightest flatter gradient has lynchets and only the steepest limbs of asymmetrical valleys have been avoided. Very similar field systems have also been plotted from aerial photographs in the north-east of the park and to the north of Danebury hillfort,[30] though most recorded examples of cohesive or coaxial field systems in regular grid patterns fall well below 200 ha in total area, so the Clarendon group, at c. 400 ha, is large.

By the later Bronze Age the Clarendon woodland landscape was already fragmented by a broad scatter of settlements with associated arable fields for cereal cultivation, pasture for stock-raising and linking trackways right across the park. Work on the chalkland of the Marlborough Downs suggests enclosures and field systems every 2–3 km,[31] and there seems no reason to expect anything different here. Several areas of activity are proposed. The best-documented of these is on Cockey Down, where occupation seems to begin around 1100 BC and continues through to the later Roman period, with a short break in the middle Iron Age.[32] No excavated feature here can be securely placed in the late Bronze Age but the struck flint from the site is

FIGURE 13.
Aerial photograph of
coaxial field systems in
Town Field, towards
the north of the park.
The date of these field
systems is disputed.
Recent work on the
Wessex chalk suggests
a middle Bronze
Age date for their
layout (1500–1000
BC). Preserved under
medieval pasture, they
have been gradually
eroded by deeper
ploughing in more
recent times. This
picture reminds us
that this is not a
static landscape but
has successively been
woodland, arable
and launds (pasture),
and has only recently
become arable once
more.
(Photograph English
Heritage copyright
(NMR 15839/01
SU1831/8))

judged to be of that date. Unworked burnt flint was also recovered here during excavation. Elsewhere at Clarendon, a scatter of 'late hollow scraper' flints was recorded by Crawford just outside the western perimeter of the medieval palace[33] while further west, towards the perimeter of the park, flint cores, scrapers, knives and flakes are also recorded from the general area of Petersfinger.[34] To these we can now add scatters of flint of middle–late Bronze Age character found during fieldwalking in central and eastern areas of the park.[35] All these could be profitably investigated further.

Hillforts are the most visible evidence for Iron Age society (from around 800 BC to the mid first century AD) and the nearest site to Clarendon is Figsbury Rings. Figsbury is a univallate enclosure, of standardised size and shape, of early Iron Age date, which apparently went out of use by the middle Iron Age, say by about 300 BC.[36] A contemporary settlement on Cockey Down is also now known from aerial photography, excavation and from recent fieldwork.[37] This exposed settlement was defined by a boundary ditch 4 m wide and 1.75 m deep, which enclosed about 1.6 ha of high ground (Figure 15). Only a small proportion of the interior of the enclosure has been investigated, including two beehive-shaped grain storage pits cut down into

FIGURE 14.
Later prehistoric and
Roman Clarendon.
Occupation is much
denser than had
previously been
suspected and many
sites continued in
use from one period
to another, though
activity in the middle
Iron Age is elusive.
Several new sites have
been discovered but no
large-scale excavation
has taken place.
(Drawn by Alejandra
Gutiérrez)

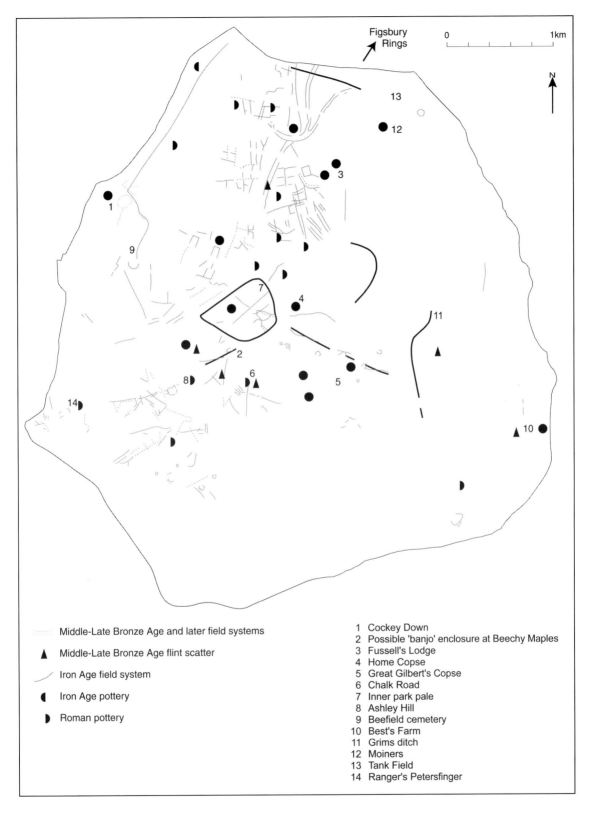

Figsbury
Rings

0   1km

N

13

12

3

1

9

7

4

11

2

8

6

5

14

10

....   Middle-Late Bronze Age and later field systems

▲   Middle-Late Bronze Age flint scatter

◿   Iron Age field system

◖   Iron Age pottery

◗   Roman pottery

1   Cockey Down
2   Possible 'banjo' enclosure at Beechy Maples
3   Fussell's Lodge
4   Home Copse
5   Great Gilbert's Copse
6   Chalk Road
7   Inner park pale
8   Ashley Hill
9   Beefield cemetery
10   Best's Farm
11   Grims ditch
12   Moiners
13   Tank Field
14   Ranger's Petersfinger

the chalk. Outside the enclosure was the gully for a roundhouse 9 m in diameter, the remains of post-built structures and a small open-sided ditched feature. A loomweight or spindlewhorl and pottery provide evidence for dating, the latter including a bipartite jar decorated with fingernail impressions. Taken together, the evidence points to this being a small early–middle Iron Age rural agricultural settlement which was approached from the north-east along the ditched trackway which can be seen on aerial photographs running along the crest of the Down. In size and shape, it might be best compared with a similar enclosure with single curving wide ditches at Hurdcott Field Barn North (Wilts)[38] and it is likely to have contained post-built houses with evidence for cooking and corn-drying, among other activities, as well as several phases of contraction and expansion.[39] More than one structure is certainly present, even in the small sample of the site examined, though this may represent rebuilding of a single farmstead. Iron Age sherds have been found further north-east on Cockey Down, at Park Corner, as well as downslope.[40] Other Iron Age sherds have been found more recently in Hockamore and Maize Field.[41]

During the early Iron Age a small oval pit was dug on Cockey Down, into which the remains of an adult were placed, in a crouched position, as part of an inhumation burial rite. Burials in individual grave pits, large enough only to contain the flexed body, are typical of the period. This individual was found lying on his left side, facing south, with the right arm across the chest and the left arm tucked underneath the legs, which had been drawn up to the chest. More human bones, including large fragments of a second skull, were found in the upper soil levels overlying the skeleton,[42] providing evidence for recutting and disturbance of earlier graves. This pit was dated by the excavators to 300–400 BC and may be part of a larger cemetery.

The general lack of middle Iron Age material from Clarendon is a feature of the archaeological record which has been noted elsewhere in Wessex.[43] This has been attributed to a shift towards a more pastoral economy, a major reorientation in the economic structure of this region. Whether or not the fields on Cockey Down were temporarily abandoned and became common grazing at this time, or whether the hiatus is more to do with archaeological visibility as the inhabitants moved into developed hillforts, by the late pre-Roman Iron Age there was once again occupation here. Iron Age pottery sherds were collected during recent fieldwork on the Down[44] and excavation has shown that the earlier sub-circular enclosure ditch was filled in. Five graves were excavated here (Figure 15). These were shallow and damaged by ploughing but sufficient survived to suggest that two of them had been reopened some years after the first burial in order to insert a second, the implication being that the grave was marked, perhaps by a cairn of flint nodules. Radiocarbon dates from three individuals produced dates in the late Iron Age[45] and these burials probably represent individuals from a larger domestic cemetery alongside a small settlement which was reoccupied in the late Iron Age or early Roman period.

A gradually increasing density of settlement and population during the pre-Roman Iron Age (first centuries BC/AD) is apparent at Clarendon. This reflects the picture seen elsewhere in Wessex, for example immediately north-west of the park, across the river Bourne, where Iron Age sites seem to be evenly spaced at kilometre intervals. Within the park several new sites now fill out the distribution map (see Figure 14).[46] It has been suggested that the inner park pale, which encompasses an area of 16.6 ha and encloses the medieval palace site and adjacent fields, may in parts be of earlier origin.[47] This suggestion has found support on four grounds. First, the unusual siting of the medieval palace at the very edge of an escarpment is noteworthy and may imply antecedent features, though this observation has to some extent been undermined by recent work which demonstrates an interest in manipulating medieval landscapes for architectural settings. Second, the overall enclosure shape is highly irregular. Third, the excavation evidence from both 1933–9 and 1961 demonstrated that the earthwork ditch pre-dated the precinct wall and may therefore have been pre-medieval.[48] Other pre-medieval features were also suggested elsewhere on the site by excavations under the Salsary and kiln.[49] Finally, Iron Age coinage and Roman material have both been found in or close to the palace precinct. The case cannot be properly addressed without further excavation but recent fieldwork recovered several sherds of Iron Age pottery from shovel pits dug through Home Copse, Great Gilbert's Copse and adjacent fields, while a single fossil-tempered sherd picked up beneath the palace escarpment probably derives from occupation above.[50]

A possible 'banjo' enclosure has been identified at the north-eastern end of Beechy Maples. The evidence for this second site is incomplete. Geophysics suggests ditches forming a small circular enclosure, about 0.25 ha in extent, with an approaching ditched trackway. A 'British' silver coin, drawn in the margin of Phillipps's early nineteenth-century plan of the palace, may have been found on that site or thereabouts, only a short distance away. It is dated to the mid to late first century BC (Figure 76).[51] During recent fieldwork, late prehistoric pottery was recovered from King Manor Field, just below this site to the north,[52] and the implication must be that there was a spread of Iron Age occupation all along the escarpment which ran right through the area later occupied by the medieval royal palace. 'Banjo' enclosures are a common settlement form in Wessex and, until recently, admittedly on the basis of limited excavation, they have been dated to the middle and late Iron Age (300 BC to c. AD 50). Given the funnel-like arrangement of their entrance ditches, a link with stock-rearing seemed plausible, but full examination of the banjo enclosure at Nettlebank Copse, Wherwell (Hants) now suggests other possibilities. Several phases of occupation were identified there, beginning with a small farmstead which was abandoned about 300 BC when the ditch silted up. When occupation began again in the middle of the first century BC it seems to have been seasonal only and the site was perhaps used for feasting. The site was finally abandoned in the first century AD.[53] Whether a similar sequence can be proposed for Beechy Maples could not be resolved without

FIGURE 15.
Cockey Down under
excavation by Wessex
Archaeology:
(a) inhumation burial
of late Iron Age or
early Romano-British
date; one of twelve
individuals of similar
date associated with
a small farmstead;
(b) in the foreground
the elliptical ditch
of an open-sided late
Bronze Age/early Iron
Age structure with
pits being excavated
behind. The substantial
ditch to the rear is of
late Romano-British
date; animal bone,
pottery, brick, tile,
metalwork and two
fragments of quern
stone were among the
items recovered from
this feature.
(Copyright Wessex
Archaeology 2005)

full excavation but the lesson from Nettlebank Copse is surely that the simple
'labelling' of these sites, in terms of their chronology and function, should not
be taken for granted. Again, Beechy Maples may not be an isolated site. Only
a few kilometres from the park there are sites of late Iron Age date which are
characterised by multiple ditches, large enclosed areas with the same suites of
finds and similar geology.[54]

Two further Clarendon sites from this period must be mentioned. From
the Fussell's Lodge area (north-east) black sandy wares of Iron Age date
were recovered from Birdfield, a single grog-tempered sherd was found during fieldchecking in woodland and disturbed ground behind Fussell's Dairy
Cottage, and three further fine calcined flint-tempered sherds were recovered

from Moiners.[55] Finally, Iron Age pottery was collected during fieldwalking on the eastern side of the estate, near Best's Farm.[56] In particular, later Iron Age–early Roman activity is suggested by several handmade sandy wares, a grog-tempered base with a pedestalled foot and possibly a lid-seated jar.

Both the Fussell's and Best's Farm sites may be farmsteads which began in the Iron Age and, as we shall see, continued through the Roman period. As for the distribution of early prehistoric sites and findspots, however, the pattern for the Iron Age is unlikely to be complete. Further sites must await discovery in the south-west and eastern parts of Clarendon Park. Nevertheless, there does seem to be a preference for ridge locations; perhaps because valley sides and bottoms were reserved for agriculture. Intriguingly, by the end of Iron Age the medieval and post-medieval settlement pattern is already beginning to emerge, with settlements being spaced at roughly equal intervals across the landscape.

Assigning field boundary earthworks to periods at Clarendon, as we noted for the Bronze Age, is hazardous and imprecise. However, several lengths of ditch and bank have now been identified from aerial photographs and possible dates may be suggested. These include stretches along the inner park pale, through Piper's Field, Ashley Hill and Warner's Copse, as well as Grims Ditch, a single bank and ditch which survives as an earthwork. All these may be grouped under the general heading 'linear boundaries' of prehistoric date, otherwise known as dyke systems or ranch boundaries, which are thought to represent territorial boundaries in a dominantly pastoral economy from the late Bronze Age to the end of the Iron Age (between 1400 BC and c. AD 50), with possible later reworkings.[57] In this context, Grims Ditch appears to define a boundary between two distinctive vegetation zones, dividing alkaline chalk soils to the west from acidic clay-with-flints to the east, this geology perhaps reflecting the distribution of arable and woodland.[58] This characteristic is shared with the Oxfordshire (formerly Berkshire) Grims Ditch.[59] At Clarendon it is not possible to cast these occasional lengths into an integrated system, as has been done north-east of the park,[60] and it should be acknowledged that different portions could have been in use for varying periods of time. However, there is every indication of an ordered late prehistoric landscape with organised and maintained land divisions between parcels of differing land use.

Romano-British Clarendon (AD 40/60–AD 400/450)

Sorviodunum (Old Sarum/Stratford-sub-Castle), 4.5 km from Park Corner, was the most substantial local Romano-British centre. Five major Roman roads converged at its east gate. One was the road from Charterhouse-on-Mendip to Venta Belgarum (Winchester) which crosses the modern A30 today immediately north of Park Corner and whose agger survives as an upstanding earthwork in pasture there.

The Roman invasion in AD 43 is invisible in archaeology at Clarendon, though the new roads which followed must have speeded local and long-distance travel and facilitated trade. Clarendon was already an intensively occupied and farmed landscape. For the moment, a total of seven settlements can be identified which were occupied through the Roman period (see Figure 14). Before 1993 only one of these was known, the successor to the late Bronze Age activity and Iron Age settlement on Cockey Down, where inter-cutting pits, post-holes and two infant burials of early Roman date have been excavated.[61] Occupation continued here until about AD 400; the structural evidence comprises pits, ditches, a corn drier, ovens and boundary ditches, which were sectioned and found to be up to 3 m wide and 1.75 m deep in places. Pottery includes New Forest Parchment and colour-coated wares, and among the other finds were brick, tile and a handful of iron objects (a square plate, a latch lifter, a rod and a ring), quernstone fragments and one possible architectural fragment of micaceous sandstone.[62] This helps fill the previous Clarendon void in the distribution of Roman sites to the south of the Roman road.[63]

Roman pottery from shovel pits and from fieldwalking has provided clear evidence of both earlier and later Romano-British activity and helped to define the limits of settlement on the Down. Among the earlier first-/second-century products are grey sandy wares from the Alice Holt kilns,[64] with a mortarium and a flanged bowl in Oxfordshire colour-coated wares marking the later third–early fourth century,[65] together with a fourth-century coin which was found during shovel-pitting.[66] Several fragments of ceramic building material were also recovered here, two of which are Roman roofing tile (*tegulae*). All of this material comes from the western side of the Cockey Down field with the highest concentrations from an area 100 m east of the covered reservoir, though Roman pottery is a regular find in the fields off the top of the Down.[67] This spread of material presents no obvious concentrations and is unlikely to reflect underlying archaeological features, so it is probably the result of manuring in the Roman period.

On the edge of Cockey Down, in Beefield, a small portion of a Romano-British cemetery has been excavated, including four adult graves, three of which were in wooden coffins.[68] Roman burials are often close to their settlements, so this is likely to be a discrete cemetery associated with the Romano-British settlement higher on the hill. There is nothing to indicate wealth in the burials; indeed the grave of one unaccompanied extended inhumation was especially shallow, which may indicate a relative lack of importance.[69] It is possible that this cemetery was placed near a track coming off Cockey Down or perhaps at the limits of the settlement.[70]

Recent fieldwalking and shovel-pit testing around the eastern end of Gilbert's Copse revealed a concentration of Roman material, including a bronze quinarius of Allectus AD 293–6 (Figure 16).[71] Together with the pottery collected from Piper's Field and Henrun, which seem to be part of the same general spread of occupation, the Roman pottery here is one of the more diverse groups from Clarendon. Among the recognisable wares are samian, Dorset black burnished ware, Oxfordshire and New Forest colour-coated wares, an Oxfordshire whiteware mortarium and one sherd of amphora. A significant proportion of the grey wares are Alice Holt products which include forms typical of the later Roman period, such as flanged bowls, beakers, flask, mortaria plain-walled dish and jars with everted rims.[72] Shelly limestone roofing slate, ceramic *tegulae*, *pilae* bricks and box flue tiles, together with many *tesserae* and metal slags, from an area of 150 m² form an assemblage which strongly indicates a sizeable and well-appointed later Roman site associated with industrial production. The existence of this site is confirmed by the discovery of a large sub-rectangular enclosure defined by a ditch 4 m wide with an accompanying internal bank, within which there is an area of terracing towards the south and, offset to the west, a range of building platforms (Figure 17). Several phases of activity are suggested, and some hints as to what these might be are now emerging from the Danebury Environs Roman Project.[73] We must consider the possibility of impressive aisled timber halls with later additions such as bath suites; subsequent subdivisions may have reflected inheritance and changes in landownership, perhaps with a later villa phase embellished by some mosaic flooring. It is also likely that there has

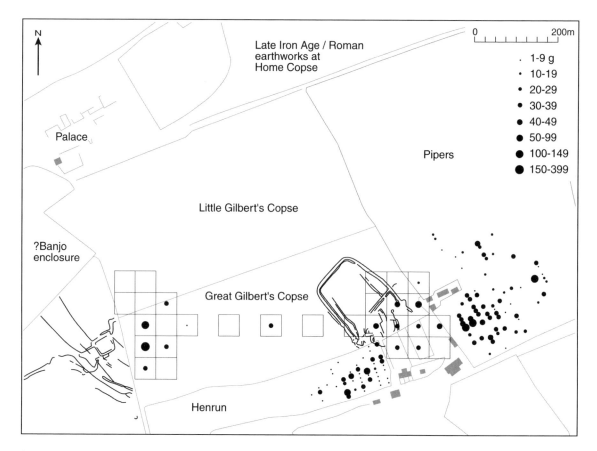

been later interference from tree growth and, more seriously, by robbers and perhaps antiquaries.[74] Confirmation of this putative villa site is of special interest in central and southern Wiltshire where, until relatively recently, such sites seemed virtually absent[75] and other sites might easily accrue from field-name evidence.[76] The location of this south-facing site is also noteworthy, as it lies 3.5 km from the Roman road, off the chalk, and is hardly ideally located to exploit arable fields on the downs. Elements of a successful economy on this site may have included cattle- and pig-rearing and coppicing of the local woodland for charcoal. The quantities of slag recovered in the vicinity do strongly suggest metalworking, just as digging for potting and tile-making clays is unproven but surely likely.[77]

There is also an extensive scatter of Roman material to the east of the medieval palace site, now under woodland in Home Copse. This third site has produced pottery extending through the Roman period and into the fourth century.[78] The spread of this material suggests a linear settlement, perhaps a Roman village, and the site probably extends as far west as the palace. Roman pottery fragments have regularly appeared among the finds from excavation and fieldwork there and Roman coins are said to have been found at the 'foot of the hill on which stood the palace',[79] though their current whereabouts and more exact identity are unknown now. At the base of the slope there

FIGURE 16.
Fieldwork in and around Gilbert's Copse has located earthworks, ploughed-out buildings and dense scatters of Roman material in woodland and arable. At least one site has an industrial component, while that to the north under Home Copse may extend beneath the medieval palace site. The plot (*opposite*) combines results from fieldwalking on arable with those from shovel-pitting through woodland to map weights of Roman pottery. The latter technique involves sampling 150 litres of topsoil on a 50 m grid where groundcover makes fieldwalking impractical. The aerial photograph (*right*) shows the site west of Great Gilbert's Copse in Chalk Road field. Trackways, field boundaries and at least two enclosures can be seen extending eastwards into the woodland.
(Line drawing by Alejandra Gutiérrez, aerial photograph English Heritage copyright (NMR 926/381 SU1829/1))

several dozen Roman sherds[80] were among recent fieldwalking finds.[81] In location and date this site shares common characteristics with settlements recently documented on the Great Ridge and in Grovely Wood, as well as on Salisbury Plain.[82] Some of these sites are also late Iron Age in origin but contain Roman earthworks, including building platforms and terraces. They are thought to have been substantial rural settlements.

A fourth site, visible on aerial photographs, lies on the western fringe of Gilbert's Copse and has been a target of recent fieldwalking and shovel-pitting in Chalk Road Field (Figure 16). Pottery of both early and later Roman date is present here.[83] The single Roman sherds from Hendon and Ashley/Chisley Hill could be derived either from this site or from Petersfinger (see below, page 35), perhaps being spread during the manuring of arable fields.

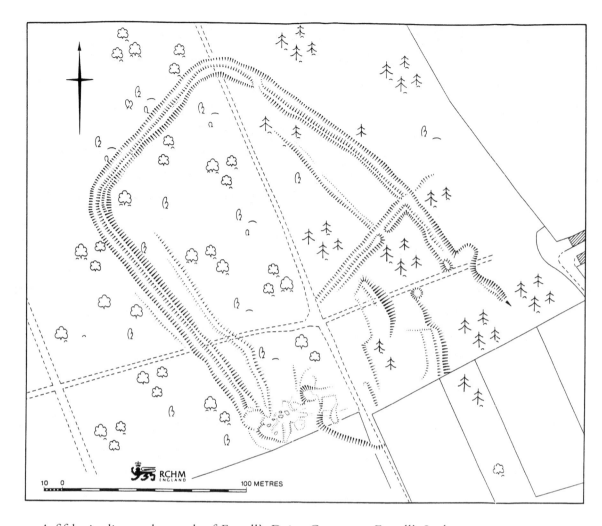

10 0   100 METRES

A fifth site lies to the north of Fussell's Dairy Cottage at Fussell's Lodge (north-east) and comprises a series of lynchets.[84] These banks delimit an area on the crest overlooking the Savage's valley, where there is a stretch of polygonal flint and mortar walling about 20 m in length associated with small amounts of Roman greyware. If the wall, the pottery and the earthworks are contemporary then a substantial complex may well lie in the immediate vicinity, though it will undoubtedly have been damaged by later building and by a Second World War bomb which fell close by. Sherds of New Forest colour-coated ware were recovered from the adjacent field,[85] but a much larger group came from Moiners, the field to the north-east of Fussell's Lodge. Since no Roman pottery was found in Tank Field, this defines the limits of the Roman site quite tightly, suggesting Roman settlement very close to the present farm on the flatter higher ground at the edge of the escarpment. Lighter scatters of Roman pottery on the south side of the valley probably reflect the extension of Roman arable in the immediate vicinity.[86]

At the eastern extremity of the park, fieldwalking close to Best's Farm has

FIGURE 17.
Earthworks survey
of Gilbert's Roman
villa and Iron Age
enclosure. This is
likely to be the
Roman site first
described by Henry
Hatcher in 1845 and
subsequently denied.
Roman pottery,
building material
and metal residues
can be found in the
surrounding fields but
the site is one with
a long sequence of
occupation. (Survey
by the former Royal
Commission on
Historical Monuments
(England), English
Heritage copyright)

revealed the western edge of what may be a substantial Roman site which straddles the south-eastern length of the medieval park pale. Significant quantities of later Roman pottery, tile and brick have been collected here previously[87] and this sixth site is also visible from the air. Oxfordshire and New Forest colour-coated wares collected during an extensive fieldwalking exercise suggest later Roman activity. In particular, a New Forest beaker[88] and flask[89] indicate occupation into the period after AD 350.[90] A small collection of Roman sherds to the south-west probably derives from this Best's Farm site.

Finally, a cluster of Romano-British pottery and a cropmark enclosure recently identified at Petersfinger probably represent another small farmstead site on the edge of the escarpment in Ranger's Petersfinger, the most westerly field in the park.[91] This is the seventh Roman site to be identified within the limits of the park but it seems to be exceptional because the pottery suggests a late Roman date.[92] There is nothing to suggest antecedent prehistoric settlement here.

The overriding characteristic of Roman settlement at Clarendon is its continuity from prehistory. Thus Great Gilbert's Copse, Home Copse and Chalk Road Field all show signs of occupation from the early Bronze Age through to the fourth century AD. A growing body of evidence suggests that parts of the inner park pale incorporate late pre-Roman Iron Age earthworks and there can be little doubt that the site of the later palace was occupied then and on into the Roman period. Cockey Down was also a continuing centre of ritual activity; every period of prehistory from the Neolithic onwards is represented by burial there, though extensive settlement began perhaps only in the Iron Age. The Fussell's Lodge and Best's Farm settlements also appear at this time and, as we have seen, all six sites continue to be occupied throughout the Roman period, being joined by the site at Petersfinger in the third and fourth centuries. Admittedly, there is some 'settlement drift' and changing form, most clearly seen on Cockey Down, but the clear implication seems to be of a long-term continuity of occupation sites, a feature of several settlements in the Salisbury Plain area, among them Figheldean,[93] Durrington Walls[94] and Butterfield Down.[95] That is not to say that the landscape was static; rather we would argue that a process of recycling is typical and, indeed, a feature of all Clarendon landscapes. Just as the later Petersfinger Anglo-Saxon cemetery incorporated Roman artefacts in several of its graves, so a small number of Romano-British pottery sherds were excavated from the upper silts of the ditch and plough soil covering Fussell's Lodge long barrow. The excavator noted that this was more than a coincidental scatter to be expected from manuring and indicated 'rather pointed Roman interest' in other Wessex long barrows.[96]

A second remarkable feature of the Romano-British landscape is the density of population. The population of Roman Clarendon exceeded that at any time in its history, but quite how these settlements related to each other is hard to say. The Roman pottery groups from these seven sites are not large; the total amounts to 1406 sherds in all, insufficient to make detailed inferences about their relative status. The high incidence of samian at the Chalk Road site should be noted, however, and the collection from the other end of Gilbert's Copse is certainly diverse, both signs of contacts and wealth which might suggest status. The idea that the villa site owned or controlled the adjacent sites is attractive and parallels suggestions made for dependent settlements on Grovely Ridge and on Salisbury Plain, but it cannot be demonstrated on the basis of the current evidence.[97] Certainly the Romano-British settlement pattern at Clarendon does not seem to be one of villas and dispersed farmsteads. There are enclosed and unenclosed sites, farmsteads and larger nucleated settlements whose sizes seem more akin to villages.[98] The proximity of higher-status Roman settlement to the later palace site is noteworthy and invites speculation on how a hypothetical Roman estate might have been reflected in post-Roman land units, and on whether we might be glimpsing lengthy periods of continuity in the Clarendon landscape. This argument suggests that the distribution of settlement and land use seen in the third and fourth centuries AD, and which itself drew upon later prehistoric patterns, might have influenced the historic Saxon and later landscape.

More could be done, particularly to place these identified sites in their contemporary landscape setting. There would be considerable value in defining the alignments and widths of palaeochannels on the eastern side of the park to evaluate any environmental potential they may hold. Localised pollen capture is certainly possible in clogged former channels though a preliminary assessment was not positive.[99] A conventional interpretation would envisage the clearing of woodland in selected locations during the Mesolithic (9000–4000 BC), with the first extensive clearance of woodland during the early Neolithic (4000–3350 BC) as a sedentary economy replaced mobile gathering and hunting strategies in an increasingly organised landscape populated by new plant cultivates and animal domesticates. There is a strong argument for this, particularly close to clusters of burial and ceremonial monuments on the chalk in the north and western parts of the park, but even those areas which now comprise the downs would have supported woodland originally, very probably dominated by small-leaved lime (*Tilia cordata*). The light, easily cultivated soils of the chalk contributed to early clearance and cultivation, and subsequent erosion has rendered the chalk downland unsuitable for the support of mature woodland, so it has remained more or less open ever since.[100] There is evidence from Wessex that some of this cleared land on the chalk reverted to secondary woodland during the middle Neolithic (c. 2500 BC) but had became grassland during the early Bronze Age (2000–1300 BC) and was subsequently organised into field systems between 1500–1000 BC, during the middle Bronze Age.[101] The frequency of settlement gradually intensified, so that by the Roman period the landscape was densely settled and exploited, a process for which we first see evidence by the later Bronze Age (1400–500 BC).

Post-Roman and early medieval Clarendon (c. AD 400/450–AD 1000)

Far less is known of Clarendon between the fifth and the eleventh centuries. It is frustrating that no pottery or finds have been recovered from recent fieldwork and, at present, nothing at Clarendon suggests other than a major dislocation of settlement, economy and land use after AD 400.

Archaeological evidence for early medieval Clarendon comes mainly from a burial ground in the Petersfinger area, on the west-facing slope of the downs, which fall away to the Avon and Bourne valleys and the expanse of Salisbury Plain.[102] This was originally thought to be one very large cemetery with seventy-one burials in all, five of which were multiple burials, but re-analysis of the plans and finds from the excavations in 1948 and 1951 now suggests two distinct cemeteries, perhaps serving adjacent communities between the fifth and seventh centuries.[103] Among the grave goods were beads in amber, quartz and glass, a pendant of drilled bone, a bronze belt-slide, buckles, purse-mounts, a bronze chain, bronze clips, buckets of yew-wood staves with iron and bronze framework, disc brooches, ear scoops, an ivory bangle, keys, knives, pottery, finger rings, shield bosses, shield-grips, spearheads, swords and tweezers. Certain artefacts with 'Frankish' affinities were identified, including a decorated bronze buckle and a small radiate brooch, from different graves, and an axe and iron buckle plate set with glass-filled cloisons from the grave of a male who also had with him a sword with a silver-plated, partially gilded pommel, a spearhead and a shield[104] (Figure 18). Recent metal detector finds from the same area include an Anglo-Saxon button brooch, together with two bronze buckles and a round bronze plaque.[105] The button brooch has a 'reasonably realistic representation of the human face with a well-defined mouth, round eyes and curved eye-rings'.[106]

Objects with fifth-century 'Frankish' links like those from Petersfinger have also been noted at Winterbourne Gunner, Harnham and Charlton, a cluster of cemeteries near Salisbury.[107] The conventional interpretation of this material is that the individuals buried were foreign, perhaps mercenaries. Thus those buried around AD 450, as at Winterbourne Gunner, are seen as isolated Germanic warriors and families living in areas of British control and perhaps owing allegiance to British rulers, while those of the later fifth century may indicate a further wave of incomers, 'a deliberate policy by the Anglo-Saxons to target British centres and subjugate them'.[108] The centre to be subjugated in this case would have been the former Sorviodunum. This 'conquest' of the region is charted in the sixth-century annals in the Anglo-Saxon Chronicle but the dates and the events they describe cannot be used as a meaningful guide to the archaeology. Indeed, whether such a simple correlation between material culture and ethnicity can be accepted at all is highly debatable.[109] Many grave assemblages like Petersfinger give 'mixed' ethnic and gender messages, combining imported material with local variants of brooches, which complicates our reading of their meaning to the extent that some scholars now favour an alternative interpretation which envisages

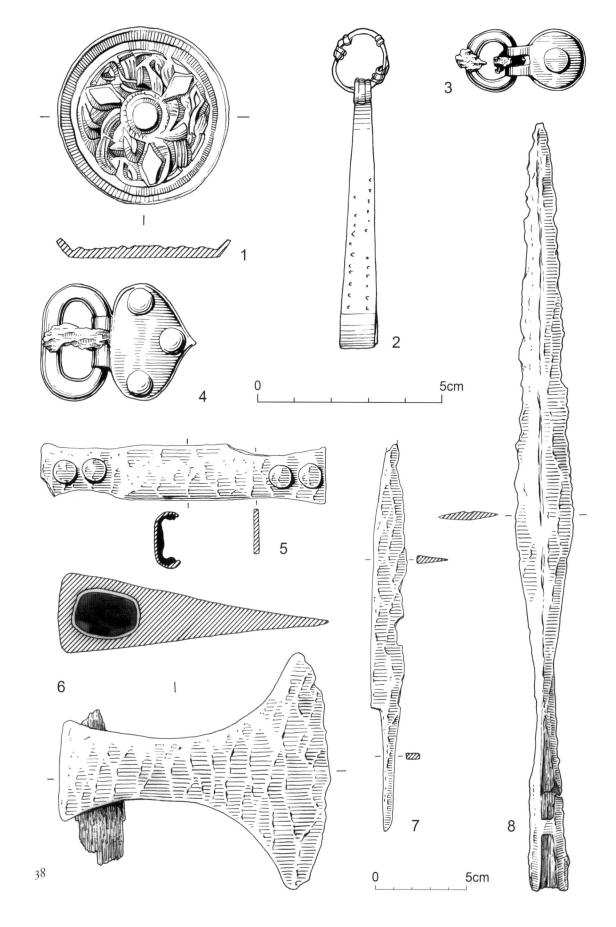

1

2

3

4

0   5cm

5

6

7

8

0   5cm

continental dress fashions spreading from Kent westwards.[110] An alternative reading of the Petersfinger cemetery, therefore, might see a new political élite taking on 'Frankish' ethnic traits as a means of marking their status. So it may be that none of the Petersfinger community was actually a Frank, nor that any one of them was genetically related to the Harnham burials. Rather, these people denoted their authority in the local area by reference in their dress accessories to other ethnicities, as well as in other ways now lost to us. The location of their cemetery immediately adjacent to the third–fourth century AD Roman site upslope may have provided a further ancestral linkage, and the discovery of Roman objects among other objects in the Petersfinger cemetery is interesting in this context.[111] Roman objects are commonly found in Anglo-Saxon graves and they were clearly selected; at least some may have been gathered from the surface at local Roman sites or perhaps they survived into the fifth and sixth centuries as heirlooms, especially where they could substitute for objects which the Petersfinger community found difficult to obtain otherwise.

The excavators' view that the Petersfinger individuals may have come from a community at Britford, across the river Avon, seems as plausible as any. Organic-tempered pottery of a similar type to that recovered from the Petersfinger cemetery has been recovered from Mumworth, just a kilometre away to the south, at the confluence of the Avon and the Bourne,[112] but there may have been a closer settlement. Searches for settlement evidence on the slopes below the Petersfinger cemetery and in the adjacent valley bottom were undertaken in the late 1960s and early 1970s, resulting in the discovery of a light scatter of Anglo-Saxon pottery but no structures.[113] More recently, excavations on a valley-bottom site produced similarly inconclusive results.[114] There is, however, every reason to believe that small early Anglo-Saxon inhumation cemeteries like Petersfinger were sited close to the communities they served[115] and it cannot simply be assumed that rural Romano-British settlements such as those at Cockey Down, Best's Farm or Petersfinger went out of use. These basic agricultural settlements might yet provide evidence of occupation into the 500s and 600s. Draper, arguing for native British continuity in Wiltshire in the fifth and sixth centuries AD, points out that Romano-British settlements become archaeologically untraceable from the late fourth century.[116] Intriguingly, two loom or thatch weights with central perforations, judged to be of possible Saxon date, are attributed to the medieval palace site, though nothing is known of the circumstances of their recovery or exact findspot.[117] Whether the location of the Petersfinger cemeteries might itself have relevance for dating the boundaries of the later park is uncertain; a notable percentage of early Anglo-Saxon burials in Wiltshire are certainly on later parish boundaries, with the obvious inference that these land-units are older than the Anglo-Saxon period and that the Anglo-Saxons showed a preference for burying their dead on boundaries in order to emphasise their territories. But this reasoning may be flawed because both burial locations and parish boundaries correlate strongly with a third variable, local topography, and this may be the key relationship in play at Petersfinger. So the location of the cemeteries is probably not helpful in proving an early date for the park's south-eastern boundary.[118]

As waves of warriors and immigrants begin to dissolve under the scrutiny of modern scholarship, so conventional interpretations of the 'early medieval' earthwork at Clarendon known as 'Grims Ditch' became doubtful. Topographical survey of this monument reveals that it is a simple ditch and bank which faces west – that is to say, the bank is on the eastern side of the ditch. The alignment seems eccentric as a defensive work against any interpretation of 'Saxon incursions'. On the other hand, there is linguistic evidence in the Salisbury area for the persistence of British populations. Though river names like the Avon, Nadder and Wylye are only the loosest indication of local Brittonic speakers, when documentary sources which refer to Clarendon Forest begin after AD 1100 an ancient British name for the area was still in use: Panshett.[119] Nonetheless, the argument for a coincidence of linguistic and/or ethnic boundaries with a short stretch of undated earthwork is extremely flimsy, to say the least, and 'Grims Ditch' might be better judged as a boundary of later prehistoric date.

By the late 600s the administration of the local area would probably have been undertaken by reeves, who operated in those districts centred on royal estates. In this area of south-east Wiltshire that social, judicial and religious role was based in Alderbury, which also gave its name to the hundred. A minster, a small monastic community of priests, was founded here to provide for the parochial needs of local people.[120] Among major clues to the former status of the church are Alderbury's relatively substantial entry in Domesday Book and its retained dependent chapels, which included Pitton and Farley, a responsibility sustained in the late nineteenth century at Pitton. Alderbury was held by 'Alweard' the priest in 1086. Reference to Ivychurch as a *'monasterium'* in 1109–10, a generation before the Augustinian house was founded there, and its hilltop site, unusual for Augustinians, hint at Saxon religious occupation of that site beside the park pale. Perhaps some functions of the Saxon minster of Alderbury had already been transferred to the new, neighbouring Augustinian priory at Ivychurch, so that King Stephen regularised the *status quo* for the specific purpose of serving the palace. Elsewhere communities of Augustinian canons (i.e. rather than monks) have suggested previous minster status.[121] The precise boundaries of the hundredal administrative unit as it ran through the forest have proved difficult to tie down – they may have been 'ill-defined'[122]– but recent research suggests that the closest links for Alderbury were to the south and west of Clarendon, while a possible separate minster at Idmiston served the north and eastern parishes of Alderbury Hundred.[123] Such an arrangement may indicate a special, possibly royal, status for Clarendon, which separated the two areas of the hundred.

Our evidence to reconstruct the middle and late Saxon landscape comes mainly from place- and field-name evidence. The area of Clarendon was known by the British name 'Panshett' meaning 'end of the wood' and, in the view of the place-name specialists, Panshett originally would have referred to a precise spot probably in the Avon valley above the present Salisbury.[124] This is the first clue that Clarendon may have partly been open land. The second clue is the name Clarendon itself, first written down as 'Clarendun' c. 1070.[125] On balance the evidence suggests an open hillside in the Anglo-Saxon period.[126] Thus 'Clarendon' first referred to 'dun', hill or sharp hillslope, a natural landscape feature which is plain to any visitor who stands on the high ground here[127] and the name Clarendon only later became associated with the royal palace.[128]

Further field-name evidence corroborates this picture of cleared areas in the Anglo-Saxon period. Ashley ('Asshelee' in 1307–27, for example), Chisley ('Chisele' in 1319) and Netley are all names found in the post-Conquest period within the park boundary, as well as Farley, adjacent.[129] Perhaps significantly, both Ashley and Chisley lie in the south-west of the park adjacent to the Petersfinger cemeteries. These 'leah' names imply open woodland, probably on the edge of a more thickly wooded area, pastures with scattered trees, perhaps of a type which might be used for wood pasture.[130] 'Clarendon', wherever precisely located, emerges as an area of open land at the edge of, or within, a more heavily wooded region.

Yet, if some parts of Clarendon remained cleared from later prehistory until the time they were named in the later Saxon period, other areas certainly became more wooded. The presence of lynchets in Great Gilbert's Copse, Home Copse, Long Copse and Pitton Copse refutes any suggestion that they might be surviving 'primary woodland' or 'wildwood' from the end of the last Ice Age and shows that even these areas were cleared by 1000 BC. The notion that no primary woodland is extant in England is certainly supported by this sample of Wiltshire landscape.[131] Archaeological evidence strongly suggests regeneration of secondary woodland over this central portion of the park after AD 400 or later, just as it does in other parts of Wessex where pre-existing prehistoric and Romano-British field archaeology is overlain by later Anglo-Saxon woodland.[132] Draper, for example, points to the concentration of villa sites under heavy woodland in the parishes of Bromham and Calne Without where the British place-name Chittoe, 'great or thick wood', indicates woodland regeneration in the immediate post-Roman period, before that area became part of the royal forest of Pewsham.[133] Closer to Clarendon, there were Roman 'villages' on the Grovely Ridge and under woodland and within the medieval royal forest of the same name. Marginal land like this on clay-with-flints must have been some of the most vulnerable to abandonment and, since we are ignorant as to precise chronology, we cannot say whether these soils were still in production even at the end of the Roman period.

One apparent difficulty with this interpretation of forest clearance is the presence of strong populations of ancient woodland indicator species (AWIS) in Clarendon woods.[134] How can this be explained when there is good evidence of clearance, settlement and cultivation? The probable answer is that ancient woodland indicator species recolonised from small pockets of uncleared woodland or from other woodlands in the vicinity, perhaps the wood of which Panshett/Clarendon formed the western end. Variations in climate might have resulted in periods of enhanced dispersion to ancient secondary sites, but a more plausible explanation is that the continuity of old trees in a suitable state of decay has ensured the survival of certain species of fauna and flora.[135] Ancient woodlands are biologically distinctive entities which have characteristic communities of species developed over very long periods: they are not to be equated with the survival of 'primary' woodland.[136]

Exactly why woodland regenerated in the centre of the later park in the period after the abandonment of settlements, which we now place at around AD 400–700, is difficult to answer. Convention has it that trees and scrub returned through lack of effective land management at a time of post-Roman demographic collapse, but neglect of former fields does not always lead to woodland and indeed woodland need not always imply a lack of effective management. An alternative interpretation might imply royal authority in south-east Wiltshire imposing order over large areas of countryside by controlling land use and, specifically, by allowing woodland to regenerate. Perhaps there were political reasons for this[137] but it is equally plausible that the decision was economic. Woodland was valued for seasonal pasture for pigs and other animals, such as cattle and horses. Animals could have grazed the pasture between the trees and, of course, there may also have been hunting.

In a wider context, an early medieval date for the recognition of a hunting reserve at Clarendon is not out of the question; Frankish kings and Lombard law were pressing royal rights to hunting as early as the late sixth and seventh centuries.[138] Areas do appear to have been designated for hunting in the late Saxon period and are known at Ongar (Essex), Brill (Bucks) and at Chippenham in Wiltshire,[139] while hunting birds and dogs are mentioned in Anglo-Saxon charters and depicted in early manuscripts.[140] Documents show unequivocally that hunting took place: for example, wild boar were hunted using hounds, and deer with hounds and nets.[141] The Anglo-Saxon chronicle, law codes and wills all stress that horses, some for hunting, were valued and gifted by AD 900.[142] Archaeology, too, adds to our understanding. To date there have been only a very few excavations in Britain at large mid to late Saxon high-status settlements where archaeologists have had the opportunity to work with large and well-dated faunal assemblages and examine the contribution of hunting, wildfowling and fishing in detail. None is local to Clarendon, but the inference from sites such as Flixborough (Lincs), where large numbers of crane, duck, deer and hare have been recovered in a well-stratified sequence between the seventh and tenth centuries, is that wildfowling and hunting were routine there at some periods.[143] Whether Flixborough should be labelled as a monastic or aristocratic site is uncertain; at different times it may have been either or both of these. In the context of south-east Wiltshire, Flixborough may be a good parallel for Alderbury at the same period, Clarendon forming part of a hinterland of diverse environmental habitats exploited by

FIGURE 19. Land use and administration in south-east Wiltshire and south-west Hampshire in the tenth century. This map combines information on Domesday manors, place-names and tenth-century charters. Entries are sparse because forest land was not liable to tax and held little to interest the compilers of Domesday. This exercise demonstrates that the later Clarendon Park lay at the northern fringes of an afforested area with woodland and hunting interests in the late Anglo-Saxon period, though Domesday refers only to the New Forest and to Melchet Wood by name. Two important church sites lay nearby, at Bredford (Britford) and Alwaresberie (Alderbury). For administrative purposes the later Clarendon Park and Forest were probably attached to Alderbury Hundred. (Map created by CMG and Simon Draper, drawn by Alejandra Gutiérrez)

nearby royal centres. Apart from the chance find of a baptismal ring of King Ethelwulf (d. 858), just possibly lost in a hunt, archaeology is blank both on Anglo-Saxon royalty and their hunting in the Clarendon area. Therefore the burden of proof for Clarendon as a royal hunting preserve rests with the surviving documents.[144]

Unfortunately, if hunting was undertaken at Clarendon, then we would not necessarily expect the documents to tell us that this was the case, at least not directly so.[145] There are, however, some clues. The term 'haga', to describe some kind of boundary feature, is usually interpreted as a pale or hurdles for the control of deer, and 'haga' features mentioned in Wiltshire charters do seem to cluster near Clarendon[146] (Figure 19). There is also later evidence which suggests Saxon hunting: in 1086 two of Edward the Confessor's hunts-men held land in vills which became part of Clarendon Forest,[147] while the 'king's forest' itself is described as intruding on the Laverstock lands owned by Wilton Abbey, as well as estates owned in Milford. At Britford, the woodland was also in the king's hands.[148] All these probably refer to Clarendon Forest,

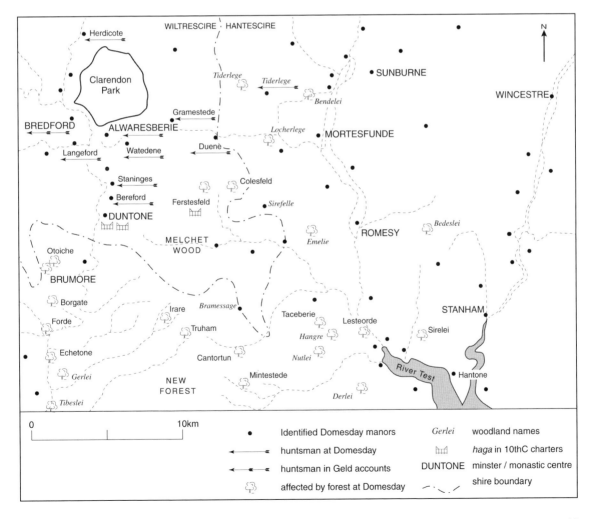

as do two references in the Geld Accounts under Alderbury Hundred, one of which specifically mentions forest.[149] Finally, like other parts of Wiltshire which were forest at this time, the average Domesday population density here was under five people per square mile.[150]

From these historical scraps and from an understanding of the later history of Clarendon, we present a case for Clarendon as a well-trodden pre-Conquest landscape, in which woodland and hunting were already priorities before AD 1000 and royal visits not unknown. The area of the later park may have been reserved for hunting as just one part of the wider Panshett Forest as early as the late seventh century and so remained free of settlement until the boundary of the park was formalised in the twelfth century.[151] As such, Clarendon may simply have formed an 'area of opportunity',[152] and this is our favoured interpretation. Clarendon was part of a region in which Roman agriculture and settlement had been abandoned and which therefore subsequently became available for other purposes and, in the late Saxon period, was conveniently situated for Wilton, from which Wiltshire took its name, and for Winchester, which emerged as a 'capital' of Wessex from around AD 900 and continued to dominate as a regional royal and ecclesiastical centre for some two centuries.

Whether there was some kind of late Saxon hunting lodge at Clarendon is unknown and could not be proved without large-scale excavation. There are certainly examples of Norman castles being raised over existing structures,[153] so the idea that William the Conqueror was legitimising his claims and setting up new buildings at an existing royal property is possible. To gain an impression of what such a complex might have looked like in the 800s and 900s, excavations at Faccombe Netherton (Hants)[154] and at Cheddar (Somerset)[155] provide archaeological clues to the range of post-holes and continuous trenches, rectangular in plan, which might be expected were this site to be excavated. Phase 5 at Faccombe, for example, dated c. 980–1070, included a timber hall (16.46 x 6.40 m), perhaps with walls of vertical boarding fitted between squared posts set in a continuous trench, a natural flinty clay floor and an oval latrine pit in one corner. Other buildings included a possible *camera*, or private building, and a possible kitchen with chalk and flint walls, all set within a ditch and bank abutting a churchyard. The interpretation of these early structures at Faccombe was not without its challenges; the dating evidence was slight, the chalky subsoil variable with colour changes hard to detect, and the interiors of timber buildings poorly preserved. Similar difficulties must be anticipated at Clarendon were any future attempt to be made by archaeologists to identify its pre-Conquest phases, not least because later buildings will have punctured earlier archaeological deposits. On the other hand, the building-up of ground levels, and the very deep accumulation of later medieval detritus and masonry across the palace site (over 3 m deep in many places) may preserve middle to late Saxon archaeology beneath later medieval remains. The earliest phases of the palace site have never been examined, but the deep unexplored stratigraphy is rich in archaeological promise.

CHAPTER THREE

Clarendon Park 1000–1500:
Laying out a Landscape

··

Henry I (reigned 1100–35) probably defined the park. Later kings embellished and may have enlarged it to reach 1737 ha by 1350. As we shall discover in this chapter, the park was defined by a bank 16 km long into which deer leaps were inserted to encourage deer to enter, and over which they could not escape back to the forest beyond. Inside, the landscape was divided into 'launds' (lawns), coppices, meadow and wood pasture, which provided grazing for deer, hare and rabbits, supplies of underwood and timber, and perhaps contained royal fishponds, all of which were managed by officials who lived in nearby lodges. The layout of the park was staged to intimidate even the most powerful of visitors, obliging visiting royalty and nobles to enter a great park, pass by an inner park below the palace buildings which dominated the skyline, before riding through the great gate and courtyard of the palace. From here, hunting with birds or with hounds could be viewed from the impressive palace garden platforms.

The making of the park

By 1070 there was already a place called Clarendon. That William the Conqueror mustered troops shows people could assemble there,[1] and presumably there were facilities appropriate for such a gathering. We argued in the previous chapter that the later palace site was already occupied, so William was enjoying a late Anglo-Saxon landscape long designated for hunting. Given his claim to love stags 'as if he were their father',[2] William must have felt an affinity with the place. Certainly, the sealing of charters at Clarendon by Henry I in 1116 and his visit in 1130, when stores were provided, prove a range of structures suitable for a royal household by that date. While documentation was prepared the king could turn his mind to pleasure. Henry was exceptionally knowledgeable about hunting; he was teased as 'Stagfoot' for being so knowledgeable about deer that he could tell how many points a stag had on its antlers by its hoof-print: for turning a 'joyous, mindlessly athletic pastime into a science'.[3] He is a prime candidate as founder of the park, a laboratory for his scientific passion (Figure 20). Perhaps, also, Clarendon was a potential retreat for the pleasures of the flesh, given Henry's uniquely large tally of bastards. Thus in the twelfth and thirteenth centuries, Clarendon grew

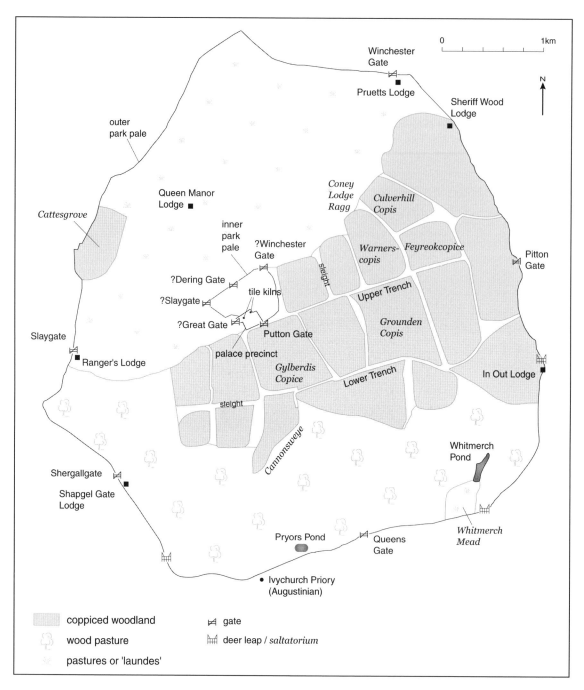

from a proto-palace or substantial hunting lodge, with private, public and administrative areas where business could be conducted by the king with his officials and the seal at his side, to a 'palatial residence',[4] making up, together with Westminster and Woodstock, the trio of major royal houses.

For earlier scholars, the origins of the park seemed simply resolved. Expenditure of £50 is recorded in 1223–8 'to enclose the park', a task initiated under

Bishop Peter des Roches in Henry III's minority.[5] However, the creation of a bank and ditch 16.5 km (10.2 miles) in length smacks of the direct royal command of a king unconstrained by regency and minority: nor was Henry III a keen huntsman. Fifty pounds does not suggest a huge earthmoving and palisading endeavour, but smacks rather of maintenance through a five-year programme. The earliest documented reference may therefore not date the park's creation and, on balance, it seems highly unlikely that either Henry I or his grandson Henry II would have showed such personal interest in the palace had there been no Clarendon Park. Henry I, therefore, probably established the park, as he did at Woodstock,[6] but documentation for the late eleventh and early twelfth centuries is lacking, so we cannot be sure.[7] However, the sheer scale of the park provides a strong clue. The giant Romanesque, even colonial, structures of Winchester Cathedral (William I, William II, Henry I) and Westminster Hall (William II) were extraordinary in their size and, it can be argued, are matched by the exceptional size of the labour-intensive park structures at Clarendon and Woodstock, with Romanesque palaces at their heart: Romanesque landscapes on a scale to match Winchester and Westminster's Romanesque extravaganzas. Henry II also spent large amounts on the palace, including the digging of the Great Wine Cellar in the 1170s. This major excavation, in terms of building work, does chime with the huge works of creating the park pale, but if he did order the embankment of the outer park then no record of it survives.

A second part of the puzzle is whether the park at Clarendon was laid out at one time. Its size and shape appear to indicate that it is a primary unit in the landscape but it has been suggested that the early park consisted only of the northern lawns, bounded to the south by the palace and the steep scarp which runs through across the park from east to west.[8] Perhaps the park did not take on its final form until the inclusion of the forest assarts in the south-eastern area c. 1319, before which, according to this argument, the palace would have been nearer to its eastern boundary.[9] In either case, there is no earthwork evidence to suggest an expanding unit and, unfortunately, the spatial location of the palace in relation to the park is no real clue. At Gillingham, for example, the King's Court Palace was at the western edge of the park there,[10] while at Woodstock the palace lay on the eastern side.[11] There is no reason to expect symmetry and the matter must remain unresolved.

FIGURE 20.
Reconstructed
medieval land-divisions
of 'launds' (north),
coppices (centre) and
wood pasture (south),
captured in retrospect
on the map of c. 1650.
Banks and ditches
served to keep deer *in*
the outer park and *out*
of the inner park, but
note the deer leaps in
the southern half of
the park. The positions
of likely gates and
lodges are indicated,
together with named
coppices and the
Canonsweye, the track
leading from Ivychurch
to the palace. (Drawn
by Alejandra Gutiérrez)

Palace and park

The medieval palace is treated in detail in the following chapter: but a brief summary of its development is necessary as a preface to any discussion of the park. The concept is straightforward. Directly derived from the Roman *villa rustica*, examples of which lay abandoned in the Clarendon woods, a medieval royal palace was undefended.[12] If he were threatened, a king would retire to a castle, where facilities were often more cramped and comfortless and where there was generally less privacy on account of a garrison and a significant permanent staff. In the reign of Henry I there were nine places outside London, including Clarendon, all unfortified, where the king sealed documents and observed the great feasts of the Christian year. By 1199, when Richard I died, there were twenty-three residences in royal hands, to which John (1199–1216) added a further six to make the largest number in royal hands in the Middle Ages. The eighteenth-century antiquarian Francis Grose (1777) registered this dry historical fact in the public mind when he observed that King John shared attributions as a builder in scale only with the Devil: John being ascribed the buildings (and as time progressed many more than he actually constructed or owned), and the Devil the earthworks, such as Clarendon's own Grims Ditch.[13] Thus in the early nineteenth century Clarendon Palace was credited to King John.[14] Some ill-gotten palaces were returned to their previous owners after Magna Carta (1215) but when Henry III inherited in 1216 there were still over twenty forest retreats, of which Clarendon received the greatest expenditure (£3600) of all the rural palaces in his long reign. Thereafter numbers generally declined to seventeen in the later years of Edward III, and Richard II had sixteen or seventeen houses all told in the realm; the Lancastrians, whose rule began with Henry IV in 1399, had about a dozen and the Yorkists, whose rule ended with the death of Richard III in 1485, had ten or fewer. This decline continued a trend which became apparent from the end of Edward III's reign: fewer, and better-appointed, houses, gradually clustered closer to London. No fewer than fifteen of Edward III's houses were within twenty-five miles (40 km) of London.[15] Clarendon Palace reached its greatest extent in the late thirteenth century, although significant additions, such as a new Chancery building under Edward II and work by Edward III and Richard II, sustained its grand scale.[16] But by 1500 Clarendon had ceased to be a royal residence.

These references illustrate the changing ways in which the palace was used between 1000 and 1500 in relation to the park and forest. Towards the beginning of this period royalty were present at Clarendon earlier in the year. For example, the Council for the Constitutions of Clarendon took place in late January 1164; King John was there on 2 January 1206; his wife Isabella was there at Easter 1207 (22 April). Typical entries for Henry III include 30 December 1225 and 14 February 1236.[17] Quantitative evidence supports these references: six of Henry II's eight dated visits to Clarendon took place between November and March. This was the doe season when a cull, carried out by professional huntsmen, would provide both spectator sport and a ready supply of fresh meat. But where both Henry II and Henry III avoided high summer, the thirty-five-year reign of Edward I witnessed a change: twenty-six days at Clarendon in January and February, but also forty days between early August and 10 September, that is to say during the fallow buck hunting season. Early in his reign Edward III visited in winter and saw to it that the pale was repaired to keep the escaping deer in, and came for buck hunting after 1333, no doubt giving rise to the traditions of hunting with captive kings and taking refuge from the summer plague in London.[18]

After Edward III's reign royal visits were much less frequent. Tudor victory in 1485 and the Dissolution of the Monasteries both changed local dynamics with the disappearance of the royal residence and of the Augustinian priory of Ivychurch in 1536. After a succession of lay owners the lordship of the manor of Ivychurch passed to the Bishops of Salisbury in 1551. The bishops let out the manor to the earls of Pembroke of Wilton House,[19] who employed Sir George Penruddock in the period 1572–80 to manage Clarendon Park, as he was doing when Queen Elizabeth visited in 1574. Penruddock, a keen huntsman, lived at Ivychurch and immediately embarked on a vigorous schedule of hunting. It was with Penruddock that Sir Philip Sidney was staying c. 1580 when he commented on the beauty of the park while composing his *Arcadia*, describing Clarendon as 'that delicious parke (which is accounted the best of England)'. Filled with Renaissance enthusiasm for Virgil's imaginary pastoral Arcadia, Sidney probably thought he had discovered it in Elizabethan England at Clarendon.

Tudor monarchs (1485–1603) focused their residential arrangements in the Thames valley and close to London. Former palaces such as Clarendon and Woodstock were no longer used as regular residences by an anxious, usurping, royal house. However, both Tudors and their successors the Stuarts – by which time there was nowhere suitable at Clarendon for royalty to live, as the palace had decayed – kept up the hunting, the key function of Clarendon.

These fragments of royal itineraries clearly indicate how the royal residences were used by medieval and early modern monarchs. Depending on age, circumstances, income and personal preference, residences were used for sport and recreation, councils and parliaments, expressions of cultural affinities in building and decoration, to cajole or impress local and foreign dignitaries, retreat from plague or merely as resting points on longer journeys. The administration travelled less with the king from the fourteenth century, once the Walton Ordinances (1338) were drafted to address the issue of how the Great Seal would be used in the absence of the king as war broke out.[20]

What marks Clarendon out from other residences is the scale of the park and buildings and the longevity of royal associations with palace and park. Helpfully, it is also the only rural palace of the medieval English monarchy for which we have anything like a complete ground plan. Comparison with, for example, Ludgershall (Wilts) is instructive:[21] the shorter time-scale of royal interest at Ludgershall, the small park, the slighter structures, the lack of significant political enactments and the lack of life-events of the royal family show its inferior status to the more grand, pivotal and venerable Clarendon.

Routes into and through the park

Early fourteenth-century documents suggest that Clarendon had, by that date, reached its largest extent; its huge encircling earthwork defined it as the largest royal deer park in England. Enclosing 1737 ha (4292 acres), it was an ambitious and costly undertaking constructed on a major scale; most other parks could boast an area of only 40–120 ha (100–300 acres).[22] Among the great estates of prelates and nobles, the lands of the bishops of Winchester were especially large but even they could only boast twenty-three parks, that at Bishop's Waltham being over 404 ha (1000 acres) in extent and Bramshill (Hants) measuring 1214 ha (3000 acres) in 1347.[23] Even modest deer parks were a virtually indelible signature of the élite on the medieval landscape, created and maintained by the wealthy as a mark of status and prestige. Imparking implied exclusivity and demonstrated command of resources, both human and animal. The very existence of a park required the annexing of large areas of otherwise profitable farm and downland. Size was clearly important in conveying this impression, but visual impact was also necessary. This was provided first by the massive fenced pale earthwork, a structure which dwarfed individuals within the landscape and put them in awe long before they reached the central palace area.

On the top of the park bank was set a pale whose classic form was a post and rail structure with cleft oak palings fastened to it. Such palings continued to be drawn on maps for Clarendon up to 1742 but long before that represented mere cartographic convention. In October 1254, only thirty years after the major refurbishment of the mid 1220s, the king was ordering the removal of some of the palings and their replacement with a hedge.[24] A notable feature of both the inner and outer pales today is the presence in several locations of large mature multi-stemmed ash and field maple trees along the crest of the bank. These have elongated trunk-bases or long horizontal sections with 'elbows' aligned along the pale, suggesting that they developed from laid hedges. Neither are typical laying species in farm hedges, however, being non-spiny, difficult to recut when mature and tending to compete with neighbouring shrubs of other species.[25] Whatever the type of hedge, the boundary earthworks themselves are still over 3 m high in places today and reference c. 1650 to the 'White Ditch', part of the south-western park pale near Shute End, reminds us how striking the bank and ditch must have looked when recently dug or cleaned.[26] The Clarendon circuit lacks natural closing features; there are no rivers or marshy areas to act as boundaries, even if some of the northern circuit made use of the break of slope on Cockey Down in precisely the same way the late pre-Roman Iron Age and Romano-British site there had done, and the Bronze Age barrows before that.

In 1272 the park was 'badly enclosed', as was frequently reported throughout the Middle Ages due to the scale of maintenance required on the exceptionally large *enceinte*.[27] Outside the pale, a survival from the Middle Ages, an 18-foot 'franchise' cordon existed in May 1650 within which owners of lands adjacent to the park were forbidden to cut bushes or trees, or to enclose land there, without the permission of 'the owner of the parke'.[28] This 'freeboard' was used as access for repairs and as a buffer against the outside world but it was the pale itself that confined that most fleet and irrepressible of animals, the deer, which could not jump out across the inner ditch and pale but might enter over a number of deer leaps. These consisted of a lowering of the paling fence,

FIGURE 21.
Conjectural reconstruction of a Clarendon deer leap, with archaeological cross-section in the lower left-hand corner. The deer shown here outside the park could leap the lowered section of pale but, once inside, the deepened inner ditch prevented them from escaping again. There were several such leaps along the outer perimeter of the park; the arrangement of ditches and bank was reversed for the inner pale. The paling fence is based on Charlecote Park in Warwickshire and the drawing adapted from Bond and Tiller (1997, 30) and Cox (1905, plate 24). (Drawn by Yvonne Beadnell)

inviting deer in, and a deepening of the interior ditch, to prevent a return to the forest outside (Figure 21).[29] Three deer leaps at Clarendon are shown on the c. 1650 map, at Pope's Bottom, Hunt's Copse and Shute End. All are likely to be medieval in origin.[30]

Entrance into the park on foot and horseback was through a number of gates. The five mapped c. 1650 were: the Queen's Gate at Alderbury, the Pitton Gate, the Winchester Gate, the Slaygate at Ranger's Lodge and the Shergallgate at Dog Kennel. During the later medieval period there was another from the south on the Canonsweye[31] which led through the park pale from Ivychurch Priory to the palace, two and a half kilometres away (Figure 22). Established in the reign of King Stephen (1135–54) on the site of an earlier chapel dependent on Alderbury minster, Ivychurch was of modest size and endowment.[32] Its Black Canons said offices at the chapels at Clarendon Palace and were responsible for the spiritual well-being of the sometimes sizeable community housed there.[33] High-status residences and religious houses were often correlated in this way, an ecclesiastical geography which was well understood

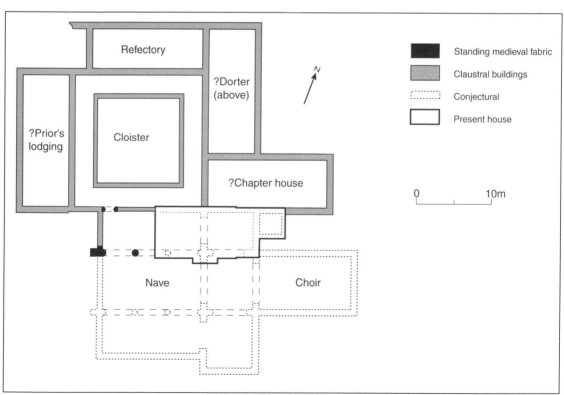

■	Standing medieval fabric
▨	Claustral buildings
┄	Conjectural
☐	Present house

Refectory

?Dorter (above)

?Prior's lodging

Cloister

?Chapter house

Nave

Choir

0 ——— 10m

and taken to express the piety of their founders, their status and paternalism.[34] A Wiltshire instance of the magnate residence/monastic combination is Bradenstoke/Lyneham castle, also twelfth-century and Augustinian. Royal twelfth-century parallels include Carlisle, Carmarthen, Dover and Southampton, all by Henry I.[35] Medieval royalty who frequented Clarendon celebrated not only religious festivals and feast days but also sustained daily mass and prayers, divided into several congregations.[36]

Perhaps the most frequently used route would have been out of the Slaygate (Ranger's) and on into Salisbury. Many newly planned towns of the twelfth century were established at the gates of castles and New Sarum (Salisbury) and Clarendon had a similar spatial relationship. This link has never been fully explored, but the move to New Sarum was decided upon before 1200, when park and palace were flourishing. The laying of foundations at the new cathedral site and the refurbishment of the park pale at Clarendon in the 1220s, along with major works on the palace, as part of a major restructuring of population distribution and infrastructure in the first quarter of the thirteenth century, created a spectacular Gothic landscape of park and palace, cathedral and city unrivalled in England. Doubtless there were economic benefits to be had on both sides, but how the bishops of Salisbury saw it is unknown. It seems unlikely to be coincidence that intervisibility was established between palace and cathedral. Indeed, in view of the Becket crisis of Church and State it seems almost perverse that the ecclesiastical authorities should decide so soon after 1170 to resite themselves so close to a major royal residence. Symbolically, the erection of the spire, at nearly 122 m in height, brought the top of the cathedral level with the palace on its hilltop, a constant reminder to visiting kings of the authority of the church; the more so as the palace crumbled into decay.

On entering the park via this route from Salisbury through the Slaygate, the traveller was confronted with a full view of the building complex on the top of the hill. Just as William the Conqueror wanted his monastic house at Battle Abbey and the made-up platforms and mottes of his castles, in both town and country, to dominate their hinterlands, so with Clarendon Palace domination of the surrounding landscapes was the intention. It is visible, imposing and high up, isolated and set against a sylvan backdrop which contrasted with the open downland landscape to the north. To arrive at the western gatehouse of the precinct, visitors passed along the now overgrown holloway parallel to the current Chalk Road.[37] Travellers from London or Winchester may also have followed this route, leaving the Roman road to the north of the park to enter by the Winchester gate, then riding along the chalk ridge and down into the valley below.[38] Anyone on this approach passed below the north front of the palace, high up on the left hand side, before circling back up the holloway. Herbert of Bosham (1164) in a bubble of ecclesiastical punning, commented that Clarendon was *'praeclara mansione'* – the clarity no doubt emanating from the prominent palace site on the hillside.[39] Regular cycles of white painting and repair – for example when the king's chamber 'towards the park' was

FIGURE 22.
The remains of the
former Augustinian
priory at Ivychurch.
This priory served the
chapel at Clarendon
Palace and may have
been established for
that purpose. The
photograph (a) looks
south and shows
the doorway which
linked the north aisle
of the church with
the cloister; the west
buttress to the church
nave is upstanding
on the right of
the photograph.
The present house
sits in the north
transept/north aisle
of the church. The
original plan (b) was
drawn by the Royal
Commission on the
Historical Monuments
of England who
also considered the
archaeology and
architecture of the
site (RCHME 1987,
149–153). (Plan redrawn
by Alejandra Gutiérrez,
photograph by
Christopher Gerrard)

'rendered over (*requirari*) with mortar and whitened' in March 1244 – ensured that the palace remained clearly visible.[40]

An alternative route to the palace from the east was via the park gate at Pitton. This provided a completely different experience of the Clarendon landscape because the approach was through woodland, riding west along the 'Upper Trench', arriving suddenly at the south-eastern corner precinct wall and entering via a gate in the southern wall, where a break in the earthwork remains today.[41] This journey was along a straight, narrow tree-free avenue, perhaps disturbing grazing deer, the path framed to right and left by coppices and taller standard trees on hedged banks, 2 m high in places. Similarly, those arriving from Southampton and the south-east through the Queen's Gate or, further west, the Shergallgate, would have travelled along the Lower Trench and then north up the 'sleight' west of Gilbert's Copse to the western palace gate.

How many of these forest tracks were regularly used by everyday medieval travellers is unknown. Perhaps many were. But once the park was created, they must have been gated at the pale to prevent deer escaping, thereby turning public routes into permitted access.[42] Tracks or 'sleights' between all the coppices enabled access to and from woodland, both for management and hunting. Matching Salisbury below, these routes networked together as regular grids which could have been used for circular rides.[43] In such a large landscape there were many options in organising routes into and across the park. What was the imperative which guided the visitor through Clarendon's woodland landscapes, or to circle in front of the palace high on the hill? Perhaps specific routes were dictated by status: royal and noble parties picked up guides at the Winchester or Ranger's entrance and were led to the palace along preferred routes. This is speculative but there seems no doubt that Clarendon was a medieval landscape selected and modified to project specific élite meanings. This display of status was played out through the arrangement of elements of royal power whose significance was understood by every Norman castle builder and deer park owner, and the opportunity may well have been taken to maximise the drama of arrival by privileging particular circuits of movement.

Land use inside the park

Based largely on the evidence of the estate map of c. 1650, together with documented medieval field and coppice names, the medieval park was divided into three main topographical and land use blocks. The chalk downland to the north-east was mostly pasture, the central portion of the park was woodland, and there was wood pasture to the south. Scattered across this carefully planned landscape were apparently 'natural' elements, such as planted trees and coppices, managed deer, rabbits and other animals, together with built elements such as banks, lodges, pales and walls. All of these were recognisably seigneurial components of an élite medieval landscape, a suite of 'natural' and 'built' elements which Clarendon had in common with many other medieval high-status estates, but which at Clarendon were exceptional in their royal scale.

The twenty coppiced and hedged compartments mapped c. 1650, which then yielded £20–35 per annum from sales of underwood from 25–40 acres (10–16 ha), seem likely to be the ancient medieval coppices documented in 1331.[44] Here poles of underwood were cropped on four- to eight-year cycles. Ash, beech, maple, oak and thorn are among the species found at Clarendon today and were familiar to medieval people.[45] In 1650 the compartments in which they grew were bounded by ditches, banks and hedges[46] and most of these are still traceable on the ground today, comprising a bank and exterior ditch, once topped with a hedge – now vanished – to prevent roaming deer from feeding and inhibiting regeneration of the coppice. There are several medieval references to this practice; one made in 1336 states 'to cause the places where such coppices are made to be enclosed with a low hay … for the preservation and defence of the wood there'.[47] As elsewhere, the Clarendon coppices are roughly rectangular, but have rounded corners to facilitate fencing and reduce costs. Some indication of past management practices is suggested by the modern ecology; Hunt's Copse is still in active management as coppice-with-standards, a familiar medieval management regime. Its canopy is mainly composed of ash/field maple with yew and oak, with a hazel understorey and a ground flora which includes orpine (*Sedum telephium*) and butcher's broom (*Ruscus aculeatus*), among twenty-two recorded ancient woodland indicator species (AWIS). Elsewhere, Canon, Hendon and Pitton Woods have intermittent old hazel coppice (Figure 23) and some ancient hazel stool-rings, suggestive of earlier practice, while Great Gilbert's Copse contains derelict ash (*Fraxinus excelsior*)/hazel (*Corylus avellana*) coppice and large old ash and pedunculate oak standards (*Quercus robur*). All have between seventeen and twenty-four ancient woodland indicator species, numbers strongly indicative of continuous woodland cover, a suggestion supported by both archaeological and historical evidence.[48]

Besides providing covert for the deer, Clarendon's woodland supplied leafy branches for their food. At other parks branches of evergreen trees were lopped and put out as fodder; as the density of deer was high at Clarendon this would have been essential, especially in winter months.[49] Coppices also provided a reliable supply of wood for domestic and retail purposes including broom handles (perhaps of fast-growing ash), skewers and spindles, hurdle fencing and building as well as for feeding the fires in the kitchens and palace accommodation. The 'log store', converted c. 1250 into accommodation for knights, highlights the tonnage of logs required for open fires, for heating kitchen cauldrons and for roasting on spits. Bavins – bundled long hazel rods for firing the bread ovens – were perhaps also dried here[50] and in emergencies underwood was sent out from Clarendon; in 1339, for example, the king instructed that Old Sarum Castle should be supplied with a load 'as his enemies propose to invade the realm', a ripple from the outbreak of the Hundred Years War (1337). Even branches, windfall and bark (for tanning)

were valuable by-products which Henry IV granted to his half-brother John Beaufort in February 1405.[51]

Of much greater value was the significant quantity of high-quality slow-grown timber from the park. Demand for Clarendon timber was steady and increased as the thirteenth century progressed:[52] from six oaks in 1222 for Gilbert de Lacy's new chapel at Britford, to thirty for the church of Wilton Abbey, forty for making shingles for the palace at Clarendon (another indication of the great scale of the palace) and sixty for rafters for Queen Eleanor's buildings at Lyndhurst.[53] Analysis of reused timbers in standing structures from trees growing from the thirteenth century onwards indicates that structural elements in Clarendon buildings were of *Quercus*. One section of fourteenth-century roof, reused at Queen Manor, probably from a nearby lodge, was composed of trees cut down c. 1330.[54] This is the earliest tree-ring sequence at Clarendon, from trees which were growing in 1218, and demand for oak continued throughout the later medieval period, for building as well as for other purposes.[55] When, in May 1378, 'the mayor and communalty of the city of New Sarum' petitioned the king for twenty oaks to help complete the 'trench around their city and wooden fence', Richard II replied that these trees might come from the park at Clarendon (or wherever the justice of Clarendon Forest deemed least damage would be done).[56] The use of timber, however,

FIGURE 23.
Hazel coppice in the snow at Home Copse. Medieval management of Clarendon woodland had two main purposes: to produce timber for building and wood from its coppices for fuel and fencing. The substantial woodbanks which once defined the coppices and kept deer out can still be traced through the modern woodland. (Photograph by Christopher Gerrard)

is not always predictable. Where one might anticipate all the timber needs of the park to be supplied from trees there, in 1244 100 logs or sticks (*fusta*) were brought to Clarendon from Grovely to 'make posts and great timbers for the king's works'.[57] These were perhaps large crucks for which suitable Clarendon trees were not available at that moment.[58] Certainly oak was not the only timber available. Large beeches of multi-trunked or pollarded form are found frequently today at Clarendon, usually at the edges of copses. Oak was the ubiquitous timber for medieval carpentry; however, on some occasions other woods were sought, sometimes specified, at others times referred to less explicitly for particular purposes. Thus beech may, as at Windsor, have been a 'special wood' sought through the forest for a royal seat at Clarendon Palace,[59] but the forked form of surviving trees suggests native planted stock rather than introduced timber stock; they may also have had significance as boundary markers and hedges.[60]

South of the coppices lay wood pasture, named as Sheer Wood on the map of c. 1650. Here oxen and cows shared the land with timber trees. Sheep and goats were excluded from royal forests without a licence because they were not thought compatible with deer and woodland but in 1317 Edward II gave pasture within his manor of Clarendon for forty beasts belonging to Ivychurch Priory.[61] Ivychurch also enjoyed a fishpond – the 'Pryors Pond' – at the edge of the wood pasture; 'a large fishpond' appears in a survey of March 1652[62] and another pond, 'Devil's Pitt', near 'Cannon Coppice', may have been another fishpond 'never without water … save for want of repair'.[63] These earthworks helped with drainage and provided water for browsing fallow deer.[64] Wood pasture there today contains a scatter of large old pollards and 'park trees'[65] of pedunculate oak with large diameters of 5 to 8 m at breast-height. Among the scrub fronting Clarendon House a very large, almost dead, oak pollard about 5 m in diameter remains, along with a large living pollard of sweet chestnut over 6 m in diameter (*Castanea sativa*), while another large, dying oak of similar diameter is found opposite the Gardener's Cottage.[66] These are venerable relics typical of a medieval deer park landscape (Figure 24).

In the south-east corner of the park lay Whitmarsh Mead, meadow valued for its grass and hay crops for deer in winter.[67] Today there is a small area of unimproved grassland flanking the southern edge of the Wild Garden which contains pignut (*Conopodium majus*), dropwort (*Filipendula vulgaris*), salad burnet and skullcap (*Scutellaria galericulata*), together with commoner species. This may represent the edge of an area of former meadowland.[68] Other activities, such as clay extraction and pottery-making, have also been suggested in this part of the park after a waster sherd was found on Ashley Hill, Petersfinger.[69] This emphasises that economic diversity in the park was wide and restricted neither to deer farming nor exclusively dedicated to conspicuous consumption. If deer parks conferred status and prestige on their owners, they also had practical purposes.

To the north of the coppices lay launds. These extensive areas of pasture are mentioned from the thirteenth century onwards.[70] In archaeological

FIGURE 24.
Old park trees.
Clarendon has a long
tradition of wood
pasture, that is pasture
for grazing animals
(mainly fallow deer,
sometimes pigs and
cattle) where there
were also trees,
particularly oaks.
Some of those which
still stand in the park
close to the mansion
are of notable girth
and age. Ancient trees
such as this were
given names such as
'Monarch' and 'King
John' in the post-
medieval period and
represent a tangible
link with the medieval
past. (Photograph by
Fran Halsall)

confirmation of this, recent fieldwalking, other than in the immediate vicinity of Queen Manor, recovered just one sherd of later medieval pottery from
the northern half of the estate.[71] Such grassy feeding areas in deer parks are
nowhere else found on the enormous scale seen at Clarendon. There were
deer ponds for watering and wallowing, deer houses to provide shelter in
poor weather and feeding troughs for hay or oats. Hares bred here and the
launds supported rabbits. This association between rabbit warrens, seigneurial
residences and monastic sites is one commonly found in medieval England.[72]
Rabbits appear in the records for Clarendon in 1355 (in conjunction with
hares), but were certainly there earlier.[73] In 1399 Nicholas Ricoun was launder

of the park and therefore supervised deer and rabbits at Clarendon, a position taken up in October of that year by Thomas Rouland, 'yeoman of the livery of the Crown'.[74] This change in tenure of Clarendon was due to the deposition of Richard II by Henry IV (Bolingbroke) on 30 September: Rouland was a Lancastrian. In 1465 'rabbits and hares without number' were seen at Clarendon by a Bohemian traveller,[75] while in 1495 the substantial sum of £100 of royal income was derived from the 'farmer of the conies' at Clarendon.[76] The industrial scale of the rabbit farming at Clarendon at that date is highlighted by the 'very large sum' of £30 a year which accrued when the warren at Aldbourne (Wilts), producing 5000 rabbits, was let out in the later Middle Ages. By analogy the annual bag at Clarendon must have been well over 15,000.[77] By the mid sixteenth century the 'coney berryes' income had doubled to £200 a year, when in 1553 William Herbert, earl of Pembroke, is mentioned as 'lieutenant of the conies … and the taking of them with dogs, nets and other engines'.[78] Like deer management, rabbits and hares provided a mix of sport (they appear in Gaston Phoebus's hunting book of 1387[79]) and commercial opportunity.

Eating rabbits enjoyed a higher status before the Black Death of c. 1350, when they were kept in specially prepared warrens. Only as they became feral, and with rising individual prosperity after the plague, does the archaeozoological record suggest they became fare for a wider public.[80] Pillow (warren) mounds have not been identified at Clarendon,[81] but the suggestion that the name 'Warnerscoppice' in 1477, later 'Warner's' or 'Warne', refers to a warren and/or a warrener's house along the ridge east of the palace seems to be confirmed by the post-medieval field-name 'Coney Lodge Ragg' which lies close by, although there is no trace today. In 1660 it was noted that William, Earl of Pembroke, 'consented to the destruction of the conies, on condition of having the forestership to himself and his heirs'.[82] This refers to Pembroke's opportunism in response to James I's personal injunction, about 1604, that the Clarendon rabbits should be eliminated because their burrows were a hazard to the king's galloping across the countryside taking his 'delight and sport'.[83]

A grasp of which animals, wild and domestic, existed inside the medieval park and where they might have been present provides a valuable picture of their positioning in the landscape. Only deer, hares and rabbits were visible from the palace and the inner park. Cattle graced the southern wood pasture; fishponds were out of sight. In 1925 sixteenth-century Breughel landscapes representing the four seasons were among pictures hanging in the Clarendon mansion, reminding the owners of a simple, rural, peasant past. Nearly 750 years earlier, in 1251, carvings of activities representative of the twelve months of the year were ordered for the overmantel of the fireplace in Queen Eleanor of Provence's hall at Clarendon Palace.[84] Images like these would have been familiar from medieval calendars and books of hours: feasting in January, cooking or chopping wood in February, sowing in March, planting and pruning in gardens and orchards, haymaking, harvesting, the vintage (or treading apples and so on), feeding and killing swine in November and December.

A series of just such cameos was depicted on the ceiling of Salisbury Cathedral in the mid-thirteenth century (Figure 25).[85] Such representations were stereotyped, of course, but real enough to any medieval villager.[86] Yet these miniature images of individual peasants were largely unfamiliar in the context of the medieval park; this was a landscape set apart from the routine of seasonal peasant digging and the cereal harvest.

The medieval hunt at Clarendon

Medieval parks were quite different in concept from modern parks. They provided occasional sport for the king and his retinue and supplied high-status royal gifts and élite meats for the table. Both red deer – from the thirteenth century – and roe deer became increasingly rare in southern England towards the fifteenth century because of increased coppicing, and the exclusion of roe from the Forest Law in 1338.[87] At Clarendon fallow deer continued to be managed, reared and hunted.[88] This was one of only a handful of parks potentially large enough to accommodate hunting fallow deer on horseback across open country.[89] It is highly likely that kings Henry I, Henry II, John and Edward III hunted at Clarendon in person, and in our view, given the expenditure on beautifying palace buildings, it is inconceivable that aesthetic considerations did not include surrounding landscapes.[90]

Medieval terms for deer are unfamiliar today. Latin terminology in medieval documents was *capriolus* (roebuck), *cervus* and *bissa* (red stag and hind), *damus* and *dama* (fallow buck and doe). As Anglicisation crept in the terms remain unequivocal: thus *unius stagg*, for example, would refer to a mature male red deer. Documents impress on us that at Clarendon Park the deer were almost exclusively *damus* and *dama* – fallow. The suggestion is that the forest was stocked from the park, whereas the more wild Grovely area of Clarendon Forest produced red deer and a few roebucks in the thirteenth century, and no fallow.[91] Furthermore, archaeological evidence is unequivocal in supporting this claim.[92] Despite murrains which in 1470, for example, resulted in the discovery of 2209 deer carcases at Clarendon, the park remained well stocked during the Middle Ages and Henry III could supply the earl of Pembroke with twenty does from Clarendon to stock a park.[93] The correspondence of royal visits with fallow hunting seasons in the late summer and autumn indicates that the owners expected to hunt at Clarendon and planned accordingly. References in the thirteenth and fourteenth centuries indicate that the hunting season for fallow bucks was 1 August to 14 September. Fallow doe hunting continued until 29 September.[94] According to Gaston Phoebus (1387), buck hunting took place from mid June to mid September.[95]

Fallow deer were grouped by medieval commentators with fox, marten and roe deer, as distinct from the hart, hare, wild boar and wolf. William Twiti (c. 1327), huntsman for Edward II, distinguished hunting practices for each group. For the latter group a lymer (like a bloodhound), was employed to seek out the quarry, whereas for the former group running-hounds (similar to a foxhound) picked up the scent for themselves. This accords with what we know of the composition of the royal buckhounds and tallies with the modern stalking practice of using a 'high sniffer' (to chase and find large prey) and a 'low sniffer' (to find prey and to retrieve small prey).[96] Fallow deer were less well regarded by hunters than the noble hart as they had less stamina and they were easier for the running-hounds to track. But at the table the fallow buck was more highly rated because its 'flesshe is more savery than is that of the herte or of the Roo bucke. The venyson of hem is ryght good, and ykept and salted as that of the hert'.[97] The meat was both flavoursome and abundant.

On occasion medieval hunting at Clarendon must have been the classic horseback chase, thundering across the launds visible from the palace site above, commands shouted, horns sounding (Figure 26). Shot from the saddle, the deer would finally turn at bay, hemmed in by dogs. Bowmen would bring the animal down and huntsmen would pierce its neck with a blade, to the sound of single long note on the hunting horn.[98] In such a large landscape as Clarendon, though, and especially through woodland, this kind of hunt was

FIGURE 25.
Labours of the months,
in the presbytery at
Salisbury Cathedral.
The original (c. 1240)
scheme of roundels
was 'restored' c. 1870.
At least five of them
are new versions taken
from contemporary
English manuscript
calendars but the
general decorative
characteristics are
correct. The original
scheme can be
compared with the
chapel of the Guardian
Angels at Winchester
Cathedral (Figure 34).
(Redrawn by Alejandra
Gutiérrez)

not well suited to spectators, who might hear but could not see. The elderly, the sick, women and children were all excluded and it seems likely that a more controlled form of hunting may have been used with beaters and dogs driving deer to prescribed locations. This is usually referred to as the 'bow and stable' hunt and is described in Edward, Duke of York's 'Master of Game' in the fifteenth century as 'the maner of hundyng whan the kyng wil hunte in foreste or in parke'.[99] There were several variants, but the basic ingredients are the same. Rather than archers chasing deer, deer are pushed towards concealed bowmen who lie in wait. At Clarendon, horsemen, beaters and hounds would have moved through the woods, where the deer would hide during daylight hours, and drive them out down the sleights. Such an operation would require large numbers of people, perhaps hundreds, but the advantages were many. The royal and noble party were stationary; they took up prepared positions ('stands' or 'standings'), drew their bows and waited. Gaston Phoebus provides guidelines for the type of bow to be used, even the length of the arrowhead.[100] Nevertheless, a single arrow was unlikely to kill a fallow deer outright, so scenting-hounds were then dispatched after the wounded animal. As Edward makes clear, the central concern was the location of the king and queen. They were the last to take their positions at their standing, where a bower might have been constructed to keep off the sun, and other spectators could either view or participate in the action.[101] After the hunt, the king inspected the carcases and gave orders as to whom they should be gifted.[102]

A question remains at Clarendon Park, as elsewhere, of how often these formalised hunting expeditions occurred. Royal parties probably participated routinely in such events but huntsmen and others at Clarendon were also charged with supplying venison on a systematic basis when the royal household was elsewhere. In that case consumption of venison would have taken place off-site. How many deer would have been taken here in a year? Calculations at other parks where more precise figures can be generated from accounts suggest that up to 10 per cent of the stock might be hunted in any one year.[103] That might mean 200–400 fallow deer per year at Clarendon on the basis that the medieval stock in the park numbered thousands.[104]

Deer were not the only wild animals to be disturbed by hunters.[105] Wolves were believed to have been hunted to extinction before 1200 in southern Britain and thus a reference to the payment of 15s paid by King John for wolves killed at Gillingham (Dorset) and at Clarendon in 1210, was assumed to have been a fossil, or payment for some other task accounted as wolf-killing. However, the existence of royal wolf-hounds (*canes luvereticos*) and recent research by Aleks Pluskowski combine to demonstrate that wolves were indeed quarry animals at this late date in these locations.[106] Wild boar (*Sus scrofa*) also lived in the Clarendon Forest, or just possibly in the park, in the Middle Ages, although dates and numbers are not known. Tellingly, no evidence has been positively identified in the faunal remains at the palace.[107] Bone assemblages recovered from the palace site suggest that hare was taken.[108] Wild birds were also hunted, generally flushed out by spaniels and brought down by hawks.[109]

The sparrowhawk and the goshawk were associated with hawking by aristo-cratic ladies and lower nobility and could be used to take partridges, pheasants and other small birds. The bones from both a sparrowhawk and its prey were recovered recently from the palace site[110] and this bird also appears in contem-porary documents. The swanimote of 1331–2 heard evidence of people breaking into Clarendon Park for the purpose of stealing the king's sparrowhawks.[111]

Mews are referred to routinely from 1154, when records begin, and clearly housed birds of prey both large and small. After 1200 King John received gyrfalcons (*Falco rusticolus*) at Clarendon from the King of Norway.[112] These birds were used at first to hunt herons, but were later put to more general use.[113] Like peregrine falcons (*Falco peregrinus*), gyrfalcons would only have been kept by individuals of the highest status, partly for their beauty and partly for hunting larger birds.[114] In 1289, for example, expenses were entered for the bringing of two cranes' heads, taken in hawking, to the Queen at the palace and for the king's trumpeter.[115] Not all wild birds, however, were taken by hawking. Fowlers were certainly present in Clarendon forest and used a 'cockshut', a large net suspended between poles used to catch woodcocks in flight at twilight.[116] Taking of woodcock dates from the Middle Ages at Clarendon, as a reference to the 'cockroads' before 1300 indicates.[117]

The most unusual recent find was a single bone from a white-tailed sea eagle, discarded by a previous excavator into a spoil heap at the West Kitchen.[118] Its natural habitat today would be coastal or estuarine,[119] so it is possible that this bird was a visitor from the south coast killed as vermin or to provide feathers for fletching.[120] A possible trade in attached primary feathers is suggested by finds of wing bones from seven Roman sites in Britain.[121] The very nature of the site at Clarendon Park, however, suggests this massive bird was kept for hunting. Medieval sources tell us that they 'by ther nature belong to an Emprowre' and that they 'will fell an Hynde calfe, a Fawn, a Roo (Roe deer), a Kydde, an Elke, a Crane, a Bustarde, a Storke, a Swan, a Fox in the playn ground'.[122] Recent research has found only one example of the white-tailed sea eagle being used in this way, in Kyrgyzstan, where the bird was used to take wolf, fox, hare and antelope. Too heavy to carry on the fist, the eagle would probably have required some kind of wood and leather attachment to the girdle or saddle to support its weight fully.[123] Once in the air, the open ground of Cockey Down would have been ideal open country, the eagle rising to a fair height and then descending at speed to crack a fox's skull at a single blow. These powerful birds are hard to train: other falcons fear eagles so they cannot be used together.[124] As a result, they are rarely used in falconry today and should perhaps be thought of as a novelty bird at medieval Clarendon, kept more for show than their killing prowess. Knights were often compared by medieval authors with birds of prey and, in this context, it is interesting to note that one medieval source from Scotland personifies the sea eagle as the king.[125]

Buildings of the park

There were certainly five, maybe eight, and possibly more medieval lodges and houses beyond the palace precinct. They were placed both at the entrances to the park and within areas of coppice, launds and wood pasture, belying the simplistic notion that medieval lodges were 'working' buildings within forests while post-medieval lodges were placed at the entrances to monitor access. The names of the lodges – like the names of certain rooms at the palace – sometimes record occupiers: Ambros, Dale, and so on.[126] Other lodges mentioned, which probably also lay either outside the park or within the palace precinct, were Biston's, Warden's, Cole's, Mille's, Nyng's and John of Clarendon's.[127]

There may have been a court function at Sheriff's Lodge, but it is more likely that judicial administration was carried out at the palace, where there was a prison and more intimidating surroundings. Sheriff's Lodge at Clarendon may simply have been the lodge near 'Shreeve's' coppice.

Queen Manor and Sharpegoregate (later Shergallgate, then Dog Kennel) may indicate both residence and function. Queen Manor is especially intriguing. This is likely to be on or near the site of the early 'Lodge on the Laund', which was being repaired in 1341.[128] During recent fieldwork a single sherd of a late medieval glazed jug and three medieval floor tile sherds were found in an adjacent field, Hockamore. The tile would seem to indicate a well-appointed building close by and since the floor tiles are both early and mid thirteenth-century in date, it is possible that there was a lodge here for at least 100 years before repairs are first documented.[129] The superficially attractive notion that Queen Manor gained its name after serving as the locus for Queen Elizabeth's dinner at Clarendon in 1574 is neat but debatable, since there are references to a Queen Lodge and a Queen Manor throughout the fifteenth century.[130] The stables and a pale mentioned then imply a separate structure[131] but quite what the role of such a building might have been is uncertain. At Woodstock there was a 'bower' adjacent to a spring which seems to have been developed as a retreat for Henry II's mistress Rosamund Clifford with buildings, a cloister, pools of water and gardens with pear trees, loosely inspired by Islamic models of the paradise garden.[132] There is no indication that anything of that kind existed at Clarendon.[133]

The lodges occupied diverse topographical locations: some, such as Queen Manor and Fussell's, were high up, commanding views over isolated tracts of the park. Others, such as Keeper's (or Ranger's) and the lodge at Winchester Gate (or Pruett's), were located at entrances/exits to the park, the first with views up the northern valley, the second commanding vistas across the north-eastern area of the park. The In Out Lodge (in Hunt's Copse, also Lez Oute Wyds) and Whitmarsh Lodge both occupied isolated parts of the park far from the palace.[134] All these were established by 1500 but they are unlikely to have been constructed at the same time. Documentation suggests that most were fourteenth- or fifteenth-century and that only Queen Manor, perhaps with a special role, preceded them.

In contrast to the major palace buildings, these lodges are likely to have been timber-framed, perhaps akin, at least in their fourteenth-century form, to that built by Edward III and still standing at Odiham (Hants).[135] They were not insubstantial. Edward III provided a hall with two chambers, garderobe, cellar, pantry, kitchen, larder and stable for his keeper[136] and surviving earthworks prove some lodges had their own pales.[137] The only structure standing from the medieval park buildings was thought to be Dog Kennel Farm, at the southern margin of the modern estate.[138] However, dendrochronology now dates the major structural phase of this house to 1588, during the Pembrokes' management period.[139] It seems highly likely to echo the site of the medieval royal kennels, and if built in 1588 may have been for hunting dogs of the kind which 'overturned' the deer during Queen Elizabeth's visit in 1574.[140] Medieval kennels, according to Gaston Phoebus, were substantial; a building 60 by 30 feet (18 x 9 m), with an upper storey and fireplace, is described. The dogs slept on hazel hurdles.[141] Several reasons can be put forward for this location. First, the kennels were at maximum distance from the northern launds, where deer grazed, so as not to disturb them or, more importantly, the inhabitants of the palace.[142] Second, before the seventeenth-century creation of water meadows, the marshy area beside the river would have been excellent for hawking from horseback with hounds putting up the birds for the riders' hawks. Medieval horseshoes and a fine fourteenth-century horse harness pendant found in the Petersfinger water meadows add substance to this supposition.[143] If this was indeed the case then dogs employed in falconry included pointers and spaniels, used to flush out game.[144]

But dogs were not absent at the palace. Characteristic chew marks were found on bones all over the site and the remains of several disturbed dog burials, both puppies and elderly animals, were found close to the western gatehouse.[145] Venison apparently contributed to their diet; parts of roe deer heads, the off-cuts from the butchered carcase, were recovered from the same area. This may provide a clue as to the identity of the dogs kept there. Lymers were housed separately from running-hounds and were used to seek out the hart on the morning of a hunt. They were also rewarded separately, with the buck's head.[146] Whether these were household or hunting dogs, they were buried on the western perimeter of the precinct close to what may have been the apartments of the deputy warden, where they may have been housed for convenience when royalty were away.[147] Cats, needless to say, roamed more freely.[148]

Medieval lodges provided domestic accommodation for officials who managed deer, other animals and woodland inside the park. The variety of appointments listed in 1553 – 'lieutenants, foresters, rangers, launders, warreners, walkers, palers, stewards of courts and swainmotes' and other officers[149] – indicates key responsibilities. Medieval documents name yet more officers, such as the 'stikkers',[150] and 'keeper',[151] among others. In the fourteenth century the warden of Clarendon also claimed 'the right to make execution touching this in the park wher of ancient time it hath been accustomed to be done'.[152] The location of the gallows is not known, though a potential site, remote, high and visible, is that later occupied by the cross in the northern extreme of the park perimeter. No evidence of it having been used has come to light, though law enforcement (particularly trespass) was clearly a concern for the officers of the park. It was they who caught John Lane, servant of the prior of Ivychurch, and John Chelseye in February 1379, who had chased a hare out of the king's park with two harriers of the prior and killed a 'pricket' which had leapt the pale in the park.[153] These men were pardoned for their transgression but others faced long-term punishment. In 1380 one trespasser was required to pay a yearly rent of three barbed arrows with peacock feathers to 'Claryndon Manor'. Three arrowheads found in the 1930s and unusually covered in copper-alloy plating, presumably to glint as they flew through the air, were other such quality hunting accoutrements.[154]

The inner park

The inner park, known variously as 'the King's park' and 'the park'[155] is marked out on the ground by a pale which defines an area of about 26 ha, if the palace footprint is included (Figure 27).[156] The pale comprises a bank with an outer ditch, designed to keep deer away from this reserved area, which was used for some purpose other than hunting. It is possible that the earthwork may have been topped with a wall;[157] a 1267 reference requests contruction of 'a wall of stone and lime around the aforesaid manor where the wall is lacking' at Clarendon.[158] The stump of a wall survives along the southern edge of the palace site where it is coterminous with the edge of the inner park.[159]

The question as to how this unusual inner park might have been entered is raised by Tancred Borenius's 'very old map' mentioned in 1935.[160] A newspaper article describing this dubious find relates that Borenius, who led the excavations at Clarendon Palace between 1933 and 1939, quoted 'several interesting facts':

> The most important of these is that the palace was surrounded by a demesne, consisting of a small park and gardens, which lay chiefly to the north, east and south of the building. Its limits were marked by some sort of boundary in which were set several gates. Apparently there were five of these, namely, the Great Gate (to Salisbury), the Winchester Gate, the Putton (or Pitton Gate), the Slaygate and the Dering Gate. The Great Gate was situated on the crest of the hill, close to the palace. Traces of the road leading from it are dimly discernible as it wends its way across the fields to the bridge at Milford. The other gates are about a quarter of a mile from the palace. Of them, Slaygate may be merely another name for Pitton Gate.[161]

If this map existed at all, then the Great Gate appears to be the western gatehouse, which Borenius had excavated in 1934,[162] while the Pitton Gate is presumably that unsuccessfully searched for in the 1960s by John Musty in the south-east corner of the palace precinct. If the other gates are only a quarter of a mile away they cannot be the gates of the outer pale, unless Borenius mis-scaled his map. It may be, therefore, that there were three further gates somewhere along the inner pale, the 'Slaygate' ('slay' = 'slea' = slope), the 'Dering gate' and the 'Winchester gate'. Detailed survey along the inner pale reveals a number of areas where there is a gap in the pale and the outer ditch is breached with a causeway, but without excavation, and without the map, it is not possible to take the matter further.

The inner park pale is certainly unusual and similar structures are not found at other royal houses. Fieldwalking within it has revealed no medieval artefacts besides a very light scatter of roofing material which probably migrated downslope from the palace site immediately above, to the south.

Various functions have been suggested, including semi-permanent grassland for tented accommodation erected during large gatherings such as councils and parliaments and events such as hastiludes. The latter may have taken various forms; either a tournament *en masse* or jousting in single combat within a 'list', an enclosed area with barriers. Records of the Field of Cloth of Gold give a general impression of the layout and suggest a field 328 feet (100 m) wide and 900 feet (274 m) long, surrounded by a ditch and bank and double railing.[163] Spectators' galleries remained on the outside with monarchs and guests in tents and wooden chambers inside the 'lists'. Retreats where knights could rest were linked to the 'list' by a bridge over the ditch. If this layout is in any way representative of what may have been in place at Clarendon then any associated archaeology, in the form of galleries and accommodation, is located outside the inner pale and there is no trace of it today. A prime view would have been from the palace gardens and the queen's tower, above.

The modern field name 'Tilting Field' is all the evidence we have, but even this may have more to do with its sharp incline than any memory of medieval jousting. The name itself cannot be traced earlier than the twentieth century; the field was called 'Old Park' on seventeenth- to nineteenth-century maps. Nor has any documentary evidence for a tournament site emerged, though local 'tourneying' did take place between Salisbury and Wilton at one of the five English 'official' sites established by Richard I.[164] In our view, the scale of the outer Clarendon Park enabled a full chase of deer to take place, obviating the necessity for ersatz tourneying.

More mundanely, was the inner park some sort of 'home farm' where cattle, sheep and pigs were stocked temporarily in a 'living larder'? This is now considered unlikely given that meats were clearly butchered into joints off-site, although without stratigraphic dating different periods of supply cannot be distinguished.[165] Perhaps part of the area was given over to garden produce and fruit trees such as apples and pears.[166] A third possibility is that tamed birds such as bitterns, herons, peacocks, pheasants and swans strolled here, though only pheasant and heron bones, and a single swan bone, have come from the palace site.[167] Peacocks are not present in Clarendon bone assemblages.[168] A final suggestion is that this was fenced pasture, perhaps for breaking or training newly acquired mounts and pasturing the baggage horses of the royal household and horses used on a daily basis by servants and park workers.[169] One large noble household kept between thirty and fifty horses, and numbers at Clarendon must have exceeded that.[170] Of the 1800 people who came in 1164, for example, many would surely have ridden. Queen Isabella's entourage, which arrived at the palace during Lent 1207, spent a very significant proportion of their outlay on oats for the horses,[171] implying large numbers on horseback, and the enormous scale of the stables also bears witness to this. At 360 m², these dwarfed the 80 m² of the aristocratic fifteenth-century stable at Farleigh Hungerford (Somerset). An average of 3 m² per horse would mean accommodation for 120 horses at Clarendon. Horse bones and teeth were scarce on the excavations, so the question of breeding must remain open,[172] but if these calculations are correct, an entourage of even 100 riders approaching the palace through the park would have been a spectacular sight, especially armed and bearing banners; they may have been a delegation of knights or attendees at a council, or escorting horse-drawn chariots carrying queens to the palace. The next chapter considers the palace at which they arrived.

FIGURE 27.
The inner park pale at the palace. There the outer bank of the palace precinct (foreground), topped by a wall in the later Middle Ages, doubled as the southern boundary of the inner park, with the ditch outside to keep deer out of the palace area. There are also more ancient, perhaps Iron Age, banks here, once proposed as enclosing an '*oppidum*', a theory not tested by archaeology to date due to the depth of later deposits. (Photograph by Fran Halsall)

CHAPTER FOUR

Clarendon Palace 1000–1500: Romanesque to Gothic

Clarendon Palace was a focus of royal visits from the eleventh to the fifteenth century, developing according to the standard manorial plan of kitchens, hall and chamber blocks to become a residence on the grandest scale. This chapter presents the evidence for the royal house at Clarendon from documents and archaeological sources, including both published excavations and more recent fieldwork during consolidation and display of ruined buildings within the precinct. In particular, these new data provide insights into the developing plan of the site, medieval diet and feasting, provision of pottery, furnishings and structural works using exotic and more local sources of stone, roofing materials and floor tile. Displays of Clarendon material can be seen at the British Museum and at the Salisbury and South Wiltshire Museum. Meanwhile, what a decade ago was a jungle of regenerated woodland and collapsing walls is now laid out as a cleared site, with public access for visitors, interpretation boards and sympathetic land management which sets the palace anew in its landscape context.

The palace

High up in the south-west corner of the inner park, and almost precisely at the epicentre of the outer park, lay the palace precinct, its major buildings aligned along the northerly escarpment edge. So far we have only examined the palace from the outside, looking in, as visitors would have done. But the location of the palace from the perspective of its occupants should also be considered. This landscape perspective has never previously been written about. Few other buildings could be seen from here, although at different times between the thirteenth and the sixteenth centuries the cathedral at Salisbury, the original Queen Manor and the deer haybarn could be seen. Looking south, the palace buildings were framed by woodland greenery. In its isolation, if we are to be reminded of any other medieval monument class, it is perhaps the Cistercian monastery which the palace most resembles, and which order's rise and fall from the twelfth to the sixteenth century was mirrored in the fortunes of the palace. It appears as a kind of eremetic retreat, a withdrawal into the forest.

Documentary references to rooms at the palace suggest that there were views out over the natural auditorium to the north. In 1244, for example, modifications to the Queen's Chamber included: 'the steps to be removed, and a winding-stair made in that corner to go up into the gallery; the gallery to be fitted with curved joists, and the joists covered with lead …'.[1]

The gallery provided very extensive views over large areas to the north towards Cockey Down, over the chalk downland launds where the deer grazed and on which hunting took place. The geography of the new layout was not lost on those who recorded further changes to 'the queen's new chamber towards the park' in February 1245.[2] Similar vistas were available at other royal palaces; in 1354 a balcony was constructed at Woodstock in order to give Princess Isabella a view of the deer park.[3] Okehampton Castle (Devon) was remodelled in the fourteenth century to provide views of the newly created deer park[4] and, as early as the twelfth century, the lord's chamber faced the deer park at Castle Rising and New Buckenham (Norfolk).[5] Clarendon was not special in realising a concept of landscape vistas in the Middle Ages; rather, it was typical in being designed with its wider landscape in mind. What is distinctive here is the *scale* of the private, managed landscape around the palace. The palace in its landscape setting was designed to impress. At Clarendon the uncertainty about function which has dogged recent castle studies[6] – that is, whether medieval castles were designed for military purposes or as stage sets – is irrelevant, as the palace was never defended. Nor is there any question that this undefended status arose through a lack of resources, as was no doubt the case with some non-royal residences. At Clarendon, the link between palace and landscape is inescapable; one cannot be understood without the other.

Less distant views from the royal chambers down on to the garden platform directly beneath were vertiginous. The main medieval palace garden earthworks lie north of the palace on a built-up terrace contained within the crook of the northern range of the palace buildings, from the kitchens to the west to the queen's apartments to the east. Despite generations of antiquarians and archaeologists shovelling at the palace, the remains of the garden platforms are remarkably intact and their earthworks were recorded for the first time by the Royal Commission in 1994. Three platforms of 25 m (east–west) by 15 m (north–south) rise from the west (kitchen) end to a small platform 5 m by 15 m, the highest point, immediately north of the queen's north chamber, after which two lesser platforms descend eastwards, each 20 m by 15 m. A large garden platform area some 25 m by 25 m, possibly the queen's 'herbour', lay east of the Queen's Chambers (Figure 28).

Documents indicate that an enclosure about the King's Chamber was turfed in 1167–8:[7] early evidence of gardens. Keyhole excavation revealed that the garden platforms were retained by a flint wall 5 feet (1.5 m) high which included a reused fragment of twelfth-century moulding, making the wall a thirteenth-century, or later, addition.[8] The west wall shielded the gardens and their occupants from the north kitchen and its middens beyond, and there are various references to a *herbarium* here. Queen Eleanor had a 'grass-plot' made in 1245, and the gardens made for her in 1247 were further improved in 1252;

Henry III, who had so much work done in royal gardens, gave orders for the wall round 'the great garden' at Clarendon to be whitewashed and for a bench to be made round the wall.[9]

The topography suggests these gardens were immediately adjacent to the royal apartments, and were designed to be seen by the king and queen, whose hall had a window inserted in 1250 especially to overlook her garden.[10] A similar range of garden features close to royal chambers is known from other pleasure gardens of the late twelfth century onwards, at Arundel (Sussex), Marlborough (Wilts), Westminster, Windsor, Woodstock and elsewhere.[11] Among the native species brought in from the wild to cultivation were dog roses, foxglove, honeysuckle and mallow.[12] Any or all of these perhaps grew at Clarendon, and foxgloves are widely seen at Clarendon today, but whether 'garden escapes' from the medieval gardens still survive in the flora cannot be proved. The hellebores on the garden platforms and elsewhere on the site of the palace today, and in the woods just below the former palace gardens to the north, are said to indicate continuity,[13] and certain rare plants were reportedly seen at Clarendon Palace, notably the giant bell flower (*Wahlenbergia undulata*) and the herb paris (*Paris quadrifolia*), both of which may have been cultivated in medieval gardens.[14] Other parts of the precinct may have been less formal gardens, particularly the courts with their covered alleys running

FIGURE 28. Reconstruction of the gardens. The north-facing medieval garden platforms, despite generations of work on the palace structures above, have remained remarkably intact and provide an unexamined time-capsule of evidence for the plantings of medieval monarchs. This reconstruction drawing marks out the plots as seen on the ground and recorded by the Royal Commission in 1994. (Drawn by Philip Marter)

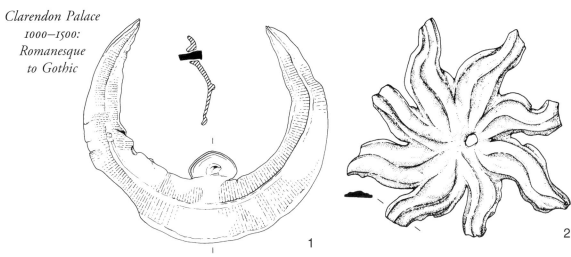

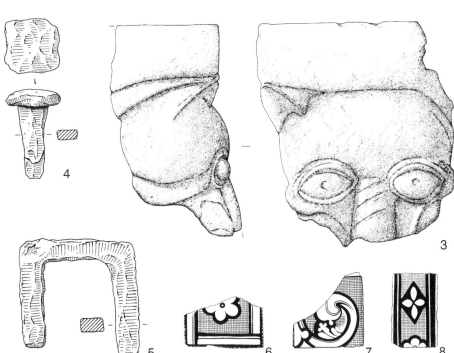

FIGURE 29.
Medieval decorative
ornaments, sculpture
and structural finds
from Clarendon
Palace.
1: Crescent (lead).
2: Eight-pointed star
(lead, whitewashed
then gilded; James
and Knight 1988,
fig. 85). 3: Springer
carved in the form
of a 'cat's head'
(limestone; Ashurst and
James 1988, fig. 91).
4: Door stud with a
square head (iron).
5: Staple, possibly a
bolt keeper for a lock
(iron). 6, 7 and 8:
glass fragments from
grisaille windows
(Marks 1988, fig. 87).
Nos 1 and 2 are shown
at 1:1, nos 4 and 5 at
1:2 and nos 3, 6, 7 and
8 at 1:4. Nos 1, 4 and
5 are all from recent
fieldwork.
(Drawn by Yvonne
Beadnell nos 1, 4, 5,
Frances Rankine nos
2, 3 and Nick Griffiths
nos 6, 7, 8)

around them. The court between the kitchens and the Salsary, as well as those to east and west of the wine cellar and to the south of the Antioch Chamber all could have been herbers: levelled, laid with turf and mown. Perhaps they were interspersed with herb-gardens such as that ordered for the south side of the courtyard near the old hall in 1244.[15]

Of all the features of the Clarendon landscape it is the medieval palace which is best understood from the archaeological and historical record.[16] Indeed, Clarendon is the largest royal English rural palace for which the plan can be deduced from abandoned ruins. Romanesque buildings were created at the palace under the Norman kings and are well documented under the first Angevin Henry II (1154–1189). No remains can be dated securely to Henry I but certain finds can be assigned to the period 1000–1216, for example, fragments of sculpture in the Romanesque style, and contemporary embellishment such as dog tooth decoration. Historiated capitals showing people, mythical beasts and foliage are of the highest order,[17] and these motifs have parallels from Reading (Berks) to Autun and Moissac in central and southern France (Figure 29, 3). Widespread use of Caen stone accords with building work at this early period,[18] while parallel evidence suggests that the interiors of the residential areas were plastered and painted. The excavators of the 1930s believed that among a variety of pieces of plaster in vivid colours, one in particular, which depicted 'part of a man in a toga', dated to the twelfth century.[19]

At a macro-level the twelfth-century arrangement of free-standing open hall and separate chamber-block is seen in its classic form at Clarendon (Figure 30). Recent work shows that not only is there a chamber block with an undercroft, but further blocks raised on piers with characteristic twelfth-century tooling (the Antioch Chamber).[20] The hall would presumably have fulfilled public functions whereas the chamber block, the *camera regis* mentioned in the 1160s, provided a more private and comfortable space.[21] The footprints of the palace's large stone structures indicate, for example, that the principal buildings were axially aligned, but there is insufficient stratigraphic evidence to give an accurate account of the palace's changing floor areas. However, hall, kitchen, royal apartments, chapels and the great twelfth-century wine-cellar (12 x 7 m), as well as structures such as the old hall adjacent to the stable on the south side of the courtyard, add up to a very extensive floor area, even if these early structures were single storey.[22]

Under John (1199–1216) and Henry III (1216–72), the floor area of the palace increased substantially. The kitchen and the Great Hall were rebuilt on a larger scale; the cellar doubled in size; the queen's apartments were more than doubled in size, and the whole complex spread westwards beyond the original earthworks to be terminated by a new gatehouse complex with additional storage and stabling facilities. Much building also took place to the east of the site in the area known to 1930s excavators as the 'Gothic suite': a complex which included ovens, barns and what may have been residential accommodation.[23] This may have been the area of the prison and the location of the permanent staff's accommodation. The documentation for this expansion is voluminous and detailed. For example, on 14 March 1244, the sheriff of Wiltshire was instructed to carry out various works.[24] The first specified is:

> A new stable … for the king and queen extending lengthways from the south wall next to the gate as far as the old hall which is now a stable for the king's horses … the old hall to be made into a chamber with a fireplace on the south side and a columned window, in the wall opposite the fireplace two windows suitably columned, and a window in the gable without

FIGURE 30. *Above*: Set between late prehistoric and Romano-British earthworks to east and west, the siting of the later medieval palace can be seen to take advantage of a pre-existing grid of field lynchets and settlement at the northern edge of a natural escarpment (see also Figure 6). Earlier earthworks may underlie portions of the precinct boundary and the inner park pale, though this has not been proven by excavation. *Below*: The twelfth-century plan of the palace. To create this figure the 1996 Royal Commission plan has been used as a base, with those structures for which there is sufficient archaeological and documentary evidence shown in bold. The boundary of the early precinct and its relationship to the inner park pale is hypothetical but adopts the line of likely earthworks. A major omission is All Saints chapel, for which the rectangular east–west building east of the 'old hall' must be a candidate. (Drawn by Alejandra Gutiérrez)

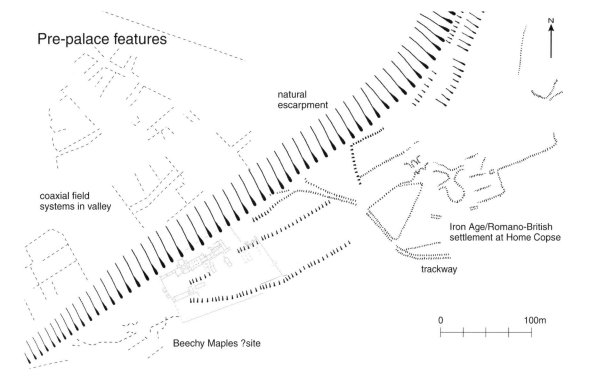

Pre-palace features

natural escarpment

coaxial field systems in valley

Iron Age/Romano-British settlement at Home Copse

trackway

Beechy Maples ?site

N

0   100m

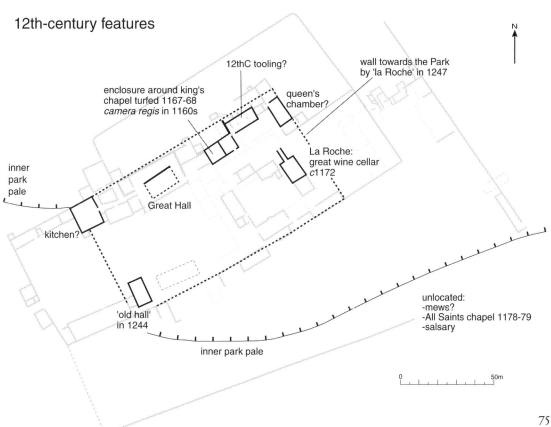

12th-century features

12thC tooling?

wall towards the Park by 'la Roche' in 1247

enclosure around king's chapel turfed 1167-68 *camera regis* in 1160s

queen's chamber?

La Roche: great wine cellar *c*1172

inner park pale

Great Hall

kitchen?

'old hall' in 1244

inner park pale

unlocated:
-mews?
-All Saints chapel 1178-79
-salsary

N

0   50m

columns, as high as may be; a privy chamber to be made for this chamber between it and the wall …

Footprints of these buildings exist today and a fireplace is still visible, though the height of the walls today is below window-level.[25] With the benefit of the documents, some features of old halls refurbished by Henry III can generally be reconstructed. But this is a frustrating process. Only a tiny proportion of the features mentioned in documents are identifiable on the ground: some doorways, fireplaces and dimensions of buildings can be traced, but grand plantings in the garden and grounds, the turfing of lawns and the provision of turfed benches would require excavations of the highest modern standards if they were to be rediscovered. For the moment, at least the continuous process of building, modification and recycling is clear enough; the palace precinct can rarely have been free of scaffolding on one range or another.

Clarendon continued to be extended and modified throughout the thirteenth and fourteenth centuries. Edward III took a particular interest here in the decade following the Black Death of 1348, when much building work was done. This included major reroofing and work in the Great Hall in 1358.[26] Characteristically, Richard II added a dancing chamber before 1400, the location of which is now unknown. As an illustration of the difficulties of integrating historical and archaeological records, we can return to the question of stables. Early in his reign Henry IV (1399–1413) repaired a 'stable by the deputy's wall'. The walls of the stable were entered at 63 feet (19 m) long, 6 feet (1.8 m) high and 2 feet (0.6 m) wide. However, the main work was the creation of a new stable, which employed no fewer than seventeen carpenters. The dimensions of this latter building are not given but it required forty-six couple rafters, twelve posts, six double beams, thirty-two '*entrelatez*' and twenty-four other posts.[27] The scale of this building would appear to correspond to the structure south of the western entrance today, which measures 45 x 8 m,[28] producing a floor area of some 360 m², an extraordinary size for a stable at the period which betokens continuing commitment by the Lancastrian dynasty to the palace. Even today, the remains of this stable are highly impressive.[29] But does this new stable really replace the mid thirteenth-century stable, or could it be that this new stable was somewhere quite different? Another candidate is the unexcavated earthwork on the eastern perimeter, which measures about 60 by 15 feet (18 x 4.5 m) and was interpreted in the 1930s as a barn. Without more exact documentary information and further excavation to establish with some certainty the position of an eastern or southern entrance, definitive answers are not easy.[30] That there were horses in large numbers stabled at Clarendon from time to time is not in doubt and an entwined silver decorative thread with silk and felt recovered here may be a relic of a grand medieval saddle.[31]

The most detailed reconstruction of the medieval palace is possible for the reign of Henry III, when documentation reaches its fullest extent (Figure 31). At this date the palace was an amalgamation of discrete functional elements

FIGURE 31. Plan of the palace of Henry III. Again the RCHME 1996 plan has been used as a base, with those structures for which there is sufficient archaeological and documentary evidence shown in bold. We can be reasonably confident about positions of the major buildings here, with the exception of subdivisions within the Queen's apartments. These are marked in grey with black outlines. The plans of buildings with a dotted outline are known only uncertainly from archaeological evidence. Buildings in grey only are certainly present but their function is not known. Many named lesser chambers, granaries, ovens, storehouses and facilities remain to be located, among them the chancellery (1247), rooms of the king's carpenter (1250), the chapel by the almonry, All Saints chapel, a 'cellar towards the park' (all 1251–60), a kitchen for the queen (1267), the house of the barber, the stewards' chamber and the foresters' building (all 1273). (Drawn by Alejandra Gutiérrez)

in which the most architecturally prominent building was the hall. Its great size, with its two arcades of four bays, announced the king's standing and, once inside, distinctions of rank were symbolically embedded in the opposition of high and low (service) ends, just as the palace's other chambers were graded visually according to the rank of their occupants. The principal spaces – the separate chambers for king and queen, multiple chapels, covered walks, hall and kitchens – were arranged axially along the north side of a series of courtyards.[32] Documented schemes of interior decoration include wall paintings of biblical scenes; glazing schemes depicting saints, historiated fireplaces for the king's and queen's chambers, carpentry for which particular woods were sought, and much else besides. Archaeological finds demonstrate furnishings and structural work of the highest quality. Growing awareness of the qualities of local stones, such as the calcareous sandstone from Chilmark/ Tisbury, is shown by its use in porches, door openings, columns and window stonework; it is found in quantity at Clarendon, as at Salisbury Cathedral.[33] Carved, painted, moulded and sculpted stone have all been recovered from

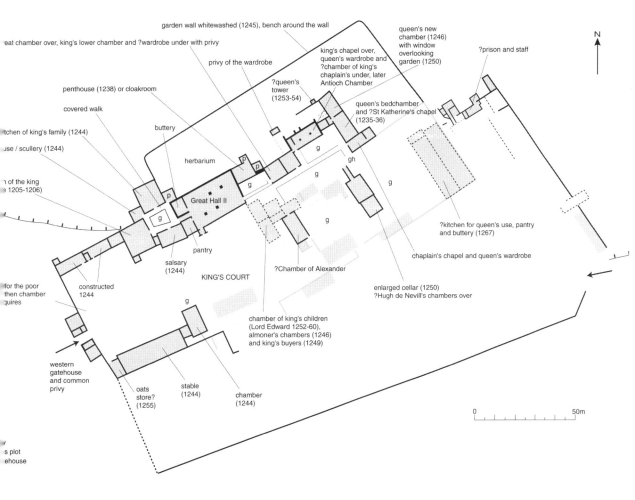

the main service and residential areas (for example, see Figure 29). The bare flintwork which remains today was decorated externally with white-painted plaster, lined in red with false-jointing to give the impression of ashlar work (Figure 32), and in places the colours were reversed to give white lines on a red ground. Internally, the major chambers were richly painted with cycles of images[34] and 'rich gothic scrolls' in bold colours – for example, rich reds, which survive as fragments, together with pieces in lighter hues of green and yellow (Figure 33). Reports of the excavation of plaster in the 1930s refer to green, red, 'sky blue' and other vivid colours; to 'brilliantly painted plaster' and to 'subdued hues' – mauve, green 'and other secondary colours'. Chemical analysis has revealed the presence of crushed lapis lazuli, brought from Afghanistan in the Middle Ages, and used for achieving deep blue effects – probably sky, as seen in the ceiling of the Guardian Angels' Chapel in Winchester Cathedral (Figure 34). Cinnabar from Spain has recently been identified. Some fragments of plaster recovered in the area of the queen's apartments were 'astonishingly brilliant' and decorated with gold leaf, including scrollwork, a human left hand, lattice-work windows and other motifs.[35]

Plaster fragments show that previous wall paintings, however grand, were subsequently whitewashed over.

The moulded and sculpted stone and the brightly coloured walls of the royal apartments were offset by tiled floors during the second quarter of the thirteenth century. The pavements from Clarendon are the only ones from an English royal palace to have survived *in situ*. The floor tiles were appropriately set, with abstract designs in the chapels and more earthly designs in private and public rooms across the complex, such as the 'Knights in Combat'.[36] The circular pavement from the King's Chapel is the earliest at Clarendon, c. 1237–45, and the finest in England of its date. Here narrow bands of green-glazed tiles alternate with wider inlaid brown tiles; this well may be the pavement mentioned in March 1244 as being ordered for the room (Figure 35).[37] The designs in this pavement were to be widely influential, both in Wessex and further afield in the West Midlands and Wales.[38] In the queen's chambers lion-tiles were found *in situ* together with abstract mid thirteenth-century designs (Figure 36).[39] Eames suggested that the Clarendon and Salisbury Cathedral pavements, which were laid before 1258, may have been made in the same place and there is a similarity in fabrics between these floor tiles and roof tiles thought to have been made at Alderbury.[40] A mixture of fanciful designs is found elsewhere on the site. Some, such as addorsed birds, are appropriate to the woodland setting; while others, such as mythical griffins, are more fantastical, reminiscent of the Savernake Forest horn with its similar mix of real and imaginary forest creatures.

These tiles were shaped in a wooden form on a sanded surface, trimmed and scoops as keying taken from their backs. Once dry they were decorated, either with a plain lead glaze (to give a brown colour on an oxidised red fabric) or one to which copper had been added (to give a green colour), or stamped with a pattern which was then inlaid with a white clay. Only then could they be placed on edge inside the kiln and fired. All the necessary resources – clay, water and fuel – could be found within the park and at least one tile kiln is known from Clarendon (Figure 37).[41] Its discovery serves to emphasise the early role of royal patronage and the possible impact of alien craftsmen in programmes of flooring and other decorative schemes, not only at this site but further afield. Although tile pavements are common at high-status medieval sites such as castles and manor houses later, at the time when the tile pavements were first laid in the royal apartments at Clarendon they would have been familiar only to monastic eyes. Commercial tileries were not in production until twenty-five years later, during the last quarter of the thirteenth century.[42] For a generation at least they would have been a striking and unusual feature for English visitors, and because they are well dated they are one of the features of Clarendon's interiors to which we can still point and say with certainty that they were in advance of fashion.

In the matter of window glass, Clarendon was also in the forefront of architectural style and taste; some of the earliest fragments of domestic glass date to Henry III's reign (Figure 29).[43] At that time the palace windows were

FIGURE 32.
The Antioch Chamber lay underneath the King's Chapel. This 1930s photograph shows twelfth-century weathering and buttress, with the plastered wall above. This fragment of the north front of the palace reminds us of the former grandeur of the building as seen from below. By the 1980s the plaster had disintegrated. (Photograph by John Charlton)

FIGURE 33.
Painted plaster.
Brightly coloured
plasterwork adorned
the interior of the
palace at least from
the twelfth century
to its abandonment
about 1500. A wide
variety of colours and
designs were recovered
in excavation, but few
fragments showed
figurative, as opposed
to abstract, designs.
Representations of
human hands, clothing
and architectural
details, found in
the 1930s, were
photographed, but
subsequently lost.
(Photograph by Peter
Jacobs).

filled with painted glass; surviving fragments with discernible decoration are all grisaille, or monochrome, and match the thirteenth-century windows of Salisbury Cathedral.[44] That cathedral, the finest example of Early English architecture, provides insights into the growth of the concept of 'Englishness' in the thirteenth century as the loss of continental possessions encouraged more home-developed styles. Internationalism, however, in this case in the form of dedications which link the English monarchy to the twelfth- and thirteenth-century growth in the cult of the Virgin, was not dead. Henry III demanded a window 'with a small figure of Mary (*Mariolam*) therein with the Child, and a queen at her feet holding an *Ave Maria*', and 'images of the Holy Trinity and St Mary' to be made for the Franciscans' (Queen Eleanor's confessors') chamber.[45] Henry would at this time have been some forty-one years old; the last recorded reference to figural glazing at Clarendon under him was in 1267, when he gave instructions for the four evangelists to be placed in the large windows of his hall. Unfortunately, none of the remaining Clarendon window glass is from these historiated windows.[46] What is certain, however, is that this figurative glass, being coloured, would have made an extraordinary contribution to the internal decoration of the palace's central building. Their impact can best be gauged by examining fragments of surviving panels in Salisbury Cathedral.[47]

Recent re-examination of the standing remains of the palace Great Hall

FIGURE 34.
The Guardian Angels'
Chapel in Winchester
is dated to 1240–1.
The 'sky' between the
'portholes' through
which the angels'
heads are seen is
represented by gilded
stars set against a blue
background. Analysis
of plaster pigment
from Clarendon shows
the blue background
there was produced
with ground lapis
lazuli, then found
only in Afghanistan.
(Reproduced by kind
permission of the
Dean and Chapter of
Winchester Cathedral;
photograph by John
Crook)

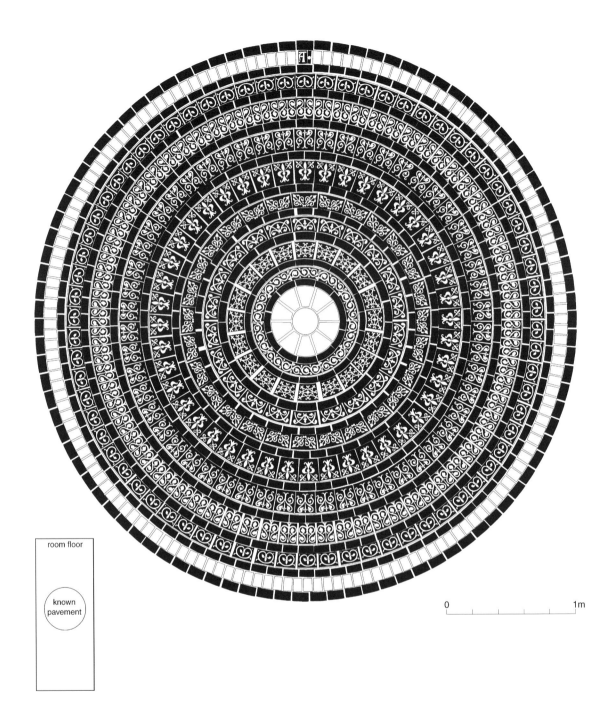

room floor

known
pavement

0   1m

suggests that they constitute elements of Henry III's hall of c. 1230. Given the scale of the structure – 100 x 52 feet (31 x 15.9 m) – with the hall, pantry and buttery areas all under the same roof, this was an exceptionally grand creation, to which the nearest contemporary parallel, also of c. 1230, is at Winchester Castle (Figure 38).[48] At Ludgershall (Wilts) a new hall 60 x 40 feet

Reconstruction of the
circular tile pavement
from the King's Chapel
ordered by Henry III
in 1244. By the early
1250s this room had
wainscoting, windows
and statues with gilded
angels above. The inset
illustrates the size
of the pavement in
relation to the known
floor plan. The tile
design traditionally
attributed to the
innermost decorated
band of the pavement
is now disputed
(Norton 1996, 93) and
has been left blank.
(Drawn by Alejandra
Gutiérrez)

FIGURE 36.
Reconstruction of
the tile pavement
from the Queen's
Chamber dated from
orders in the Liberate
Rolls issued between
1250 and 1252. The
inset illustrates the
footprint of the
surviving pavement
in 1939 and 1957 in
relation to the known
floor plan (James and
Robinson 1988, plate
LIVa; Eames 1960).
Similar designs are
also known from
Winchester Castle and
Cathedral as well as
Salisbury Cathedral.
This pavement, like the
one in the 'chaplains'
chapel' to the south,
was laid in panels.
(Drawn by Alejandra
Gutiérrez)

(18 x 12 m), some 75 per cent the size of Clarendon, was ordered in May 1244.[49] The timber roof there may have been supported by timber arcades carried on painted wooden piers. By contrast, at Clarendon the 1930s excavators found evidence of stone pillars on the pier bases of the Great Hall, as at Winchester. The standing portion of the east wall has the remains of a corbel with a rectangular slot above it, which may suggest a wooden arcade post, but the arcade is more likely to have matched Winchester's stone.[50] In 1244 the east end of Clarendon hall was wainscoted 'for the space of 5 pairs

of rafters over the dais', reminding us how often spaces were remodelled and redecorated.[51] Decorative schemes were subject to rapidly changing fashion then as today.

So many of the royal houses of medieval England were acquired from other owners that the full extent of the part the Crown played in their architectural form is problematic and varied. At Clarendon, continuously in royal ownership, the situation is atypical, as while there may be individual buildings and monuments elsewhere which better show off royal patronage of architecture, given the later history of Westminster and Woodstock it is now only at Clarendon that we have the opportunity to examine, both in the landscape and in the palace, royal arrangements in their established setting. Thus we can see the king's arrangements, with apartments for receiving guests, chapel and sleeping chamber; the queen, with similar accommodation (though on a smaller scale); and, at a distance, children's accommodation, when monarchs had young children: for example, John and Henry III, Henry III as a minor, Henry III with his own children. The 'Prince Edward' chamber, c. 1250, is notable in this context: Edward III made arrangements for the birth of his daughter Isabella there, and the Black Prince was in his bachelor twenties in the 1350s when his mistress probably bore him Roger at Clarendon. Unlike Guildford, which appears to have been especially favoured as a location for children – and which, as a result, was the place where certain royal children died, Clarendon

FIGURE 37.
In 1937 this kiln, accompanied by waster tiles matching those in the King's Chapel circular pavement, was discovered under the south-west corner of the later Salsary. In 1964 Elizabeth Eames led a team from the British Museum Research Laboratory to re-examine and remove it for display. The reassembly of the kiln was a pioneering exercise in reconstruction for exhibition. (Photograph by John Charlton)

FIGURE 38.
The Winchester
Castle Great Hall
parallels the hall
structure at Clarendon.
This picture shows
the sense of space
and the impressive
now fragmentary
'upstanding' (*stantivis*)
windows ordered
by Henry III for
both halls. Elias de
Dereham was involved
in works at Clarendon,
Winchester and at
Salisbury Cathedral.
(Photograph by John
Crook)

was further away from London and appears to have enjoyed the status of a family home when the family was in residence, but without such unhappy associations.[52] Indeed, the enthusiasm in particular of Henry III and Edward I for Clarendon as adults quite probably stemmed from happy childhood memories of the place. No one was obliged to use Clarendon and it is noteworthy that the later medieval dynasties – Yorkists and Tudors, who seized the throne and who had been brought up elsewhere – did not come here.

Food, feasting and dining

If hunting was the major pleasure of the Clarendon parkland, food was among the key pleasures of the palace buildings and it is important to see the link between activities outside in the park and those of feasting. At the end of a day's hunting, Gaston Phoebus (1387) tells us:

> Back in his hall, while a supper of suet, venison, and wine is being made ready for him, he strips off his clothes and shoes, washes his legs and some-times his whole body. Once he has eaten and drunk, he is thoroughly warmed and contented, and can lie down in his bed between fine, fresh linen, and sleep wholesomely through the night, without any thoughts of committing sin.[53]

At Clarendon, feasting imposes itself forcefully on the architecture, most obvi-ously through the provision of ample kitchen accommodation to the west of the great hall. But there is also an archaeology of feasting to be seen through the bags of medieval pottery and animal bone from the palace site.[54] The noble status of the site is immediately apparent from the high proportion of deer bones, principally fallow, which outnumber those of cattle. Bones of sheep are more numerous but, given the disparity in size between fallow deer and sheep, venison must have contributed more to the larder than mutton. Two bones of young spring lamb are of interest as an indicator of seasonality and they may be associated with feasting at Easter.[55] Overall, the distribution of skeletal elements suggests that the palace was being supplied with dressed carcases of mutton and beef which had already had their feet and heads removed at the skinning stage. The mutton was probably fresh but the beef might have been salt cured and dried or smoked and came from younger animals between two and four years of age. Together with this quality beef, a small number of bones from veal calves were also present.[56] By contrast, pig remains are least abundant. From the North Kitchen came three bones from sucking pigs, a specific dish associated with élite diners, though fresh pork from younger animals and cured bacon were also regularly available for the table. Pigs from Clarendon were mostly slaughtered in the first year of life, with none surviv-ing beyond two years.[57] Butchery might have taken place on site, as it did at other great households, but perhaps a local slaughterhouse and butcher were hired in Salisbury or elsewhere.[58]

Red deer were among the faunal remains recovered at Clarendon but it seems more likely they were taken in the forest. Roe deer, too, were recovered, but again they were minor components of the palace larder and, like the red deer, probably only took on importance when they were to be hunted by royal residents.[59] Fallow deer is outstandingly the most commonly represented spe-cies among the animal bones at Clarendon and the analysis of the assemblage recently recovered from the spoil heaps casts new light on how venison was used.[60] The distribution of body parts is telling; for while metapodials and phalanges are common, showing that butchery of whole deer carcases took place on site, forelimbs and scapulae are scarce or absent. Dressed carcases of fallow deer were evidently being prepared but were not always consumed at the palace; rather, they were being sent away from the site.[61] A chief function of the park was clearly food production, and fallow deer were ideal for this purpose as they carry more venison in proportion to their size than red deer.

Other bones in the Clarendon assemblage include the beasts of the warren: hare, rabbit, pheasant and partridge. With the notable exception of rabbit, their bones were only present in modest quantities. As we have seen, there was a rabbit warren close to the palace site during the medieval period and its careful management seems to have ensured a continuous supply of meat to the royal household. Unlike the pork, beef or venison, rabbit meat could not be cured, it does not travel well and has to be supplied fresh. The same is true of chickens, which were also commonly consumed at the palace.[62] Far less common were goose bones, though it is not clear what proportion derive from domestic or wild birds,[63] and there was a single swan bone. The large and valuable swan was perhaps reserved for consumption at Christmas[64] and may have come from the royal swannery adjacent to the southern border of the park on the river Avon. Large numbers of swans were kept on the river and were occasionally stolen during the fourteenth century,[65] commissions being issued to search for and recover stolen birds regularly between 1327 and 1345.[66] Other smaller wild birds among the bone assemblage included an undiagnostic wader and a jackdaw, the latter perhaps a casualty from a colony on the palace roof.[67] Heron/bittern type birds, mallard and a golden plover may all have found their way to the palace table as result of hawking expeditions in and on the margins of the park.[68] On a national scale, wild birds like these are much more common on sites of high status, such as castles, where they were more important as symbols of wealth and aristocratic style than as a meaningful contribution to subsistence. The Clarendon evidence supports this.[69]

Emphasis on fish as well as meat was another characteristic of the aristocratic diet. Fish was eaten two or three days a week, during Lent and at certain feast days.[70] In contrast to previous investigations, during which the technique of floating out small bones and seeds from bulk soil samples taken from excavated deposits was not used, recent spoil heap work has now produced a modest assemblage of medieval fish bone and the results show a pattern which contrasts with that found in documents. The remains were mainly of marine fish, mostly herring, though there were also cod and hake bones and a range of other species, including conger eel, grey mullet, possibly whiting, gurnard, wrasse, flatfish and sea bream. The hake and cod vertebrae were from large fish at least a metre in overall length which came from deep sea fishing, and the recovery of only one dentary fragment in the sample analysed suggests that these fish were supplied processed: perhaps dried or smoked, pickled or salted.[71] Herring, which was prominent in the assemblage, is unlikely to have been fresh and may have been lower-status fish, and, likewise, conger eel could have been pickled. Herring and mackerel appear in a Clarendon Lenten account of 1207,[72] but this one mention in the documents gives us no sense of the frequency or range of marine fish eaten. Most, if not all, the fish could have come from markets in Southampton and there is much documentary evidence of importation of fish there; hake were landed from Penzance, for example, and conger eel from Jersey and Guernsey.[73] There are no detailed port or overland (brokage) trade records for Southampton for the period before c. 1425, and only intermittent records for the remainder of the medieval period.[74] However, brokage books show onward destinations for port produce to towns like Salisbury and Winchester, either or both of which might have been the source of kitchen supplies for Clarendon.[75]

Further evidence of contact with the coast comes from oysters recovered during re-excavation of the spoil heaps.[76] The shells show pervasive evidence of infestation by worms which attack oysters. One of these, *Polydora hoplura*, is found only on the south and south-west coasts of England, which helps to locate the origin of the shellfish. Heavy infestation by parasites, particularly on large individuals, is also good evidence that the oysters lived in an open marine environment and, since the shells are regularly shaped and fall into the three- to five-year age bracket with no evidence of distortion, the balance of probability favours a managed population. Poole or Southampton are likely sources.[77] The valves must have been opened with a special instrument which left notches cut into their outer edge[78] and oysters were obviously a common sight on the Clarendon table, though documentation for them is rare. By contrast, other marine species, including the common whelk and the common mussel, are poorly represented.[79] Whelks appear in the 1207 account,[80] but there is no hint there of marine products from further afield, such as the large European oyster shell (*Ostrea edulis*) and a scallop shell (probably *Pecten sp.*) or the large edible crab (*Cancer pagurus*) which were recovered from outside the North Kitchen.[81] Crustacea were eaten only rarely by noble and aristocratic households, or so their accounts would lead us to believe.[82]

No royal fishponds are documented at Clarendon: freshwater fish came from elsewhere. In 1244 Peter de Wakering caught forty bream 'in the stew' at Taunton and sent them on to for Henry III's table at Clarendon.[83] Likewise, for Christmas 1255, eighteen bream 'in paste' were supplied from Marlborough.[84] Again, archaeology and documentary evidence complement each other; infrequent documentary references imply a steady movement of fresh fish across Wessex, whereas freshwater fish are rather rare in the archaeological record. Among the fish remains recovered from palace spoil heaps only eel and trout, both migratory species, originated in freshwater. The king enjoyed rights on the river Avon,[85] perhaps the source of these fish. Lamprey and salmon, which are documented for Christmas at Westminster in 1240, were no doubt enjoyed at Clarendon as well.[86] However, lamprey are absent and salmon scarce in the Clarendon archaeological record as problems of preservation exist for remains of both these species. Lamprey have a cartilaginous skeleton which does not survive and salmon bones have a high fat content and are generally under-represented in archaeological fish assemblages.[87] The combination of archaeological and historical evidence creates a new and more diverse picture of fish consumption.

Some of the earliest daily expenditure which can be assigned to a particular household includes records for Clarendon in 1207, already cited. This roll was drawn up for the household of Hugh de Neville, master of the royal hounds, chief justice of the forests and a close adviser to King John. Just before the Feast of the Conception (25 March) 1207, and six months before the birth of Henry III on 1 October, Hugh de Neville was escorting the pregnant Queen Isabella to Clarendon by way of an arduous and tortuous route. Sometimes they were in the company of the king, sometimes with his hounds. In 1207 Easter Day fell on 22 April, so the journey was taking place well into Lent. Lenten fare is clear in the diet consumed at Clarendon: bread (6s), ale (2s), oysters (2s), herrings (14d) and mackerel (9d). A few days later *quando dominus ivit apud Clarend' pro regine'* for bread (5s), for ale (27½d), for wine (16d), for mackerel (9d) and for salmon (20d). These were clearly fish-days. Oats, valued at 5s 5d, were by far the most expensive item and indicate the requirements of that itinerant lifestyle with its horses and, given the queen's condition, possibly carriages. Hay ('*feno*') cost 13d. The final Clarendon entry in this fragmentary roll includes bread (6s 9d), ale (29d), herrings (20d), '*mulvello*' (possibly cod, 25d) with 4s 4d for oats and hay: '*de stauro H. de Wylbi*'.[88]

The detailed evidence from the 1207 visit is unique: for other periods the balance of the food economy between the palace and the park and forest beyond, and the wider country and continent, has to be pieced together, particularly where archaeological evidence is absent. For example, the 1207 household account shows that ale was available and this may have been brewed on site or purchased locally. Buying in ale may have been more sensible, given that it only had a shelf-life of a week or two. We can also be sure that wine was brought in from Gascony, as well as local brews such as mulberry, raspberry and '*ferrati*', presumably an iron tonic. Wine supplies began to roll to Clarendon in earnest after Henry III came of age in 1227: two tuns were supplied from the port of Southampton in 1228. The wine was being bought in bulk at the port; in 1236 four tuns were ordered on 10 December with a further ten to be sent 'with speed' on the following day, and yet four more during the following week. Ten years on, the figure had risen to over fifty, a number sustained almost yearly until the political troubles of the late 1250s, and picking up again in the late 1260s after Henry had defeated Simon de Montfort (Figure 39).[89] All these tuns of wine necessitated the doubling in size of the wine cellar in 1252. Fragments of wine glasses from a context below the north windows of the king's apartments are of a type used in the reign of Edward I (c.1300).[90] In Edward III's reign the lord of the manor of East Winterslow (a manor founded by Henry II's falconer in 1187) was bound to provide a barrel of '*Clare*' (Clarendon wine or claret?) from which to serve the king a cup at his coming, after which the donor could keep the barrel (perhaps to the king's relief?).[91] Wine-drinking could not be afforded by most

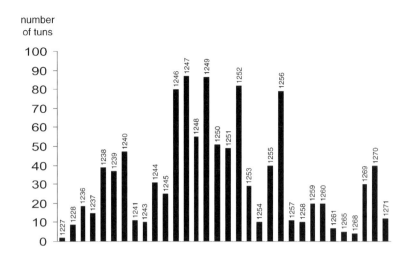

number
of tuns

FIGURE 39.
Barrels of mainly
French wine were
carried down the
stone steps into the
magnificent wine
cellar carved out of
the hilltop for Henry
II, and doubled in size
by Henry III, whose
supplies are shown
here; see Figure 82.
(Drawn by Alejandra
Gutiérrez)

of medieval society and consumption on this scale and regularity was wholly exceptional.[92] But it is perhaps only through wine consumption that there is any real hint of the enormous volumes of food which must have been consumed at Clarendon. Archaeological evidence hints at wide variety but not the great quantities of foodstuffs required each day nor the frequency with which feasting took place. Where other great households may have eaten venison at major feasts, at Clarendon the impression is that its provision was unlimited, and the same was true of wine; few other households could have counted on a regular supply and perhaps no other in such quantity.

Among the small number of household objects found and kept during excavations at the palace were a pan from a candlestick and locks and keys from doors or caskets (Figure 40), for which there were also binding strips, hinge loops, drop handles and fragments of silver gilt, with which one box was decorated.[93] From these we get only the most oblique understanding of the type and quality of furniture and fittings. Tables, seating, tapestries and curtains; the colours and textures of all these must be imagined. The most sumptuous rooms were royal chambers. Evidence elsewhere suggests that the hall itself would have been simply furnished, with covered trestles, forms and stools laid out only for meals.[94] Slightly more can be said about tableware, though even here the record is partial. There are no silver or silver gilt bowls and spoons, for example, a regular entry in the inventories of the medieval aristocracy[95] and surely a feature of the high table at Clarendon. It is the breakables and the commonplace which survive, such as scraps of copper-alloy rim bindings for some admittedly very large wooden dishes or leather jugs,[96] though by far the most common item is pottery.[97] The palace was provisioned with most of its pottery from the local kilns at Laverstock, just outside the bounds of the park. Among the coarsewares are globular jars with their characteristic scratched surface, used for storage as well as cooking, and green-glazed jugs of globular and baluster shape with rod and strap handles which would have held ale or wine. Few of these are decorated but there are

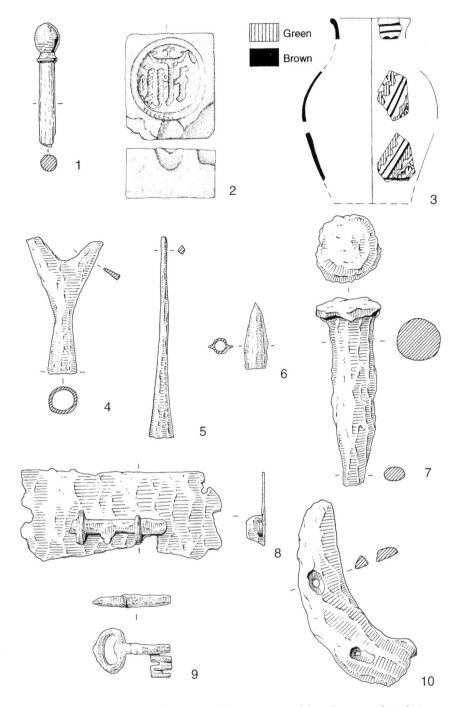

FIGURE 40.
Selection of objects illustrating daily life of the household at Clarendon Palace. 1: Pin or parchment pricker, for setting the spacing of lines on manuscripts (bone, medieval). 2: Seal matrix with IHS trigram, representing the Holy Name of Jesus (stone, thirteenth- to sixteenth-century; Ashurst and James 1988, fig. 95). 3: North Italian archaic maiolica (pottery, thirteenth- to fourteenth-century; Gutiérrez 2000, fig. 5.7). 4: Arrowhead with V-shaped head or 'forker', possibly for fowling (iron, late fourteenth-century; Jessop 1996). 5: Arrowhead with long point for hunting/military use (iron, early thirteenth-century). 6: Arrowhead with cone-shaped head and attached wings (iron, twelfth- to fifteenth-century). 7: Blacksmith's punch (iron, medieval). 8: Mounted lock, probably from furniture (iron, medieval). 9: Key with kidney-shaped bow, possibly for an item such as 8 (iron, medieval). 10: Horseshoe arm with countersunk nail holes (iron, eleventh- to thirteenth-century). Nos 1, 4, 5, 6, 7, 8 and 9 are all from recent fieldwork. No. 1 shown at 1:1, the rest at 1:2. (Drawn by Yvonne Beadnell)

examples of dot-and-ring decoration, brown vertical bands painted with iron, applied thumb strips, combed walls and a face jug.[98] Other products identified include Crockerton-type glazed jugs and globular jars in a distinctive micaceous fabric from south-west Wiltshire, a Kennet valley flint-tempered jar from near Newbury in Berkshire, green-glazed jugs from Southampton and other products from Hampshire, such as an early Verwood-type cistern; there was also a London-type jug with white slip and a green glaze, and a group of Surrey whiteware jugs.[99]

Among the imported pottery, the Rhenish imports reported in 1988 are now considered post-medieval in date, but to the thirteenth–fourteenth century archaic maiolica jar from Italy previously published (Figure 40) may now be added a Saintonge polychrome jug from France and two sherds of Malagan lustreware from southern Spain, a jug and an *albarello*, or straight-sided jar.[100] The use of Spanish lustreware has been linked to the arrival of Eleanor of Castile in England in 1254,[101] and her visit to Clarendon in 1290, the year she died, is well documented.[102] Indeed, the lustreware *albarello* was found in the spoil heap near the queen's apartments and could have been used to hold flowers or as a container for sweets, preserves, compotes or medicines such as treacle, which was used to treat colds.[103] Pottery of this type is not common and has been found at only about twenty-five sites in Britain and Ireland.[104] Locally, Faccombe Netherton is one such site.[105] Imported condiments were expensive, exclusive and accentuated differences between the Clarendon household and others in south-east Wiltshire who had to make do with locally grown produce.

With the possible exception of the *albarello* and the more highly decorated boxes or caskets, there is very little here which might be categorised as a personal possession. Leaving aside the medieval coins[106] which would have been used to pay officials and for provisions, there were strap ends, buckles, an annular brooch, scabbard fittings, a dagger, a group of iron knives and a bronze ring.[107] The collection is neither high quality nor numerous though, unlike the iron tools, there are occasional exceptional pieces which would certainly be out of place on, say, a deserted medieval village excavation. They include a seal matrix, three knives with decoratively finished blades,[108] two military arrowheads, three hunting arrowheads with copper-alloy plating, keys and locks for chests and a variety of horse fittings, such as a harness pendant decorated with the arms of Sir Robert Fitzpaine,[109] gilt bronze bridle bosses and more mundane horseshoes (Figure 40).

Two points are noteworthy about this finds assemblage. First, archaeological evidence for many aspects of palace life is slight. There is little to show for all the practical administrative tasks of running the household, or indeed the state. To indicate literacy there is one bone object: a broken pin with a lathe-turned spherical head and shank found near the kitchens which may be a parchment pricker used for pricking holes to set the spacing of horizontal lines on a manuscript (Figure 40). Alternatively, it may have been a stylus, for writing on waxed tablets, or a pointer, as an aid for reading manuscripts.[110] Other evidence for literacy and administration includes the pierced scallop shell (*Pecten maximus*) containing azurite and the ceramic vessel containing minium or red lead, both associated with manuscript illumination and suggestive of a scriptorium, though red lead was also applied to plaster as well as directly on to stone (Figure 41).[111] Documentary evidence from and about

(a)

FIGURE 41.
Pierced scallop shell
containing azurite (a),
pot base containing
minium (red lead) (b)
and cut stone painted
with red lead (c). Shell
palettes like this one
are rare; examples
from London contain
the red pigment
vermilion (Pritchard
1991). Azurite was
commonly used as a
blue pigment for panel
and wall paintings
and manuscripts from
the early medieval
period until the
eighteenth century.
Its main source was
Hungary. Red lead was
used on manuscripts,
polychrome sculpture
and panel paintings
but was less suitable
for mural paintings
because it darkens
on exposure to light
and air. Its use has
been identified on
wall paintings from
Westminster Abbey
dating to around 1400.
(Photograph by Phil
Clogg)

(b)

(c)

Clarendon is much more voluminous, and includes the many texts written and sealed there throughout the Middle Ages. The early graphic example of the text of the Constitutions (1164), which Henry II had written on the spot and presented for sealing to Becket, highlights scribal activity at the site. As for leisure beyond hunting, other than a Jew's harp there is little in the archaeological record to suggest recreation, games and pastimes. There are no dice or gaming counters, for example, both common finds on high-status sites in medieval Europe. However, there are two marbles, one found in the royal apartments, finds which are 'extremely rare in contexts from before the mid-seventeenth century', which may hint at their élite status.[112] On the whole, the finds speak loudly of hospitality, hunting and riding; the main activity which took place at Clarendon was, in a word, patronage, and patronage in which food, drink and horses played a central role[113] and formalised group activities took precedence over individual pursuits such as games of chance – until the latter become visible with the betting associated with deer-coursing and the grandstand. Second, not every single object on the site speaks of expense and status – quite the opposite; most of the dress accessories and household items are ordinary. Many of them could have belonged to the servants who manned the kitchens, stables and the cellars.[114] Notably, they are also largely male items, probably a fair reflection of the composition of the household and royal followers.

It is common for high-status sites at this period to produce restricted finds assemblages of this kind.[115] The restricted range is usually attributed to intermittent occupation by the household and assiduous cleaning both prior to and after sporadic visits. High-value items were also curated carefully and are unlikely to be found in waste deposits sifted by archaeologists. As a result it is the scale of the permanent structural fixtures and their documented creation and maintenance, with surviving fragments that were not carried away, which tell their special story here. This story is supplemented by assemblages such as the animal bone which hint at particular functions of park and palace, and occasional high-status products such as paints, with their far-flung origins – in Afghanistan for lapis lazuli and Hungary for azurite – together with chronicles of events such as the 1164 confrontation which emphasise the status of Clarendon.

Recently a medieval roof tile was found with a piglet footprint on it. This detail conjures up a picture of tiles made for the palace roofs lying out to dry, and the young pig running freely there. The tile must have been nearly dry or 'cured' when it was jumped on; the cry of frustration from the tiler can well be imagined.[116] Such an incidental detail is illustrative of an important point; industries were attracted by the presence of the park and its royal clients. The main tilery was at Alderbury, while the fancier glazed ridge tiles found at the palace site came from the nearby Laverstock kilns.[117] A major reroofing project in 1354 involved the purchase of 64,000 roof tiles for £12 16s; 1000 hip tiles for 15s and 50 crests (ridge tiles) for 2s 6d.[118] While some building materials were lighter and easier to transport, such as the 40,000 wooden shingles which came from the royal park at Gillingham in 1244,[119] roof tile is heavy and there were benefits to both client and supplier in having local manufacture. Thus Laverstock potters were granted rights to wood for fuel. In 1318–23/4 John and William le Potter, perhaps the Laverstock potters, were entitled to a rood of brushwood (*subboscum*) in Clarendon Park and Forest, while John le Potter had a specific claim in the park at Asshele (Ashley), Chesil (Chisley) and at Cattsgrove. All these coppices are towards the Laverstock side of the park. Nor were these the only Laverstock kiln products which interested the palace. In 1268 1000 Laverstock pitchers (20s) were dispatched from Clarendon to Winchester with a charge of 5s 10d for their carriage. Royal officials supplied colleagues by buying Laverstock pottery and sending it to Winchester.[120]

Another important local resource was stone. In the eleventh and twelfth centuries, Caen stone was brought to Clarendon from Normandy: considerable quantities are reused in thirteenth-century buildings right across the site. As supplies dwindled the kings increasingly sought out local stone beyond Clarendon forest, and Tisbury/Chilmark limestone became the main source of dressed ashlar work at the palace from the thirteenth century. Carving, moulding and sculpture are all of this stone and they were complemented by polished Purbeck (Dorset) limestone, which is also found as fragments at Clarendon. A document of 1174 refers to 'marble columns', presumably Purbeck, being brought by sea to Southampton and thence overland.[121] This was just at the time the Purbeck industry was rising to national importance.[122] Some twelfth-century stone buildings were also finished with Hurdcote, a local greensand from Fovant, west of Wilton, with a dramatic green hue which was popular in local parish churches, but this seems soon to have gone out of fashion, probably because of its lack of durability. The greensand is found in a number of locations in the standing structures: for example, it was used for the quoins of the old hall abutting the great stables; it is abundant in the lowest levels of the King's Chambers, and forms the paved area at the top of the wine-cellar stairs; and it is also found in the West Kitchen and scattered across the site in archaeological spoil. Almost the only material for construction which could not be supplied locally was lead. In the thirteenth century supplies ordered from Derbyshire's royal 'Bailiff of the Peak' for roofing sheetwork and for decoration were shipped round the coast to Southampton and carted to Clarendon. Fragments of lead window cames (ventilators) were recovered from demolition layers.[123]

The first habitable structure in brick on the palace site, the brick kitchen, is traditionally dated to the mid fifteenth century, and has been associated with Henry VI's mental breakdown at Clarendon in August 1453.[124] Early brick was used two centuries earlier in the tile kiln and had been used in the previous decade at the 'Queen's Lodge'.[125] The brick kitchen contained a number of hearths and was heavily plastered, with red painted walls lined in white to match interior to exterior.[126] The brick here is contemporary with its use on other high-status sites, including Caister (Norfolk), Esher (Surrey) and

Tattershall (Lincs).[127] Late fifteenth-century documentary evidence indicates 'moche newe buylding of stone and breke' at the neighbouring priory of Ivychurch, which could indicate a developing brick industry in the adjacent park and ties in with revitalisation of the priory, although no structural brickwork is now upstanding there.[128] By contrast, at the palace site after 1450 there was much decay, and a more agricultural role emerges at the less frequently used palace.[129] Nonetheless, in the year of Bosworth Field (1485) repairs were being carried out and ovens retiled. The traditional materials of stone and timber framing were becoming old-fashioned in their medieval form, which further contributed to the increasing lack of interest shown in Clarendon by the Tudor monarchy. Not only were its facilities old-fashioned, but its appearance was outmoded as well.

The economic relationship between palace, park and forest was an evolving one. Park and forest responded to the demands of the palace, particularly in the supply of goods and services. Yet, in the longer term, it was the palace which was to decay, the park which was to survive. Political change in late Lancastrian, Yorkist and early Tudor England led to a change in the disposition of royal residences. Clarendon was too remote to be safe for kings and their families during the kaleidoscopic changes in the monarchy which followed the madness of Henry VI in 1453. Clarendon had to adapt to fill a new primary role, or be disposed of. The next chapter charts its fate.

CHAPTER FIVE

Cultivating Change 1500–1800: Property and Parkland

....

In 1500 the palace was still largely complete, though no longer used, but by 1800 it had long since disappeared into a jungle of overgrowth, its buildings plundered and carted away. James Harris, trying to measure the 'parliament hall' in 1769 found it 'so truly ruins that it is difficult to form an idea of any single part of it'. The park survived, however, initially as a setting for deer-coursing and later as home to several tenanted farms for which evidence of their contents and inhabitants survives. When the antiquary William Stukeley visited in 1723 he found 'Chlorendon … a sweet and beautiful place' though the medieval landscape was by that time considerably changed. Coppices had been dug up, oaks removed, much of the launds turned to arable and the deer population decimated. A change of ownership in the early eighteenth century was followed by the building of a mansion in the southern part of the park among the relict wood pasture.

People and perspectives

In 1496 the office of Clerk of Works at Clarendon lapsed, an acknowledgment that the Crown saw little value in maintaining the palace. No longer frequented by royalty, provincial houses had fallen out of favour with Tudor monarchs.[1] During the sixteenth century the local ecclesiastical and forest infrastructure was also fractured when Ivychurch was dissolved in 1536 and the Melchet area of Clarendon forest was disafforested between 1577 and 1610. Clarendon remained a royal possession but its uneasy journey through the next century was a low point.

Henry VIII probably visited Clarendon in 1535 and Elizabeth I came from Wilton in 1574. By this date the palace buildings had so deteriorated that she dined in a temporary 'banquett house',[2] but the park itself was far from redundant. 'A very large thing and hath many keepers' commented the antiquary John Leland around 1542,[3] and a decade later the medieval attractions of deer-hunting were being further developed there by the Pembrokes of Wilton.[4] From this date until the Commonwealth they and their heirs appointed the court stewards, foresters, rangers and warreners who occupied the various lodges in the park and had their own wages and rights to grazing, firewood and venison. The earl of Pembroke used the pasture for his own cattle or let it out, took wood for his own use as well as profits from the 'conie berryes'.[5] The advantage to the Crown in retaining Clarendon is not so immediately apparent, but whereas her father had taken in great tracts of monastic land, which had all but left royal hands by Elizabeth's reign, she attempted to keep the remaining royal estate intact and to sustain it so far as her limited means allowed. Its privileges could be used to reward supporters, while the queen enjoyed their hospitality.[6]

So it was that while the palace and outer forest became redundant during the later sixteenth century, Clarendon Park continued to thrive. Tradition has it that the poet Sir Philip Sidney (1554–86), in political exile, wrote his first *Arcadia* at neighbouring Ivychurch towards 1580, commenting at the time that Clarendon was 'a delicious parke (which is accounted the best of England)', while his Oxford contemporary William Camden commented in his *Britannia* (1586) that it was 'very commodious for keeping and breeding Deer, and once beautified with a royal palace'.[7] James I seems to have agreed, for he initiated a complete overhaul of the park and its buildings then surviving: 'needefull and necessarie Rerapacons speedily to be done in and upon the Lodges pales and Rayles within the Kinges majesties Forest of Pauncett and park of Claryngdon'.[8] Much work was done at King Manor and Queen Manor, at several of the other lodges and at 'The heybarne in the great Rayles'.[9] Further works were put into effect in the summer of 1607, when weekly costs were recorded for felling, cutting, knifing and squaring the trees; for making and hanging fourteen gates, twelve in the launds and two at 'Iveschurch', and for repairing the rails of the pound at Whitmarsh Lodge.[10] The circuit of the palings is recorded on Saxton's map (1576), where the scale of the park dwarfs Salisbury: King Manor and Queen's Lodge appear on a map of c. 1610 (see Figure 73). These records demonstrate continuing royal commitment to Clarendon Park in the early seventeenth century, though a closer reading of the documents reveals that much was being recycled. In the week ending 9 May 1607, men were paid for 'digging stone at the king manor' at 8d a day – a total of 8s – on top of which was carriage of the same at 6d per load, a further 2s: twelve man-days moving four loads. This shovelling at the palace to supply works at Queen Manor continued until the middle of June[11] and must have removed many cartloads of stone.

The account of preparations for James I ends with reference to a day's work for Robert Walker 'att Claringdon about the Rayle against the kinges coming' for making the pound, setting the posts and for a lock and irons for the door, and finally there is a mention of John Randall and John Smyth 'for driving the parke against the kinges coming'. Eventually the costs escalated to £262 11s 6d between January 1606 and October 1607, and subsequently even more still.[12] King and queen both enjoyed Clarendon and were there together in August 1607 with their horses for hunting:[13] 'The queen doth ride every day in the coach with the king to Clarendon Park and there they both do take their horses to hunt'.[14] Afterwards they went their separate ways, the king to Thruxton and Andover, the queen to Wherwell and on to Basing (Hants).

FIGURE 42.
By c. 1650 the medieval land uses of the park were beginning to change. 'The Standing' and 'Pady Course' are marked here across the northern 'Lanne'. The 'Dear Lyps' and lodges are shown too, including some buildings now lost, such as Hunt's Lodge and Palmer's Lodge. The latter was at one time thought to be a precursor to the present mansion but it seems to be positioned too far north on what is otherwise a very accurate piece of cartography. (Reproduced by kind permission of Andrew Christie-Miller; image from a copy at Wiltshire and Swindon Record Office)

A further £86 spent in 1609 indicates the costs of their enthusiasm for keeping the park in top condition.[15]

Had Clarendon not been favoured personally by the king it might well have been disposed of, but Charles I saw the matter rather differently. While he 'was excessively affected to hunting and the sports of the field' and made his chaplains get up exceptionally early for services on hunting days,[16] Charles also saw the forests as assets to raise money for his cause, and he stirred up opposition by attempting to force the creation of a great red deer park between Richmond and Hampton Court in 1636, partly on the grounds that

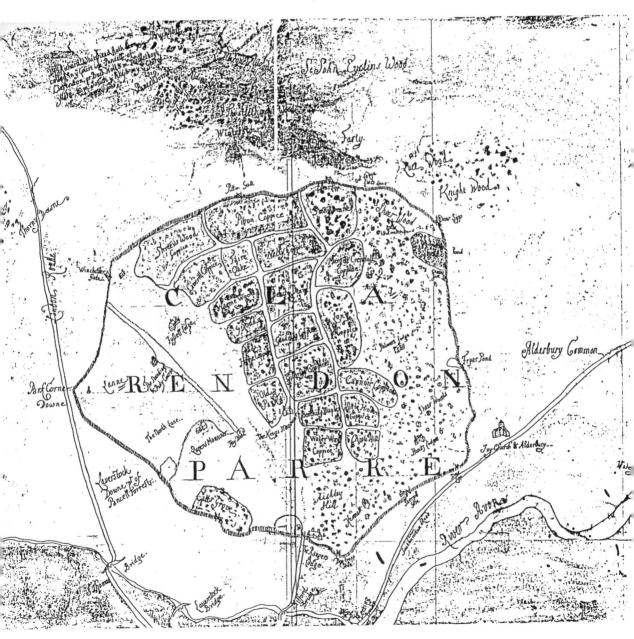

Clarendon Park and Grovely Forest only contained fallow deer.[17] Perhaps there was already an intention on the king's part to dispose of Clarendon to raise money, for soon afterwards, in 1643, he mortgaged the estate to 'Lord Hatton and others' for £20,000.[18] From Edward Hyde's papers of the late 1640s, we learn that Charles, encumbered with debt from the Civil War, proposed to 'Grant and Convey' (sell) Clarendon together with other royal parks and forests to a number of creditors round Oxford, which had been a centre of his resistance,[19] and it is from the latter part of his reign, or soon after his execution, that the earliest map of the estate survives (Figure 42), perhaps when the park was surveyed prior to being broken up.[20]

After the execution of Charles I in January 1649, Clarendon remained out of royal hands until the Restoration of 1660.[21] During the Civil War, Charles I had appointed Clarendon Park as a rendezvous for troops in October 1644, intending a sortie thence to surprise the parliamentarians at Andover (Hants). Then, in October 1651, after the Battle of Worcester, Charles II, 'pretending a hunting party' came to Clarendon and walked alone there with Humphrey Henchman (later bishop of Salisbury and then London) to Park Corner, where the Becket Cross stood, before setting off for Sussex and exile: a monarch and a churchman both defeated after a civil war which saw the eclipse of both, gathering at a monument to the martyr of a previous struggle of church and state.[22] Four years on, on Sunday 11 March 1655, Colonel Penruddock gathered 180 men at Clarendon Park during the Rising in the West, and was joined by Mompesson with forty more. Four days later the group was scattered in the failed rising; Penruddock and his leading accomplices were executed at Exeter.[23] Royalist estates were generally sold to settle arrears of army pay, with crown estates being sold off at a higher price,[24] but Clarendon was held back by parliament from disposal, reserved with other royal parks as security for the payment of the trustees appointed to carry through the sales (Figures 42 and 43). Thus 'all the coppices, cordwoods, Pollards and underwoods' could be sold towards the 'satisfaction of their salaries'.[25] The handsome Philip, fourth Earl of Pembroke (1584–1650), one of James I's early favourites and a friend of Charles I, had joined the parliamentarians in 1641. After the death of Charles, Philip began to amass lands, reinforcing his family role as Warden and Keeper of the forest and park of Clarendon, and that of Chief Ranger, which his brother had assumed in 1606. On Philip's death on 23 January 1650, the Pembrokes were reputed to have 'the most complete and absolute control over a royal hunting preserve ever possessed by a subject'.[26] This death was the opportunity parliament sought to dispose of Clarendon and the property was now surveyed for sale.[27]

Prominent among the buyers were London merchants, perhaps because at this early stage the lots were larger than they were to be later.[28] The first of the five divisions of the estate, Palmer's, was sold to Lawrence Steele, merchant of London, who sold it on in 1655 to 'George Cowper Esq. of Bow'.[29] The Clarendon oaks were especially valuable as saleable assets and George Cooper was soon defending his rights. 'Importunately urgent' with a Navy Commissioner apparently claiming his trees at Clarendon, Cooper soon found that much of what he believed he had bought was 'reserved for the use of the Navy'.[30] He tried to secure a deal whereby he distinguished trees already cut down from standing trees, but he was clearly unhappy because in 1658 he presented a petition, via Cromwell himself, to the Admiralty Committee, claiming that trees to which he had a right in Clarendon Park had been bought from the contractors at Worcester House, but had been disposed of without reference to his interest in them. In 1660 he was still petitioning but this time for a grant of the fifth part of Clarendon Park, presumably Palmer's Division, excusing his previous purchase of land by saying that he 'was enforced to purchase it, to recover 3000*l* of his money which the Parliament got into their hands', presumably a reference to the disputed timber.[31] It has been suggested that George Cooper MP 'acquired a country seat at Clarendon Park, Wiltshire' and that he 'lived at Clarendon Park near Salisbury'.[32] Given that Palmer's Division is the south-east division of Clarendon, if Cooper did live there then it was probably either in Palmer's Lodge, or in a new-built house on the site of the later mansion. Fine brickwork and a roof dendro-dated to c. 1654 in the 'motor garage' west of the mansion indicate quality building activity in Palmer's Division at that date.

In contrast to those at Palmer's, who benefited from the Restoration, the Ludlows at Ranger's (west side of the park) were at first in some danger from the return of the monarch. After the death of Charles I, Ranger's was leased to Rowland Hill in 1652 for eleven years but was sold on within a year to Henry Manning of Baynard's Castle, London. However, in 1660, in compensation to the earl of Pembroke for the sale of Clarendon he was assigned a fifth of the park, which he then leased to 'Mr Ludlow and Mr Hawles'; both these men had an interest in the park or the neighbourhood and were therefore induced to deal for the land, although 'holding the purchase unlawful'. Thomas Hawles clearly wriggled free of any claim of unlawful dealing and was later appointed a commissioner for Clarendon Park in 1660,[33] while the house at Ranger's was occupied by the Ludlow family, William Ludlow being sub-ranger in 1650. Edmund Ludlow, William's cousin, was a staunch parliamentarian. In his diary of 1660–2 he records his and others' opposition to 'that torrent of tyranny and popery which was breaking upon us' – the Restoration and its aftermath. Edmund hid his family with the Ludlows at Clarendon while he lurked in the countryside hoping for the release and uprising of Major General Lambert, who had been Cromwell's effective successor in the late 1650s before 'the comming of Charles Steward', who Ludlow feared would have had him executed.[34] The Clarendon Ludlows survived this testing time and still lived there when Catherine Ludlow died in 1677.

These cameos of the families who obtained interests in Clarendon during the Commonwealth and survived the collapse of Cromwellian government and the Restoration illustrate the detail of life at Clarendon during those turbulent decades. Of the other divisions, Hunt's was sold in February 1653 to Nicholas Skynner, merchant of London, and John Dove, a local (royalist)

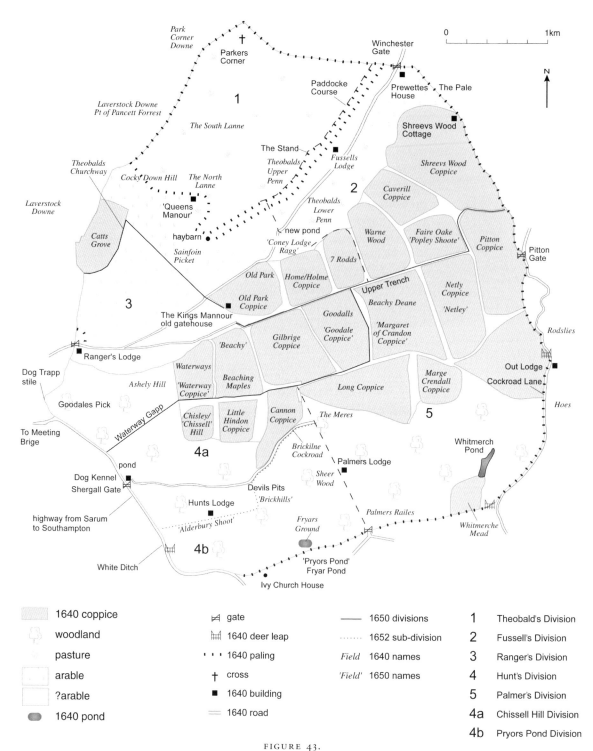

FIGURE 43.

Land use 1540–1707. Between c. 1550 and 1800 the park towards Salisbury was dug up for arable, in response to growing population locally and nationally. New features included the brick kilns in the southern half of the park and the paddock course in the north-east. The divisions shown here were those drawn up by the Parliamentary Commissioners c. 1650 when Clarendon, as an asset of the deposed Charles I, was parcelled up and sold off.

(Drawn by Alejandra Gutiérrez)

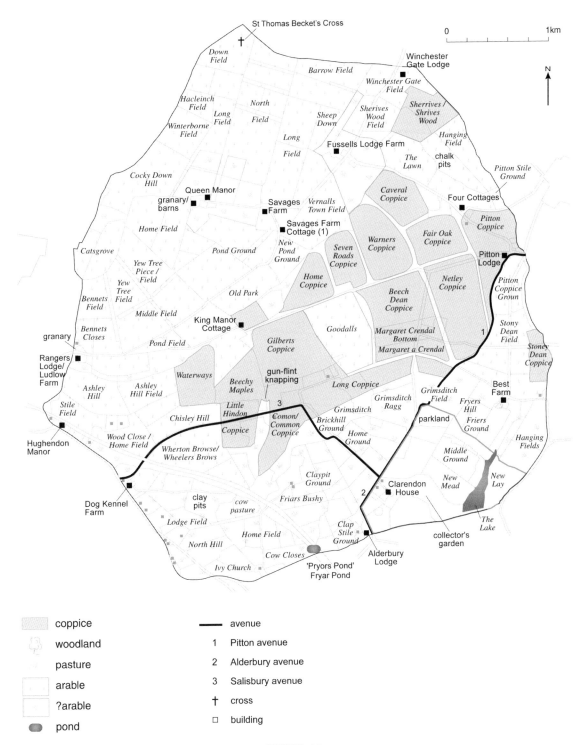

St Thomas Becket's Cross

Winchester Gate Lodge

0　　　　　　　　　　1km

N

Down Field

Barrow Field

Winchester Gate Field

Hacleinch Field

North Field

Long Field

Sheep Down

Sherives Wood Field

Sherrives / Shrives Wood

Winterborne Field

Long Field

Fussells Lodge Farm

Hanging Field

The Lawn

chalk pits

Pitton Stile Ground

Cocky Down Hill

granary/barns

Queen Manor

Caveral Coppice

Four Cottages

Pitton Coppice

Home Field

Savages Farm

Vernalls Town Field

Catsgrove

Savages Farm Cottage (1)

Warners Coppice

Fair Oak Coppice

Pitton Lodge

Yew Tree Piece / Field

Pond Ground

New Pond Ground

Seven Roads Coppice

Pitton Coppice Groun

Bennets Field

Yew Tree Field

Home Coppice

Netley Coppice

Old Park

Beech Dean Coppice

Stony Dean Field

Bennets Closes

Middle Field

King Manor Cottage

Goodalls

Margaret Crendal Bottom

granary

Pond Field

Gilberts Coppice

Margaret a Crendal

Stoney Dean Coppice

Rangers Lodge/ Ludlow Farm

Waterways

gun-flint knapping

Long Coppice

1

Ashley Hill

Ashley Hill Field

Beechy Maples

Grimsditch Ragg

Grimsditch Field

Grimsditch

Fryers Hill

Best Farm

Stile Field

Chisley Hill

3

Little Hindon Coppice

Comon/ Common Coppice

Grimsditch

Brickhill Ground

Home Ground

parkland

Friers Ground

Hughendon Manor

Wood Close / Home Field

Wherton Browse/ Wheelers Brows

Middle Ground

Hanging Fields

Claypit Ground

New Mead

New Lay

Dog Kennel Farm

clay pits

cow pasture

Friars Bushy

2

Clarendon House

Lodge Field

Home Field

Clap Stile Ground

collector's garden

The Lake

North Hill

Cow Closes

'Pryors Pond' Fryar Pond

Alderbury Lodge

Ivy Church

coppice	——	avenue
woodland	1	Pitton avenue
pasture	2	Alderbury avenue
arable	3	Salisbury avenue
?arable	✝	cross
pond	☐	building

FIGURE 44.

Land use 1707–1812. The main changes, when compared with Figure 43, are the massively increased arable acreage within the park and the pasture fields around the dairies at Fussell's Lodge and Queen Manor. The new 'parkland' at Clarendon House, with its eighteenth-century avenues and lake, can also be clearly seen.

(Drawn by Alejandra Gutiérrez)

gentleman from Ivychurch.[35] Towards the east, Prior's Pond also went to Dove on a twelve-year lease while, to the west, Chissell Hill went to Skynner.[36] What underlay the disposal of Ranger's Division is less clear: it was bought in December 1652 by the Londoner, Henry Manning, possibly on behalf of the earl of Pembroke, or the purchase may have been made 'through' the fifth earl in his role as Warden/Keeper. The Pembrokes' motive in purchasing the estates was recorded by Edward Hyde, with hindsight, as being fear rather than profit.[37] Some of the purchases, for example that by the royalist Dove of Ivychurch, echo purchases of monastic lands at the Dissolution intended to facilitate any subsequent return of the monks, for Ivychurch House had been a royalist base in the 1640s for successful forays into Dorset against parliamentarians.

Just as Clarendon was excluded from the tenants' 'right to buy' scheme after the execution of Charles I in 1649, so royal estates and parks were excluded from purchasers' compensation at the Restoration when all these purchasers' rights lapsed.[38] The question now was whether Clarendon should be reimparked. Commissioner Hawles thought it too dilapidated and in a report in late 1660 it was stated that 'by the footpaths the deer can easily be stolen; that the woods are reduced from 1000 acres to 60, so there would be no pasturage for deer, which would have to be supplied with hay'. Income from the land was by now estimated to be as high as £1200 a year, all of which would be lost if the deer park was reinstated.[39] The arguments seem persuasive, but it was reimparkment which prevailed, chiefly on the grounds that, although the income would be much reduced, the coppices could still be exploited and 'it is an ancient royal residence, a place where Parliaments have been held'.[40]

In the event, reimparkment was to last less than five years, but the result was that the complex web of ownership and tenantry in the divisions was broken and the park could be used by the grateful Charles II to reward the two architects of his reinstatement. General George Monck (1608–70), created duke of Albemarle on 7 July 1660, was gifted Clarendon Park by royal warrant to the duke of Albemarle on 22 March 1661,[41] the 4329-acre (1,752-ha) estate being valued at £1580 a year, a quarter of the income of £7000 a year granted to the duke.[42] Meanwhile, Edward Hyde (1609–74) had become Baron Hyde of Hindon on 3 November 1660 with a royal gift of £20,000[43] and was, until his dismissal in 1667, the first minister of the restored monarch. Only a month after Monck received the estate of Clarendon, Hyde was created Earl of Clarendon on 20 April 1661.

For the land appropriate to his new title, the earl of Clarendon now waited some three years until, on 22 April 1664, Albemarle assigned him Clarendon Park for a down payment of £12,000 with a final concord in the same year, and a quitclaim on 20 April 1665, when Clarendon made a final payment of £3000 to complete the £18,000 he had agreed to pay the duke.[44] Reimparkment had apparently affected Monck's income adversely, the income from the estate being valued at only £1000 a year,[45] over a third less than the £1580 a year promised in 1661, but disparkment coincided with the Hydes' gaining possession of Clarendon and provided potential for a better future. Thereafter, until his dismissal by the king, impeachment and flight into exile in 1667, Edward Hyde enjoyed the estate whose name he had first taken in 1660.[46] Despite exile for life, he was to be deprived of neither lands nor title.

The question arises that if Hyde was not the first owner of Clarendon Park after the Restoration then why he did he take the title 'Clarendon'? He was son of a local squire, and was born at Dinton, near Salisbury, in 1608. He therefore knew Wiltshire and Clarendon well and this may be part of the answer. His father Lawrence had taken over the neighbouring manor of Melchet from James I. To this it should be added that Hyde, a successful barrister and parliamentarian, had joined Charles I before the outbreak of the Civil War and was Chancellor of the Exchequer from 1643–6, after which he became chief adviser to the future Charles II. In the 1640s, Charles I was attempting to capitalise on his assets, of which Clarendon Park was one, and perhaps Edward Hyde's eye was drawn there then, especially as he loaned money to Charles I. Thus, at the end of the Commonwealth period Edward Hyde, returning to Wiltshire and seeking a title for his new earldom, selected Clarendon, which in the fullness of time he came to own. The coincidence of the £20,000 mortgage in the 1640s, the £20,000 gift to Hyde after 1660 and the £18,000 paid to Albemarle for Clarendon Park as an asset of declining value all contribute to this interpretation.

Hyde had little time to enjoy his new estate. Rewarded with the office of Chancellor, he was a central figure in government,[47] head of the University at Oxford and led a busy life in London and at Cornbury, his Oxfordshire home. His appointment as Lord Lieutenant of Wiltshire in 1667 might have meant he spent more time on his Wiltshire estate, but it was not to be. In the same year his life and work fell apart, first with the death of the earl of Southampton, his remaining friend in the ministry, and then two of the children his daughter had given the duke of York (the future James II). Almost immediately, his wife died, as a result of which he ceased to attend the Privy Council; as it turned out, he never did so again.[48] He lost the support of the king, and although he found allies in both Lords and Commons, Charles II was determined to be rid of him and threatened trial and execution. Hyde fled into exile, where he died in 1674, but not before he had raised to himself the greatest possible monument of self-justification in the form of his *History of the Great Rebellion*.

All agree that Hyde's character is elusive, despite his huge written output. There is a curious paradox between his consummate political and intellectual skill and his unworldliness. In the matter of his great house in Piccadilly, for which Charles II had donated the ground, Hyde had wished for 'a good ordinary house' costing around £17,000, but 'not understanding such things' had allowed the creation of a vast pile costing over three times that sum.[49] Taking his eye off the builders also cost him dear politically, as his Clarendon House achieved notoriety as 'Dunkirk House' and 'Holland House' – allusions to supposed bribes from enemies, one of the major causes of his downfall.[50]

While his house in Piccadilly was being constructed Hyde lived at a number of London houses including Dorset House, Fleet Street, Worcester House (at £500 rent a year), and Berkshire House as well as York House, Twickenham, after his daughter married the duke of York.[51] Shortly afterwards, rather than build at Clarendon, he began a new house at Cornbury in Oxfordshire in the spring of 1667 so that he could be 'very commodious both in town and country, though perhaps much envied'.[52] It was at his 'house and parke' at Cornbury in January 1666 that he wrote his will,[53] which refers to 'lands in and about Clarendon' and settled income from his Clarendon lands on his 'deerly beloved' wife. There is no reference to a house, though this does not mean there were no houses at Clarendon; clearly there were, as there were at the other extensive manors, spread across the midlands and the south, which he owned. Nor is it proof that he had done no building at Clarendon; he might well have done and some architectural details of the present Clarendon mansion suggest that he did (Figures 45 and 46), an idea now supported by dendrochronological evidence. What *is* clear is that he did not have a capital mansion at Clarendon, and compared to Clarendon House in London and to Cornbury, the seventeenth-century house at Clarendon whose remains exist today would have been a small place to this larger-than-life character – indeed, his girth was such that towards the end of his life he found it difficult to cross the room. Like his patron Charles I, Hyde seems to have seen Clarendon Park as a financial asset above all else. Even while he was abroad he continued to raise money by mortgages on the Clarendon estate: thus his signature subscribes documents in November 1670 by which, in return for an unnamed capital sum, he acquits and discharges the 4300 acres (1740 ha) at Clarendon Park, valued at an income of £1000 a year, for one peppercorn to a disparate group of trustees. This transaction may have been associated with the second marriage of his son Henry Hyde to Dame Flower, widow of Sir William Backhouse.[54] Had he lived to witness it, he would no doubt have been delighted that his grand-daughters Mary and Anne both became queens of England.

Following Clarendon's exile, the estate passed to his son Henry (1638–1709), the Viscount Cornbury, who became second earl in 1674 on his father's death.[55] Cornbury's pressing concern on inheriting seems to have been to raise money so that he could carry through his father's plan for a country place at Cornbury.[56] To achieve this, Henry rapidly sold Clarendon House in Piccadilly in 1675 to Christopher Monck (Albemarle's son) who, to pay his own debts, sold the great London house for development and saw it demolished in 1683.[57] At Clarendon Park Henry Hyde continued his father's policy of raising loans by leasing the Wiltshire estate;[58] for example, on successive days in 1675 he leased the estate to and from Edward Hales of 'Tonstall' (Tunstall), Kent, in return for a loan, a mechanism which provided badly needed funds.[59] In that year canal fever gripped the bishop and corporation of Salisbury, and they wrote a request for support from, among others, the earl of Clarendon, which – not surprisingly, in view of Henry Hyde's finances – received no response.[60] In 1683, through an exemplification of common recovery (i.e. Henry Hyde broke

FIGURE 45. Clarendon House, London, shared a number of architectural features with Clarendon Park mansion (Compare this with Figure 46). Edward Hyde built in London between 1660 and his exile in 1667, which occurred just as the house was completed. John Evelyn was minded to criticise this extravagant pile, but on seeing it had to concede it was 'the finest house in England'. (Photograph from the Conway Library, Courtauld Institute of Art)

PROSPECTUS CELEBERRIMÆ DOMUS ILLUSTRISSIMI DUCIS AB ALBERMARLE

the entail on the estate, entering into a legal fiction of disposing of Clarendon), he 'conveyed' Clarendon Park and over 2000 acres (809 ha) of nearby lands to Anthony Beck, no doubt as security for yet another loan.[61] This process of raising money against the value of the Wiltshire estate continued for the remaining quarter century of his ownership. Increasingly long leases are recorded, including one of 1000 years in 1687.[62] Through these means the Clarendon Park estate as received by the first earl remained intact, so that by the time of Henry Hyde's death on 31 October 1709, Clarendon had been sold as a unitary estate.

George Monck and Edward Hyde had been almost direct contemporaries, in their early 50s, when the Clarendon estate became, successively, their property. Significantly from the point of view of the development of the estate both men were firmly established in their lives and careers when they gained possession. Their focus was elsewhere: for Monck Clarendon was part of his

FIGURE 46.
The eastern elevation
of the mansion at
Clarendon, with
its raised steps and
matching window
details, is strikingly
similar to the entrance
to Clarendon House
in London, built by
Edward Hyde before
1667 (Compare Figure
45). (Photograph by
Fran Halsall)

income; for Hyde it was a lesser possession in support of his great house in London and his Oxfordshire creation at Cornbury. Both, in a sense, downgraded Clarendon as an estate and allowed it to fall further away from the pinnacle of its medieval status. Neither did the male heirs of Albemarle nor of Hyde sustain a direct interest in Clarendon for long, though other members of the Hyde family did live there. William Hyde of Clarendon Park, 'weake in body ... of sound memory', made his will early in 1691 and was dead by 17 July that year when it was proved. The principal beneficiary, receiving £20, was Mary Hyde, possibly a daughter of Hugh Hyde deceased. No wife or children are mentioned, his executrix being his cousin Mary Ewer 'of Clarendon Parke', who received the residue of his goods, monies and chattels after his funeral and legacies had been paid.[63] William Hyde seems a prime candidate to have been living in the mansion at Clarendon at that time, perhaps with his cousin Mary Ewer. He did not own the house, but it is likely he was installed there as one of Henry Hyde's family.

From the early eighteenth century the Hydes retained the Clarendon title in name alone.[64] Their successors were the Bathursts, who bought the estate from Henry Hyde in the summer of 1707 for £24,000. In order to secure possession Dame Frances Bathurst was immediately involved in settling a complex web of Henry Hyde's loans and mortgages on the Clarendon estate; in the case of a debt of £2000 judged to be owed by Hyde to Richard Rose, she had to pay Rose's widow the money to clear the debt secured against the estate.[65] Dame

Frances Bathurst was the widow of Sir Benjamin Bathurst MP, of Pauler-spury in Northamptonshire, and she moved quickly to settle the estate on her second son Peter Bathurst (1687–1748), then aged 22, in December 1708.[66]

Peter Bathurst went to Eton about 1700 and to Trinity College Oxford in 1703. He was a Tory returned 'on petition for Wilton, near his estate' in 1711–13, suggesting that he was already living at Clarendon then. He tried unsuccessfully to enter parliament for Salisbury in 1722, but sat for Cirencester until 1734 when, as 'Peter Bathurst Esq., of Clarendon Park'[67] he was successful at Salisbury, for which constituency he sat until 1741.[68] His eldest brother, Lord Bathurst, declared him to be 'quite free from party zeal', but what he lacked in political interest he made up for in his enthusiasm for his family. He married twice, first in 1709 to Leonora-Maria (d. January 1720), by whom he had two daughters, and second to Lady Selina Shirley, daughter of Robert, first Earl Ferrers, by whom he had five sons and ten daughters: seventeen children in all from his two marriages. But where on the estate did he live before the rebuilding of the mansion house? The presumption is that he lived in the 'Cowper' or 'Hyde' mansion on the same site, perhaps the house formerly occupied by Mary Hyde,[69] though how this family managed in the early eighteenth-century mansion at Clarendon, with its limited space and rooms, can only be guessed at.[70] At the end of his life, with so many children, not to mention living expenses, Peter Bathurst also used his Clarendon property to raise money. Between 1745 and his death in 1748, with his eldest son, also Peter, he raised various sums by mortgages on the estate to, for example, Allen Lord Bathurst and Selina, Dowager Countess Ferrers, in May 1747, for £5000. This was for the marriage portion of Selina Bathurst, daughter of Peter Bathurst and Lady Selina Bathurst, on her impending wedlock to Arthur, Lord Ranelagh.[71] Peter Bathurst senior died in 1748 and his heir was contemplating an advantageous marriage soon afterwards. Pre-marriage articles with Elizabeth Evelyn in 1750 proposed a settlement of £5000 on Bathurst, who was to pay her £100 for each £1000 annually from his estate at Clarendon Park. In 1751, quite probably with this capital sum, young Peter discharged the mortgage to Lord Bathurst by a payment of £5300. Between 1754 and 1773 Peter Bathurst accumulated a debt of £9000 secured on the estate by a series of mortgages, the largest of which, in 1754, was for £4000, which was raised from a tenant, Thomas Hayter; this may represent the point at which Peter paid off his sister, Selina, who surrendered Clarendon to him in 1755. These details are found in a schedule of deeds of 1773, which John Jacob, a doctor, promised to deliver to Peter Bathurst on payment of £9000 (plus interest) 'secured unto me a mortgage of said Peter Bathurst's Estate, Clarendon Park'.[72] These mortgages enabled Bathurst to retain the unity of his landholding without the sale of parcels of land, and with it the symbolic attribute of being a landowner. Thus the former royal estate at Clarendon was exploited by successive owners in the century following the Restoration to finance family, political and social ends: a new pattern of values after centuries of royal stewardship.

Deer-hunting and the Pady Course

Between 1500 and 1650, hunting remained central to park life. In the 1570s Sir George Penruddock, on behalf of the earls of Pembroke, engaged in the traditional chase and his 1574 hunting book records the taking of bucks, prickets and sorrels across the Clarendon estate from Whitmarsh in the south to the Out Woods and the launds/paddock/Shreeve's Wood areas in the north and east. Pembroke hunted with his wife: she is recorded as killing a pricket and a fawn,[73] and carcases were distributed to visiting dignitaries in the neighbourhood, among them the earl of Leicester, local gentry (many of whom themselves hunted), and others such as John Crooke, a merchant and mayor of Southampton. The book shows a flurry of activity for ecclesiastical dignitaries (and for keepers) in the week leading up to Christmas: for the 'Queen's warrant' (four does), the canons of Salisbury (two) and the Dean of Winchester (one).[74] Even when Charles I was trying to dispose of Clarendon in the 1640s hunting continued, ceremony was honoured and obligations met. On 27 June 1646, the occasion of the appointment of a new Ranger of the park,[75] the officers met at 10 am to begin their day and, in May 1650, the Dean and Chapter of Salisbury Cathedral were still demanding 'a brace of bucks and a brace of does yearly in their proper seasons in name herewith of tyth' – the annual Christmas does. Until royalist reverses in the Civil War it is generally true to say that political life and ownership upheavals had made little impact on the ground.

It is in the Tudor period that the use of the Clarendon landscape for deer-coursing is first implied. In the 1530s Henry VIII may have commissioned a permanent Standing from which to watch hunting. When Queen Elizabeth came in 1574 there was slaughter on a large scale; 340 deer were taken 'when the queen was here', but it is not clear how many were coursed and how many rounded up and killed elsewhere in the park.[76] It is quite possible that a grandstand might have existed at this date without a 'paddock course'; there are surviving examples of just this kind of isolated observation tower at Chingford (1543) and in Hatfield Forest (both in Essex).[77] Whenever it finally came to be laid out, the 'Pady Course' was in the northern part of the park (see Figures 42 and 43) and comprised a fenced course about one and a half miles (around 2.5 km) long and eighty yards (around 70 m) wide, rather like a modern horse racetrack, on to which single deer were released, pursued by dogs. Initially the deer was pursued by a slow-running 'teaser' dog, but once the deer was past the 'Law Post' at 160 yards a couple of racing dogs, usually greyhounds, were released. The dog nearest the deer when it passed the post was the winner and bets were then paid out. Sometimes the deer used were allowed to escape, often into a special paddock, but sometimes they were killed, either by dogs or bowmen or with guns (Figure 47). Given the unusual length of the course at Clarendon, the position of the grandstand and the way in which the course flares out at this point to allow spectators a better view, the races may have been started from either end with the grandstand located at the finish in the centre.[78] The slope on the south side of the course would have given excellent views at this point and although almost the whole length of the enclosed Paddock Course is visible from the palace site, where the roof of the residual gatehouse might have provided a platform from which to view from afar, the best view was undoubtedly afforded from the grandstand with its 'terrett' which lay 'in the course'.

The creation of the 'Pady Course' and its grandstand was expensive. The course was evidently railed off,[79] and one document of 1630–3 refers to 500 oaks, a huge number, having been felled in Sheer Wood for, among other tasks, 'making the Paddock Course'.[80] Perhaps some of the timber was destined for the haybarn which stood near the western start of the course.[81] A building with the same name occurs in documents from the mid-fifteenth century,[82] also appearing on the map of c. 1650, and was still extant in 1692 when, as part of Queen Manor Farm, it was let with 250 acres (101 ha)[83] next to three sizeable fields listed as Upper and Lower Penns and the 'Launes' in the 1650 survey.[84] Their names suggest these fields were used for grazing deer during events, and perhaps the banqueting house for the 1574 royal visit was sited here.[85] Presumably there was a dog pound in this part of the park too, though none is mentioned. The hounds were perhaps more permanently housed in 'the house called Dogg Kennell', possibly the present Kennel Farm, dated by dendrochronology to 1588 and consisting c. 1650 of 'one roome below stayres and two chambers above stayres, with a yard walled about with bricke … and one dogg kennell about fiftie foote in length and fifteene foote in breadth … also a well neere the said house and a garden plot hedged in …'.[86]

The date of the Standing on the paddock course remains uncertain. At the earliest it dates from c. 1537 and at the latest, taking dendrochronology and documents together, about 1610. In 1651 it was described as being built 'with timber and bricke and part covered with tyle', at which date the same document refers to brick kilns present on the estate, which may have reduced building costs.[87] It consisted then of two rooms with a staircase and a turret and even though 'much decayed … [and] unfit to be repaired' was still valued at £30, valuable when compared with the 'tenement or Gate House called Kings Manor' – apparently the only surviving fragment of the palace buildings – which was worth only £15.[88] Fragments of these buildings may still survive, incorporated into later building projects. A large quarter oak reused in a fireplace at Queen Manor Farmhouse had begun to grow in 1347 and was felled in the spring/summer of 1537, rendering it contemporary with Henry VIII's interest in Clarendon.[89] Two other sixteenth-century timbers in Queen Manor Farmhouse have been dated by dendrochronology: one is perhaps contemporary with the 1537 beam, while a principal rafter felled sometime after 1544, suggested a later phase of building or repair at that date.[90] Most notably, there are pieces of the grandest oak cyma (traditionally dated typologically from 1530–40s onwards) and ovolo mouldings (traditionally 1550s, 1580s–1620s) reused both in the granary and in the farmhouse

at Queen Manor. These match aspects of the Chingford standing of 1543 (Figure 48). If contemporary with the Chingford mouldings these cyma and ovolo mouldings would be precocious, as ovolo mouldings would be more likely to date from the late sixteenth century in central southern England.[91] However, Clarendon was a royal estate and such precocity cannot be ruled out.

Not all activity in the park was lawful at this period of lessening royal control. During Henry VIII's reign, Margaret York of Laverstock became so infuriated with the park officials, claiming they had wrongly enclosed her land, that she not only encouraged her servants to hunt inside the park and resist the keepers but issued an invitation to all local gentry to join her.[92] On another occasion, three poachers set out with a horse from the Green Croft, Salisbury, at 11 pm one night in the early summer of 1606, perhaps taking advantage of a disruption of the management regime at the park. They hid their horse near Laverstock and proceeded with two greyhounds to take a 'male deare', which was taken to the house of Thomas Raye, a clothier, and there 'broken uppe', part being cooked for an Ascension day feast. After being apprehended, the poachers and receivers were sent to the Quarter Sessions.[93] Then, in 1610, a 'fearsome affray' between two Salisbury men was threatened when a duel was scheduled for 14 September at the

Clarendon Park pale, well beyond Salisbury city limits. The affray had arisen over a combination of matters – ostensibly a pair of bowls, but also cheating at cards, pistols and 'bastinadoing', not to mention the upholding of the honour of the sister of one of the duellists. The affair ended in the Court of Star Chamber.[94] Two years later, in the summer of 1612, poachers Leonard and John Moggeridge had their hounds captured by the park keepers. Lest their identity should be revealed the brothers broke into the keeper's lodge (presumably the In Out Lodge just outside the pale on the east side of the park), smashing down doors as they went from room to room, until they discovered their dogs upstairs.[95]

The Moggeridges may have had no better luck if they had returned fifty years later. In 1661 there were said to be no deer in the park, partly because of the derelict pale, partly due to unmanaged hunting during the Interregnum.[96] It was said by the two underkeepers, Hunt and Palmer, that there had been 7000 fallow deer at Clarendon in Charles I's time.[97] Parliamentary surveys of 1650 and 1651 show a sharp contrast between the 3000 deer counted in 1650 and a figure of only 500 in the following year.[98] Although Charles II's 'pretended hunt' in 1651 suggests that it was still reasonable to expect to find deer at Clarendon,[99] these figures represent a count at the end of the highly damaging and disruptive Civil War, when deer stocks on the royal estate were plundered and the ploughing up of woodland by new owners and the loss of trees generally to the Navy was probably at least as damaging to their habitat.

There is no evidence of formalised hunting at Clarendon during the Hyde years though it may be assumed that deer were taken illicitly and by tenants living in the park. Approved hunting of any kind probably resumed only under Peter Bathurst and then only once he had a larger house in which to entertain after 1715. Decorative fallow deer appear in front of the mansion house in the 1791 picture (see Back Cover) but from the eighteenth century it was probably pheasant which provided the major game in the park. Friends and family could be invited to shoot and presents of braces of birds cemented both social and political relationships, though the organisation of shoots would not at this point have been as intensive as it was to become in the nineteenth and twentieth centuries. The lake may have supplied fish as well as having an important aesthetic function. Presumably there was boating from the boat house shown on maps at the south-western corner of the lake. In Peter Bathurst's will (1796) we gain a glimpse of his key officials, and the esteem in which they were held: John Toomer, bailiff (£200); wearing apparel was left to his *valet de chambre*, James Simmons; and the gamekeeper, George Wort, was left the testator's dogs and guns.[100] By that date the medieval chase and wagers at the paddock course were long since a part of Clarendon's past.

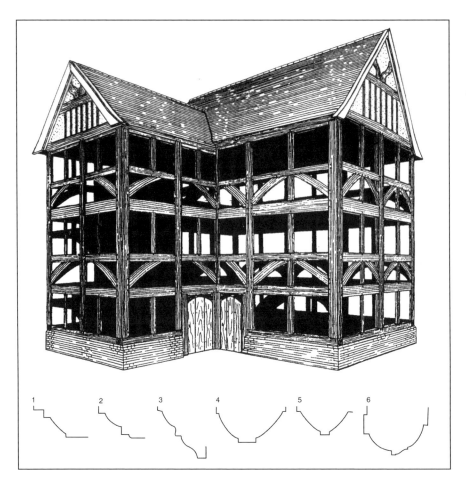

FIGURE 48.
This surviving
grandstand, or
Standing, is at
Chingford in Essex.
The early Standing by
the Paddock Course
at Clarendon may
have looked like
this before it was
replaced by the brick
and lead structure
extant in 1650. Large
cyma (1–3) and ovolo
(4–6) mouldings
(below), in situ at
Chingford, match
Clarendon examples
discovered reused in
later structures (scale
1:7). (Building drawn
by Douglas Scott,
modified by Susan J
Brown; by courtesy
of John McCann.
Mouldings from
drawings by Dorothy
Treasure, Wiltshire
Buildings Record)

Changing land use in the park

Throughout the sixteenth century and the first half of the seventeenth century, there was little reason to change the basic land use compartments which had developed at Clarendon during the medieval period. Woodland, for example, was still divided in May 1650 between timber trees, underwoods (mostly 'thornes'), a two-acre nursery of young oaks and coppices 'usually fenced in'.[101] To the north and west there were grazing lawns on the chalk downland. Visually the park landscape remained much as before. Access routes into and through the park were unchanged, though walkers, welcome or uninvited, could now make use of two stiles, both on the western pale: the 'Dog Trapp Stile' at Ranger's Petersfinger,[102] necessary with all the new gates and locks installed earlier in the century; and another at Cattsgrove, accessed along the Theobald's Churchway from Queen Manor Farm. Peter Theobald, one of the under-keepers in 1650, probably made his way to Laverstock church along this path, but for those traversing the woods, impressive or unusually shaped trees provided important markers and were occasionally individually named: the 'Two Sisters'; 'the little maple tree'; 'Kytes Ash'; and the 'Cross Oak'.[103]

One of the benefits enjoyed by the mid-seventeenth-century occupants of the Innelodges (lodges within the park) were rights to herbage, pannage, portions of coppicing and meadow, as in the medieval period. The 16-acre (6.5 ha) Whitmarsh Mead, hedged 'to protect the plantes', in the south-eastern Palmer's Division, was available to the park's officers in 1650. Each of the four quarter keepers and the Out Keeper was allowed an acre of the Mead each, and they were also permitted to keep eight cows (the Out Keeper was allowed only six) in the park, together with one bull and their horses.[104] Other land use, too, continued much as before: for example, rabbits were kept until after 1600. Smaller feral animals included mice, rats, squirrels and voles as well as moles – the latter recorded as a problem during, and before, the seventeenth century, when 'wontodge' (mole-catching) was a designated task in the park. Management of fox, badger, marten, otter and squirrel, all of which could be hunted as vermin, was probably the warrener's responsibility.[105]

Following the execution of Charles I, the wider economy external to Clarendon Park began to impinge. Oak was needed for shipbuilding and the 1650 survey dismally reveals 'wast and spoyle done and committed upon the woods' and mentions trees 'marked out and cutt down for the use of the Navy'. Most of the destruction had been done in the southerly wood pasture of Sheer Wood: £200 of damage in Hunt's Division, £150 in Palmer's Division, £100 in Ranger's and £50 in Fussell's. Theobald's division, in the north of the park, escaped because it contained no woodland.[106] Nevertheless, there were still 15,961 trees left, of which 12,638 were timber trees and the rest mostly 'old dotterels and decayed trees good for little save the fire'. In addition there were 'Underwoods' (mostly thorns) and twenty-one coppices, usually fenced in.[107]

Over the next decade timber-cutting must have been continuous. By 1661 there were as few as 2500 old oaks 'yet left standing' (20s each), which were fit for the use of His Majesty's navy; 2000 younger oaks (30s apiece) growing in the coppices; 3000 oak saplings 'of about tenne inches square'; and many other trees not valued. The 1000 acres (405 ha) of woodland had been reduced to a mere sixty.[108] Pepys's diaries firmly blame the Navy Board for the disappearance of timber resources, describing the displeasure of the earl of Clarendon on learning in July 1664 of the 'trees in Clarendon Park marked [with the Navy's broad arrow] and cutt down'. In a lengthy passage the earl accuses Pepys of being 'most ungentlemanly-like with him' and of having 'sent the veriest Fanatique that is in England to mark them [the trees] on purpose to nose him'.[109] The timber trees for the use of the Navy, 'to be taken at convenient times', were reserved to the Crown.[110] The New Forest provides a local parallel for increasing seventeenth-century demand,[111] and at Windsor Great Park the position was also comparable, with 2664 trees deemed fit for use by the navy, and a further 4333 old and largely decayed trees 'good for little save the fire'.[112] A rise in the provision of both merchant and naval ships has been noted in the period 1660–1700, and it clearly involved large-scale felling of timber across southern England.[113]

The 'severall purchasers' between whom the estate was split during the Commonwealth period, c. 1650–60, occupied rather than developed their properties in the park. With such an uncertain future they were unwilling to commit to large capital projects, but they began by dividing the land up among themselves 'and ploughed up a great part thereof'.[114]

The chalk downland pasture must have been among the first areas to be converted. Before this time the unenclosed launds in the north of the park would have looked bleak to our eyes. Now, with arable came enclosure, permanent fencing and hedging. Finds from recent fieldwalking provide archaeological evidence of this process. There are, for example, fragments of seventeenth-century stoneware pottery which may have been introduced during manuring from fields to the north-east and west of Fussell's Lodge and from fields at Best's Farm.[115] Four out of five pipes recovered from fields near Best's Farm also fall into the period 1620–1730 and there is a late seventeenth-century stamped stem from King Manor Field.[116]

After the Civil War buildings, farms and houses within the park were leased out to tenants who farmed different divisions of the park. It seems likely, although it is not possible to prove it beyond doubt, that the divisions of the second half of the seventeenth century became the basis for all later tenurial arrangements until after the Second World War. Thus, in 1703, two years before his death, Henry Hyde tops the Clarendon land tax list of eleven taxpayers.[117] Likewise, in 1707, when Dame Frances Bathurst purchased Clarendon, twelve taxpayers are listed in Clarendon Park.[118] Each of these tenants turned their attention to improving their profits within their own farmland so that, although the park continued in single ownership, its management was now divided. With the deer in apparent terminal decline the future lay with arable and restoration of the woodland to productivity.

Clues as to exactly how the later seventeenth-century farms were worked are embedded in probate inventories. There are only three of these, but the major Clarendon crops were clearly wheat, barley, oats and peas. Linseed and flax are also mentioned; linseed oil was used in paints and soap, and hemp could be woven into cloth and wound into rope. There was evidently some specialisation because while all farms kept horses, only two kept sheep while the third was clearly a dairy and beef unit with 'milch cows', bullocks and a bull. This last farm, run by Henry Hayter in 1680, also kept seventeen pigs fattened on the whey while the peas he grew could have been fed to the pigs to harden off their flesh before they were sold for bacon.[119] Above all, Hayter and his fellow tenants seem to have found little use for the Clarendon coppices. Large blocks of coppiced woodland disappeared at Shreevewood Coppice, Cattsgrove, Beechy, Goodalls, Chisley Hill and Old Park, as well as parts of Cannon Coppice, Pitton Coppice, Stony Deane, Marge Crendall Coppice and Long Coppice. Timber trees in Sheer Wood were mostly removed too by 1750 and the area ploughed. This was a key moment in Clarendon's land use history. The reduction in woodland may have begun during the Civil War, but it certainly continued later. Much of the clearance apparently post-dated

FIGURE 49.
The 1713 map: Peter Bathurst's guide to the estate he came to own after 1707. It shows boundaries and field names overlaid by the names of tenants. Notice, for example, 'Clay Hills Ground' and 'Claypit Ground' in the southern half of the park, tenanted by Stephen Maton. Buildings are tantalisingly schematic but include what must be a house in the location of the mansion and an avenue running north-west, as well as several structures near the palace site. (Reproduced by kind permission of Andrew Christie-Miller)

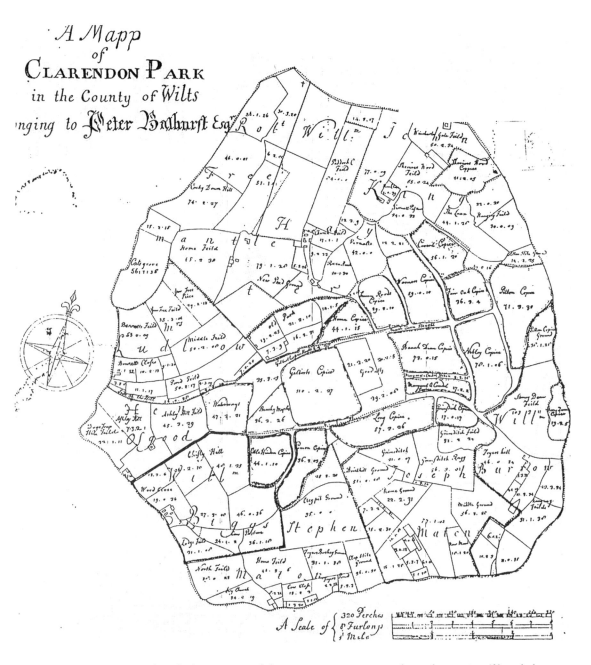

A Mapp of CLARENDON PARK in the County of Wilts ...nging to Peter Bathurst Esq...

Aubrey's description of the twenty coppices, made in about 1684,[120] and changes pre-date the 1713 map (Figure 49).[121]

Industries such as weaving were secondary employment for small farmers. This may have been the case at Clarendon, with the proximity of cloth-making at Wilton. Certainly the extraction of fuller's earth was already in progress towards the south of the estate in Hunt's Division in 1652 and is referred to by the antiquarian John Aubrey in about 1684.[122] A brick kiln is also mentioned at the same date and field names such as 'the Brickhills' and 'Devill's Pits' suggest waste heaps, pits and ponds (Figure 50).[123] The lease in 1773 of Brick Kiln farm to John Newman for fourteen years referred to 'fullers claypits brick kiln clay pitts sandpitts, Chalkpits', tile clay, brick clay, and so on.[124] Substantial clay pits are still common earthworks right across the park. In addition, evidence of gun-flint knapping has been found at King Manor from about 1750. The flints were extracted from a chalk-pit beside the road and carried to the sunny bank opposite to work them into gunflints.[125] All these activities provided potential supplementary income for Clarendon households.

By 1800, and certainly by 1812, the pattern of land use seen today was established. From the analysis of maps and finds from fieldwalking, it is clear that in the north and west, on the chalk downland, most fields were ploughed.[126] Although we are ignorant about details of the crops sown there, the estate's three major arable farms, at Ludlow Farm/Ranger's, Queen Manor and Fussell's, were all equipped with granaries for the surplus of more disease-resistant crops.[127] Unnamed buildings were also found at Town Field, Piper's Field, to the north of Whitmarsh Pond, and between Ranger's Lodge and King Manor and to the south of Queen Manor. These were presumably barns for hay and machinery. In the centre of the estate was residual medieval woodland, and throughout the eighteenth century a continuing source of income came from wood and timber. Doubtless the woodland provided cover for game birds too but unfortunately no distinction is made on either Andrews and Dury's map of Wiltshire of 1773 or the 1812 estate map (CEA) as to the different forms of management. As far as can be judged, the overall proportions of land use remained roughly constant, with a slight increase in the wooded areas at Shreeve's Wood, Waterways and Beechy Maples, decreasing with the clearance of Goodalls (Piper's Field) between 1773 and 1812. Again, these land use changes are reflected in the finds from fieldwalking survey, so that pottery of seventeenth- and eighteenth-century date is absent from Beechy Maples, a field which was probably only converted from coppice to arable late in the eighteenth century. Other income came from the dairy at Best's Farm[128] and perhaps others at Dog Kennel Farm, Fussell's Lodge and Queen Manor. These four farms are shown surrounded by pasture fields on the 1812 map (possibly under- or mole-drained by this date), though some pasture may have been for sheep rather than cattle.[129] A possible dewpond at Fussell's Dairy Cottage lies near to 'Ram Close', at the end of 'Sheep Down' field on the 1812 estate map, and sheep kept here were probably folded on the adjacent ploughed land, a practice recognised to be beneficial to the light chalky downland soils.

What emerges by 1800 at Clarendon are five semi-independent mixed farming units situated at Best's Farm, Ludlow Farm/Ranger's, Queen Manor, Dog Kennel and Fussell's Lodge, reflecting the lines originally envisaged in the temporary break-up of the park in 1650. Between about 1500 and 1800 some features of medieval Clarendon had decayed, the palace being the most notable victim of neglect and the target of plunder. Other features, like woodland and timber trees, were ripped out because they could generate cash quickly, and were then replaced by more speedily profitable arable. All that was new, in the way of building stock, new crops, increased enclosure and subdivision, and the extinguishing of common rights, was designed with more efficient exploitation of the landscape in mind. But there were also echoes of former lives and landscapes: hunting survived in an altered form; the basic divisions in the medieval landscape also existed in post-medieval land use, even if the detail had changed – where there had once been pasture launds there was now more ploughed land and where there had been wood pasture there was now to be a new kind of park and mansion.

Officers and testators

From 1553 the administration of the park was vested by the Crown in the earls of Pembroke of Wilton. To overcome this inconvenience of non-residence the earls appointed a sub-ranger.[130] In 1647 that was William Ludlow esquire, who lived at Ranger's Lodge, one of the grandest houses on the estate. Reporting to him in 1651 were four quarter or underkeepers: Peter Theobald at Queen Manor; William Fussell; Thomas Palmer; and James Hunt, all at their eponymous lodges, as well as Henry Hunt, who was based at the Out Lodge, beyond the park pale. They were each waged at between £4 and £8 a year but were also entitled to £3 6s 8d in lieu of their 'fee wood' from the annually cut coppices.[131] John Walker, at Dog Kennel Farm, earned £4 a year from the Chief Ranger for killing moles and also kept up the hedges on the coppices, for which he received four marks a year.

Other posts were more nominal. The escheator of Clarendon Park and 'bow bearer', a term first recorded in England in 1538 (*OED*), developed into a position as an under-officer in the forest who looked after trespasses affecting vert and venison. These posts were, by the patronage of the earls of Pembroke, in the hands of the Nicholas family in the 1630s and 1640s. John Nicholas, appointed escheator of Clarendon Park by the fourth earl of Pembroke, obtained the position of bow bearer for his cash-strapped, London-based son Edward, who was a royal secretary. When his father died in December 1644, old and worn down by billeting of soldiers and the plundering 'of all my horses … by the chief commanders of the Parliament forces', Edward Nicholas made over the bow-bearer's privileges at Clarendon to his mother to enjoy it as she had done in his father's time, advising her to 'take care that the said place be upon all occasions executed by some of your servants, that you will be pleased to receive for your own life all the fees, profits and perquisites belonging to the said place …'.[132] Not that the park was entirely safe, as revealed a generation or so earlier when, in March 1579, Edward Appleford, the 'keeper of the beasts' in Clarendon Park, had 'accidentally wounded Dyer' there. John Dyer died ten days later.[133]

These individuals were primarily officials rather than farming tenants, and one reason for the government's exclusion of the royal parks from sale to tenants becomes clearer: the officials could continue to extract income from the park on behalf of the government, while being waged for their duties.

Gradually the posts and their authority were downgraded, though they were still valuable for the influence and the customary rights they carried. The Parliamentary Surveys state rights in a form which could be interpreted as a disposable asset and sometimes build them up in a generous interpretation of their true value. Thus the former royal rights over swans on the Avon, for example, were expressed as extending from Warminster to the sea, much wider than anything found in medieval records.[134] The 'place' of bowbearer – long since honorary so far as carrying the king's bow was concerned – amounted to permission to keep eight cows, one bull and two horses (like the underkeepers, with a similar in *lieu* fee wood payment). Royal nomenclature too was allowed to fade. After the Civil War the Queen Manor division took the name of its underkeeper. This personalised naming of parts of the landscape was the culmination of Renaissance individualism and self-fashioning, combined with the need for new titles for posts which reflected a post-monarchical society.

Occasional glimpses of the events of ordinary life are offered by documents. Regular bastardy suits involving Clarendon people remind us that there was more to the eighteenth century than the Enlightenment, and a clutch of coroners' records bring us face-to-face with a death by falling from a horse while riding home and three drownings, two accidental and the third, of a person unknown, attributed to lunacy.[135] Rather more detail on the network of society on the estate can be extracted from eight Clarendon wills, all from the seventeenth century.[136] To these may be added the three wills and/or inventories mentioned below.[137] Anne Pile's will of 1656 lists bequests of three sums of £100 apiece, and three of £50 (the latter to Thistlethwaite uncles, a high-status family from Winterslow, and a Ludlow aunt, which betoken the testator's local status) clearly demonstrate her wealth. Her maid, Joan Titchborne, received a large bequest of £50 (more, for example, than the combined value of the remains of the ruined palace and the hunting grandstand in 1651), even if it was tempered by £14 already owed her by the testator.[138] 'Mrs Dove at the Exchange' received £24 and may have been a relation of the Doves of Ivychurch. Possibly the puritanism of the 1650s, coupled with anxieties about the many-headed monster of the poor and the potential of pastors to spy for the government, or perhaps the plain generosity of Anne Pile, resulted in bequests of £20 to the local parson, bequests to 'all the servants in the houses and with me 20s apeece', and £100 to the poor. For Anne Pile, as for other seventeenth-century Clarendon female testators, mourning was important: she leaves the residue of her wealth 'to bury me and to buy mourning for my friends in the house with me'.

Anne's 'Aunt Ludlow' may have been Katherine Ludlow, spinster, who died in 1677 and who also made provision for family and the poor (though not the parson).[139] Katherine Ludlow's brother William was the first beneficiary and her executor, and received £10, as did each of her four nephews and nieces (Edmund – whose name echoes his republican uncle of the previous generation – John, Anne and Elizabeth), while there are legacies to her married sisters surnamed Corbett (and to her sister's son and four daughters) and Barry, and to others.

FIGURE 50.
View of The Meres. These artificial ponds, previously known as the 'Devill's Pits', are either medieval features to provide water for deer, fishponds or early post-medieval pits for clay extraction for brick-making. The 'Brickilne Cockroad' ran directly here in the mid-seventeenth century; later the Salisbury avenue originally ran to their west, but during the nineteenth century The Meres were planted up and the avenue diverted to bisect them. (Photograph by Fran Halsall)

These wills provide several useful insights. First, they highlight markedly Protestant burial arrangements: Margaret Dunch, Christopher Ewer and William Hyde, the other three individuals for whom wills survive, enter the puritanical 'to the earth' instruction for burial, while both Katherine Ludlow and Anne Pile provide for mourning apparel to be provided, in Ludlow's case specifying that there should be black cloth made available 'for mourning' for her two nieces Anne and Elizabeth, whose probable father William Ludlow, as executor, would have had to be prominent at the funeral, as he was charged with the choice of burial place. George Monck's spectacular, snaking procession of mourners, recorded in a contemporary print, was the ultimate expression of such arrangements. To succeed in puritan England, demonstrative Protestantism was essential.

Second, these wills give some clues as to the connections maintained between Clarendon people and adjacent parishes, Clarendon having no parochial status of its own. Anne Pile is listed as of Clarendon Park, parish of St Martin, Salisbury. Parochially, therefore, she looked south-west and made reference to Mr Eaire(s) 'the Parson'. John Alford asked to be buried on the north side of Pitton Churchyard (east of Clarendon), Christopher Ewer and William Hyde demonstrated a family and Clarendon connection with nearby West Grimstead, the latter with a request to be 'decently buried' there, near the Ewers.[140] Neither Margaret Dunch nor Katherine Ludlow specified a burial place, and instructed their executors to bury them 'as they see fitt'. These varying arrangements suggest uncoordinated religious affiliations of the Clarendon community in the post-Reformation period, as seen above in the varied political outlook of the Coopers and the Ludlows, and serve as a reminder of the scattered nature of the residences across the estate, and the problems of communication such a large estate posed when most people lived more or less at its margins.

A third point to be noted here is the provision the testators make for the poor, despite the introduction of the post-Reformation poor law. Margaret Dunch reveals local poverty in a reference to the 'poor people in and near unto Clarendon', and Anne Pile's bequest of £100 is outstanding in this respect; Katherine Ludlow likewise made provision for the poor (unspecified, at the discretion of her executors) while William Hyde left a very modest 20 shillings to the poor of West Grimstead. The three women's wills provide evidence that they were wealthy in their own right (the Prerogative Court of Canterbury was intended to be the preserve of the wealthier members of society). Margaret Dunch left total bequests of over £130 and Catherine Ludlow a similar amount, while Anne Pile left some £650 of bequests, and her references to 'houses', her maid and to 'all the servants' suggests she was living in a grand house on the estate – possibly in view of her Ludlow connections, with her relations in the Ludlow Lodge at Ranger's.

Finally, these wills also highlight gender networks among women. Half of the £100 set aside for the poor by Anne Pile in 1656 was to be dispersed by her grandmother, Catherine Ludlow. The majority of the beneficiaries of the will were women, including one sister whose husband remains unnamed, and they were also chief beneficiaries – for example, by far the largest individual bequest by Margaret Dunch, one of £50, was to her sister Bridgett Tremaine. Women also took their place as executrixes (cousin Mary Ewer for William Hyde and Judith, 'my loveinge wife', for John Alford). Nine witnesses were listed in these wills, three of whom were women; two of these, Margaret Hayter and Dorothy Whatley, made marks rather than signatures, betokening illiteracy.

Houses and their contents

Park officers occupied their lodges as before. Ranger's Lodge[141] was refurbished in 1607–8, requiring twenty-five days' work by a mason and two men, and helliers (roofers) for twenty-eight days, at a total cost of £36.[142] In 1618 a deposition records 'the decay of Ranger's Lodge, want of tiling so that rain beat into the house these last three years'.[143] The 'chief of the Innelodges' was described in 1650 as:

> a hall, a fayre wanscoted parlor, a buttery, a kitchen, a larder, a washhouse and a milk house below stairs. And in the first storey a large dining roome, three lodging chambers with a closet and two other roomes. And in the second storey one lodging chamber and one garret. Also a courtyard and a garden (both paled) with a well therein, and adjoining to the said house a fayre stable with two roomes over it and a little paled yard and a well therein.[144]

An orchard and a six-bay barn with paled yards are also mentioned, so this was a sizeable house with agricultural buildings, all with their own individual pales. No wonder William Ludlow was reluctant to lose it; between the end of the fifteenth century and the building of the mansion in the first half of the eighteenth century Ranger's Lodge was, with Queen Manor, the best appointed of the Clarendon houses.[145]

Other medieval lodges survived but proved expensive to maintain. In 1618 Queen Manor was 'so ruinous that sixty pounds will hardly repair it' and that it was 'likely to fall to the ground'.[146] Yet by 1650 the same lodge is described as 'consisting of 8 roomes and a cellar below stayres, and seaven chambers above stayres', together with a stable and 'two little garden plots paled … and also a commodious well'.[147] The oldest parts of Queen Manor Farmhouse today, the rear north-east wing and the central rear parts, are perhaps early seventeenth-century, a date suggested by the brickwork and the carpentry there.[148] Other former lodges were refurbished too. In 1607–8 £29 was paid for 'new building up of walls, parlour, kitchen and stable' at Shergallgate Lodge/Kennel Farmhouse; Whitmarsh Lodge was rebuilt after it burnt down; and the Sherriff Wood Lodge had its roof repaired.[149]

During the sixteenth century and the first half of the seventeenth century there were apparently significant additions to Clarendon's building stock; several new names are documented. Thomas Palmer, who lived at the lodge to which he seems to have given his name, was 60 years old in 1618 and if he was the first occupier then his lodge may be mid-sixteenth-century in origin. However, it seems more likely that the lodges were named simply after the head of household at the time the reference was made, rather than after the family which had first occupied them. Fussell's Lodge, Hunt's (Out) Lodge and Palmer's (Whitmarsh) Lodge were ancient enough to be listed in a deposition of 1618 as being 'in great decay and like to fall down', despite all the work done on them only ten years earlier, Hunt and Palmer being parkers before 1650.[150] They did not collapse, for they reappear in 1650, all three lodges apparently substantial dwellings.[151]

None of the Clarendon lodges has been investigated archaeologically and assemblages of pottery and other finds from fieldwalking nearby are meagre. Seventeenth- or eighteenth-century Westerwald stoneware, post-medieval slip-wares, wine bottle fragments and clay pipe dated 1620–1700 were among the finds from Hockamore field near Queen Manor (Figure 51).[152] Clay pipe of the same date was recovered at Fussell's Lodge Farm but, even taken together, these objects give little impression of life in Clarendon houses in the seventeenth century. It is fortunate then that documentary inventories and surveys are more revealing. Overall, the Clarendon properties listed in about 1650 were of three types: large houses with seven to sixteen rooms (Ranger's had fifteen, Queen Manor sixteen, Fussell's twelve, Hunt's ten, Palmer's seven), smaller tenements or cottages with three rooms and a specific function past or present (King Manor, Winchester Gate Lodge, Dog Kennel), and non-residential properties (the Stand). Noteworthy beyond these is the Out Lodge, with five rooms, where the keeper, Henry Hunt, lived. These properties had barns, outbuildings, gardens and, in some cases, additional land: thus Palmer's had 'two garden plots and one parcel of meadow ground called the Orchard, and a little court yard on the east side of the house', while Ambrose Pruett, by 1650, had rebuilt Winchester Lodge, in the north-east corner of the park, at his own expense, where he enjoyed 'a little garden plot'.[153]

To this basic listing of buildings of different sizes, we can also add information from three inventories of 1666, 1680 and 1684. All three were of the larger-house category: one described the contents of over seven rooms and the others, over ten rooms. There are hints as to which houses they may have been, but no certainty, no personal names being attached to a particular property. Henry Hayter had goods valued at £320 19s in March 1666. His inventory opens with his 'backsyde' containing his beasts, crops and a few tools. The house contained a Parlour, Hall (with hangings, spits, bellows and so on), pewter and brassware, kitchenware, flitches of bacon and so on. There follows a Brew House, a Buttery and a Milk House. Probably upstairs was a Parlour Chamber (high bed, hangings, cushions, carpet and a rug), Hall Chamber (ditto plus chest, chair), the back loft (mainly bedsteads) and 'Lumbar goods', and finally 'bookes in house', which were worth a total of £1 10s. Described here were some seven rooms in all, plus the milkhouse, in what appears to be a ceiled-over medieval hall.[154]

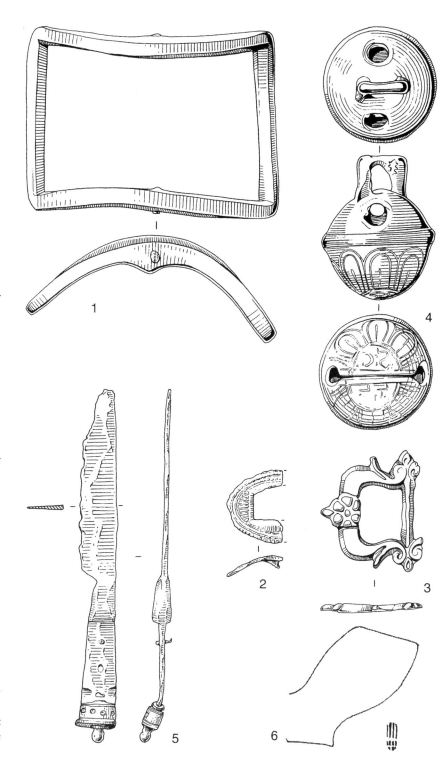

FIGURE 51.
Selection of post-medieval finds. 1: Shoe buckle (copper alloy, eighteenth-century). 2: Shoe buckle, pin bar missing (iron, post-medieval). 3: Buckle, double-looped and decorated with scrolls and rosettes (lead/tin alloy, eighteenth- or nineteenth-century). 4. Rumbler bell, initialled 'S [reversed] C' (copper alloy, eighteenth-/nineteenth-century). 5. Scale-tang knife with bolster, end cap with dot-and-ring decoration (iron, seventeenth-century). 6. Clay pipe, stamped with trade mark of the Gauntlett family of Amesbury (seventeenth-century). All these finds were recovered from the palace site during recent fieldwork with the exception of 3, which came from near Queen Manor. Nos 2 and 5 at 1:2, the rest at 1:1. (Drawn by Yvonne Beadnell)

Christopher Ewer's inventory of 1680 was valued at £293, of which goods to the value of some £50 were in a leasehold house beside the prison in Salisbury. His appraisers at Clarendon began in the Lower Kitchen (brass, latten, ironware, a table, and so on), passing afterwards to the Buttery; the Other Kitchen (jack and weights, brewing vessels, and so on); the Great Chamber (iron pot, lumber, a close stool); the Long Chamber; the Cheese Loft; the Parlour; the outer and inner milkhouses; the Best Chamber (bed); the Womans Chamber (feather beds and other items); the Dungion Chamber ('goods'); and, finally, the Closet (watch and other plate £12). There was also a Bird Room, Room within the Stable and, intriguingly, a 'parliament Hall', in which goods worth £1 10s were recorded. Crops and beasts are also mentioned. The reference to the 'parliament hall' suggests that Ewer may have lived close to the palace site and that there was possibly some continuing use there. A post-medieval hearth in the Great Stable and post-medieval finds there and elsewhere on the palace site (discussed below), and the possibility that the 'dungion chamber' could be the wine cellar, add to this new interpretation of continuity of use at the palace site.

New archaeological evidence also suggests that the western end of the palace site continued to be used, in some form, into the eighteenth century. Spoil heaps in and around the medieval gatehouse produced post-medieval pottery (mid sixteenth- to mid eighteenth-century) from Verwood, German stonewares of Raeren and Frechen and Westerwald types, redwares decorated with sgraffito, all-over white slip, trailed slip and bands of encrusted quartz, possibly from South Somerset, and Bristol/Staffordshire slipwares, including a mug or posset cup.[155] Among the post-medieval metalwork is a fine scale-tang knife, shoe buckles and a rumbler bell of eighteenth- or possibly nineteenth-century date (Figure 51).[156] From the same area fragments of early 'onion' wine bottles were recovered, together with the rim of a late seventeenth-century glass phial. These types of pottery and glass are common and widespread, but much more refined dating comes from the fourteen clay pipes found. All but one are pre-1750, with a bias towards the period 1690–1720. Three are stamped, one bearing a crude cross within a heart-shaped frame dating to 1690–1720, and another an illegible stamp on a stem of the same period. The latest pipe to which an accurate date can be given is from the north wing and garderobe of the gatehouse and bears the stamp of Edward Higgens of Salisbury, which can be placed accurately between 1695 and 1716. Higgens was 24 when he married in 1698 and is unlikely to have been running a business before 1695, when he was 20. He died in 1716.[157] If the Higgens pipe was among the last to be smoked at the old gatehouse then it may well have been owned by someone in Christopher Ewer's household. In that case, there was a substantial, if dilapidated, building which probably included medieval structures at the gatehouse site until about 1720 – on the eve of Stukeley's drawing (see Figure 74). This building, which had some ten rooms as well as its Cellar Milkhouse,[158] also made use of the 'parliament hall' and the old stables nearby. The post-medieval hearth inside the stable, together with seventeenth-century clay pipes found there, further support the hypothesis that this building was being used, while single stems of seventeenth-century pipes recovered from the Antioch Chamber and near to the Queen's Chamber are proof that these areas too were at least visited. Sherds of Verwood pottery, Somerset slipwares and German stonewares in that same area hint at other uses, possibly even habitation. Stone robbing is a certainty, but the concentration of pottery here seems rather more than accidental. Of these finds, among the clay pipes there are several makers' names present, including three quality products by the Gauntlett family of Amesbury, dated 1620–40, whose products cost considerably more than the average pipe and were restricted to a wealthier market.[159] Such a profile could fit Christopher Ewer.

The piece of the puzzle yet to be finally resolved is that, in 1650, the 'Gate House lying in the middle of the park', always previously assumed to be the western gatehouse of the former palace precinct, is dismally recorded as consisting of 'one room below stairs, with two chambers above stairs, which will not be made habitable without great changes'.[160] Yet we are suggesting that within thirty years of this description Christopher Ewer slept in a comfortable and large house on the same site. Perhaps the 1650 document is an exaggeration, down-valuing property to secure a lower price, or possibly it was drawn up without visiting Clarendon, though if that is so it is hard to explain Stukeley's 1723 drawing, which shows the only ruins at the palace. The most likely explanation is that Ewer was living at 'The King's Mannour' shown on the 1650 map (Figure 42), a now-lost, grander precursor to the present King Manor Cottage, and domestic rubbish from that building was dumped into the area of the medieval gatehouse.

One further point can be extracted from Ewer's documents. Appended to his will is a substantial list of the debts he owed, to be settled by his daughter Mary, his executrix. The debts to the hundred creditors exceeded the value of the inventory by over £20. They included many familiar names: William Hyde, Hayter, Bristow and others, and listed 'the Earle of Clarendons Coachman and groome' as being owed 15s, with the largest debt being £80, owed to the 'Earle of Clarendon'. The Hydes were apparently soft on their debt-ridden relations, but these references clearly show that the owners maintained a presence on the estate at this date, the mention of the coachman providing a further clue to the existence of some kind of mansion on the estate c. 1680.

The final inventory is that of John Bristow of Clarendon in 1684, whose (probable) wife appears among Ewer's creditors as 'Mrs Bristow for money owing to her husband'. Bristow was the wealthiest of the three inventories we have. Much of his wealth, in July 1684, lay in his crops. Besides his crops and animals, ricks, 'water stones' (possibly millstones), well tackle (£95) and wool (£40) are all listed. The house included a Parlour, Hall (brass, fowling pieces, and so on), Little Parlour (bed, along with other items), books of all sorts worth 10s, a Nursery, 'Queens Chamber' (where there were two bedsteads), Middle Chamber, 'Chappell Chambers' (beds and other items), Dining Room, Cheese Loft, Stair Head ('A Mill and other lumber'), Maid's Chamber (eighteen pairs of sheets among other items), Milkhouse, Passage, Cellar, another Cellar and Flesh House and a Kitchen.[161] Bristow's wearing apparel, at £6, was 20 per cent more valuable than that of Ewer and Hayter, but it would seem that all three were modest dressers. Bristow's house amounts to some ten rooms, cellars and Milkhouse. Was Bristow at the Queen Manor, with its 'Queen Chamber' and its 'Chappell' rooms? It seems possible that he was.

Queen Manor Farmhouse, typologically, is a late seventeenth-century structure with a stone façade hiding the timbers. It seems to have been reconstructed after 1660, its timbers mostly derived from oak-framed buildings of previous centuries, just as the front wall reuses ashlar stone.[162] Dateable details are the polyhedral finial on the staircase newel post and the carpentry of the main roof with its lapped collars.[163] Timbers with narrow chamfers and ogee stops appropriate to the late seventeenth century, with the appearance of being in their original position, consist of fast-grown oak which did not date by dendrochronology. This is disappointing, but may reflect the stripping of the oak-assets of the estate in and around the Commonwealth period. A further

FIGURE 52. Queen Manor Granary is at first sight a standard eighteenth-century staddle granary. Closer examination revealed it was constructed of timbers from exceptionally grand previous structures. Dendrochronology and study of mouldings, together with timbers and mouldings from the adjoining farmhouse (see Figure 48), date these earlier buildings to the century following Henry VIII's visit in c. 1535, especially James I's reign. In addition, the farmhouse roof contains an 'A' frame from a building dating to before 1350. (Photograph by Fran Halsall)

issue is that whereas the medieval reused timber found in the buildings of the seventeenth century dates by dendrochronology, the beams from trees *felled* in the late seventeenth century were fast-grown and not susceptible to tree-ring dating. This is suggestive of a different timber regime at the time of or following the Civil War which may explain the 'useless' (for dendrochronological purposes) timbers in the lower floor of the granary, and a group of 'exceptionally fast grown timbers' found in the mansion house.[164]

The small staddle granary which adjoins Queen Manor Farmhouse has been variously dated to between about 1660 and 1800 (Figure 52).[165] An example of the agricultural vernacular designed to store grain in dry, well-ventilated conditions, it too is constructed from fragments of previous, grand, buildings. The Department of the Environment listing matches it to the late seventeenth-century farmhouse, doubtless on the visible evidence of its half-hipped roof, a feature which became fashionable at that date.[166] Recent work on its reused timbers suggests these may well have come from grand Tudor/Stuart buildings on the estate, buildings which were derelict in about 1650–60 and redundant after disparkment in 1664.[167] Missing mortices in the timber frame indicate timbers replaced by brickwork and this may have coincided with the rebuilding of the structure to secure it as a granary as the brown rat (*Rattus norvegicus*) became more common in the eighteenth century.[168] Changes of ownership and land use were mirrored by – but were also sometimes the cause of – changes lower down the ecological chain.

At the southern extremity of the estate, Dog Kennel Farm is listed as partly seventeenth-century by the Royal Commission, but has some framing dating to 1588 and more which dates to the reign of James I, and therefore represents an element in his royal building and refurbishing campaign.[169] Thus, as well as the brick and stone 'head' house, there is a brace of farmhouses which tie into the Hyde/Albemarle period, after the estate left royal hands in 1660 and before the Bathursts obtained possession in 1707. To these can be added various repairs to existing buildings, such as the weatherboarding of the Out Lodge in 1678 when, in addition, 600 bricks were bought to repair the oven and chimney there as well as structures elsewhere, such as Queen Manor granary.[170]

By 1750 a medieval and post-medieval deer park at Clarendon had been transformed into a large agricultural estate worked from farmsteads. Pruett's Lodge survived as a gate lodge but buildings which no longer served any purpose became defunct and eventually disappeared. Both Hunt's and Palmer's Lodges seem to have been demolished sometime between 1640 and 1773,[171] Hunt's Lodge being remembered in Lodge Field in 1812. This residue of medieval lodges was, however, insufficient for the effective functioning of such a large estate. The south-eastern sector was an inconvenient distance from any of the major farms and to remedy this Best's Farm was built between 1713 and 1748. This comprised a small two-storey residential farmhouse with an attached service wing to the south, containing a dairy.[172] Savage's Farm may have been constructed 1640–1773, but a more likely date-range is 1700–50;

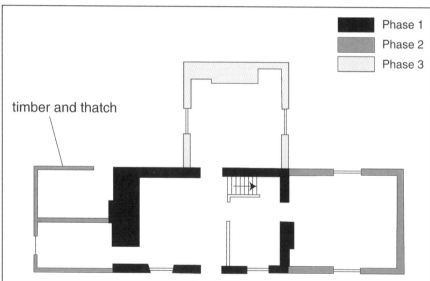

timber and thatch

Phase 1
Phase 2
Phase 3

FIGURE 53.
King Manor Cottage, formerly Keeper's Cottage. Picture and plan. On the basis of recent archaeological study we would refine the construction date for King Manor Cottage to about 1716 or shortly thereafter, tying in neatly with a date for the Bathurst mansion. It is therefore the earliest surviving cottage on the estate, as distinct from the mansion and Queen Manor Farmhouse. (Plan redrawn by Alejandra Gutiérrez; photograph English Heritage copyright, 11W/34)

at the same time several houses on the south-western edge of the park, at Ashley Hill and Hughendon Manor, were built. Some new buildings, like Four Cottages, built between 1640 and 1773, were originally thatched, and today are white, rendered two-bay cottages under slate with modern window frames, projecting rear wings and lean-tos; these housed agricultural labourers, presumably engaged in ploughing, seed drilling, harvesting and threshing, as well as shepherding and livestock work. Other buildings, like Keeper's Cottage (1821), now called King Manor Cottage, had more special-ised functions. This single-storey two-room building was probably built for a bachelor keeper and takes its name from the western gatehouse of the palace precinct which lies adjacent (Figure 53). It is estimated to have been built in the period 1700–66, probably about 1716, though a kitchen was added to the north later in the eighteenth century and there are more modern extensions to west and east.[173] The dimensions of the original King Manor Cottage are not generous but the occupants may also have made some use of the old pal-ace site. Certainly they dumped their refuse into some of the nearer derelict buildings and they were still doing so a century and a half later. Among the post-medieval pottery discarded into the stables area were Verwood products, Nottingham and Bristol-type stonewares, eighteenth-century creamwares and factory-made slipwares. The eighteenth-century clay pipes provide something of a contrast with some of the high quality seventeenth-century pieces from the gatehouse area. All the stamped pipes are from local Salisbury makers, described as of the 'ordinary sort' in a Salisbury grocer's inventory.[174]

One issue facing all eighteenth-century landowners was the control of access into their parks. Gatelodges already existed at Ranger's and Winchester Gate and the first additional gatehouse lodge was Pitton Lodge (by 1750); Alderbury Lodge, built to control access from the south, followed perhaps a generation later.[175] Alderbury Lodge was a thatched two-room building, perhaps closely modelled on King Manor Cottage. Unlike the mansion, Alderbury is not a classical venture, not an arch or a temple, but neither is it obviously neo-medi-eval Gothick. It is an understated building, never intended as an eye-catching feature of the park, but a mood-setter, a keeper's house signalling the park and woodland beyond and contrasting with the geometry of the mansion. Pitton Lodge was also modest in scale and pretension, 'a picturesque *cottage orné* to a bosky landscape'.[176] The lodges could house a widow or widower, perhaps a mother and daughter in humble circumstances, or even a family in cramped conditions. Children were not encouraged.[177]

The mansion

It has hitherto been assumed that the Hydes had no residence on the estate during their period of ownership, but the recent and significant discovery of fragments of brick façade with stone banding and window decoration on a house of the Hyde period embedded within the structure of Clarendon House (Figure 54) has suggested otherwise. This building, the brickwork of which suggests a 'mid- to late seventeenth-century date', was in contemporary high fashion, with a *piano nobile*, as found in houses in the cathedral closes at Salisbury and Winchester created by patrons whose architects were familiar with similar buildings from their exile on the continent during the Civil War. The Clarendon house was probably single pile.[178] Materials and techniques common to both these town-houses and the Clarendon fragment include penny-struck pointing, stone string-courses and – possibly – a rusticated quoin or pilaster strip, which was found in the fragmentary Clarendon house.[179] Both brickwork and stone dressings are visible at first-floor level in the north-east part and, below, beneath the floor of the north-east *piano nobile* room of the eighteenth-century house.[180] A reasonable indication of a date for the seventeenth-century building is suggested by twenty-three samples taken for dendrochronology, including from the large under-floor beams on the ground and first floors, which suggested that, while earlier timbers had been reused in the building's construction, no timbers could be dated later than 1667.[181] A

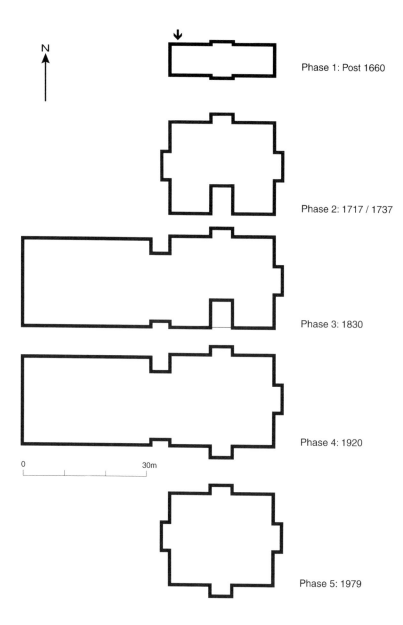

N

Phase 1: Post 1660

Phase 2: 1717 / 1737

Phase 3: 1830

Phase 4: 1920

0   30m

Phase 5: 1979

Clarendon: Landscape of Kings

FIGURE 54.
Phasing of the mansion house. The mansion house has complex phasing. The first phase was a single pile house of c. 1660, built of brick with stone dressings and possibly a stone east façade. This may be the structure mapped in 1713 (Figure 49). In the early eighteenth century it was extended to give its present aspect. Nineteenth-century building campaigns grafted on a substantial double-pile wing on the western side, and a ballroom was added in 1926. Most of the later accretions have since been removed. ↓ marks the drill spot of Figure 55. (Drawn by Alejandra Gutiérrez, based on an original by Ross Turle from plans in the CEA)

132

combination of the results of three samples suggests that they were all felled 1604–29. One other ground-floor beam and a first-floor lintel represent a later phase at 1638–67, though reused timbers of fourteenth- and fifteenth-century date were also present. If this is the Hyde house, rather than one built by Cowper, then its discovery is of considerable interest, for it would have placed Wiltshire Clarendon once more in the forefront of style and modernity. The reused timbers are likely to have come from other buildings on the estate, the obvious choice in that area of the estate being Whitmarsh Lodge, which may have been nearby.[182]

Detailing of doors and windows, especially on the east front of the mansion, strongly resembles Clarendon House in Piccadilly (Figures 45 and 46), and the central portion of the east front is aligned with the brick and stone façade. In other words, there was a brick and stone north front, but also (as at Queen Manor) a stone aspect as well, designed to overlook the lake and to be seen from there. Such a mixture of brick and stone facades is found quite frequently at the period; for example, locally at Petersfinger Farmhouse and, further afield and more grandly, at Mottisfont in Hampshire, in a mixture of ruined medieval ecclesiastical and post-medieval functional Protestant architecture.[183] The reference to the second earl's coach and coachman, in 1680, suggests there was also accommodation for servants and storage for vehicles.

Changes in ownership are commonly a catalyst for building and rebuilding, and between 1708 and 1713 shortly after the estate was gifted to Peter

FIGURE 55.
A sample of brick being taken, using a diamond-faced core drill, from the north façade (east end) of the post-1660 building (see Figure 54) for luminescence dating tests. A luminescence signal emitted by crystal grains (e.g. quartz) extracted from the brick core is measured in the laboratory and, together with the results of other tests, the date of firing of the brick is determined within a calculated range of uncertainty. The results produced from several cores taken from Clarendon House are contributing to an on-going programme of dating bricks from late medieval and early modern buildings in England conducted by the Luminescence Dating Laboratory at Durham University. (Photograph by Fran Halsall)

Bathurst, there may have been a substantial (re)building of the mansion. In terms of the family dynamic, it was also about 1713 that the present day Cirencester House was built by the first earl Bathurst.[184] An 'illegible datestone' was seen by RCHME inspectors at Clarendon; their notes debate whether it read 1717 or 1737, with the last entry in the file strongly favouring 1717, drawing on a parallel at nearby Britford.[185] Cases can be made for each date (Figure 55). The 1717 date ties in with the change of owner and may be supported by a dendrochronology date from a substantial beam in the cellar underpinning the main building which was reported as 'cut down in the Spring of 1714'.[186] Peter Bathurst certainly heads the land tax returns soon after 1708 when 'My Lady Bathurst' is listed for the first time. In 1710 Peter Bathurst is listed alone, and sometimes 'for ye woods', as in the 1712 tax return.[187] When Peter Bathurst first lived at Clarendon is unknown. Unfortunately, architectural opinion wavers: all are agreed that the style is that of Vanbrugh or Hawksmoor but both Thomas Archer and John James are considered likely architects, with James favoured since in the 1730s he was involved with buildings locally;[188] this was at a time when Bathurst would have wanted a convenient local base after his election as MP for Salisbury (1734–41). Either date – 1717 or 1737 – would make the patron Peter Bathurst (d. 1748), but on balance we favour the earlier of the two, meaning that the architect must remain, for the moment, uncertain. The first picture of the Clarendon mansion survives from 1791, showing the house very much as it appears today from the north, with fallow deer grazing and fashionably dressed people enjoying a stroll.[189]

The mansion's landscape context

Although building records are lacking for the eighteenth century, a good deal of the landscape context can be reconstructed from cartographic and standing-structure evidence. Clarendon is shown as the only paled park in Wiltshire marked on Badeslade's county map of 1742;[190] by this time the creation of a lodge (before 1700) and subsequently a mansion had changed the focus of the landscape from the centrally placed medieval palace to the south-east margin of the estate. The park surrounding the mansion, called 'Clarindon Lodge Peter Bathurst Esq' on Andrews and Dury's map of 1773, extended to some 120 acres (49 ha) in the south-east quadrant of the estate (Figure 56). A formal parterre garden, seen in 1773 adjacent to the 'Lodge' (mansion), probably lay within the area now enclosed by the walled garden of the Stable House, with geometric beds and stable block adjacent to the mansion. Geometric beds followed the precepts of the Frenchman d'Argenville as set out in his influential *La Théorie et la Pratique du Jardinage*.[191]

This geometric garden would have been bordered by Scots pines, which are depicted as mature trees on the view of Major General Bathurst's Clarendon Park in 1791 (see Back Cover), indicating planting before 1750, perhaps at the same time as the oak avenues. It is likely that the Bathursts introduced to Clarendon the Scots, or, as it was then known, the 'Scotch' pine (*Pinus sylvestris*), which spread from a base in Scotland to naturalise in England.[192] This garden has today entirely disappeared; however, a fine eighteenth-century brick and render garden seat survives and is now adjacent to the mansion, no longer in its original position, which was at the south end of the lawn, squarely facing the south elevation of Clarendon House.

Bounding the enclosed park to the east is a major ornamental lake, formed by damming the stream running through Whitmarsh Mead. This water feature is part of the eighteenth-century landscape, dating from the period following the craze for canals (for example, as at Hampton Court after 1660), when the mode had moved on to favour informal water features. The lake, more prosaically, was also a water supply for the main house, another reason for developing that area of the estate, though this was also the least profitable part of the Clarendon land, on heavy clay soils and away from the eyes of the tenanted farms across the estate.

The development of Clarendon's eighteenth-century park was too late to be included among Leonard Knyff's bird's eye prospects of great English houses,[193] but the outer landscape features of the garden area surrounding the house can be dated on map evidence. The origins of the collector's wood north-east of the mansion may date to the eighteenth century on the evidence of a labyrinthine path which leads through the trees and resembles a

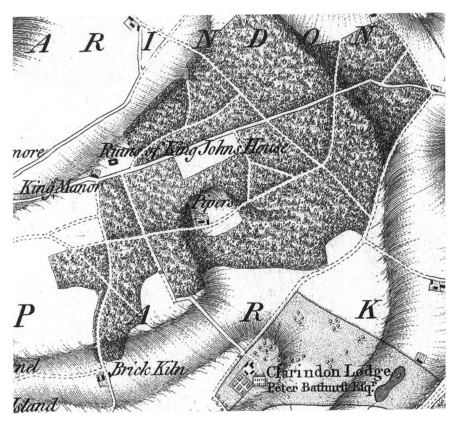

FIGURE 56.
The inner landscape park around 'Clarindon Lodge' in the later eighteenth century, with its lake and scattered clumps of trees inside a fenced perimeter; an arrangement much influenced by the prevailing fashion for 'natural' parkland. Although by this date walled kitchen gardens on large estates were often placed well out of sight, at Clarendon they remained adjacent to the stables, which provided manure, and were convenient for the mansion's kitchens. The exit north-west towards Pitton Lodge skirts the woodland rather than cutting through it, as it does today. The avenue to the north-east is aligned on 'The Ruins of King John's House'. Other buildings shown are Brick Kiln, King's Manor, Piper's, Best's Farm, Pitton Lodge, and Savage's Farm. Extract from Andrews and Dury's map of Wiltshire 1773. (Image from Wiltshire and Swindon Record Office)

FIGURE 57.
The Wild Garden. The 'Wild' or collector's garden at Clarendon may have been begun by the Bathursts in the eighteenth century, on the evidence of a serpentine walk there. Many of the plantings seen today date to the Hervey-Bathurst era before 1900, when it was called 'The Rookery'. In the twentieth century a swimming pool was added on its southern edge, complete with a 'Chinese-style', thatched, changing room, now no longer extant, but recorded in a fine architect's colour-washed drawing in the possession of the Christie-Miller family. (Photograph by Tom Beaumont James).

serpentine walk (Figure 57). Such curvilinear features were pioneered before 1750.[194] More certainly, three extant avenues radiated from the mansion: one westwards towards Alderbury, one to the north-east to Pitton, offering sweeping views of the park, and a third, the Salisbury avenue. These are likely to have been planted at the time the mansion was built or during the tenure of the second Peter Bathurst after 1748; oak trees sampled in the avenues and in the park are 200 to 300 years old, (i.e. between 1700 and 1800), with some going back 400 or 500 years (that is to say to 1600 or 1500), suggesting they were already established when the site of the mansion was first developed.[195] By contrast the beech avenue, which runs east of the mansion park, and the lime avenue, which runs northwards from the drive into the mansion, are shown by dendrochronology to be only about a century old, placing them in the Garton or early Christie-Miller period (see below), though it is likely that these are replacements of earlier plantings which, if third generation, would carry them back to the Bathursts' era, or, if second, to the early Frederick Hervey-Bathurst years after 1824, possibly when the rebuilding of the mansion was in progress and work was being undertaken on the 'pleasure gardens' (Figure 58).[196]

*Cultivating Change
1500–1800:
Property
and Parkland*

FIGURE 58.
Avenues at Clarendon
are key elements in the
'military landscape'
of the Bathursts and
Hervey-Bathursts
and their successors,
the radiating avenues
representing the 'thin
red line' of British
soldiery. Today Sir John
Hervey-Bathurst recalls
these avenues being
described as matching
military dispositions at
Waterloo. They contrast
with the compact
block coppices of the
medieval landscape.
(Photograph by Fran
Halsall)

How far back the walled gardens went towards the seventeenth century is also unclear, but Edward Hyde was especially interested in the walling of his garden at Cornbury in about 1670. South-east of Clarendon mansion is a dovecote, that unique stamp of manorial lordship, erected, accompanying the new great house, to house doves which would consume tenants' and others' crops (Figure 62). This octagonal brick building in Flemish bond has twenty-three tiers of nest holes and a surviving timber potence but it too cannot be tightly dated on either architectural or dendrochronological evidence.[197] The fine staddle barn and granary outside the stables has been dated by dendrochronology to 1765[198] and may well be of contemporary build (Figure 59).

Perhaps the most remarkable thing about the Bathursts' new Clarendon mansion and its park is its apparent modesty. At Cirencester Park, Sir Benjamin Bathurst's eldest son, Allen, was assembling land to create a new estate on which he too could build.[199] Like Peter, Allen Bathurst also recycled, purchasing Sapperton in April 1730 in order to demolish its manor house and provide stonework for his buildings, and incorporating Roman stone coffins into the ha-ha. Like Peter, Allen lacked water in his new park[200] and, it appears, both brothers faced the challenge of what to do with earlier mansions. Coincidentally, given the controversy over the date of Clarendon mansion, Allen Bathurst seems to have begun structural alterations at Cirencester House in 1715–18, work which was not deemed entirely successful. Allen was not overly interested: 'I think any house good enough to sleep in'. The work was carried out by William Townesend, a master-mason from Oxford.[201] But that is seemingly where the similarities end. Allen was truly creating a new estate rather than modifying existing territory and he probably moved in different social circles; he was friends with Alexander Pope,[202] Lord Robert Digby of Sherborne Castle and others who expressed views on park monuments and design, and he became highly influential in the evolving design of parks and gardens in the early eighteenth century, in a manner that Peter may have understood but not wished for.

At Clarendon, apart from the octagonal dovecote, there was little in the way of up-to-the-minute landscape design: no ha-ha, pillars, obelisks or octagons and, though a single seat has survived, there were few cross vistas and engineered lines of sight, no model working farms, no icehouse, no attempt to broach views to buildings outside the estate. It all seems very understated. Given Peter Bathurst's single parliamentary utterance on clandestine marriages and his unassuming estate landscapes, it is noteworthy that in Colman and Garrick's comedy *The Clandestine Marriage*, first performed in 1766, much space is devoted to mockery of the created landscapes of the *nouveau riche* Sterling, who drags his unwilling social superiors round his landscaped garden telling them 'The chief pleasure of a country house is to make improvements' and that they should see 'my water by daylight, and my walks, and my slopes, and my clumps, and my bridge, and my flowering trees and my Dutch tulips' … 'My grand Tower, as I call it' … 'a pinery', 'an octagon summer-house … raised on the mast of a ship' ... 'the pleasantest place in the world to take a pipe and a bottle'.[203] Lest we need reminding, people's aspirations for their eighteenth-century parks and gardens were not fixed, not even within the same family. And yet elements of Cirencester's experimentation may perhaps be found. Contrasts between the brothers' estates may signal more complex social and family relations, now lost to us, than a simple interpretation allows.

Clarendon had no need for false ruins – it already had the real thing.[204] Nor was there any need to plant; Clarendon had areas of existing woodland 'wilderness' cut through by 'trenches', though these do not seem to have been focused on monuments new or ancient.[205] Stephen Switzer's volume *Noblemen, Gentlemen, and Gardeners Recreation* (1715) advocates the idea of a simple inner garden extended by rides and avenues through working farmland, in a manner which is familiar at Clarendon. In their early phases of park design, Clarendon and Cirencester are perhaps not so different, especially if the slight evidence for a serpentine walk is accepted;[206] both provided the contrast between well-managed house and garden and the irregularity of the landscape beyond. What we do not know at present is the extent to which the palace was open to the new landscape tourists of the mid-eighteenth century, who held an appreciation for the Picturesque. We imagine that the antiquarians were not alone and that the ruins were visited and enjoyed, especially once war put paid to the Grand Tour in the 1790s. As we shall see in Chapter Seven, Clarendon fitted the sense of rediscovery of English tradition and of 'sensibility', a reminder of the transience of man and architecture perhaps, even a sense of isolation and danger in the woods. Emerging from the woods near the ruins, whether in the Middle Ages, in the age of enlightenment or today, the spectacular view of Salisbury Cathedral remained a constant feature.

By 1800 the Bathursts had begun to cut themselves off from the surrounding community. Access to the park was slowly being controlled by lodges and funnelled down avenues. Views into the park were limited, views of the house and its private gardens all but impossible. The estate was managed by an agent and meetings between Bathurst and his tenants were probably few and far between, other than in the context of the hunt.[207] By now the Bathursts' community was not Alderbury, not even Salisbury, it was other members of the land-owning class who lived in similarly depopulated private spaces, protected by the deterrents of their tasteful lodges. When the Bathursts sought to visualise their space it was the house, their mansion, a geometric classical box and the parkland which surrounded it, which they chose to have represented, not the ploughed fields of Cockey Down. As far as we know, like the majority of eighteenth-century country estate owners, the Bathursts were not interested in showing off their house and its pleasure grounds to a wider public. Barriers of distance, class, exclusive taste and education ensured that Clarendon remained a mostly private place where its Tory owners, by 1800, were isolated from the populace, secure in their Tory landscape. Major General Peter Bathurst saw action in the Seven Years War (1756–63) in which Britain, with her Hanoverian and Prussian allies, successfully faced a coalition of France,

FIGURE 59.
Mansion staddle barn
and granary, with the
granary component
of the structure in
the foreground. This
three-bay timber-
framed staddle barn
and granary, adjacent
to the stables beside
the mansion, has
been dated by
dendrochronology. The
oak trees from which
it was built were cut
down in the spring
or summer of 1765.
(Photograph by Fran
Halsall)

Russia, Austria and Spain.[208] Success in that war, although at the time by no means assured, would make Britain the most powerful world power. But that position was not secure, either in terms of the nation's sphere of influence or the security of the social order, for by 1800 the American and French Revolutions had provided graphic evidence of the potential changes of fortune which could occur.

CHAPTER SIX

A Working Estate 1800–2000:
Survival and Revival

A major remodelling of the mansion, its gardens and planting schemes was undertaken under Frederick Hutchinson Hervey-Bathurst, Clarendon's main nineteenth-century patron (1824–81), who also commissioned a lodge from the architect Pugin for the principal carriage entrance. Later, sales of land to the railway allowed further investments in the park's building stock, underpinned by rents from tenants' farms and income from forestry, woodland products, the extraction of gravel and clay, and hunting and shooting. But when farming entered a deep nation-wide recession, the equilibrium of the estate finances was upset. By 1900 Clarendon had to be sold, as it was again in 1919. Since that date new legal regimes, especially death duties, have made inheritance increasingly problematic. Two world wars took their toll of people and buildings; social change saw the decline of households with large numbers of servants. Today there are new issues to be addressed, conservation, public access and the transformation of farming practice among them, but Clarendon has survived and remains a landscape for pleasure as well as production.

The Hervey-Bathursts

After Peter Bathurst's death in 1801 the mansion remained empty for perhaps thirty years. During this period the estate passed to Frederick Hervey (owner ?1801–24) on condition he took the name Bathurst. Frederick lived elsewhere and Clarendon was rented out.[1]

Throughout this period, the principal source of income for Clarendon's tenant farmers was wheat,[2] though there was still money to be made from the complex pattern of letting and sub-letting of different combinations of farms and lodges. For example, in 1813 Savage's Farm and Ranger's Lodge, at 427 and 303 acres (173 ha and 123 ha) respectively, were both in the hands of Thomas Marchment, who presumably then sub-let either house or farmland as he wished; other farmers – Ainsworth and Parsons, for example – enjoyed similar rights.[3] Despite the apparent impermanence of these arrangements, the impression from census documents is that several generations of the same family were involved with some of the farms. The principal beneficiaries, however, were the Hervey-Bathursts, who thus received a regular income – £1500 in 1813 – and minimised their involvement with land management.

Some continuing investment in the park can be seen in the building and rebuilding of the gatehouses. The Pitton and Alderbury lodges were there by 1812. Their non-classical style followed King Manor Cottage, characterised by a thick mantle of thatch, an organic rounded form 'like sweet syrup' which made rooms dark against the wooded backdrop.[4] Evidently there was also some interest in the history of the palace. As we shall see in Chapter Seven, it was Frederick Hervey-Bathurst who had dealings in 1821 with the young antiquarian and bibliophile Thomas Phillipps over excavations at the palace site, which revealed so much of its plan. The ageing and rheumatic Sir Richard Colt-Hoare commissioned this work, which was published in his *Modern Wiltshire* (1837), still a mine of information on Clarendon and its documentation, although the copious finds of tiles, window glass, and other artefacts are lost. All this accorded with a rising intellectual interest in things 'Gothick', reflecting particularly a national interest in well-documented high-status secular and monastic sites which was fuelled especially by the publication of administrative and financial records as the century progressed.[5]

Frederick Hutchinson Hervey-Bathurst

After Frederick Hervey-Bathurst's death in 1824 the estate passed to his son Frederick Hutchinson Hervey-Bathurst (FHHB), who was owner from 1824 to 1881 (Figure 60), and, at once, plans were afoot to extend and remodel Clarendon House. The 'Lodge', as it had been known in the eighteenth century, was to be doubled in size under the eye of Sir William Fremantle, who was referred to as 'proprietor'.[6] Fremantle, who was FHHB's grandmother's second husband, was then Treasurer of the Household to George IV and in 1830 became Deputy Ranger of Windsor Great Park. At Windsor he kept meticulous records of his building and park works, and this attention to detail shows in correspondence left by John Peniston, the Salisbury architect who became contractor for the works at Clarendon.

Peniston as contractor and Fremantle as client were, on paper, an ideal pairing. Peniston was involved with brickworks at Clarendon for decades – for example, drying sheds for bricks appear on his plan of the railway cutting in the 1840s.[7] The contractor therefore knew the site and could supply basic materials, as well as being an architect with quantity surveying skills. Fremantle, busy elsewhere, had to provide direction without engaging in detailed briefings, but he certainly brought considerable experience to the table. Bricks stamped CLARENDON are found on and around the estate and their manufacture was possibly inspired by Fremantle's knowledge of Windsor Park, where similar bricks were stamped with a crown and royal initials.[8] Also at Windsor, Fremantle oversaw the erection of various lodges of the *cottage orné* type and it may have been he who was behind the development of lodges at Clarendon.[9] But Fremantle was 'not the easiest client' for Peniston, leaving the youthful FHHB to judge 'if the expenditure is fairly shown to be more than the estimate'. Hervey-Bathurst, it seems, took a particular interest in

FIGURE 60.
Frederick Hutchinson
Hervey-Bathurst
(1807–81) inherited
Clarendon when aged
17 in 1824 and died
there in 1881. He
married Louisa Smythe
in 1832, and occupied
the refurbished
mansion. (Photograph
courtesy of the
Marylebone Cricket
Club Library, Lord's,
London)

the furnishings of the billiard room and, at least while his instructions were followed, declared himself happy with work there, pleasing Peniston.[10]

Work began on 25 May 1825. Initial estimates for the extensive alterations and repairs were £3883, with an additional £1000–2000 required for the coach house and stables; this was equivalent to some four years' income on the basis of the 1813 figures. Inside the mansion there was to be significant structural remodelling, especially in the basement, where new 'offices' included the

FIGURE 61.
The mansion hall, with its 'Scagliola' columns, and marble floor, installed by John Peniston for FHHB during major structural works in the years 1825 to 1832. (Photograph by Fran Halsall)

FIGURE 62.
Dovecote and greenhouse. The dovecote was built before 1800, but the clock, to face north and south, was probably added under FHHB. A stylish green- or peach-house stands in front of the dovecote. (Photograph by Fran Halsall)

FIGURE 63.
Grecian Temple. The date of this structure is uncertain, but it was there by 1880, then approached by a gravel path between banks of kalmia and rhododendron. In recent years it has provided a quiet retreat for Barbara Neil to write her successful novels, which draw on the Clarendon landscape for inspiration. (Photograph by Fran Halsall)

kitchen and 'Servants' Hall' visible today.[11] On the first floor, the hallway was to be paved and ornamented with 'Scagliola' columns; that is to say, plaster-work imitating stone (Figure 61). A 'metallic hot-house' from Jones and Clark of Birmingham, manufacturers, which matched a similar structure supplied to the nearby house at Norman Court, Tytherley, was installed between the southern wings of the mansion. This massive contraption included a 32-foot (9.6 m) balcony on each side, with steps and a furnace.[12] Garden conservatories were becoming increasingly popular in the early nineteenth century and provided the attraction of exotic plants all through the year; they only came within reach of the middle-class gardener when tax was abolished on glass prices after 1845.[13] Elsewhere in the mansion there were alterations to the Library[14] and to the room above, which raised the cost from £8000 to £10,000, over twice the original estimate, and led to the necessity to raise a mortgage of £8000 in 1829–32.[15] February 1829 even saw the entire 'old roof' being replaced, with plumbers at work there and slaters ready, but by January 1830 the billiard room was nearing completion. Work evidently slowed once Sir Frederick left Clarendon and instructions were not always followed.[16]

Meanwhile, work began on a new west wing. This too was a considerable operation, for when heavy rain intervened in November 1828 we learn that 100 men employed for three or four weeks were discharged. Such delay explains Peniston's urgency in November 1830 in coming 'up to Clarendon to put the roof on' and staying until it was finished. The extension was probably completed that winter. There were clearly several tasks happening at once: work on the stables, coach house and exterior offices,[17] as well as on a bakehouse and a brewhouse. These were not inconsiderable works in their own right. The brewhouse, for example, required 170 feet (51 m) of piping to carry beer from there to the cellar; additionally, a new well had to be dug to supply the brewhouse, the washhouse and the dairy. There was also much to be done in the gardens: walling, the completion of fencing and planting.[18] The Hervey-Bathursts clearly saw houses, gardens and landscapes as an integrated whole.

Peniston's final choice of building materials was in part limited by what could be made available. Ironically, given its timber-producing past, the estate itself seems to have provided nothing, so timber was imported, including 'many loads of memel timber and a considerable number of deals'. The standing remains of the mansion still contain extensive softwood roof trusses, no doubt from this very campaign.[19] Peniston would have preferred well-seasoned 'Christiana' deals, red and white, but found them unavailable outside London. Other new materials included Somerton (Somerset) stone and slate for the roof, which was preferred to tile on aesthetic grounds. Interior lighting was contracted to Jones's chandelier manufactory in Birmingham[20] and there were bills for gilding work on brackets, for marbles, and for bronzing three eagles, possibly for the centre and corners of the north façade.[21] Finally, there was a bellhanger (seventeen bells for main house; six for the office) and a clock to face north and south, to reflect the orientation of the mansion. This may have been attached to the roof of the dovecote (Figure 62).

The slate roofing, usually associated with the coming of the railway, and the transport of the ironwork for the conservatory from Birmingham, are both noteworthy as aspects of élite building before local railway transport. We also know that finances were not unlimited. With costs escalating, attention was paid to finding secondhand materials, including the 'Scagliola' columns and several marble fireplaces.[22] For the garden walls, old bricks and tiles were stacked and covered for reuse.

After its restoration Clarendon House was occupied from his marriage in 1832 by FHHB (b. 1807). He was a JP, sheriff and Deputy Lieutenant of Wiltshire, Colonel in the Wiltshire Yeomanry and, not least, Clarendon's main landowner during the majority of the nineteenth century.[23] The estate was the venue for 'A grand review of the rifle Volunteer forces of Wilts and some adjacent Counties' in September 1860.[24] FHHB was also an outstanding cricketer, a president of the MCC and a patron of Hampshire county cricket in the 1860s.[25] He died in 1881, exactly 50 years after he played his first game at Lord's aged 24.

Clarendon was not on the Wiltshire treasure-houses tour of the mid-nineteenth century as Wilton House was, with its van Dyck portraits, or Longford Castle, south of Clarendon, where there were Old Masters on view twice a week. The mansion had not been as grandly refashioned as Wilton was under Wyatt c. 1800, nor was it antique Tudor, as was Longford (1591), nor expanded in the classical style, like Stourhead c. 1800. The succession at Clarendon of the young FHHB, coupled with long periods when the house lay empty or inconvenienced by building works, all militated against Clarendon becoming a visitor attraction.[26]

One visitor in 1880, however, did note personal impressions and was particularly taken with the Clarendon flora, its ancient oaks and its recent additions. On arrival he was struck first by the approach to the house:

> the principal entrances to the park, which are through avenues of towering Fir, elm and oak, are Alderbury, Pitton and Salisbury – the latter drive, which with one or two exceptions is uphill the whole length is two miles long from the lodge to the mansion, passing on the way thither in the bend of, and on either side the road, several detached bushes of Rhododendrons, growing in a kind of ravine, each specimen being surrounded by water.[27]

He had clearly entered by the Pugin lodge drive, where the ponds and rhododendrons at 'The Meres' are still visible today (Figure 50).

In the gardens round the mansion the visitor noted the 'flower garden and grounds' opposite the south-west front of the house, which consisted of numerous beds, including carpet beds, which were a fine sight from the terrace with the woodland beyond. In the adjacent 'collector's wood' there were well-grown young specimens of Cedar of Lebanon (*Cedrus libani*) (with girths of 10 to 11 feet (3–3.3 m) measured at 4 feet (1.2 m) from the ground) and evergreen oak (girths of 6 to 7 feet (1.8–2.1 m) at 4 feet from the ground). In addition there were good specimens of Japanese Cedar (*Cryptomeria japonica* 'Elegans'),

Greek Fir (*Abies cephalonica*), Lawson's False Cypress (*Chamaecyparis lawsoniana*) and Wellingtonia (*Sequoiadendron giganteum*). Further south, beyond the lawns below the terrace, the visitor was again impressed by a broad gravelled walk 220 yards long (now grassed) leading to the Grecian Temple, the walk framed on the south side by flower beds and *Chamaecyparis lawsoniana*, with the most spectacular bank of rhododendrons, hardy azaleas, kalmias and other plants 'that I have ever had the good fortune to see' (Figure 63). The kitchen gardens stretched to four acres (1.6 ha), with walls supporting a variety of espaliered fruit trees (supplemented by a four-acre orchard elsewhere in the park). Here there were glasshouses and frames – two unheated peach-houses, with young and well-established trees, and two young plant stores containing a varied collection of decorative and flowering plants.[28]

When accounts begin in 1832 as much was spent on the 'gardens and pleasure grounds' as on the coppices[29] and the young age and novelty of certain of the collector's items recorded by the 1880 visitor is striking. The Lawson variety of cypress, for example, is first recorded only in 1852 and the Wellingtonia became available in Britain after it arrived in Scotland in 1853. Rhododendrons, an import from south-east Europe, became abundant in England in the nineteenth century.[30] Undoubtedly these recent exotics and outdoor plantings were the work of FHHB, as were the tree ferns and palms in the new heated conservatory. Reflecting the gardening fashions of the Victorian age, it was he who introduced the formality of colourful bedding schemes, terraces and gravel paths to Clarendon, though he continued to enjoy unrestricted views

Clarendon:
Landscape of Kings

FIGURE 64.
A. W. N. Pugin designed and occupied 'St Marie's Grange', across the road from Clarendon. He designed this Clarendon lodge, which was built in 1837, the year he moved away. Its main details are eclectic: a moulded string-course and parapet, nail-studded main door and shaped Dutch gables. Internally, there are planked doors and stone fireplaces with Tudor-arched heads. The overall impression is remarkably non-Catholic, given Pugin's dedication to the architecture of the old religion. In 1851 Peter Bundy, a 69-year-old widower lodge keeper, lived here with his daughter (29 years old), a native of Clarendon; in 1891 it was occupied by Isaac Bungay, 'Labourer', a widower of 76, who lived there with his unmarried daughter of 30 and a cowman lodger (TNA:PRO HO 107/1846; RG 12/1618). (Photograph by Fran Halsall)

FIGURE 65.
The arrival of the railway at Clarendon in 1846 was the first incursion into the medieval park. The railway company erected a suitably impressive viaduct, and dug a cleverly hidden cutting. Judging from the flurry of building and refurbishment on the estate which followed, the £3600 they paid was valuable income to the estate (TNA:PRO TR 58/73292). In the 1990s Railtrack, the railway infrastructure company at the time, continued to refer to this structure as 'Sir Frederick's Bridge'. (Photograph by Fran Halsall)

over the parkland, enriching its appearance with new plantings of native and exotic trees.

In the 1830s, following the work on the mansion and at West Grimstead church, FHHB created a new westerly lodge, at which great iron gates remind us that this was the principal carriage drive entrance. This lodge, known originally as the Clarendon Lodge but today as the Southampton Lodge, was designed by A.W.N.Pugin. Pevsner dates it to 1837[31] and indeed, the lodge and its occupants are listed in the 1841 census[32] (Figure 64). The style of the new lodge, with its 'protestant' attributes, contrasts with Pugin's own local residence, St Marie's Grange in Alderbury, of 1835,[33] and it is possible FHHB also had a part to play. Pugin was dedicated to Catholicism, but when a wealthy, Protestant neighbour asked for a lodge, and Pugin had bills to pay, he obliged his client. Like his father, FHHB took an interest in Clarendon's history and was soon involving himself in the erection of a 'historical' stone plaque at the palace site in 1844. This memorial, known as the 'Protestant fragment' to excavators in the 1930s, celebrates 'the first barrier raised against the claims of secular jurisdiction by the See of Rome', thereby commemorating the site at which the first spark of the English Reformation had been struck. We shall return to its significance in the next chapter.

Building on the estate and nearby, at Alderbury Church, were FHHB's first major contributions to the Clarendon building stock in the quarter-century between the end of work on the mansion and 1860, when he set to expanding the mansion once more.[34] In explaining the twenty-three 'Absentees' on census night in 1861 the census enumerator reported that the mansion was 'under repair'. Although there are no building accounts for this activity, local directories record that the mansion was extended 'by the addition of a new wing to the west front about 1864'.[35] This took the mansion up to twenty-nine bed and dressing rooms and five reception rooms. As the 1881 census shows, this could be a sizeable household at times. Thirteen members of the family were recorded then, as well as an 'instructor' and twenty-six servants.

In 1846 the railway arrived in the south-western corner of the park through a cleverly sunk cutting, bridging with a fine three-arched viaduct of brick and stone the avenue north of the Pugin Lodge (Figure 65).[36] Improvements and new houses suggest that profits from the sale of land to the railway were reinvested at Clarendon.[37] Among these building works, a second rebuilding at Pitton Lodge included Arts and Crafts elements (Figure 67) with fancy barge boards, like those at Piper's Cottage (Figure 68). The period 1850–75 was a healthy one for owner and tenants alike with rising profits and rents, as it was throughout British farming (Figure 66). But this would be the final opportunity for the Hervey-Bathursts to invest at Clarendon. From the later 1870s, agriculture entered a long-term depression fuelled by falling prices caused by cheap imports, which particularly affected the corn prices on which Clarendon's owners and tenants were by then so dependent.

To grasp why the Hervey-Bathursts became so badly affected financially, we need to understand that during the nineteenth century land management inside the park was split into two. About half the estate, some 2,000 acres (809 ha) in 1881, was kept 'in hand', including the woodland and the parkland around the house. Shooting, or the letting of shooting, was reserved for the owners who maintained their gamekeepers (Figure 69).[38] The distribution of their homes suggests that they each took responsibility for different parts of the estate. No game books are known for this period but the number of gamekeepers surely reflects greater organisation and expenditure on pheasant and partridge. The remainder of the estate, some 2344 acres (948 ha), was let out to a number of tenant farmers who lived in properties scattered across the estate.[39] The more important of these were Queen Manor (456 acres; 185 ha) and Fussell's Lodge (444 acres; 180 ha), followed by Best's Farm, Ranger's and Dog Kennel (around 300 acres (121 ha) apiece), Ashley Hill, Hole Farm and Beech Tree Cottage (this last at 133 acres; 54 ha).[40] Statistics for mid-nineteenth-century crops show how these farms were organised. Wheat and

FIGURE 66. Nineteenth-/twentieth-century map of land use at Clarendon. In the last two centuries the ratio of arable to woodland has changed little. What is noticeable is the military landscape of avenues established by the Bathursts was followed in turn by a growth in military installations, especially many Second World War facilities, as Clarendon, in common with the country as a whole, was heavily drawn into successive war efforts. (Drawn by Alejandra Gutiérrez)

barley went for bread and malting, and oats and rye perhaps also went for human consumption, though they had other uses too, as horse fodder and green compost and forage respectively. Beans, peas, vetches and a range of root crops such as turnips, swedes and mangolds, as well as the potatoes, were grown as livestock fodder for winter and spring. Turnips were grown chiefly for sheep-folds, and clover, as spring fodder for sheep, was the dominant crop.

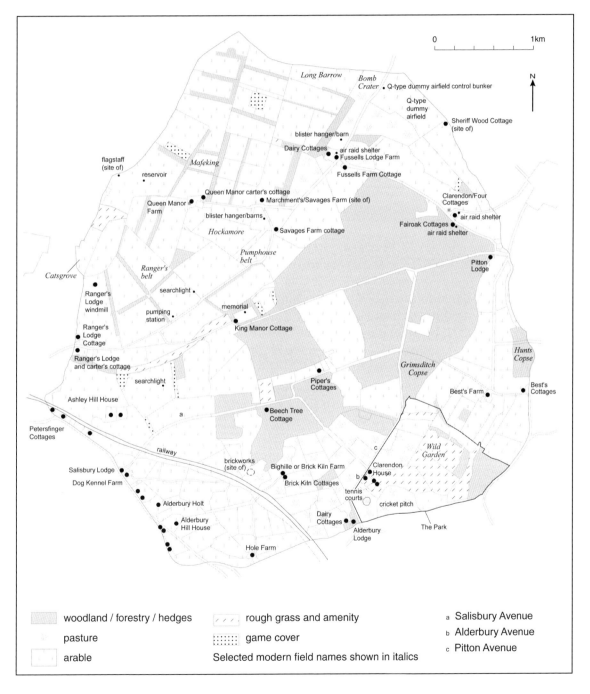

0   1km

N

Long Barrow

Bomb Crater • Q-type dummy airfield control bunker

Q-type dummy airfield

Sheriff Wood Cottage (site of)

blister hanger/barn

Dairy Cottages   air raid shelter
Fussells Lodge Farm

flagstaff (site of)

Mafeking

reservoir

Fussells Farm Cottage

Queen Manor carter's cottage

Queen Manor Farm

Marchment's/Savages Farm (site of)

Clarendon/Four Cottages

air raid shelter

blister hanger/barns

Hockamore

Savages Farm cottage

Fairoak Cottages
air raid shelter

Pumphouse belt

Catsgrove

Ranger's belt

searchlight

Pitton Lodge

Ranger's Lodge windmill

pumping station

memorial

King Manor Cottage

Ranger's Lodge Cottage

Hunts Copse

Grimsditch Copse

Ranger's Lodge and carter's cottage

searchlight

Piper's Cottages

Best's Farm

Best's Cottages

Ashley Hill House

a

Beech Tree Cottage

Petersfinger Cottages

railway

Wild Garden

brickworks (site of)

Bighille or Brick Kiln Farm

Clarendon House

c

Salisbury Lodge
Dog Kennel Farm

Brick Kiln Cottages

b

tennis courts

Alderbury Holt

cricket pitch

Alderbury Hill House

Dairy Cottages

Alderbury Lodge

The Park

Hole Farm

woodland / forestry / hedges   rough grass and amenity   a   Salisbury Avenue

pasture   game cover   b   Alderbury Avenue

arable   Selected modern field names shown in italics   c   Pitton Avenue

FIGURE 67.
Originally a new
gatehouse in c. 1750,
Pitton Lodge was
extended twice, once c.
1812 and later following
railway construction
after 1846. Features
to note include the
main windows, which
are lattice-glazed with
chamfered mullions,
arched heads and
moulded labels. The
chimney stacks have
octagonal shafts
of white and red
brick, and there are
shaped barge boards.
Internally, the plank
doors have strap
hinges. Isaac Lock
(47), labourer, his wife
(39) and two labourer
sons were there in 1851;
in 1891 William Gower
(51) gamekeeper, his
wife (48), his three
sons – one, 16 years
old, an apprentice
carpenter – and his
daughter appear
(TNA:PRO HO
107/1846; RG 12/1618).
(Photograph by
Christopher Gerrard)

All fields at Clarendon would have been farmed under a four-year rotation of root crops, barley (with grass and clover undersown), fallow for hay and grazing by sheep, and winter-sown wheat.[41]

What emerges from this pattern of Clarendon land use is a balance of arable and stock production in which sheep and cattle both played an important role. Sheep numbers, in particular, were seemingly impervious to the dramatic decline elsewhere in the county[42] and some 2237 head were counted in 1875.[43] Looking after them were the two shepherds who regularly appear at Clarendon in the nineteenth-century census returns, one being based at Fussell's in the period 1871–1891. The sheep would have been sold increasingly for meat rather than for their wool but they also fulfilled another purpose. Grazed on the down during the day, they were folded on the arable at night to fertilise the chalky soils. At the same time, names such as Dairyhouse Farm and Home Dairy indicate the importance of liquid milk production to the tenant farmers. In 1866 there were seventy-six milk cows and thirty other cattle, twenty-four of which were under two years old.[44] Judging from the map evidence, Clarendon cows were grazed on the pastures near the farmhouses and milked twice a day, supplying Salisbury dairies and more distant markets by rail.

The core of the agricultural workforce which worked these farms was overwhelmingly young and local, as the records of the decennial census (1841 to 1901) make clear. In 1881 each farm employed between four and eight men: a total of fifty-three males for the estate as a whole. These carters, cowmen and farm servants were natives of Pitton, Alderbury and the surrounding villages and only more skilled workers were drawn from further afield. Thus, in 1891, the gamekeeper was a native of Mildenhall in Suffolk, the gardener was from

FIGURE 68.
Piper's Cottage (or Farmhouse) was built between 1812 and 1841. Its *cottage orné* style, with scalloped bargeboards, is delightful and its slate roof is unusually early at Clarendon, showing the aesthetic influence of the similarly slated mansion at that period. In 1851 John Gartery (39), a labourer, his wife Ann (41) and their five sons (all aged 10 or under) were in Piper's Cottage; in 1891 Stephen Lock (58), a general labourer, his wife Eliza (60), and their daughter and son appear (TNA: PRO HO 107/1846; RG 12/1618). (Photograph by Fran Halsall)

FIGURE 69.
Beech Tree Cottage. This thatched lodge with its tall brick chimney stacks dates to the first half of the nineteenth century and is probably a contemporary of the latest modifications at Pitton Lodge. In 1851 a labourer, George Lock (aged 57), and his wife Ann (63), with their children Hannah, Thirza and Elijah, were here; in 1891 Arthur Mussell (63), a farmer and one of the park's five gamekeepers, lived here with his wife (53) and their four children, who included a milliner and a 'mothers' help' (TNA:PRO HO 107/1846; RG 12/1618). (Photograph by Fran Halsall)

Dorking in Surrey and the forester was Scottish. Among these Clarendon families standards of living were not always high. Various of the park's residents ended up in the records of poor relief and in the workhouse at Salisbury: for example, in 1816–19 the widow Mary Saunders, aged 29, with her sons William, 11, and Charles, 9, and in 1848 Charles Bundy, 57, and his wife, Ann George, 31.[45] But it is only at the forester's house at King Manor that we have any insight into the possessions of daily life on the estate, because here domestic waste from the nineteenth-century lodge was dumped into the old

stables at the palace site, from where it has since been excavated. As might be expected, pearlwares of various kinds were the most common tablewares, though there were occasional fragments of porcelain and bone china as well as two early nineteenth-century lead glass rummers or wine glasses,[46] so perhaps those employed directly by the Hervey-Bathursts were rather better off than some of the tenant families.

Clarendon woodland was recovering and continued to be productive, remaining 'in-hand'. Underwood was cut and sold:[47] nearly 4000 oak bavins and just over 2000 oak faggots were sold at 10s 6d and 20s per 100 respectively in one year.[48] All this implies a regular crop of young wood through coppicing as well as routine local demand. Decisions about woodland management were the responsibility of the park's forester, who was answerable to the estate owners. Woodland was never rented out, the thriving coppice production providing a quicker return than timber; sales of bark were especially profitable. In 1832, for example, forty-three tons of bark were sold at £6 a ton, bringing in £258.[49] Bark was a valuable commodity in the dyeing and tanning industries before chemically prepared substitutes for tannin became available after 1850.[50] Oak coppice bark was richer in tannin than timber bark,[51] and provided an important source of income on woodland estates;[52] the profit from bark was equivalent to the annual rent from four of the estate's nine farms. Ash trees were grown for sale, although whether for transplanting or as cut wood is not clear, and sales of wood from fir trees testify to cropping of this variety.[53] As the century progressed there was less interest in timber and declining profits led to neglect but the need for thick game cover for profitable shooting kept drastic clearance at bay.

To add to the underwood, timber, sapling and bark sales, the names Great Withybed and Rag Withybed indicate the growing of osiers (*Salix viminalis*), which would have been harvested for basket-making. The product of Rag Withybed was worth £8 10s annually to the estate when it was sold to Stephen Bell of Fisherton in 1832 and the ground there is still wet, with the presence of ditches and substantial earthwork banks suggesting that it was intentionally kept so. There was also a third 'willow bed' listed in mortgage documents of 1889 at the Dairy Cottages, and different species may have provided shoots of varying flexibility and colour. Certainly there has been a long tradition of willow cropping in the area, from the Osier islands in the Avon owned by Clarendon in 1650 to Tom Cox, basket maker and repairer, who is listed at Clarendon Road in 1931.[54]

Other natural resources from which the estate benefited were gravel, which was being extracted near Hole and Dogkennel farms on the 1891 sale map, and clay. Brick-making, flagged by the name Brick Kiln Farm, had continued at Clarendon throughout the nineteenth century in the southern part of the park and had been a part of the Clarendon landscape for at least two hundred years.[55] In 1894 Frederick Hand, the former manager, took over the brick-making.[56] Here, as in most other aspects of the estate's management, the Hervey-Bathursts preferred to rent rather than risk investment.

In 1832, when he moved into Clarendon House, FHHB paid £10 to Richard Elkins, his gamekeeper, 'for the dogs', and 4s 8d for 'Dog Tax and birchbroom',[57] indicating at the outset an interest in the game and sporting side of the estate's activity. Medieval royal rights to fishing and to swans on the river Avon remained attached to the estate and during the nineteenth century FHHB let the fishery annually to G. P. Jervoise of Longford Castle.[58] Shooting and fishing were largely managed by the élite and the pleasures of Clarendon were enjoyed by Edward, Prince of Wales, in 1880, the year before 'Old Sir Frederick's' death.

Frederick Thomas Arthur Hervey-Bathurst (FTAHB, owner 1881–1900)

FHHB's heir was his 48-year-old son, Frederick Thomas Arthur.[59] The precise details of the family's financial history after FTAHB took over at Clarendon remain private, but rents must have been declining[60] and contributed to an unwelcome turnover of tenants, even resulting in some farms becoming untenanted. Many farmers had to make do with older buildings and the economic climate was such that the new owner was unable to borrow money and so raise the capital to improve his properties.[61] Encumbered with debt, he set about rationalising the family's situation, and the railway now provided the obvious line of amputation.[62] Events indicate the obvious anxieties. Occasional plots were disposed of south of the tracks[63] but, despite gloomy agricultural forecasts, the introduction of death duties and pressure from the bank, there was no sale. The reason was FTAHB's declining mental health: from the early 1890s he could not give consent for trusts to be broken. Although the estate was advertised for sale from 1894,[64] it could only finally be disposed of once FTAHB had died on 20 May 1900. Meanwhile, the family evacuated to their Somborne Park (Hants) house.[65] FTAHB died at his London residence at 28 Half Moon Street in Mayfair. He was described as being 'of Somborne Park' and left five sons, three daughters and effects worth £2647.[66]

When Clarendon was advertised for sale in 1894 its attractions as 'one of the finest residential and sporting domains in the southern counties' were highlighted, not its agricultural or woodland potential. The particulars stated:

> The estate is absolutely within a ring fence and forms an exceptionally fine sporting property, affording excellent partridge and cover shooting, the woods extending to upwards of 1000 acres … The lake in the winter months abounds with wild fowl … and is well stocked with pike and other fish. Clarendon is in the centre of a good hunting district being within reach of the following packs of hounds: The earl of Radnor's, the Tedworth, two packs of New Forest Foxhounds, also the New Forest deerhounds and Netton Harriers so that a variety of hunting may be had every day of the week.

The wording stresses privacy, fieldsports and location; the estate was at the nexus of several hunt boundaries. Clarendon certainly had promise in that respect; for a start, it had the capacity, boasted by its stalls and boxes, for eighteen horses, and 'ample accommodation for carriages and men',[67] not to mention tangible social cachet. Here was a passport to 'superior' social occasions such as Hunt Balls and lawn meets, enhanced by the exclusivity of the private shoot. The heir to the throne returned to shoot at Clarendon in 1899, by coincidence the year before FTAHB's death, just as he had visited the year before FHHB's death. Much had changed, however, in those twenty years: FTAHB was failing fast, and the only option now for the future of the estate was sale.

James William Garton (owner 1900–1919)

Captain (later Major) J.W. Garton (1864–1940), aged 36, bought Clarendon Park in 1900 for £80,000. Garton was a director of the Wiltshire and Dorset Bank, the mortgagees of FTAHB's Clarendon, and managing director of the Anglo-Bavarian Brewery in Shepton Mallet (Somerset),[68] which he is said to have sold to raise the capital to buy Clarendon.[69] At first sight the decision to buy appears incomprehensible for a bank director, but was probably based on several premises. As an exceptional shot he wanted to indulge his passion for shooting and perhaps he thought his young family would benefit from the space round the mansion: tennis courts are visible south of the mansion in photographs during his ownership, and archery targets, 'Box of croquet' and cricket kit were listed in 1919 when he came to sell.[70]

Garton's period of ownership was brief and not without controversy. His most visible contribution, reflecting his personal passions, was to plant up the northerly shooting belts which provided cover for game birds.[71] These belts enhanced partridge and pheasant shooting by forcing birds higher. Elsewhere at Clarendon (for example, between Ranger's Lodge and Savage's) hedgerows often exist on one side of the road only – another element of the created shooting landscape, designed to encourage birds to stay where they can best be driven and most easily be retrieved. Garton improved Clarendon's building stock with some red-brick houses which share common features of architectural detail and dressings.[72]

But if the shooting and the properties were enhanced under James Garton, other aspects of his ownership did not go so smoothly. His vigorous stewardship of the estate revived a long-standing local grievance in a 'right of way case' which was tried at the Wiltshire Assizes, Devizes, in 1903.[73] In court Garton explained that public access along rights of way 'interfered with the privacy and subsequent enjoyment of the park, and also disturbed the game in the woodlands'. Three paths were at issue: from Pitton (east), from Farley (south-east) and from Alderbury (south) via Hole Farm. Garton's case was partly historical, in that the 18-foot (5.4 m) leap round the medieval beast-hunting park, and its circular nature, had precluded paths; therefore, during Clarendon's time as a royal park there had been no rights of way. The situation between 1707 and 1900, under the Bathursts and Hervey-Bathursts, continued the Hydes' arrangements, with strict entail to son and the owner as life tenant, thereby securing the families' ownership of the estate through successive generations. These circumstances had been broken only twice: between 1747 and 1800 and when the estate was mortgaged latterly for a sum of £8,000 by FHHB in 1829–32. Such continuity of ownership presumably suggested the survival of original, royal, exclusion of any rights of way in the park. The issue went back generations: Enclosure Commissioners' evidence of 1819–20 was cited about the path in Hunt's Copse, and it was noted that Col. Hervey-Bathurst had diverted the path round Piper's and had ploughed the area. Evidence was adduced about notices against trespassers. Witnesses included Mr Lock (aged 74), a former keeper and son of a previous keeper, who denied that gamekeepers had impeded walkers in his experience. On the other hand Moses Welstead (80 years old) had been instructed eighteen years previously to hang footpath gates designed to 'shut and catch the passer-by by the heels'. James Lampard, a grocer from Quidhampton, had been stopped in 1883 and accused of trespass, and in 1892 had removed the padlock at Pitton Little Gate. It was noted further that the estate was often let, for example to Mr Hartmann, who 'had entertained the present king there' and had put up notices threatening the 'rigour of the law'. Local people had attempted to reach the palace site, 'merely a heap of ruins', as it was described in the case. Both John Forward and John Williams testified they had been turned back by Col. Hervey-Bathurst's gamekeeper from visiting the ruins even though Williams had left his dogs tied at the bottom of the hill.[74] Although the action against the landowner was successful and cited as one likely 'to encourage local authorities to resolutely resist any attempt to illegally curtail the public rights of way over great estates',[75] Garton could also claim victory. He was able to exclude walkers along the Farley and Alderbury paths (the latter he seems to have found particularly irritating because it came close to the back of the house) but local people continued to use the established right of way from Pitton. The judge pronounced the case 'tedious' (Figure 70).

Like the Hervey-Bathursts before him, James Garton enjoyed Clarendon's history, as captured in a 1906 photograph where he appears with others among the palace ruins.[76] In 1914 it was he who encouraged the publication of the seventeenth-century estate map.[77] But despite his investments, by the end of the First World War Clarendon's finances were again in trouble, largely as a result of continuing agricultural depression after the Armistice. Rather than sell large chunks of the estate to tenants or advertise to let, both patterns followed elsewhere – for example, at Knole and Montacute – Garton decided to sell everything. Successful public auctions of personal effects from country-house collections had featured since the 1880s, with much interest abroad, especially in America and Germany,[78] and this was the route he now chose, moving to a smaller property at Lilliput (Dorset).

The Clarendon sales catalogues of 1919–20 bring to life farm and house contents, and include extraordinary items such as a 'varnished Dogcart with rubber tyres, cushions and three lamps … suit a horse about 15 hands' and

an 'Old motor-car with 7 h.p. De Dion engine'.[79] There was also a veritable museum of firearms; the sporting side of Clarendon inevitably looms large.[80] The kit for rearing, protection and management of birds was especially extensive, including many pigeon traps, sparrow nets, vermin and rabbit traps.[81] For managing fish there were galvanised fish screens, together with a 'Hampshire punt' and a 'Shooting punt'.[82] In 1909–10 Major Garton had commissioned detailed investigations into 'Clarendon Park Fishery Rights'[83] which concluded that 'the fishery in the Avon between Harnham Bridge and Longford appears to have been divided between the owner of Clarendon and the owner of Britford', some islands (e.g. the Osier islands) belonging to Clarendon, and others to Britford.[84]

Gardening tools of one sort or another were also many in number (Figure 71). Four mowers, one with a twenty-seven-inch cut which was drawn by a pony, indicate the fashion for mown grass areas round the mansion. Sprayers, watering cans, hoses, wheelbarrows, pruners, a six-foot crosscut saw and a hand-saw, ladders and steps, shears, scythe, rakes, hoes, edging irons, a garden roller and an eight-foot spirit level are all indicative of order and symmetry. There were also dung forks, four '5-grain prongs' and four spades for digging, while equipment ranging from small metal labels for plants and 'A Box of slug traps' to a 30-foot range of garden frames elucidate pest control and planning. The requirement for manual labour was not, however, restricted to the mansion gardens. No fewer than 611 pot plants were also to be disposed of,[85] from which it seems that the conservatory was still in use.

FIGURE 70.
This photograph, taken in Devizes in 1903, followed the battle over public access to routes across the park. Locals won the right to continue to use the established rights of way from Pitton, Major Garton the right to exclude people from the Farley and Alderbury paths. The latter crossed the railway from Hole Farm and came close to the back of the mansion along part of a carriage drive. (Image from Salisbury and South Wiltshire Museum collection)

FIGURE 71.
The Edwardian
parterre garden, south
of the mansion, in
about 1906. Bedding
plants and exotics
are interlaced with
gravel walks to create
intricate colour
'pictures'. (Photograph
by Winifred Garton,
1906; reproduced by
kind permission of
Robert Corbett)

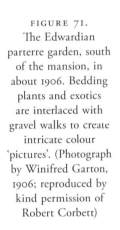

Sydney Richardson Christie-Miller (owner 1919–31)

In 1919 Clarendon's new owner was Sydney Richardson Christie-Miller (1885–1931) of Britwell Court (Buckinghamshire), from a family with business and political experience, an estate in Scotland and long-standing literary and historical interests. The purchase price was £138,500 (to which would be added certain additional sums for farm valuations of hay and other materials), bought against a valuation of £140,000 which Christie-Miller noted for his own purposes as 'Land £77,000, Woods £50,000, House £13,000'.[86] Even at that price, the house was probably the least satisfactory part of the bargain. Garton was lucky to be rid of it for more than the price of the land it stood on.[87] *The Field* at the time advised readers to demolish their mansions; others were converted into schools; at Warwick Castle and Stowe, for example. Unwieldy classical mansions such as Clarendon, with a very few, large, rooms, even with its nineteenth-century extension, were hard to heat and required numerous staff. This had been fine in the 1890s, when servants were the largest occupational group in the national census, but after the Great War staff were scarce. Large mansions were simply unfashionable, criticised as foreign and ugly.[88] However, an inventory of 1925 shows that Clarendon House was quickly transformed from a saleroom into a home filled with comfortable, elegant furnishings, art and antiques. Some of the finances for this refurbishment came from the sale of the famous Britwell Library, which was dispersed in a series of twenty-one sales between 1916 and 1927.[89] The *Times* reported that the sale was 'almost like an empire falling ... the sale of the Library has been a continuous story of high prices and large profits – profits which have scarcely any parallel in fact or fiction ...'. In all, £605,000 was raised, more than any library had ever fetched at auction. A 1599 edition of Shakespeare's *Venus and Adonis* reached the highest price ever paid for a printed book. Much of the library was bought by the Californian magnate Henry E. Huntington.[90]

In 1925 the mansion house was in its heyday: the list of the contents of the house and adjacent service structures enumerates fourteen bedrooms along with other rooms identified by personal names or positions within the household. Eighty spaces were identified in all, from the main bedroom through the Drawing Room, children's rooms and nursery, down to a telephone room and bottle store. Space was attributed according to gender and age. Specifically identified areas for men included the Bachelors' Landing, the Butler's Room, the Footmen's Bedroom, and the valets' rooms in the 'Outbuildings'. For women there was Mrs Christie-Miller's Sitting Room and separate rooms for Miss Veronica, Miss Rosemary and Miss Lavender.[91] For female servants there was the Housemaids' Sitting Room, Cupboard, Closet, Young Ladies' Maids' Room, Head Housemaid's Room, Scullery Maid's Bedroom, Head Kitchen Maid's Bedroom, three Housemaids' Bedroom and a Housekeeper's bedroom. Outside there were a further thirty-one outhouses, including stables, dog kennels and a bicycle room. Some of these outbuildings also contained bedrooms.

The mansion contained a wide range of European art, including Breughels, recalling the park's medieval heyday. Diverse ceramics (Chinese porcelain, crackle ware and so on) and other materials echo the worldwide trade networks of the nineteenth and early twentieth centuries. Clarendon mansion was a global showcase: from cotton and linen bedsheets and table coverings (including '156 D'Oyleys'), to mahogany (some Spanish) and Chinese teak furniture, bamboo screens, Indian (maybe the source of two large Tiger skins), Turkish, Persian and Brussels floorcoverings, French furniture and china ornaments, Vienna teacups, Imari bowls, Egyptian porphyry, ebony and ivory, and a great deal else. There was also much that was British, from Crown Derby and Devon ware to Minton, Spode, Wemyss ware and Wedgwood; English furniture and furnishings included Chippendale, Hepplewhite and Sheraton, an Old English chiming clock, and Axminster and Wilton carpets and mats. The world's goods were offset by finest British products in an uniquely grand English landscape setting.[92]

Plenty of evidence of sporting activity is found in the 1925 inventory: polo clubs, croquet equipment, golf clubs and skipping ropes, cricket kit, tennis racquets and maintenance kit for both grass and hard courts. In 1925 a well-appointed Billiard Room is found indoors, probably that established by FHHB;[93] there was also a Bluthner Boudoir grand piano in the Drawing Room together with a wireless,[94] a His Majesty's Voice table gramophone in a mahogany case with 100 records, and a Jazz set of drums. Elsewhere in the house fencing foils and a 'Model Yacht and Sundry Mechanical Toys etc' are listed. These may have included a clockwork Alfa-Romeo 'about a foot long which steered by hand', Michael Christie-Miller's prized possession at his prep school, West Downs (Winchester), in the early 1930s.[95] In the servants' quarters entertainments were more subdued: only draughts are recorded with which to while away the hours.

Samuel Vandeleur Christie-Miller (owner 1931–68)

When Sydney Christie-Miller died in June 1931 his widow, Evelyn Nora (née Vandeleur), continued to live in the mansion, where in her widowhood she encouraged the excavations of the medieval palace which lasted annually, under Tancred Borenius and John Charlton, until 1939.[96] The estate passed to their elder son, 'Sammy' Vandeleur Christie-Miller (1911–68), who, after Oxford, became a major in the Wiltshire Yeomanry. Sammy Christie-Miller was not an old-fashioned landowner; his modern tastes stretched to the purchase of two Hudson Terraplanes, 'the first car to have an American stream-lined concept of a swept back rear'. These unusual cars impressed young Guy Mills, a friend of the family, 'used to … 40 to 50 mph' with an 'exhilarating 70 mph, over the switch backs via Stockbridge' back to the severe prep school life at Winchester which the country boys Michael Christie-Miller and Mills, used to home lives spent in the open air, found restricting. Mills thought the chauffeur would have preferred the standard country-house Rolls-Royce or Bentley. On a later visit the boys went out shooting pigeons on the Clarendon drives from an old tourer. The aim of the game, achieved only by Sammy Christie-Miller, was to shoot a pigeon and accelerate so as to catch the falling bird in the open dickey seat.[97]

The Christie-Millers enjoyed a substantial outside swimming pool, now disused, which lies north-east of the mansion in the shade of the Wild Garden. The Mills memoir of 1934 records boys' carefree swimming there, 'baked by a southern sun and sheltered by beeches on the north', sustained by separate bowls of white and black cherries, while the Sunday papers were 'rattled' at the poolside on that hot late-June afternoon. There was a Chinese-style changing room north of the pool.[98]

The Hervey-Bathurst tradition of allowing skating on the frozen lake (see n. 26, this Chapter) was honoured by the Christie-Millers.[99] Young people also visited and some took part in archaeological work at Clarendon. In particular, the palace excavations of the 1930s, run by the youthful John Charlton, attracted a range of guests, young and old, not least Tancred Borenius's children, who dug with vigour at the palace. Intellectuals who signed the Borenius visitors' book had a wide range of cultural interests, principally archaeology

(Figure 72). In September 1938 forty children from Alderbury school thronged the excavations at the Palace.[100] Photographs show the workers in their waistcoats and flat caps, and occasionally visitors such as Sir Bruce Richmond, editor of the *Times Literary Supplement*.

For those who worked in the park, little changed between 1900 and 1950. A young farm labourer beginning work at Clarendon about 1900 would have seen few changes in the 1920s and 1930s from his father's day in the nineteenth

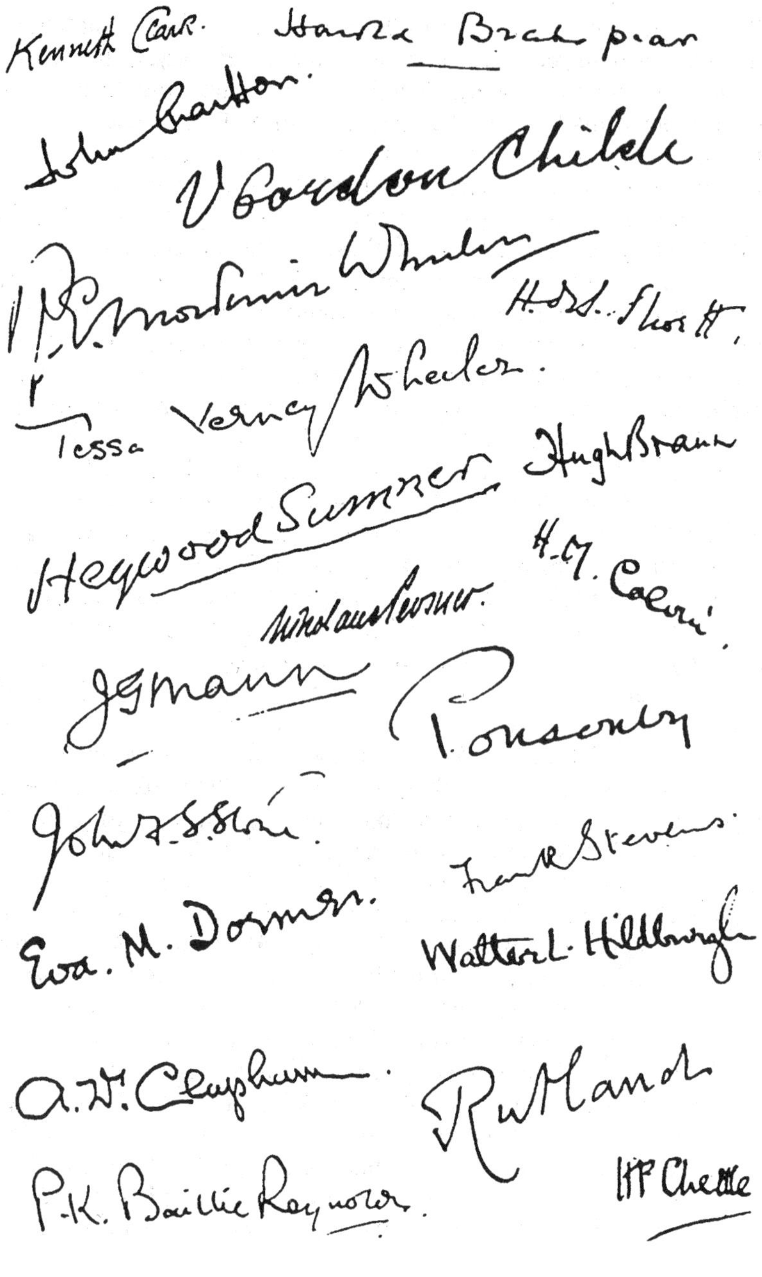

FIGURE 72.
Visitors to Tancred Borenius's home at nearby Coombe Bissett, 1930–39. Among the local archaeologists who came were Frank Stevens, from Salisbury Museum; J. F. S. Stone; Heywood Sumner; and John Charlton, recommended by Wheeler as site director at Clarendon Palace. Those from further afield included Kenneth Clark; V. Gordon Childe, the Edinburgh prehistorian; A. W. Clapham and Nikolaus Pevsner, the architectural historians; the Wheelers; James Mann, Keeper of the Armouries at the Tower of London; Walter Hildburgh, the American expert on medieval alabasters; the ninth Duke of Rutland and Lord Ponsonby of Shulbrede, both medieval tile experts; Harold Brakspear, the veteran excavator; G. H. Chettle, an expert on Hampton Court Palace; and Howard Colvin, a teenager, later to be the distinguished historian of medieval royal buildings.

century, and by retirement in the 1950s the park would not have seemed much different to the day he began work. He would have lived through the introduction of tractors,[101] combine harvesters, some agrochemicals and the wiring of electricity on the farm, and perhaps he would have noted that Clarendon seemed less self-sufficient[102] but the numbers employed as 'labour' across the estate were not all that different. There were only ten fewer in 1951 than the seventy-nine employed in 1925 (sixty-seven of them men).[103]

Employment was varied. Shooting continued as a major activity though with some novelties. Guinea fowl were raised in the 1930s among the northerly shooting belts to act 'as sentries against poachers and foxes'.[104] Elsewhere in the park livestock enterprises had become prominent. There were two tenanted dairies and three estate dairies.[105] A prize herd of Ayrshire cattle was introduced to Clarendon just prior to the Second World War,[106] with pigs being fattened on the dairy by-products and kept for market.[107] The estate also continued to run a large sheep flock,[108] but the change most noticeable to the visitor was the 14,000 poultry running free-range at Queen Manor/Ranger's.[109]

The war saw considerable changes at Clarendon, as elsewhere. Unlike the First World War, the Second World War brought more involvement of civilians in the landscape because of the dangers of invasion and bombing and, latterly, preparations for the D-Day invasions. Wartime military installations at Clarendon included the tank-trap ditch dug between Petersfinger and Alderbury Common in 1940–1 amidst invasion fears; searchlight stations operated at Ashley Hill, King Manor and at 'Searchlight Field',[110] and a K/Q-type dummy airfield to distract enemy aircraft from Old Sarum aerodrome nearby.

The 'control bunker' of the dummy airfield by Winchester Gate still exists and lay in the quadrant south of Old Sarum where Lysander, Mustang and Tomahawk aircraft operated. It was originally manned by three airmen and equipped with a generator which powered lighting patterns imitating that of an airfield when seen from the air at night (a Q-type decoy). 'Tank Field', meanwhile, contained dummy tanks (a K-type decoy for daylight deception) and possibly 'Blister' aircraft hangers as well, though the two which remain on the estate may have been a post-War acquisition. These decoys seem to have done their job at least on one occasion, when bombs fell at Fussell's Lodge Farm, killing 'a couple of horses and damaging an Austin Motor car', and also across the road from Tank Field. Today ploughing still turns up fragments of the Drem circuit lights, posts, buried ducts and cables. The dummy airfield went out of use about 1942.[111] Elsewhere, a stick of bombs also fell north of the mansion, leaving a series of craters; a Dornier DO17 came down in Tank Field 'during harvest time', according to Clarendon estate workers, and in 1944 Henry Maidment of Alderbury recalls salvaging part of the radio of a German plane which had crashed on Ashley Hill 'almost vertically' into the chalk and had all but disappeared. Another account records that two Mark XII Spitfires collided over Ashley Hill and crashed there.[112] Various young men from Clarendon and its neighbourhood fell in the War, among them Michael Christie-Miller, who was killed in Normandy commanding a

Note Baillie Reynolds who later, as Chief Inspector of Ancient Monuments, despaired of Clarendon Palace (xvii). Among other friends, and friends of friends, were the young composer William Walton; the Egyptologist Alan Gardiner; the painter Henry Lamb; Diana Cooper; Pamela Mitford; and Bruce Richmond, founder of the *Times Literary Supplement*. This remains an unusual glimpse into Britain's inter-war intellectual élite and the social side of archaeology. Most, though not all (for example, Walton), progressed to the palace site. (Reproduced from the Borenius family visitors' book, from the collection of the late Clarissa Lada-Grodzicka)

tank after D-Day, a far cry from those carefree days in the Clarendon pool ten years earlier.[113]

Evacuees came from Portsmouth to Clarendon early in the War. One letter provides glimpses of the life of a young boy in 1941 a – request for supplies of tuck ('running low'), his enjoyment of the weekly Mickey Mouse – but a lack of news led to a request for the *Sunday Graphic*: 'the wireless is only used for such things as nature talks ... for scools', with the suggestion that his parents listen to the next one, on 'Trees'. A recreation room contained a stove, a stage, bookcases, cupboards and tables, rocking horse, piano and 'mecano table'. Children are one of the least-visible social groups in both the archaeological and historical record of Clarendon but its landscape is perhaps as well adapted for the enjoyment of children as of any social group, whether the seventeen children of Peter Bathurst or the smaller families of more recent times.

The recent past (1968–)

Sammy Christie-Miller farmed the estate until his premature death on 21 January 1968. He is buried in a private cemetery near the ruins of the medieval palace. His widow, Esmée (née Fraser-Urmston), lived on in the mansion house until she remarried in 1971 and moved to Shaftesbury. At this point the mansion house ceased to be the main residence at Clarendon, the focus moving to the adjacent Stable House. The nineteenth-century extensions were demolished in 1979.

In recent years agriculture on the estate has been transformed and, as we shall see in Chapter Seven, conservation, public access and landscape issues have all taken a high profile. Financial constraints imposed by death duties have led to the further disposal of properties, mainly south of the railway, in the 1980s, and Savage's Farmhouse, further north, was demolished in 1989. Nevertheless, at the heart of the current management strategy is the determination to retain the core of the medieval estate intact and that, together with the preservation of the park's buildings, has been achieved.

When we look back at the events of the twentieth century, it was the 1970s and 1980s which were the important watershed in the story of agriculture at Clarendon. These two decades saw the introduction of plant breeding, fertilisers, livestock management and farm machinery on an altogether different scale, influenced by the Common Agricultural Policy and its associated subsidies, improvement grants and market demands. These measures and introductions have radically affected the variety and management of crops, increased crop yields and milk production and, in probably the most striking change, massively reduced the number of people working on the land.[114]

There have also been major changes in the way the landscape is managed. Where in 1960 a large acreage of farmland was rented out to tenants, just as it had been since the seventeenth century, in 2003 the only tenanted farm at Clarendon was Brick Kiln (90 acres; 36 ha). Queen Manor/Ranger's and Savage's are now farmed in hand; Dog Kennel and Hole Farm have been sold.

Only Home Farm, with 170 milking cows, remains as the relic of commercial livestock operations[115] though ducks, geese and chickens are still kept in backyards, together with twenty-nine sheep which graze the palace site. The prize herd of Clarendon Poll Herefords was sold off in 1980[116] and the pigs followed in the early 1990s. Against these losses, the total farmed arable acreage 'in-hand' is now 2450 acres (992 ha), nearly two and a half times what it was thirty years ago, with a far greater variety of crops, including oilseed rape for vegetable oil, linseed, and protein crops such as beans, lupins and, most recently, peas.[117]

Today a quarter of the Clarendon Park estate (1200 acres; 486 ha) is managed woodland. There is a visible contrast between the southern area of the estate, where timber trees are found in avenues and scattered through the park and pastureland, and the central and northern areas. In the central woodland area timber trees are found in groups and standing as single trees among new coppice and conifer plantations. They fade to nothing in the northern area. What we see today is a relict landscape that broadly reflects that of the Middle Ages: wood pasture with scattered oak trees (Front Cover), coppices, and the medieval launds, now arable and shooting belts. Some older oaks near the mansion were named specifically in order to promote this link with Clarendon's medieval past: two ancient oaks were known in 1880 as 'Monarch' and 'King John', respectively then 18 and 19 feet (5.4–5.7 m) in diameter at 4 feet (1.2 m) from the ground.[118] Above all it is the trees and the blocks of woodland which provide the clearest visual link with the past. Many place-names remain in use today with only minor spelling changes. Names of c. 1650 such as Hendon Copse, Cannon Copse, Gilbridge Coppice, Stoney Deane, Netly Coppice, Faire Oak, Caverill Coppice, Beachy Dean and so on compare well with their modern equivalents. The unusually-named Marge Crendall Coppice (also c. 1650) is now Crendle Bottom Copse. All this contributes to a very strong feeling of continuity of residence, names and landscape forms at Clarendon which has proved such a key element of this study. There are still several hundred deer at Clarendon, mainly roe.[119] About 40–50 roe bucks and 80–100 does are culled annually, together with a few fallow and muntjac.

Today's garden focus has moved away from the terrace south of the mansion to the former walled vegetable garden south of Stable House, which is now a flower garden with some remaining nineteenth-century glasshouses, a tennis court and a swimming pool. The relocated fountain – formerly on the terrace south of the mansion (see Figure 71) – provides a feature in this late twentieth-century garden. The ruins of the palace and the uninhabited mansion, both with abandoned gardens, the one conserved, the other with an emerging restoration plan, may have a brighter future than at any time in the last half-century: for as we finalise our text in the Summer of 2006, news is breaking that the Clarendon Park estate is sold, that new owners will be in possession by the late Autumn and that there is an intention to repair and occupy the mansion. A new era is beginning.

CHAPTER SEVEN

Valuing the Landscape

In this chapter we leave behind our sequence of prehistoric to modern land-scapes in favour of a thematic approach which examines some of the different values placed on the park by owners and visitors. We look at the motives of the antiquarians, archaeologists and historians who have had interests at Clarendon, stressing the recent influence of heritage management, conserva-tion and presentation. Aesthetic value was promoted by the architecture and setting of the medieval palace and the later mansion, while economic worth ranges from income generation from the park's many products to the use of the estate as a legal entity to raise mortgages. Clarendon Park proves more than a mere financial workhorse, however; it also conferred social advantages through ownership and title, delivered recreational value through shooting and other sports, and has developed a multiplicity of meanings which go beyond the utilitarian. Of particular importance in the medieval period was the literary image of the forest and the hunt together, with the natural and religious themes developed through interior decoration in the royal palace. The symbolism of later landscapes is also considered. The purpose of this chapter, therefore, is to consider the many different ways in which Clarendon Park has been treated by those who have owned and visited it. We are mainly concerned with attitudes, ways of thinking and exploiting what the park may represent, rather than, for example, the fine details of its natural resources. To do this we have grouped the different values we can recognise into six main categories: *academic, economic, aesthetic, social, recreational* and *symbolic*; and these are examined below.

Academic value

Antiquaries, archaeologists, historians and art historians have a long, if flawed, involvement with Clarendon and the palace site provides an interesting case study of their motives.

Knowledge and invention
Some antiquarians, among them, in the first half of the sixteenth century, John Leland, did little more than note the existence of Clarendon.[1] Like many later commentators, such as the eighteenth-century topographer Thomas Cox and his contemporary, the travelling diarist Richard Pococke, Leland may never have stepped inside the park, preferring to rely instead on local knowledge and

existing accounts.[2] Their interest was casual at best, noting only Clarendon's former glories. Likewise, neither William Camden in c. 1590,[3] nor Daniel Defoe a century later, could claim intimate knowledge of Clarendon's archaeology. The detail they record, like that on the first maps of south-east Wiltshire (Figure 73), is scant and, as was typical of accounts of their day, somewhat biased towards the pedigrees and landed interests of local property owners.[4]

Wiltshire-born John Aubrey, however, does seems to have known the park for himself. In his *Monumenta Britannica*, compiled in 1688–9 from earlier notes, Aubrey mentions the discovery of Iron Age and Roman coins as well as later finds.[5] The ending of royal ownership and disemparkment provided Aubrey and others with an opportunity; William Stukeley, for example, visited on 3 August 1723 and sketched the palace site in pencil and watercolour,[6] with the figures of Captain Thomas and Lady Betty Herbert strolling among the ruins[7] (Figure 74). It was, he thought, 'a large place … unfortified and built mostly of flint tho they have been pulling it down for many years'.[8] The first effort to make a more detailed record of what had survived at the palace followed later in the century and was led just after Christmas 1769[9] by James Harris, together with his friend Thomas Warton.[10]

Chlori dunum.

Harris and Warton's visit reflects the new eighteenth-century fascination with roots, nationhood and, more specifically, the constitutional importance of the medieval period. In this case the inspiration was Charles Lyttleton, an antiquarian of aristocratic standing with an interest in 'Saxon' and Gothic architecture who encouraged his correspondents to decipher the architecture of medieval buildings for themselves.[11] This was an important intellectual shift from those who saw historical evidence as the only reliable guide to a building's age. The significance of Clarendon in Lyttleton's mind was probably linked with his belief that Saxon architecture had persisted until the reign of Henry II, when it became more Gothic in style. Lyttleton's argument was that if continuity could be proven in architecture and the Norman Conquest had had no impact on architectural forms then it was likely that the same was true for the constitution. Thus it could be 'proved' that feudalism and a representative system of government were present in Saxon society, beliefs which were shared by Whigs and Tories opposed to Robert Walpole, who was seen to have upset the constitutional balance. During the 1760s Lyttleton was absorbed in writing a history of Henry II specifically intended to explore these issues[12] and it was he who had asked Harris to go up to the palace ruins.[13]

This visit is also striking because it marks the development of the romantic view of the palace site which we see echoed throughout the nineteenth century. Warton, Professor of English at Oxford, would have been especially intriguing company. He knew about the paintings of Richard the Lionheart in the Antioch Chamber, and was no doubt able to relate, when in their original setting, to the medieval 'Romance of Richard', and his own poem 'The Crusade', which extols 'English Richard'; he was also aware of Henry II's

FIGURE 74.
William Stukeley wrote 'Chlorendon … a sweet and beautiful place' when on 3 August 1723 he sketched the palace ruins with the figures of Lord and Lady Herbert strolling among the ruins. Thomas Herbert, eighth Earl of Pembroke (1656–1733) was a collector of 'statues, dirty gods and coins' and was involved with Stukeley in other antiquarian activities and in the Royal Society. Stukeley's view apparently shows the western gatehouse to the left and the east gable of the Great Hall on the right. 'Chlori dunum', on the horizon, is Figsbury Rings, with Queen Manor directly below. (From Stukeley, 1724)

168

FIGURE 75.
The upstanding crag
of walling at the
Great Hall was John
Buckler's focus when
he made his romantic
watercolour in 1805
amidst Britton's owl-
and raven-ridden ruins.
(Photograph from
the Conway Library,
Courtauld Institute
of Art, by permission
of the Wiltshire
Archaeological and
Natural History
Society)

encounter with Becket at Clarendon. So while Harris measured the 'Parliament Hall', so he tells Lyttleton in his letter, Warton conjured up the memory of these great men and their Clarendon associations just as he had done elsewhere in his poems such as 'Written at Vale-Royal Abbey, Cheshire' or, more locally 'Written at Stonehenge'.[14] Such intellectual fancies were commonly indulged at medieval monuments, which allowed Protestant visitors to bask in the 'progress' of their own times, thankful that they had escaped the suffering (and Catholicism) of the Middle Ages. In this case, 'a flight of imagination' took over, conjuring King Henry and the 'great Becket' before him and in a flight of pure Whig history he concludes 'but the scene soon vanished, I returned to my self and thanked providence for having destined me to a happier more enlightened period'.

Clearly, a medieval monument like Clarendon Palace could be 'read' by visitors in a variety of ways, some of them rather obscure to our eyes, others somewhat objectionable. Here there was political, social and religious meaning to be had, not to mention the broader appeal of the romantic ruin. 'The habitation of Kings is levelled with the dust' wrote the Wiltshire-born antiquary John Britton in 1801, 'and all the proud revelry of a court has given way to the hooting of the owl and the croaking of the raven'.[15] By now the park had

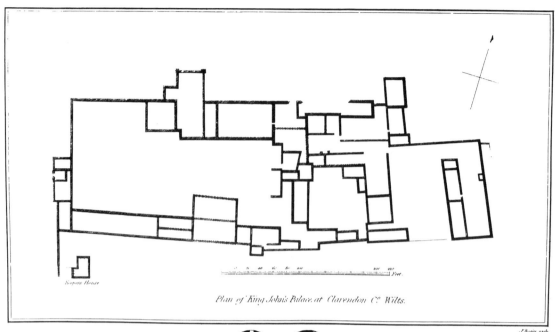

Plan of King John's Palace at Clarendon C.° Wilts.

'British Coin found at King's Manor Farm.

FIGURE 76.
Thomas Phillipps's brief was to try 'to ascertain the Ground Plan of King John's House'. 'Coins and other Treasure Trove' were to be delivered to Sir Frederick Bathurst, who entreated Phillipps not to damage the woods and to return the 'earth and rubbish … to the places from whence it was taken'. In the event Phillipps exposed more walling than was uncovered in six years of excavation in the 1930s and provided a more extensive, if partial, plan of the palace. The site was never fully reinstated. (Bodleian, Phillipps-Robinson MS b108, f34–7)

been remodelled with the mansion as the key feature and the ruins of the palace were a 'Gothick' sideshow. The crags of walling were all that interested John Buckler when he came to do his watercolours in 1805 (Figure 75) but neither he nor Britton could claim to have an advanced understanding of the palace site. The overgrown walls and the melancholy, even fear, they inspired were the main attraction, though perhaps Clarendon also represented a native Gothic architecture that was peculiarly English, something which the classical designs of the day could never be.

All archaeological excavations must be seen in the context of their time, and those carried out in 1820 at Clarendon palace by the young antiquary and bibliophile Thomas Phillipps are no exception (Figure 76).[16] This was an age when medieval monuments, particularly those with links to national histories, were just beginning to be routinely investigated and the Constitutions of Clarendon (1164) were becoming widely acknowledged as a key event *en route* to the English Reformation; the latter was in part due to Protestant reaction to a resurgence of Roman Catholics in public life, especially after the repealing of the Test Acts in 1829.[17] Today we find Phillipps's plan invaluable, though the credit should probably go to his agent, Hensley, who also sketched the remains he saw (Figure 77),[18] and to Richard Colt-Hoare, who assembled an eclectic mix of documents to accompany the new plan for his *History of Modern Wiltshire* (1822–45). Colt-Hoare's publication undoubtedly led to a flurry of activity, with some people exploring the documents further

an arch, once underground at Clarendon

FIGURE 77.
The vault in the wine cellar, sketched by William Hensley in 1820. Hensley was Thomas Phillipps's agent and probably organised the 'excavation' on the palace site. Described by Phillipps in 1833 as 'an arch once under-ground', the vault in fact marks access to the extension of Henry II's wine cellar dug out for his grandson in the thirteenth century. The cellar itself is cut down through the solid chalk and there were no doubt chambers above which have collapsed into the void. ('Ruins of Clarendon Park 1821' from the Hensley album, Wiltshire Archaeological and Natural History Society, 1982.7933 Hensley 66)

for evidence of decorative schemes at the palace,[19] and others engaged in the discovery of earlier sites.[20]

During the eighteenth and nineteenth centuries, Clarendon conjured diverse emotions for those who visited. Scholarship was intensely bound up with political, religious and philosophical views in a way which may be surprising to us today. Motives were never neutral and results were intended to convey messages of an elusive kind, specific to their age. When the historical associations of the site were further celebrated by Clarendon's owners in 1844, a stone plaque was erected at the east end of the Great Hall at the palace site (Figure 78).[21] FHHB, the sponsor, was both a Protestant and a military man. No matter the historical inaccuracies in his inscription,[22] the woodland visitors who carved their names and left their initials there (Figure 79) could not leave doubting his patriotic, religious message.[23] For others it was the leafy atmosphere of the site which attracted them. 'Netley Abbey', inscribed in capitals on the Hervey-Bathurst monument, was a popular companion venue for those in search of the authentic 'Gothick' experience.

Enter the archaeologist

From 1850 until the 1930s, Clarendon and its monuments stirred little interest,[24] and when large-scale excavations were undertaken at the palace site between 1933 and 1939, the inspiration came from a fresh direction. Tancred Borenius, the instigator, was a Finn who became Professor of Art History at London University and had already published widely on English medieval wall paintings.[25] His curiosity was driven by his research interest in Clarendon's place in the history of art. He 'developed the conviction that Clarendon Palace offered a field of study which is of prime importance for the medieval archaeology not only of England but of the whole of Europe'.[26] Initially, he

171

FIGURE 78.
The Great Hall,
looking east: (a) *above*
shortly after excavation
in the 1930s; (b) *left*
the kitchen area after
the clearance of trees
in 1994; (c) *opposite top*
the kitchen area after
consolidation, in 2004.
(Photographs by the
late John Charlton,
Tom Beaumont James
and Fran Halsall).

FIGURE 79.
In the period between 1844 and the removal of the collapsing remains of the 'porch' in 2001, some 300 separate graffiti appeared. The earliest date is 1847 (W.S or w.s S), with other dated contributions clustering before 1875, and 'W.K. 1907'; dated inscriptions continued to 1969. (Photograph by Christopher Gerrard)

expected to recover medieval fine sculpture, artefacts and wall paintings to further his research, and the interim reports on the excavation reflect those interests. Practically the first information to emerge from the excavations was the publication of an early Gothic sculpted head (Figure 80), and even details of sculpture and floor tiles appeared before 'the configuration of the palace'.[27] It was Borenius's charm, enthusiasm, social (and royal) connections and academic gravitas which had made the project possible and attracted so many luminaries, as well as public interest, to the site.[28] In point of fact, relatively little of the medieval levels at Clarendon was actually *excavated* and only the final phases of demolition were reached in many places.[29]

Other than the work of Borenius, there have been two further campaigns of excavation at Clarendon which have been driven by what we might think of as purely academic considerations. The first, by John Musty, involved the digging of small trenches at targeted locations inside the palace precinct with the intention of recovering a stratified pottery sequence for comparison with the Laverstock kilns and examining hitherto poorly understood areas such as the garden terrace and the south-east entrance.[30] The second, by Elizabeth Eames, was inspired by the re-examination of the archaeological and documentary record for tile production at Clarendon as part of her national survey of floor tiles in the late 1950s. This led, in 1964 and 1965, to the removal of the mid thirteenth-century tile kiln which had fired the tile pavement in the King's Chapel by a team from the British Museum Research Laboratory.[31]

All three of the twentieth-century excavation campaigns on medieval targets at Clarendon were focused on the palace site. No interest was shown in the lodges or the deer park pale, for example, in spite of an awareness of wider landscape stimulated by work on prehistoric field systems and monuments in the park. More specifically, both Borenius and Eames firmly targeted the thirteenth-century phase of the site driven by art historical interests, while historical research, particularly Howard Colvin's two volumes on *The History of the King's Works*,[32] which included reference to Clarendon's royal building accounts. Although Borenius was excavating at the tail end of the era of great 'restoration' projects, when massive campaigns at castles and monasteries had cleared sites which were then opened to the public, there was never any explicit ambition to create neat walls and smooth lawns. Two major obstacles to further investigations then emerged. First, there was never a satisfactory scheme for access which would have been a prerequisite for State intervention and funding; and, second, the war intervened and put a stop to archaeologists' and historians' aspirations.

Threat, rescue and heritage
From the day that the Borenius excavations were abruptly halted, at the outbreak of the Second World War on 3 September 1939, the major concern became the conservation of the palace site. We are able to piece together from surviving documents the measures that were taken. To begin with, there is no doubt that Borenius fully expected to return and complete what he had

begun. To this end the wine cellar was timbered and the Queen's Chamber tiled pavement and the tile kiln were protected *in situ* under corrugated tin and sand, but thieving (attributed to the military, as was wall damage) and the weather soon took their toll. On visiting the site, the Ministry realised that the costs of repair would be considerable and 'must therefore await better times'.[33] Borenius, feeling 'personally responsible for the decay', provided funds from his own pocket and, once 'Out of Bounds' notices had been erected, repair work focused on a limited portion of the site.[34] The worst falls of walling were to be treated and turfs placed on other wall tops in order to protect them. This took time, since building and farm labour were almost impossible to obtain locally in a time of war, but the repairs were complete by November 1942. Two years later all was well, though there was a forewarning of what was to come in one Ministry memo: 'I am rather alarmed at this attempt to preserve, with sticks and staves, a composition of saturated masonry of the flint and chalk variety ... I anticipate some disappointment when struts, etc. are removed'.[35] In fact, they were never removed; rather, they rotted away and when Borenius died suddenly in 1948, the champion of the Gothic Clarendon and the essential link between Ministry and estate was gone. There were calls for the excavations to be reopened as late as 1952 and for earlier results to be published,[36] but the only step taken was the Scheduling of the palace as an ancient monument on 12 January 1950.

By the late 1950s the palace site was in a poor state and the owner, Major Sammy Christie-Miller, now intervened. A prolonged correspondence with the Ministry about the condition of the site followed, which questioned the Ministry's operational priorities. When excavations began at Fussell's Lodge long barrow in 1957, the owner was perplexed and frustrated by what he saw as dual standards at play. How could a long barrow be excavated when the palace was in such a poor way? The long barrow, explained the Ministry publicly, was 'under threat' and had to be 'saved', though internal memos reveal their academic interest in the first earthen long barrow to be excavated since before the War and the first on Salisbury Plain since the early nineteenth century.[37] In 1957 the Chief Inspector (who had previously visited in the 1930s, see Figure 72 and xvii) concluded 'it would be nice to lay out the plan of Clarendon', but 'it is hardly an exaggeration to say that deterioration can go no further'.[38] He might have added that, with other monuments in the park suffering extensive plough damage, immediate and radical intervention was essential there if anything was to be recovered before the remaining evidence disappeared altogether.

Less significant issues flared up from time to time which simply made relations worse. Lines of communication were formal, with ample scope for misinterpretation. In 1957 the Ministry had refused to contribute to a fence to protect the palace site and were unsupportive two years later when a metal detectorist accompanied by 'a woman with excavating tools' were discovered at the site. A year later, in 1960, the Major wrote again, pleading that the whole palace 'is disintegrating'.[39] Then, adding further insult, a second 'rescue'

FIGURE 80.
The first major find
to be published from
the 1930s excavations,
the thirteenth-century
Gothic Head of
a Youth indicates
Borenius's interest in
schemes of decoration
and cycles of images
under Henry III, on
which he published
his final word in
1943. The head is
perhaps too small to
be architectural and is
more likely to be from
a piece of furnishing
such as a fireplace. The
furrowed brow, closing
eyes and large nose
suggest a character on
the brink of a sneeze
and he may represent
Winter, perhaps to be
matched elsewhere by
the caricatured smiling
face of Summer (Paul
Binski pers. comm.).
(Photograph by
Salisbury Museum)

campaign financed by the Ministry began in November 1961, when Major
and Mrs Vatcher excavated the plough-damaged round barrow on Cockey
Down.[40] At this point Major Christie-Miller's letters ceased. What becomes
clear from the correspondence is that the Ministry were simply not willing
to take over the ownership and management of the palace site because they
feared the costs involved. They saw their priorities in archaeological sites of
different sorts and from other periods; sites which could be resolved through
an established procedure of excavation. Nothing was further from their minds
than the suggestion made by Nikolaus Pevsner in 1966 that Clarendon should
be entirely rebuilt.[41]

Over the next twenty years, Clarendon occasionally resurfaced as a 'heritage' issue. In the royal jubilee year of 1977, correspondence in the London
Times once again referred to the poor state of the ruins of Clarendon Palace,
overgrown and decayed in the Wiltshire countryside.[42] At that point, work
began on the backlog of finds and records of previous work at the palace. In

FIGURE 81.
The palace site looking
west in 2006 with
the queen's chamber
in the foreground,
the declivity of the
wine cellar to the
left and the king's
chambers, hall and
kitchens stretching
away westwards along
the scarp of the hill,
which drops sharply
away from the garden
platforms north of the
palace. The grey gravel
leads eastwards from
the holloway from
Salisbury, finishing at
the former medieval
western entrance.
(Photograph by
Elisabeth Barton)

the meantime, finds from the 1930s excavations were placed on display when the Salisbury and South Wiltshire Museum moved to a new location at The King's House in 1982[43] and, in 1984, Romanesque sculpture from the Clarendon royal apartments was shown at the English Romanesque Art exhibition at the Hayward Gallery.[44] Reburial of the standing remains was among the solutions suggested by the newly established English Heritage in 1984.[45] Two years later a letter from the Chairman of Rescue to the *Times* took English Heritage to task for proposing a further excavation of Maiden Castle for the pleasure of the World Archaeological Congress in the UK rather than the re-excavation of Clarendon, so that it might be displayed, and 'where the excavations, conducted 50 years ago and still unpublished, are in a scandalous state'.[46]

With the site in a perilous state, matters now came to a head quickly. The first intervention was not welcome. The October 1987 'Great Storm' took its toll both on established trees and on shallow-rooted ash trees which had self-seeded since the 1930s and were perched on medieval walls and spoil heaps at the palace. This caused a significant amount of very visible damage (Figure 78b). A year later the results of the 1930s and 1960s excavations were published,[47] providing the platform for further negotiation; this began in 1994, when the estate received a grant from English Heritage for removing fallen wood and cutting down the remaining trees (compare Figures 78b and 81). This exposed

other fragile walls and spoil heaps to the weather; rain washed out finds, some of which were recovered by limited fieldwalking. A survey of the archaeology on the wider estate was then financed by English Heritage in 1996, with the aim of reviewing all the archaeological, architectural and historical data available for the whole medieval park.[48] A 'landscape management plan' followed in 1998[49] which assessed threats and included proposals for the future management of all archaeological sites at Clarendon. This work then provided the basis for further grant applications,[50] including one for the palace site, which had by then been placed on the English Heritage *Buildings at Risk* register.

The essence of the 1998 proposals was to remove some excavators' spoil heaps and consolidate major walls at the core of the medieval palace complex.[51] Most controversially, nineteenth-century Hervey-Bathurst additions were partially removed, including three ineffective buttresses and the 1844 plaque, which was reset so as not to detract from the original structure. Away from the core buildings, where weed-blocking geotextiles were overlaid with gravel to denote interiors, crumbling masonry was reburied for protection. Chalk grassland, grazed by sheep within a newly fenced area, replaced the woodland jungle of a decade earlier. These works, it is hoped, will significantly reduce degradation of the masonry, enhance the legibility of the site and address safety (Figure 83). Six interpretation boards now show reconstructions of different aspects of the palace and though frequent visitors will see a difference, those discovering the site for the first time should not find a triumph of 'heritage' over 'sense of place'.[52]

Of course, the legacy of cultural monuments at Clarendon has been, and will increasingly become, associated with wider public concerns for the 'heritage'. This incorporates a quite different set of public interests which must be negotiated: demands for access, education, and more emotive needs such as the desire to set down cultural roots. These are not strictly academic values but they impinge upon them and have already significantly influenced current management strategies. The starting point for the modern research described here has been conservation and the keys to releasing funds have been the creation of permissive access from the existing Clarendon Way on to the site, the improvement of safety and the rendering of the ruins intelligible to the visitor by focusing attention on the more complete areas of the site and those with a clear function and historical identity. More academic research, while desirable, has been a low priority in this scheme, a by-product of the conservation strategy and not its key objective. This represents an important shift in mentality.

Clarendon Palace provides a case study for the integration of archaeological research with conservation and presentation. It has not been undertaken without difficulty, however, and it is worth illustrating key debates which have arisen as a result of conflicting values at play. Because of ongoing damage to masonry the decision was taken to remove tree cover on the site to reinstate its chalk downland appearance. This decision had four impacts.

First, the removal of trees and scrub adversely affected a prized shooting drive and this had an economic impact on the estate. Second, the tree clearance altered the visual appearance of the site. Given that the general public perception of the site was as a romantic ruin with a sense of seclusion, the treatment of the surroundings of the site was as challenging as that of the crumbling foundations. Third, the maintenance of the chalk grassland would require grazing by sheep and therefore fencing would be necessary; the latter has a certain visual impact and both involve additional long-term costs and care. Fourth, clearance of the site created an opportunity for a detailed topographical recording and provided the essential basis for making decisions about what to preserve and how to proceed. Each of these four issues required transparent discussion and a trading of economic, academic and heritage values. Fortunately, there was far more to agree upon than to dispute. Our watchword at Clarendon is resistance to over-presentation of the site. The setting of the palace site is paramount, both in its modern appeal and to the medieval mind. Therefore it was essential that visitors should be pedestrians, with no car parks or other facilities provided. This controls the numbers of visitors to the fragile site while allowing the monument to be appreciated in something like its original landscape context. Thus there are no paths, there is uneven ground and the site will never entirely easily accessible to all, though by selected provision of some steps major health and safety issues have been addressed.

Thus academic values are now considered via a quite different route than has traditionally been the case at Clarendon and it is the management and future care of the monument which have finally taken centre stage. One by-product of this reorientation of values has been the aligning of archaeology and history more closely with other countryside concerns. For example, a common area of interest between archaeologist and botanist has been the restoration of the chalk grassland across the precinct of the medieval palace. In addition, by removing trees and reintroducing grazing, scrub and coarse grass invasion should be minimalised, which will benefit birds, butterflies and moths.[53] Our interests have perceptibly widened to encompass wildlife and botany and the improved management of habitats.[54]

Another history

Finally, it should be stressed that archaeology, architecture and history are no longer the possessions of the academic minority. Filming for historical television programmes is almost an annual event at Clarendon,[55] while works of a more overtly fictional character have recreated aspects of Clarendon's historic and more recent past. These include Edward Rutherfurd's *Sarum* (1987), which gives an atmospheric account of the palace in the days of Edward I (1272–1307); Clarissa Reeve's *Roger of Clarendon* (1793) fictionalises the Black Prince's illegitimate son (c. 1355–1401); and, more recently, *The Possession of Delia Sutherland* (1993) exemplifies the work of Barbara Neil, the only owner to write fictional accounts using the modern Clarendon setting.

FIGURE 82.
The wine cellar,
looking south: (a)
above, Tancred
and Anne-Marie
Borenius arrive for the
excavations in 1933;
(b) *left* excavation
underway in the
1930s; (c) *opposite top*
the same view today.
(Photographs by John
Charlton and Fran
Halsall).

Aesthetic value

It is hard to imagine that kings and queens, and their successors in the Clarendon story, did not derive huge pleasure from their surroundings – and on the whole it was the longest-lived monarchs, including Henry III (65), Edward I (68) and Edward III (65), who loved Clarendon most. Christmas holidays, fauna and flora, sunshine, vistas, recreation, patronage of buildings and of landscape are all recognisable through the ages. Henry III's anger at officials' failure to complete works on time surely contrasted strongly with the enjoyment which he and his family derived from their commissions. Clarendon provided a setting for art, architecture and gardens under Henry III and Queen Eleanor of Provence, for example, and there is evidence, too, for novelty and experimentation. The painted grisaille window glass, dating to Henry III's reign, is among 'the earliest examples of English domestic glazing with painted decoration', its 'historical importance' far outweighing its 'intrinsic merit'.[56] Clarendon was a place for English kings to impress visiting foreign royalty and aristocrats.

As Chapter Five showed, values other than the purely aesthetic took precedence in the uncertain decades before 1660, when the estate was sold and many trees cut down before Monck, followed by Hyde, took possession. As a Tory, Peter Bathurst (d. 1748) was not then able to cash in on government office to create landscapes on the scale of those great Whig enterprises at Blenheim, Castle Howard, Chatsworth and Stowe. Like his cousin Henry Bathurst at Richings/Riskins (Bucks), Peter Bathurst's landscape kept him in touch with the practical necessities of land use (farming to fuel his finances) without being excessive in his landscape works. The aesthetics of his fashionable house, his geometric gardens, his lake and his avenues were planned, developed and enjoyed without disturbance, either from those who laboured on rented farms in the north of the estate or from travellers and diarists, who remain silent on the merits of Clarendon's eighteenth-century landscape. Privacy was clearly important and this was still the case in the nineteenth century, when Clarendon was never rated among the Wiltshire treasure houses. Quite possibly the Hervey-Bathursts simply never thought to encourage public access because this was the family's principal mansion, often being built and rebuilt. They preferred to build, develop the landscape and enjoy hosting and playing cricket.

Today some who have appreciated Clarendon's visual landscape have helped bring it to a wider public. Film crews have used the mansion as a set for film and television, most notably in Stanley Kubrick's candle-lit adaptation of Thackeray's *Barry Lyndon* (1975), the eighteenth-century tale of the rise and ruin of an Irish rogue who gambles and duels his way up the social ladder.[57] More locally, views are expressed by parish councils, district and county authorities, national agencies, specialist groups and interested members of the public, not to mention the owners. Much of their concern centres upon the woodland and the balance to be struck between its recreational and visual properties and economic necessity. A focus for many who live outside the estate is to guard against visual change. Conifer plantations, in particular, attract hostility,[58] and there is certainly a tendency to regard the park today as mere scenery. Taken to its extreme, this wish for enduring changelessness in the landscape is impractical and reveals serious misunderstandings about both historic and modern woodland management and landscape evolution in general. Reacting to this need for stability in the Clarendon landscape, however, the owners avoid clear felling wherever possible, adopting a shelterwood system in both conifer and broadleaf woodland; in other cases, a proportion of the trees are retained beyond their optimum rotation length in order to minimise the visual impact of felling. The views of all parties on woodland management are appraised in the cycle of meetings and documentation which shape future plans for the park.

Economic value

The third theme to be considered is economic value. During the medieval period many people worked at Clarendon, converting the woodland into a profitable and convenient resource on behalf of the king, supplying timber for construction and underwood for a variety of purposes as well as managing pasture for grazing animals. The income derived from the woodland was supplemented by fees paid into the Exchequer by stewards and other officers for entries into their posts, though by far the largest form of income from the royal forests were payments of fines.[59] In the late twelfth and early thirteenth centuries royal forests provided just less than one tenth of all the income received by the Exchequer, so Clarendon's economic importance in the Middle Ages cannot be doubted even though so much of its output was given away.

That the boundaries of the Clarendon estate remained almost static in the Middle Ages and survived down to the nineteenth century, encompassing approximately 4300 acres (1737 ha), illustrates that one of the main achievements of successive ownerships was keeping the estate intact. The value of the land was greater than the sum that could be raised by selling off its component farms. Because the estate remained intact this enables easy comparisons of sale prices and annual income and therefore some estimate to be made of its economic value. In 1660 Edward Hyde was given £20,000 by Charles II; the estate cost him £18,000 in 1664–5. In 1707 the Bathursts paid £24,000 for Clarendon. In 1900 the estate was sold for £80,000 and in 1919 for some £138,500. These crude figures, however, do little justice to the real economic worth of the estate, for the run-down state of Clarendon, as of other royal parks such as Windsor, set post-medieval owners a different agenda. They were not required to restore the estate, but they could use it, as Charles I tried to do and as Monck and Hyde did, as one element in a wider portfolio, to finance their lives elsewhere. These were new men who had risen through their personal abilities as generals and statesman. Initially they were busy London people, and in any case they had no suitable living accommodation at Clarendon. For Edward Hyde and his son Henry, Cornbury was the major project and Clarendon a financial workhorse they exploited to raise mortgages and capitalise on leases. As a result, these owners were to leave little impact on a landscape which now became a source of revenue, a neutral asset (perhaps one largely liberated from any cultural meaning) against which to borrow for other projects – for living and building expenses (as did the first earl Clarendon), for building expenses (the second earl), for marriage settlement (Peter Bathurst senior) and so on. It is fortunate for the landscape historian that this was so, for the grapplings of successive owners with assessments of the financial value of their inheritance or purchase generated documentation and maps, which are so important today for understanding how and when the park developed.[60] In many respects the park as it survives today is a product of benign neglect, that most gentle of management régimes, between c. 1660 and 1900.

At moments of financial crisis, most notably at the end of the nineteenth century, Clarendon was reduced to a legal entity – an estate, mapped and documented, rather than a living park and home. Parliaments ancient and modern have often seen it that way: the seventeenth-century parliament brought royal ownership to an end, nineteenth- and twentieth-century parliaments have

FIGURE 83.
The Antioch Chamber:
(a) *oppostite top* as it
was in the 1930s, once
excavation was halted;
(b) *opposite* invisible
under regenerating
woodland c. 1980;
(c) *above* after
clearance and with
consolidation of the
walls under way in
2004; (d) *right* the
Antioch chamber in
2006. (Photographs
(a) John Charlton, (b)
Annie Robinson, (c)
Tom Beaumont James,
(d) Fran Halsall)

battered owners with the demands of death duties.[61] For that reason death has been such a catalyst for change: the death of an individual king, such as Henry II, Henry III, or Edward III, who favoured Clarendon affected its fortunes; Henry Hyde sold up in 1707 as death approached; while Sir Frederick Hervey-Bathurst, too sick to manage, was obliged to hold on until his death in 1900. Conversely death also brings renewal, from the replanting of fields through the regeneration of coppices to the replanting of trees, while 'new blood' among owners has brought change and development – the building programmes of Henry III and Edward I in the thirteenth century, or those of FHHB and his mentor Sir William Fremantle following 1824.

This is not the place to make any analysis of the financial régime of the modern Clarendon Park estate, sold in 2006, as reported in *The Sunday Times*, for c. £30 million. We highlighted in Chapter Six the changing rural context in which the economy of the estate must now function. The major changes have occurred within the last thirty years as labour has been substituted by machinery, with a resulting decline in the agricultural workforce. Clarendon's major income is from agriculture and once the United Kingdom entered the European Community in 1973 so there were changes in farming practice at Clarendon in response to the Common Agricultural Policy. The economic matrix in which Clarendon functions today is still rapidly changing. The last decade has seen the phased reduction of support for output in favour of compensation payments based on areas of crops and the numbers of animals kept. In the future there is likely to be further emphasis upon environmental values, including rewards for archaeology, biodiversity and a greater reliance on renewable resources grown under more 'sustainable' conditions. Clarendon appears well placed, especially as there is to be increased support for the conservation of natural and cultural heritage, and preference given to landscapes judged to have local character and variety.[62] Heritage and economic values are drawing together.

Social value

The estate's owners and their managers today work within clear financial constraints but from the eighteenth century onwards the estate was more often a drain on family fortunes than a boon, and to compensate for losses there was a regular need for injections of capital from mortgages, the sale of land to the railway, advantageous marriages and other sources. If owners ever totalled up the economic value of their estate, they knew that money was only part of the equation. Perhaps as important was the social value conferred by ownership and title. At Clarendon these two things were only coincident for a short period during the second half of the seventeenth century, when Edward Hyde was earl of Clarendon. From the early eighteenth century onwards the Hydes retained the Clarendon title but no longer owned the estate. For the Bathursts and subsequent owners, social value was to be extracted in other ways. Most obviously, post-medieval owners engaged in establishment activities, from shared schooling (Etonians) to regiments (nationally, Guards; locally, Yeomanry), to being representatives in parliament. These biographical interests were occasionally written directly on the fabric of the landscape – the field name Mafeking and the room called Ladysmith at the mansion evoke the South African war of 1899–1902 (Figure 66).[63]

The crudest expression of the relationship between ownership and landscape occurred in 1710 when Peter Bathurst attempted to take the seat of Wilton and enter parliament, and threatened to withhold 'blue clay', or fuller's earth, from the park from the feltmakers of Wilton if he did not receive their votes.[64] More subtly, features of the landscape had for many years played a vital role in controlling access and the use of space to create a particular impression and so enhance social illusion. Medieval buildings and landscapes exuded intimidatory power and emphasised a physical gulf between royalty and the rest in which social distance was exaggerated rather than minimised. Likewise, access to the Bathurst mansion was funnelled down avenues and controlled by lodges; the social exclusivity of its occupants was underlined by their physical segregation. Thus when the Bathursts sought to portray their lives they did so by commissioning a drawing of the mansion, not the working parts of the estate to the north, and when county cartographers wrote the names of landowners it was the 'lodge' they indicated, not the wider park.[65]

If social value was centred on the mansion in the eighteenth century, then during the nineteenth and early twentieth century attempts were made to extend the privacy of that inner sanctum to the park as a whole. By this time the leisurely shooting of partridge and pheasant enjoyed by Peter Bathurst in the first half of the eighteenth century had become a more organised affair, with large numbers of birds being reared for the woodland cover. Where footpaths crossed the new Clarendon game coverts there was an inevitable clash. In an attempt to insulate the park the Bathursts diverted paths, locked gates and put up notices restricting access. The judge at the Wiltshire Assizes may have found the whole affair 'tedious', but the case struck at the heart of the social values that the Bathursts and Garton considered theirs by right. By contrast, in order to avert confrontation, the modern estate manager rarely takes decisions on access without wider consultation with interested parties outside the estate, local parish councils in particular, though care must be taken to ensure that privacy and the agricultural and sporting interests of the estate are maintained. Several public footpaths run through the park, most notably the Clarendon Way, and ride widening and edge management are routinely required. Nevertheless, there have been several significant concessions made in recent years to allow walkers access along 'permissive' routes, one of them looping through the ruins of the medieval palace.

Social value is emphasised in other ways. The 1919 sale catalogue floodlights provision for entertaining and cooking: sixteen dozen pheasant pattern 'meat and pudding' plates among much else besides, while in 1925 there was a full range of kitchen equipment for baking, boiling, poaching, roasting and stewing, and much specialised equipment for carving ham, icing, the making of jellies and soufflés, and so on.[66] What is striking about the comparison between palace and mansion kitchens is how much remained in common between the two so far as the central issues of bread, meat and fish consumption were concerned, and in the provision of specialised items such as wine glasses and knives. The ingredients of these 'food events' remained strikingly similar, though much of course changed over time, as betokened by the potato masher and the aluminium coffee pot in the kitchens.

Viewed in a more anthropological fashion, the ownership of a large estate conferred the privilege of several different types of 'exchange'. It could generate credit, as we have seen, and it could generate profit in the form of rent or commercial trade, usually in dairy products or cereal crops. But there is another type of exchange which does not involve money directly and which has an important social value: gift-giving. At Clarendon this might have taken several forms. Timbers used in important new buildings, for example, enhanced royal status and formally marked major construction projects like Salisbury Cathedral with the monarch's approval and charisma. The giving of plants, dogs, horses and particularly venison and pheasant created a kind of debt obligation for those in service, not to mention a sense of reward, while affirming shared social status for members of the élite.[67] Gift-giving appears to involve no financial sacrifice on the part of the owner but it is not necessarily done because the owner cannot afford a more substantial gift. Instead its value is social; such gifts pass between people (owner and male heads of households normally) already bound in other ways and they serve to underwrite social divisions and hierarchies over many generations.

Finally, forest and park also had legal meaning. It represented that land over which the king had hunting rights and it was subject to special laws which could be a source of conflict, both because laws might be unpopular and were disputed, and because they blanketed large tracts of apparently useful arable land. Thus the forest demonstrated power over landscape, a message which became stronger as woodland settings disappeared across much of the landscape in the thirteenth century. It is estimated that by 1334 the area of royal forest had shrunk to about two-thirds of its extent in 1250, with some jurisdiction disappearing altogether.[68] Owning forest and woodland was a privilege, an exception, implying control over and unlimited access to natural resources. As the Middle Ages advanced so forest law was less strictly applied, but within the park a greater degree of enforcement was possible.[69]

Recreational value

These academic, aesthetic, economic and social values are linked by a fifth theme: recreational value. The origins of the deer park and medieval hunting have been discussed in some detail in Chapter Three and were the core of the park's activities. Stable hunting was complemented by the paddock course, the latter probably marked out in the sixteenth century. The openwork of the surviving Standing at Chingford, Essex, of 1543, has much in common with Tudor and Jacobean tournament standings: designed to be hung with rich tapestries when in use, but otherwise left as a shell. At tournaments and at paddock coursing, whether at Hampton Court or Clarendon, royalty were determined to be seen prominently in their extravagantly appointed temporary buildings.[70]

If the principal object of estate management in the nineteenth century was 'a life of leisure with freedom to pursue occupations that were not dictated by the compulsions of economic necessity',[71] then that life of leisure at Clarendon continued to revolve around hunting. In this book we have seen evidence for other outdoor sports, among them archery, cricket, croquet, swimming and tennis (with golf and polo off-site), as well as billiards, cards, dancing, the gramophone and music indoors, but the combination of military and sporting threads forms a continuum which runs through the whole historic period, shading from the shooting of deer under medieval warrior kings into 'military' landscapes under the soldier owners and their tenants during the eighteenth, nineteenth and twentieth centuries. Until 1831 shooting was restricted by law to those with land to the value of at least £100 per year, and only in 1881 could tenants destroy rabbits and hares without the permission of their landlord; thus the law dictated who could and could not enjoy the recreation of shooting.[72] It is shooting and hunting which provide an important link between owners and their landscape, as well as friends and visiting dignitaries. These are activities for small groups in large landscapes, so they reinforced social value as well as bringing economic benefits.

Symbolic value

By this point it should be plain that to construe medieval and post-medieval landscapes, fauna and flora, as geared wholly to matters of utility and economy is a misrepresentation; if the full multiplicity of meanings is to be understood, the landscape must be viewed in the context of other images with which it was intimately associated in the eye of its beholders. Our sixth and final theme in this chapter, therefore, is symbolic value. For the medieval period there are two main conceptual themes: woodland and the hunt. Here we consider each in turn.

Woodland
Richard Fitz Nigel's *Dialogus de Scaccario*, written in 1176–77, evokes the royal use of woodland, park and palace:

> It is in the forest too that 'King's chambers' are, and their chief delights. For they come there, laying aside their cares now and then, to hunt, as a rest and recreation. It is there that they can put from them the anxious turmoil native to a court, and take a little breath in the free air of nature.[73]

As a royal palace Clarendon provided a prime example of what it seems medieval kings thought of as a 'pleasure dome'; Fitz Nigel undoubtedly had

Henry II in mind when he wrote. What he chose to emphasise was the physical attraction of the 'chambers' in the forest as the focus of kingly pleasure. This image is overwhelmingly a positive one and had corresponding resonances in contemporary literature, where the forest is the setting for many of the quests of chivalric romance. In the twelfth-century Tristan romances, for example, lovers are exiled to the forest, and in the Grail romances the forest is seen as a symbol of the human need for regeneration, while the castle or palace is the place from which the hero begins the quest and to which he ultimately returns.[74]

In Becket's day the picture of a palace on the hill, framed from the road below against a backdrop of woodland and the sky, is a realistic one. At that time it would have taken under half an hour for a group of horsemen to reach the gates of the palace precinct from the outer boundary of the park, longer if travelling with a burdened cart or 'chariot' bearing royalty; time enough in either case to absorb the surroundings. All was birdsong and rustling leaves until within earshot of the hive of activity at the palace. If riding through the woodland from Pitton the precinct wall would appear suddenly in front of the visitor and the opening gate would reveal unexpectedly large buildings. For visitors to the palace, their journey through the landscape had an active part to play in creating a particular atmosphere and mood. We think of the palace's remoteness, its isolation, of its proximity to Nature, of the relevance of that juxtaposition in a religious context and of the literary qualities of the forest as a place of conversion.

This quality of 'separateness' is one which was understood by Fitz Nigel and it is often echoed in the literary presentation of lonely forest characters. A generation before Fitz Nigel, Geoffrey of Monmouth (d. 1154) situated his Merlin in exile in the forest 'glad to be hidden beneath the ash trees'. Merlin pleads:

> Before the other buildings build me a remote one to which you will give seventy doors and as many windows, through which I may see fire-breathing Phoebus with Venus, and watch by night the stars wheeling in the firmament; and they will teach me about the future of the nation.[75]

This building reflects Merlin's wish to stay close to nature[76] and we are reminded of the darkness of the forest. The Romanesque palace at Clarendon provided only limited pools of light in a pitch-black night world but it was a positive symbol, a place from which to observe Nature at night and so reveal the workings of God.[77]

The interior of the palace provided a canvas to develop related themes and symbols. Sadly, there is little to say of the twelfth-century interiors but of the thirteenth-century palace of Henry III there is more detail (Figure 84). The upper floor of his chamber, beyond the east end of the Great Hall, had a green wainscot spotted with gold stars like the ones still extant in the Guardian Angels' chapel at Winchester Cathedral (Figure 34).[78] There has been debate about what these symbols might represent; they may be the moon and stars,

FIGURE 84. Iconography of the palace in the reign of Henry III. (Drawn by Alejandra Gutiérrez)

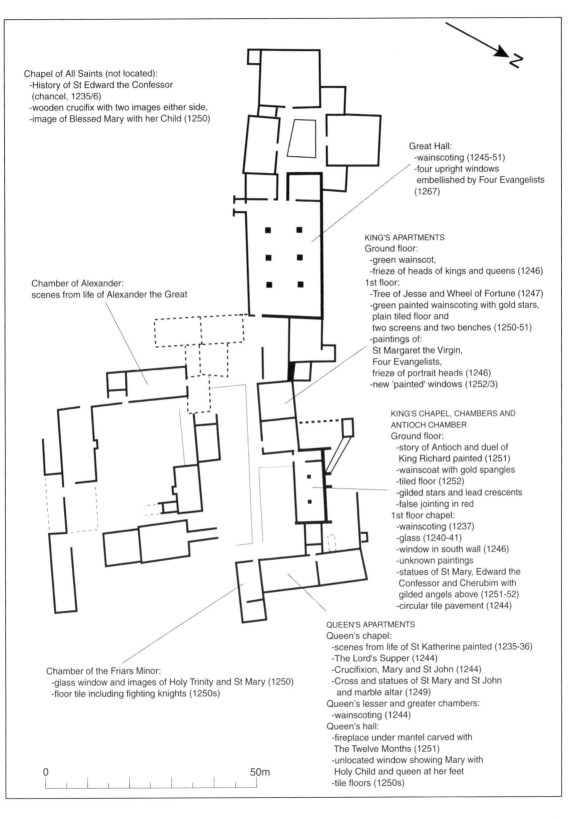

or sun and moon, above an earth clothed in green, and recent work has suggested that the crescents might date to earlier Romanesque decorative schemes (for examples, see Figure 29).[79] The layers of potential meanings and the varying locations of the finds of stars and crescents hint at a complex web of meaning which we do not as yet fully grasp. In a general sense, however, this decorative scheme served to emphasise the proximity of Nature and perhaps the dominance of sun and moon in the cosmos, both themes to which the location of Clarendon was well suited.

Religious themes also featured regularly in decorative schemes. Around 1250, window glass in the Queen's chambers contained an image of the Queen praying to the Virgin and Child.[80] The Queen's chapel, at the southern end of her chamber, was dedicated to St Katherine and had scenes from her life painted on the walls.[81] Eleanor of Provence, Henry III's queen, may have identified particularly with these two female images.[82] Whether these scenes were embellished with local motifs cannot now be known, but other religious themes echoed Clarendon's woodland setting. Among the Marian imagery, for example, was the Tree of Jesse, which conventionally shows a recumbent Jesse with a tree growing from his side and in its branches various kings and prophets; at the apex is the Virgin Mary and the infant Jesus.[83] Among the other wall paintings commissioned by Henry III for his chambers were the Four Evangelists, Matthew, Mark, Luke and John, usually differentiated by their symbols, a man, lion, calf and eagle respectively. Four windows in the Great Hall were embellished with the same subjects. There were scenes from the life of St Margaret of Antioch, among the most venerated female saints, who is usually depicted emerging from the dragon which is said to have swallowed her and from whose bowels she escaped unharmed – hence her adoption as the patron saint of women in childbirth.[84] Curiously, this image, usually associated with women patrons, was painted in the King's Chambers rather than the Queen's,[85] presumably echoing the position of the Antioch Chamber below as well as the symbolism of the woodland setting, with its connotations of life-cycle rituals. More directly, in 1251 the Queen's new fireplace had the twelve months of the year carved over the mantel (Figure 25).[86]

As a counterpoint to the positive natural and religious associations of palace and park there was an alternative, grimmer view of the medieval forest which emphasised it as a place of darkness and disorder, a wild place with 'resonances of exile, escape, prophecy, penance, vision and temptation'.[87] In the late fourteenth-century *Sir Gawain and the Green Knight*, a contrast is made between the safety of the court and the danger of the landscape beyond, an opposition between inside and outside worlds. At Clarendon any fear of what danger might lurk there was more imagined than real. It is hard to imagine that the deer park was ever a dangerous place physically, even if, as Becket discovered, it could be very dangerous politically, and it was even more safe after the park ditch and bank were dug. The park was a sanitised forest. There were strangers, thieves and even murderers lurking in the forest, as the Conqueror's sons Richard and Rufus had discovered, but of such wickedness at Clarendon little reaches us through documents and, in the historic period, nothing at all through archaeology. Poachers and illegal wood cutters were perhaps more likely at Clarendon: though while forest law and adequate food supplies prevailed they too seem to have been kept mostly at bay.[88]

Within the precinct was a different world in which nature was entirely controlled, the perimeter wall marking an important symbolic divide. Inside was a tamed forest,[89] quite literally since wild plants were probably taken from the woodlands into the gardens, where there was no reason to fear attack or the possibility of becoming lost; outside were dark brooding trees. Archaeological, topographical and documentary evidence from Clarendon combine to suggest that the precinct housed one large and many smaller gardens by 1250. Some appear to have been royal and exclusive; archaeology shows us they were walled, with restricted access, offering respite from the communal hall. Two gardens – the Garden of Eden and the Garden of Gethsemane – are familiar in medieval iconography, and as the Gothic era proceeded these became known to ordinary people through window-decoration and wall paintings, and to the élite through books of hours. The idea of the garden as a place of paradise, a refuge where all the senses are indulged privately, is one commonly alluded to in medieval romances.[90] In *Cligés* (c. 1180), by Chrétien de Troyes, the lovers Fenice and Cligés have a walled garden:

> Fenice passed out through the door into the garden … In the middle stood a grafted tree, loaded with blossoms and leaves … beneath the tree the turf is very pleasant and fine … And the garden is enclosed about with a high wall connected with the tower.[91]

Whether the flowers in the gardens at Clarendon were grown for their symbolism is unknown. Roses, red and white, quite apart from their later political symbolism in England, could signify love/martyrdom and purity and were employed in panel paintings of Mary and Christ, as well as St Katherine.[92] Such allusions were well understood and combined in contemporary wall paintings or glazing schemes. It is significant that when, in 1268, Henry III ordered work to be done in the Queen's herber at Guildford, he arranged the work through his court painter, William Florentyn.[93] Life and art were entwined in decorative schemes.

Who was aware of these allusions? While we make no case here for a purely ideological reading of the Clarendon landscape at any stage in its evolution, élite visitors were well aware of literary allusions and romances. The Arthurian enthusiasms of Henry III's son Edward I included his attendance with Queen Eleanor at the reopening of the supposed tomb of Arthur and Guinevere at Glastonbury Abbey in 1278, and the famous dinner at Winchester in 1290, for which it is possible that the surviving Round Table, now hanging in the thirteenth-century hall there, was made.[94] Through readings and performances of poems and texts the deeds of kings, past and present, were associated with mythical heroes. This familiarity continued in the fourteenth century in the reign of Edward III, who, early in his reign, received gifts replete with the romance iconography of Roland and Oliver, Gawain and Lancelot, such as a ewer given to him by Queen Philippa.[95] Among the possessions belonging to Edward II's French widow, the Queen Isabella, on her death in 1358, were a large Arthurian text as well as a copy of *Tristan and Isolde*.[96] An awareness of these romances reinforced the monarchy's image as chivalric heroes, and could provide political advantage. Objects, together with information on book ownership and panel painting, give a clear impression of contemporary taste and patronage and reveal 'the widespread interest in and knowledge of literature of this [romance] kind'.[97]

Trees and woodland also took on cultural significance and symbolic meaning in the post-medieval period and continue to do so today. During and after the Civil War the cutting of trees was linked with republican politics and portrayed in opposition to planting and the restoration of the king. Oaks were a patriotic emblem, a symbol of strength, durability and stability – even of safety for the fleeing Charles II.[98] Later, in the early eighteenth century, the Bathursts' new park towards the south of the estate was established in an area already sprinkled with oak trees.[99] The oak trees in the avenues leading to the mansion, however, were probably planted contemporaneously with the building of the mansion, and the tidiness and organisation of these plantings exemplify the military of that date who created the British Empire. As we saw in Chapter Six, their planting schemes drew on flora from all over the globe. These were a 'side effect and, indeed, a symbol of imperial power' as the Empire spread across the world.[100] Then, old soldiers could dominate the world in miniature in their own gardens with global plantings; today, a global economy and democratised politics have once again changed the way in which woodland is regarded. Woodmanship has been replaced by forestry, an economic vision based largely upon coniferous plantations, not upon the oak. Even so, the issue of identity remains closely bound up with modern attitudes. Conifers are said to lack the individuality of oaks; they can be seen as foreign intruders and even tap into contemporary ethnic concerns.[101]

The hunt

Developments in hunting went hand in hand with those in tournaments: both allowed the practice and display of riding – part physical virtuosity, part military training – and through a demonstration of excellence gave the opportunity for prestige to be earned by a successful hunter. Aesthetically too, in colours and textiles, speed and form, there must have been much to please the eye and ear. At a social level, part of the purpose of both activities was to extrude hierarchies and status onto a wider stage beyond the palace precinct. Merely participating had an ennobling effect but to do so successfully required proficiency in a set of highly formalised procedures.

Certainly martial imagery was not out of place inside the palace.[102] Beneath Henry III's chapel was the Antioch Chamber with its green wainscoting with gold stars, also decorated in 1251–2 with the History of Antioch and the Combat of King Richard and Saladin (Figure 84).[103] The combat refers to the Third

Crusade in which Richard I took part, ending with the reconquest of Acre (1191), though not of Jerusalem itself, and the imposition on Saladin (1137–1193) of a treaty guaranteeing freedom of pilgrimage. Richard and Saladin did not meet at Antioch, suggesting that there were two different scenes, or that what the king requested was unhistorical. The thirteenth-century 'Richard and Saladin' image found on tiles at Clarendon was revived a century later during 'costume' jousts for Edward III (Figure 85). Thus the 'knights in combat' theme on inlaid tiles may have been a general literary cue, rather than being a specific historical reference.

At first sight it is puzzling that we find no specific references to tournaments at Clarendon. But it may have been the case from the twelfth to the seventeenth century that there was no need here for the mock tournament to test that increasingly essential element of chivalry, 'prowess', as the park provided the real thing. Buck-hunting genuinely tested people's ability, whether visiting kings, nobles or others, to ride and slaughter; moreover, this took place in a grand setting, overseen by royalty and visiting ladies, which had the facilities to prepare and eat the prey. The plastic complexities of the tournament might be appropriate for an urban setting or for a traditional, small, deer park: Clarendon was neither of these.

Current knowledge of medieval hunting, and the distinctions between open-country stag-hunting and the pursuit in the park of fallow bucks and does, is imperfect. Clarendon was also highly unusual because of its size: it was a park, but also a chase, perhaps sufficiently large for bucks either to be pursued across the open launds, or driven at armed hunters. The structure listed in 1650 as the 'Standing', may therefore have originated as a grandstand where kings and others stood and towards which deer were driven across the park, later being developed as an element in a formalised course. In either case much of the etiquette was shared, whether stags or bucks were the quarry. The giving of commands would mark out the senior roles of hunts-men, reinforcing status, as did various traditions: one such was that the right forefoot of the game be presented to the most eminent person at the hunt, another that the head should be reserved.[104] The assembly of the participants had much in common with theatre, with particular conventions and an eti-quette and a terminology to be learnt. Hunting manuals, such as George Turbevile's *The Noble Art of Venerie or Hunting* (1576), coming within a year or so of the great Elizabethan hunt at Clarendon, provided exclusive termi-nology and correct forms of language, address and procedure. For example, after the kill, special preparations for the ride home might require the party to ride two by two bearing the deer in the correct order of body parts, head first, then breast, legs and ribs and hide last. The hunters sounded a fanfare as they approached the 'hall', the venison was dragged onto the floor of the hall and a slice held up for the household to cheer.[105] The story of a hunt like this is used by Chrétien de Troyes and his successors to add a notion of adventure, of quest, in literature;[106] it can act as a metaphor for the search for individual destiny, drawing characters deep into a specific landscape setting, woodland, removing them from the conventions of court and regal process, taking them on a wondrous adventure in which the hero is led away from the norms of medieval society into another world in which anything goes. Thus the chase acts as a metaphor for the tragic fall of a noble victim; the wounded deer a trope for lost maidenhood.[107]

At Clarendon, we suggest that the medieval hunt carried meaning at a number of different levels. First, at a spatial level, it moulded circulation pat-terns around the centrally located palace, the place from which hunters left early in the morning and to which they returned at the end of the day. The palace provided the ideal platform from which to view the drama of the hunt underway in the valley below. If bow and stable hunting was used for fallow deer at Clarendon, then stands to the north of the woods would have provided the ideal location for royal bowmen as the deer were driven towards them by beaters, horsemen and dogs. Alternatively, the drive might have taken place down the valley. With beaters positioned along the sides of the valley this would have channelled the quarry towards archers stationed immediately below the palace or below Fussell's Lodge, roughly at the location of the later 'grandstand'. Curiously, it is an almost identical topographical situation which is described in the fourteenth-century poem *Sir Gawain and the Green Knight*, in which Sir Bertilak undertakes a bow and stable hunt:

> Before the first beam of the sunshine brightened the earth
> He and his knights were in the saddle, high on their horses …
> The wild beasts quivered at the cry of the questing hounds;
> Deer ran through the dale, distracted by fear,
> Hastened up the high slopes, but hotly were met
> By stout cries of the stable, staying their flight.
> The hinds were held in the valley and hey! and ware!,

The does driven with din to the depth of the dale.
Then shimmering arrows slipped from the bowstring, and slanted,
Winging their way from every tree in the wood.
Their broad heads pierced the bonny flanks of brown;
The deer brayed and bled, as on the banks they died.

This passage imagines a valley lined by beaters, the 'stable', with does, separated from bucks, driven towards the archers.[108] Our hero is among those on horseback driving the deer with the 'brachets' (perhaps spaniel-like dogs) and the hunting horns, and has given orders that stags and bucks be released before they reach the archers.[109] In a Clarendon setting, this kind of hunting provided greater scope for entertainment simply by virtue of the fact that it was highly visible, controlled and predictable, and offered a variety of roles to the visitor, even if the true huntsman might prefer to be after the hart in the classic chase. It also suggests an awareness of the Clarendon hill and valley terrain was as important then as it is today and that modern pheasant drives may have far more in common with medieval hunting than might be thought. It is the same disposition of woodland, open land and breaks of slope which attracts the shoot to some of these parts of the estate today.

Second, at a social level, the hunt provided communal, shared experience, though etiquette probably enforced segregation between participants of different status and underlined differences, excluding those of lower rank through the complexities of its terminology and procedure. And third, at a symbolic level, any understanding of the hunt would depend upon education and, in particular, the knowledge of literature. Even at a physical level the mere existence of this huge park and its palace, remote from London and yet undefended, sent out a message emphasising the control that the monarchy had over the realm of England – possibly demonstrated to two visiting prisoner-kings in 1357 by their conqueror.

In this section we have focused on the hunting of deer because this was the main activity undertaken within the medieval park. There is less evidence for other forms of hunting with birds, for example, though they certainly featured here. Hunting birds appear, too, in romance literature. In Chrétien de Troyes's *Erec*, there are hawking competitions, knights and ladies tend falcons; the hawk is an integral part of the 'love chase'. In the Tristan romances, a woman's elegance may be compared with the falcon's refined grace,[110] but we know of no specific images at Clarendon which echoed this activity other than the archaeological evidence of hawk, eagle and dogs. However, the decorative schemes in the palace were certainly appropriate to a woodland retreat: the green and brown of the glazed tiles, both floor and roof, and more especially the foliage in the sculpture, along with motifs such as addorsed birds.[111] Similarly, we have encouraged the suggestion that the location of the Clarendon rabbit warren was carefully chosen to be visible on the same north-facing scarp as the palace. This seems inconveniently sited for hunting and riding and there seems little reason for its placing there other than to

FIGURE 86.
The wheel of fortune
from Rochester
Cathedral, c. 1270.
(Borenius and Tristram
1927, no. 38; redrawn
by Alejandra Gutiérrez)

be seen. Medieval rabbit warrens are associated with high-status sites across Europe and were linked with clothing and landownership, as well as having an erotic significance. These were also vulnerable creatures which required care, so implying benevolence.[112]

Not all the imagery within the medieval palace directly reflected the Clarendon natural environment. Among the decorative schemes which Henry III had painted in 1247 was a Wheel of Fortune, in which the female figure of Fortune turns a wheel with figures on the rim representing the future king ('I shall reign'; 9 o'clock), the present king at the summit ('I reign'; 12 o'clock), the once king ('I have reigned'; 3 o'clock) and the lost king ('I have no kingdom'; 6 o'clock). The last is usually shown being thrown from the wheel or otherwise suffering, as at Rochester Cathedral (Figure 86). Hagiographic images, too, are common to other royal palaces of Henry III. In 'the king's lower chambers', probably undercrofts below his principal suite, Henry III had the wainscot painted green in 1246, and in 1251 similar green wainscoting, with gold spangles (*scintillis*), was supplied to the adjacent Antioch Chamber.[113] Nearby, the king's new chapel, built in 1234–7, had gilded angels and images of St Mary and Edward and circular tile paving in banded rings of green and yellow tiles.[114] The story of St Edward the Confessor also appeared in the chancel of the chapel dedicated to All Saints, together with a wooden image of the same saint, while in 1235–6 the Majesty of Our Lord was painted in the nave.[115] St Edward the Confessor enjoyed a substantial cult in medieval England and was associated with piety and devotion, and was the patron saint of England in Henry III's reign.[116] In another chamber the walls were painted with scenes from the life of Alexander the Great,[117] a popular figure in medieval Romance and one of the classical heroes of Dante's *Inferno* a century later.

Other evidence of Henry III's artistic inspirations and interests survives at Westminster Abbey and can also be partly reconstructed for the Painted Chamber at the Palace of Westminster.[118] This chamber was destroyed by fire in 1834, though not before watercolour copies of the wall paintings had been made. From these, as well as texts and other images such as the royal Great Seal, it has been argued that images of St Edward the Confessor are sufficiently commonplace during Henry's reign to begin to identify a clear pattern in which the king discloses that he views himself as the successor to the sainted Anglo-Saxon ruler.[119] The thinking was allegorical and intended to strengthen Henry's English royal lineage. Yet at Clarendon the mood is not entirely contemplative; the wider range of images of Alexander, Antioch and Richard I suggest past heroic deeds. Clarendon was one site at which generous patronage could help to establish the notion of some kind of Golden Age reborn. This 'character of self-address', as it has been referred to by one writer,[120] is an identifiable characteristic of the English royal court – images of court designed for the court by the court, without the wider populace in mind. Clarendon, cut off from medieval society and cocooned in its own landscape, was a place in which the past was remembered, an aid to constructing a past in order to substantiate claims for the future. But if this was the case then the vision did not last, at Clarendon at least, for in the years of Henry's struggle with the barons the buildings seemed to have become run down and, according to the survey for Edward I after Henry died, had not been returned to pristine condition in the last golden years of the old king's reign between 1266 and 1272. Perhaps for later Plantagenets, who visited more infrequently, Clarendon was less adequate for the promotion of a new royal mythology based by now on new, more active, ancient and therefore manipulable heroes like King Arthur. Edward I was more tempted by British (rather than English) mythology, and employed new visual reference points and foundation myths inclusive of both Wales and Scotland as he concentrated on emulating the kings of France, who had subdued and brought their outlying provinces into the royal fold.[121] Edward III found defence the best form of attack and engaged the French head on in a struggle for supremacy from 1337, using Clarendon as an occasional retreat in bad times, such as during the plague, and good times, according to the tradition of the hunting party with David II and John II in 1357. His successors kept the palace in order and made peripheral additions, so that when the Tudors abandoned the draughty, remote, old palace after 1485, there was a wealth of building material to be carted away; but the life of the palace was over.

CHAPTER EIGHT

Time and Landscape

This final chapter provides a critical overview of our research on Clarendon and identifies the major changes in the landscape from prehistory to the present day. Under a series of thematic headings, we consider settlement, land use and infrastructure as well as the diverse and sometimes hidden ways in which the park has been exploited. It is apparent that there have been long periods of stability punctuated by dramatic shifts in the historical trajectory of the whole study area. In particular, we emphasise the importance of royal ownership during the Middle Ages in determining the social and economic shape of Clarendon down to the present day.

Overview

This volume results from the application of a wide range of techniques. Analysis of maps and documents has led us to previously unseen archives and sources, including family records, antiquarian accounts and national registers. Of particular importance from the archaeological fieldwork are the results of recent fieldwalking, geophysics and standing building surveys, as well the specialist reports on the artefacts recovered from the removal of spoil heaps left behind by previous excavators. All these have contributed to an interdisciplinary study of Clarendon which provides as clear and detailed a picture of its various landscape components as is presently possible.

Four achievements in particular are noteworthy. The first is to have gathered disparate accounts into a single integrated archaeological and historical analysis. The second is to have applied modern fieldwork methods to the park landscape; and the third is to have drawn previous research on the medieval palace site not only *outwards* into its landscape context but also *across* a much wider chronology, from prehistory to the present day. Blocks of woodland, pasture and arable have been mapped, buildings and routes placed in their correct locations and alignments, flora and fauna are reconstructed in our mind's eye to give a secure impression of medieval and later colour and landforms, sounds and vistas, and of how earlier landscapes and their buildings looked and worked. Finally, as we have seen in Chapter Seven, the geographical and natural resources of the park are not merely a background with a passive role. The economics of a large estate like Clarendon are vital, of course, but we must also press home the importance of hidden agencies. Woodland and hunting, for example, form the critical link between environment, on the one hand, and culture, on the other. A mere descriptive digest, the mapping and phasing of landscape features, is not an end in itself for us.

There are, however, weaknesses in our data set, most glaringly the absence of any detailed account of vegetation history in prehistory; a lack of appreciation of pre-medieval economy or diet; the inadequacy of the archaeological record for the late Saxon period, and for post-medieval material culture outside the palace site, an inability to link documented seventeenth-century houses in the park with standing buildings and earthworks; and the lack of an all-embracing ecological appraisal. All these concerns and more would have to be addressed before this account could be thought comprehensive.

With these caveats in mind, the final challenge is to stand back and consider the major lines of development in the Clarendon landscape, to seek out and explain the disruptions, innovations and continuity which have taken place over time. This can be best done from the perspective of three different time scales; geographical time, measured in centuries and millennia; social time, up to a couple of generations; and individual time, the specific moment.[1]

Geographical time

This, the longest of our time frames, can be adduced in this Clarendon study through archaeological techniques, and particularly results from fieldwalking, as well as from the study of documents and maps. Four major themes in particular can be tracked over extended periods within the study area. They are continuity of *settlement, land use and infrastucture*; exploitation of the park for *pleasure*; *mentalities*; and *deep historical memory*.

Settlement, land use and infrastructure

In broad terms this work has revealed the chronology and location of settlement and provides superficial data on craft production, trade (mainly in pottery, the commonest artefact type, and in woodland products) and the treatment of the dead. Viewed on this long timescale it is clear that population density grows steadily from the Neolithic through to the end of the Roman period, with a possible break for perhaps two centuries in the middle Iron Age. Continuity of occupation cannot be proven conclusively at any pre-medieval Clarendon site but it is certainly the case that settlements and ritual activity recur in the same vicinity. Though vegetation changed in response to climate and human actions, topography, water and land use resources continued to enhance the opportunities for settlement in certain locations. In this and in all other characteristics of the archaeological record, pre-medieval Clarendon shares its defining features with the surrounding Wessex countryside. By the late Saxon period Clarendon was archaeologically invisible; we believe, though we cannot yet demonstrate, that the population had dwindled and dislocated. This is the period of change, of innovation, between about AD 700 and 900, when a special status for the landscape set in train the creation of specific land uses and building complexes dedicated to hunting and to sport. Within the broadest parameters of demography, settlement location, land use and function, Clarendon has remained unchanged since then. Seen on this timescale, the events of history are diminished. To take one example, continuity through historic periods can be exemplified by one land use in particular – woodland. While in its detail woodland management has evolved, the fundamental landscape characteristic of the estate, the one which forms a part of the everyday experience of the visitor or the resident today, is the presence of trees. A monumental millennium sculpture on the edge of woodland at Clarendon celebrates this today. Trees are well adapted to the specific geology and soil type at the heart of the estate and, as we have seen, they can be more than simply an economic resource.

Pleasure

This brings us to the second of our major themes which can be traced over the long term during medieval and later life at Clarendon. Pleasure is taken in landscapes and vistas, oaks and coppices, in buildings and furnishings, in entertainment, food and sport. Clarendon was and remains a visual feast and a sporting landscape.

Of course, each monarch enjoyed Clarendon in a slightly different way. If Henry II and Edward III were manly heroes who loved physical activity and valued Clarendon for that, Henry III and Richard II were happily married monarchs with more aesthetic tastes, the former and his wife especially enjoying the decoration and beautification of the royal apartments and gardens for their special pleasure, the latter adding a dancing room. Queen Elizabeth, James I and Anne of Denmark all came hunting here. The works carried out here in the early years of James I echoed the punctilious delight expressed 250 years earlier by Henry III. For post-medieval owners the pleasures were to an extent similar, if never on the same extraordinary scale. Hunting and shooting, with their sharp social divisions and leisurely pace, as well as the accommodation and dining offered at the mansion, have been enjoyed by every owner since before 1700, and remain to this day key elements in the survival strategy for Clarendon Park.

Mentalities

A third product of Clarendon's medieval royal status and its continuing function as a country estate after the mid-seventeenth century might be thought to be a well-differentiated and clearly structured social and economic hierarchy, with owners at the top and their employees beneath, but such an analysis has never been entirely satisfactory. While there is today one community at Clarendon tied, in one fashion or another, to the maintenance of the estate, just as there has been since late Saxon times, there is also another constituency of houses rented to individuals whose livelihood does not depend on the estate. This is nothing new, and was a feature of the park in the later Middle Ages – the clergy, for example, occupied buildings at the palace – but manifests itself most clearly in the naming during the Interregnum of houses and farms after their owners or occupiers – Fussell, Ludlow and so on. Identification of these people is a ripple in the pool of late Renaissance individualism but it is a burst of individuality which is then fossilised by the coming of the Bathursts in the early eighteenth century, since when naming of buildings and farms after individuals declines sharply.

Clarendon differs from nearly all other communities in that it is not derived from the common currency, parish or village. It was designated as a civil parish only in 1858, and has not, since the Middle Ages, when its palace chapels variously served spiritual needs of owners, staff and visitors, had a church or chapel within its bounds. The palace was described as a 'towne' in the late fifteenth century, but soon afterwards that great complex vanished, leaving a focal hole which has remained ever since, only partly filled by the emergence of lodge and mansion from the late seventeenth century. The park's medieval status as demesne land in which the occupants served the sporting purposes of the royal household was highly exceptional and it was an identity not easily shrugged off. The park retained its vestigial political meanings right through to its final moments of royal ownership. After the demise of the palace and the coming of the Reformation Clarendon fell into various parishes, recorded in 1650–1; Alderbury, Laverstock, Pitton and St Martin's Salisbury, and, a relic of its royal past, 'part thereof in no parish but relating to the Lady Church of Sarum'.[2] This varied parochial affiliation is clearly seen in the Protestant wills of the residents at Clarendon in the seventeenth century, so that in 1625 John Fussell asks merely to be buried in the parish church of the parish where 'I shall decease', a wish which betrays both perceived social status (to be buried inside the church) and a lack of any clear loyalty to a local church.[3] Since then, with the notable exception of a single Protestant flourish in the mid-nineteenth century with the erection of the memorial at the palace site, religion has taken a back seat: owners have commissioned no chapels on the estate nor religious iconography within the mansion. The Christie-Millers have established their own burial ground within the estate, the first burials at Clarendon in the Christian era since Roman Christianity in the fourth century AD. In this the Church has conceded a right previously jealously guarded and certainly not generally available.

The Clarendon community, then, has long been diverse in its parochial affiliations and never wholly cohesive in any sense, though ultimately all the residents on the estate relate to the central household in one form or another, even if they are only tied by rental agreements. They cannot, for example, expect to express their wealth or status exactly as they might wish, especially in as far as changes to building stock are concerned. This element of centrality, together with shared spaces and activities, has fostered the growth of a civic sense of community and an interdependence among families who live on the estate today, and we consider this cohesiveness to have been an enduring long-term feature of life at Clarendon.

Deep historical memory

The fourth binding tie is the sense of deep historical memory. Today there are lineages of gamekeepers, for example, and lineages of house occupants, though these stretch back in the memory no more than a hundred years at most. Cycles of family and children in each individual household have always been of closer concern. However, more enduring than any of these is the palace site and what that has represented, and continues to represent, for owners, inhabitants and visitors. The collective focus of that memory is not archaeology at all but the association of that specific location with the historical events enacted there and the individuals who were present at the time. In particular, the Becket/Clarendon connection swithers between evidence and fantasy. Becket was there in 1164 at the sealing of the Constitutions of Clarendon, but beyond that little is certain. His murder in 1170 was the most-written-about event in the Middle Ages, bringing archbishop and king, their story and Clarendon, to the widest national and international audience. Not surprisingly, powerful local legends associated with Becket have grown up, and his name is attached to several local landmarks: St Thomas's Bridge, St Thomas Becket's well and St Thomas Becket's Cross near Clarendon Corner; and also church and chapel dedications, such as St Thomas's Salisbury, and the nearby Gomeldon chapel. Among the more persistent stories, and one which can be traced back at least as far as the seventeenth century, is that of a 'wonderful' path taken by Becket between Winterbourne and Clarendon which remained etched into the landscape no matter the crop or the season.[4] The Becket tradition was given added dynamism in the mid-nineteenth century when the site of the Becket story was commemorated by Frederick Hutchinson Hervey-Bathurst in the 'parliament hall'. His was a Protestant statement in stone which sought to encourage visitors to the palace site to interpret the ruins and the world about them as a key site for the origin of English Protestantism, that religion which James I hoped to make the basis of a world faith equal and opposite to Catholicism. Though FHHB's knowledge of history was imperfect, his intention is clear – to create a 'genesis' myth and in so doing to draw attention indirectly to the social and religious importance of what he owned and had preserved for future generations. His reasons for that perpetuation of memory are not ones obvious in today's post-imperial and secular age, but the dual sentiments of religion and patriotism are ones we might recognise.[5]

Social time

Social time, those processes which have a life of a generation or two, seems hard to recognise at first in the landscape record. Because of its peculiar social and tenurial structure Clarendon has never been obviously at the whim of rises and falls in national demographics which are so much a feature elsewhere. Nevertheless, we can pick out the impact of the personal preferences of Henry III and Edward III, which led to large-scale programmes of decoration and refurbishment over their lifetimes in the thirteenth and fourteenth centuries.

Building materials and artefacts survive to demonstrate these investments. One destructive upheaval within the scale of 'social time' was the change in land use at Clarendon during the second half of the seventeenth century, and it is the 1640s which have the best claim at Clarendon to be regarded as the economic and social origin of the exit from the medieval world. Within the space of a few decades, we can identify a striking fracture in the dendrochronological continuum of tree-ring sequences indicating a change (or abandonment) of the long-standing forestry régime of the previous half-millennium and more, the effective eradication of traditional wood pasture and the ploughing-up of pasture on chalk downland. As the focus shifted away from the palace and from royalty, it was tenants who took charge of these changes in the park, and the special circumstances at Clarendon, in the form of a range of structures of no further practical use – palace, grandstand, ruined lodges and so on – provided a ready quarry of sites and materials in the century after 1650.

Later examples of changes in the medium term must also include several of the imprecisely dated changes to land use and building stock, as various as the cricket pitch at Clarendon laid by FHHB and the investment he probably made in brick buildings across the estate in the mid-nineteenth century. Indeed, it might be thought easier to identify owners who left no mark on the landscape, building stock or vegetation history. Several monarchs might be candidates for such a list – William II and Edward VI among them – but, of course, absence of interest can have the most dramatic of all signatures in the archaeological record – decay. Exactly the same point might be made for the late nineteenth century, when the last Hervey-Bathurst owner was quite unable to invest in his estate and began to sell off land south of the railway. This land was quickly developed, so his nineteen-year period of ownership is now distinctively visible in the architecture of residential buildings in that former part of the estate. Indeed, his distressing personal and financial circumstances meant that he had one of the more dramatic impacts of any owner at Clarendon.

Individual time

Individual time is perhaps easiest for the historian to capture. Seventeenth-century probate records link named people, places and possessions; letters written home by twentieth-century evacuees also do so. The difficulty comes in linking these moments, crystallised in a document, with events on the ground. It is soon apparent that some 'events' on the ground exist only the documentation rather than in the actuality. The Constitutions of Clarendon of 1164, to take one example, were an 'event' of national and international significance, but one whose signature in the landscape is invisible, although the documents, as archaeological artefacts in their own right, are dramatic enough to see and to hold. To take another, more recent example, in spite of the impact of British and European Union grants, land use patterns at

Clarendon have not changed significantly since the early eighteenth century. Crops and their management have been transformed,[6] as we saw in Chapter Six, but unlike other farms around Salisbury, only a small number of hedges have been removed to create larger fields because of the added value they give as wildlife corridors for game birds.

Of course, there are some individual events which do leave traces: the investment in the mansion between 1825–32 is one example for which there is good architectural and documentary evidence; a second is the erection of the extension to the mansion after 1860, a physical expression of an expanding Victorian household in which, by 1881, servants outnumbered family by a ratio of two to one. A third example is the Second World War buildings such as the K/Q-type dummy airfield. Yet, without the benefit of historical records, we doubt whether any of these three events could be dated so precisely.

In the absence of a Vesuvius or a major battle, most landscape archaeologists struggle to identify specific events. Even documented and dated renovations and repairs at the palace, where the precise quantities of medieval nails and tiles are known, cannot easily be linked with certainty to trays of archaeological finds. There are two main reasons for this: stratigraphy has never been effectively explored at the palace site (or, arguably, elsewhere at Clarendon, with the exception of Fussell's Lodge long barrow), and artefact chronologies are rarely refined enough to detect these processes of minimal duration. Some dating techniques, like dendrochronology and thermoluminescence, applied to Clarendon for the first time during the course of this study, offer that potential, but only under specific conditions.

However, some artefacts may have more intimate stories to tell. For example, two sherds of Malagan lustreware may hint at the visit of Eleanor of Castile to Clarendon in 1289. Even this is tenuous, however; lustreware of this type and date is not exclusive to sites with royal Spanish connections and stratigraphical data from Clarendon is almost wholly lacking. Another example is more curious: during excavations in the 1930s a coronation medallion of William and Mary was recovered.[7] This was struck in 1689 and the pewter has been pierced, causing damage to the lettering (the L of ANGL). Presumably it was suspended as a decorative amulet, perhaps for some talismanic purpose, before finding its way to the palace site. But exactly who might have placed it at Clarendon Palace, and why, are unresolved mysteries. Queen Mary was daughter of Anne Hyde (d. 1671) and James Duke of York (James II to be). She was born on 30 April 1662, some eight months after her mother's precipitate marriage which caused such fury to Anne's father Edward Hyde, Earl of Clarendon. Mary married William of Orange in 1677. As her father and mother were both long dead by her coronation in 1689, and Mary herself died only five years after she ascended the throne, it is likely – unless it was a bizarre chance loss by a visitor – that she or her family were associated with the deposit of the artefact.[8] We can never be sure exactly why it was done, but perhaps burial symbolised the end of the royal/Clarendon bond at the death of Mary, the ending of a lifecycle for both object and queen?[9]

What can we learn about the Clarendon landscape when it is studied over so many millennia? In our study area there have been two long periods of coherence, each of which is characterised by a broad stability in land units and in social and tenurial relationships. The first began in early prehistory and lasted until the end of the Roman period or shortly afterwards, with a brief period of instability in the middle Iron Age; the second began in the late Saxon period and endures to the present day. These two periods are punctuated by a series of events in the early medieval period which, on the one hand, put an end to the first phase and, on the other, created the conditions or structures for the second. This was a complete shift in the historical trajectory of the study area and if we were to rewind the tape of Clarendon's history and play it again without that imposition of royal ownership by the eleventh century, events would have not have been the same. Instead, the weight of social and economic structures since that time have been such that, while unpredictable episodes have certainly occurred, some imposed from the exterior world and others generated from within, they have not damaged the core. The social and economic shape of Clarendon has persisted right through to the present day. In this sense, as in so many others, Clarendon cannot be regarded as typical.

Notes to the Chapters

....

Notes to Chapter One: Themes for a Landscape

1. In the 1930s Professor Borenius prefaced a lecture by stating 'every schoolboy' knew Clarendon through the Constitutions, while the popular history, *1066 And All That* (1930) devoted its entire section on Henry II to the Assize of Clarendon and the quarrel with Becket. More recently, these enactments make no appearance, for example, in Norman Davies's monumental *The Isles* (2000).

2. The Press drew its income from the first earl's posthumous *The History of the Rebellion and Civil Wars in England* (1704; 1839), the proceeds of which were assigned to the Press in perpetuity and which funded the Clarendon Building, by Hawksmoor (1713), and the Clarendon laboratories (1868).

3. Clarendon Plantation is in Beaufort County, South Carolina. Clarendon, Tasmania, is the property of the National Trust of Australia (Tasmania); a Clarendon Stores (1836) and Clarendon Hotel (1847) are also found in the neighbourhood, as are Blenheim and Marlborough (CEA Historic Sites; CEA Text relating to Clarendon, Tasmania).

4. James and Robinson 1988, viii.

5. Colvin 1963.

6. Binski 1999.

7. James 1990; Thurley 1993.

8. Rackham 1980.

9. Young 1979.

10. Bond 1994; Cantor 1983; Richardson 2005.

11. Saunders 1993.

12. Thomas 1984.

13. Liddiard 2000; Johnson 2002; Taylor 2000.

14. Jones and Cloke 2002; Tsouvalis 2000.

15. Pollard and Reynolds 2002.

16. Fowler and Blackwell 1998; Fowler 2000.

17. Tingle 1991.

18. Gingell 1984.

19. Barrett *et al.* 1991; Green 2000; McOmish *et al.* 2002.

20. An important influence on our thinking has been the *Annales* school of historiography (Bintliff 2004;

Knapp 1992). *Annales* scholars, especially Braudel (e.g. 1972), strike a chord with any historian or archaeologist who might wish to document a more anthropological kind of past and in particular investigate the processes that have shaped a particular landscape at different time scales.

21. That is, 'an open space among woods'; 'pasture'; 'untilled or grass-covered ground' (*Oxford English Dictionary*).

22. Lewis 1994.

23. Aubrey 1847; 1969, 35. Digging fuller's earth and brick-making occur in surveys c. 1650. TNA:PRO E317/Wilts. 27.

24. Anon. 1952, 222–3.

25. That is, the liberty of Clarendon, and an Extra-Parochial Place. In 1884 part of Laverstock and Ford Civil Parish (pop. forty-five in 1891) was transferred to Clarendon Park (Pugh and Crittall 1959, 326, 331, 345 and n. (b); and see TNA:PRO RG 12/1618, where these additional people are entered).

26. The bounds of the forest are discussed in Pugh and Crittall (1959, 427–31) and Bond (1994, 116). For forest administration see Young 1979, and for a recent detailed discussion of the wider forest see Richardson (2005), who also discusses the teams of wardens, foresters, verderers, regarders and agisters who formed the hierarchy of forest officials and the courts which administered decisions.

27. *CPR 1334–38*, 5.

28. For cases of forest trespass see Richardson (2003b) and *CPR 1330–34*, 189. The legal identity of the two land units, forest and park, grew apart during the twelfth to fifteenth centuries, as the king sought to raise revenue first by strengthening and later by lifting the restrictions of Forest Law in return for fines as he presided at Clarendon Palace (Bond 1994, 132; Maddicott 1984, 33).

29. *CLR 1240–45*, 314 (1245). On another occasion 'the king's fat' (rendered deer carcasses?) from Clarendon was to be salted, placed in tuns and carried to

the Tower of London (*CCR 1337–39*, 500 (1338)). We thank John Steane for discussing this reference with us.

30. *CPR 1330–34*, 112.
31. *CCR 1339–41*, 158 (1339). Southampton had been sacked by the French in October 1338.
32. *CCR 1333–37*, 254. Clarendon (forest and park)

provided 40 of the 581 trees needed for the building of Salisbury Cathedral and windfallen wood also fuelled the burning of lime to make mortar (Simpson 1996). No Clarendon timber has, to date, been identified in Salisbury Cathedral (Tim Tatton-Brown, pers. comm.).

33. *CLR 1240–45*, 266 (1244).

Notes to Chapter Two: Clarendon Before AD 1000: Beginnings

1. Harding and Bridgland 1998.
2. Tranchet axes are straight-edged tools, flaked parallel to the edge. A recent national survey of handaxe finds identifies Shute End (SU 175280) as the provenance for a handaxe in Salisbury Museum (Wessex Archaeology 1993, 101).
3. Clay-with-flints is reworked chalk, mixed with other deposits and disturbed by permafrost. These geologies pre-date the river terraces.
4. Arnold *et al.* 1988.
5. Ashbee 1958; 1966. Long barrows on Salisbury Plain mostly range in length from 25 m to 75 m, clustering at around 50 m; most widths are 12–23 m, clustering at 18–23 m (McOmish *et al.* 2002, 21); so Fussell's is typical. The pair of long barrows on Milston Down also have restricted views (McOmish *et al.* 2002, 22).
6. For long barrows generally see Simpson 1968; Ashbee and Simpson 1969; Thorpe 1984; and Kinnes 1992. For correspondence related to the excavation of this site see TNA:PRO WORK 14/1777. The uncalibrated radiocarbon date for Fussell's is early – 3230 bc +/- 150 (BM–134) – but there is only one.
7. The excavator's interpretation of the roof construction is not universally accepted today and further parallels for Ashbee's findings are now available. For example, see Whittle 1994 and Cleal and Allen 1994.
8. NMR aerial photograph: Crawford, AP 4672; for a recent analysis see Palmer 1984, 76–77.
9. In Well Bottom and in Boundary fields: identification of the former depends upon unconvincing interpretation of aerial photography, the latter upon an unexplained divergence of the northern deer park pale. There is no clear earthwork at this location and the site remains doubtful. OS card SW13SE37. Some geographical references have been withheld for security reasons.
10. This site was partially excavated in 1924 (Cunnington 1925). For further comment see Guido and Smith 1982; Palmer 1984, 27; Harding and Lee 1987, 295–6.
11. Fussell's is an outlier (to the east) of a major clustering of long barrows south-west of Stonehenge

(Ashbee 1984). Other long barrows in the same notional 'territory' include those at NGRs 20493481 (Idmiston), 22003426 and possibly 21573296 (Pitton and Farley), whose settlement sites are as yet unlocated. A suggested causewayed enclosure of Neolithic date at Fussell's Lodge Farm can probably be dismissed: map work shows the low semi-circular bank in Birdfield to be an eighteenth-century field boundary.
12. Two endscrapers on flake blanks showing parallel laminar removals are probably earlier Neolithic, for example, while a bifacially pressure-flaked projectile point roughout may have been intended as a leaf-shaped arrowhead. Earlier Neolithic flintwork is poorly represented within fieldwalking assemblages and this concentration may reflect an early Neolithic site which is being truncated by the plough (Scott 2004).
13. The distribution of flints represents two foci; Scott 2004.
14. A broken fabricator and a chisel arrowhead from Best's Farm are later Neolithic, as are three scrapers from Wild Garden field, not far distant. A carefully worked multi-platform core and a flake with a trimmed platform, both typical of late Neolithic/earlier Bronze Age technological practice, were also found on Cockey Down (Scott 2004).
15. Fasham 1985. The ditch itself was found to be 21.6 m in diameter and 0.91–1.22 m in depth.
16. Timby 2004.
17. Palmer 1984, 79. This penannular monument was first seen in 1924 but discounted in 1950 when fieldwork identified nothing on the ground.
18. Soilmarks observed by Richard Price in 69K and Maize Field; aerial photography transcription by Richard McConnell has identified a sub-circular cropmark in 69D.
19. For examples see Fowler 2000, 222; McOmish *et al.* 2002, 43.
20. No excavation is recorded at any of the Pitton group. The largest barrow has perhaps been reused and heightened at a later date. For other examples see Williams 1997. Five others are in woodland to

the south, one of which is dubious (Corney and McOmish pers. comms), and two further examples are visible as earthworks in the adjacent field, together with a probable ring ditch a little way to the east. The latter makes a plausible windmill site.

21. Piggott 1945–7.
22. Formerly in the Morley Hewitt collection at Rockbourne Roman villa; not seen by the authors.
23. Eleven sherds in all; Timby 2004.
24. For Wiltshire Beaker pottery generally see Case 1995.
25. A large bifacially worked knife of early Bronze Age date was found at Best's Farm (Scott 2004).
26. Around Avebury an intensification of land use was identified during the Beaker period, when boundary features were established over limited areas (Evans *et al.* 1993).
27. See, for example, Catt 1978.
28. McOmish *et al.* 2002, 53; Gingell 1984 for the Marlborough Downs; Barrett *et al.* (1991) for Cranborne Chase; well-targeted excavation at Clarendon would enable examination of the chronology of land divisions and field systems.
29. For example, north of Ranger's Road.
30. Palmer 1984, 130.
31. Gingell 1984.
32. Lovell *et al.* 1999.
33. OS card SW13SE40.
34. Pugh and Crittall 1957, 101.
35. Specifically from Best's Farm, Chalk Road, Beechy Maples, Crendle Bottom, Grandstand (Gooseneck) and King Manor fields; generally speaking, Clarendon flint of middle Bronze Age date or later seems uncommon, though no technological analysis of the flint assemblages has been carried out (Scott 2004).
36. Cunnington 1925.
37. Palmer 1984, 20, 31; Trott 1991; Lovell *et al.* 1999.
38. Palmer 1984, 46.
39. Recent published parallels for Cockey Down are Pimperne and Gussage All Saints (Harding *et al.* 1993).
40. The Park Corner finds were made by the Vatchers in 1961 while excavating the Ford Down bowl barrow (Fasham 1985).
41. Timby 2004.
42. Trott 1989.
43. Cunliffe and Poole 2000a at Suddern Farm, Middle Wallop; also at Nettlebank Copse and Houghton Down (Fowler 2000, 225–6).
44. Timby 2004.
45. The dates were 390–110 cal BC, 2190+/–50 BP (GU–4959); 340 cal BC–cal AD 20, 2070+/–50 BP (GU–4961); 350 cal BC–cal AD 60, 2070+/–60 BP

(GU–4969); the remains of at least twelve individuals were identified, ranging in age from neo-natal to mature adult. Gum disease, osteoarthritis, sinus infections, a possible infection of the meningeal membrane and a break on an adult female scapula, possibly the result of a blow, were all identified (Lovell *et al.* 1999).

46. Previously only one Iron Age site other than Cockey Down had been found at Clarendon. Identification of rectangular or L-shaped flint flakes found near Petersfinger and dated to the Iron Age has been disputed and, on the basis of fieldwalking results from that part of the parish, can now be discarded.
47. Anon. 1962; James and Robinson 1988, 1, 75.
48. James and Robinson 1988, 76; Musty 1961–3.
49. James and Robinson 1988, 74–5, 137.
50. Three fine flint-tempered sherds and one shelly sherd, plus eleven black handmade sandy wares of Iron Age/early Roman date, came from Home Copse. Six possible later Iron Age/early Roman sherds came from Great Gilbert's Copse, nine similar sherds came from Piper's, to the east, and one later prehistoric sherd was found in Henrun (Timby 2004).
51. Colt-Hoare 1837/44 following 162h; Allen 1978, 242; an unascribed south-western coinage, silver or billon, attributed to the Durotriges. We thank Paul Robinson and Colin Haselgrove for their advice on this identification.
52. There are three sherds here, one in a sandy fabric with flint (Timby 2004).
53. Cunliffe and Poole 2000b.
54. The sites are Blagdon Copse/Doles Wood, north of Andover; Hamshill Ditches, Hanging Langford camp, Ebsbury and Stockton, west of Wilton; the Gussage Hill complex in Cranborne Chase, north Dorset; and the Forest Hill/Savernake complex (Corney 1989).
55. Flint-tempered pottery from the Clarendon assemblages has been ascribed an Iron Age date. Some of the sherds are tiny, however, and the use of flint tempering is also known in Neolithic and Bronze Age pottery (Timby 2004).
56. Including fine flint-tempered fabrics, grog-tempered and sandy wares (Timby 2004).
57. McOmish *et al.* 2002, 56–66.
58. We thank Mark Robinson for this suggestion.
59. We thank John Steane for this observation.
60. Palmer 1984, 127.
61. Trott 1989.
62. Anon. 1973; Trott 1991, 118; Lovell *et al.* 1999.
63. Corney 2001.
64. Lyne and Jefferies 1979.

65. Timby 2004.

66. Constantius II, Caesar. Rev: PROVIDENTIAE CAESS, Trier mint, AD 326. RIC VII, 480. We thank Steve Minnitt for this identification.

67. Hockamore produced thirty-nine Roman sherds, mostly of later Roman date, as well as a handful of ceramic building material; Fields 69D, 69K, Grandstand, Maize Field, Pumphouse Belt, Pumphouse and Winterbourne also produced Roman pottery in small quantities (Timby 2004).

68. Anon. 1973, 133.

69. Esmonde Cleary 2000; Foster 2001. This last grave was a little way from the others and undated (Anon. 1973, 132–3).

70. Small clusters of Roman burials like this one, set apart and apparently marginal, have been argued to be low status, but this is disputed (Pearce 2000). The contemporary landscape context is not sufficiently well understood here to make such a claim.

71. We are grateful to Danny Darwish for this identification.

72. Timby 2004.

73. Cunliffe 2003.

74. The Gilbert's Copse site must be the Roman villa site referred to before 1850 and later dismissed. 'Mr Hatcher, of Salisbury, asserts that the site of another unexplored Roman villa exists in Clarendon woods …' (Anon. 1846).

75. Villas are known at Downton, West Dean, Winterslow, East Grimstead and Winterbourne Stoke, for example (Mark Corney pers. comm.).

76. Simon Draper pers. comm.

77. Paralleling medieval forests at Braydon and Savernake, for example. We thank Simon Draper for this suggestion.

78. Timby 2004; the 267 Roman sherds from shovel pits include products from Alice Holt, Savernake, samian, a Dragendorff type 31 bowl, Oxfordshire colour-coated and white ware, New Forest colour-coated ware and Dorset black burnished ware. Necked jars, plain rim dishes, beakers, bowls, mortaria and jugs are all present.

79. Borenius and Charlton 1936, 56.

80. Seven sherds are also recorded from earlier excavations at the palace (Robinson 1988, 177).

81. Timby 2004. Ceramic building material was also recovered from both fields, including a piece of box flue from the latter, to add to that mentioned by Robinson (1988).

82. Corney 1989; McOmish et al. 2002, 98–100.

83. Including a handmade/wheelmade lid and jar of early Roman date and Oxfordshire/New Forest colour-coats dating to the later third–fourth centuries

(Timby 2004); this site is clearly visible on aerial photographs as it extends into the adjacent field, Chalk Road, where further finds collected during fieldwalking include tegulae and a relatively high percentage of samian, suggesting a settlement of higher status.

84. Towards the top of Birdfield and through the adjacent scrub woodland.

85. From Birdfield (Timby 2004).

86. From Town Field and Rex's Field.

87. By Sue Creasey, living locally.

88. Fulford 1975, type F30.

89. Fulford 1975, type 23.

90. Also of note at Best's Farm was a Dorset black burnished ware flanged bowl, a sherd of samian and a pierced rim from a large Alice Holt storage jar. This may be a ceramic beehive of the type described by Clark and Nichols (1960) (Timby 2004).

91. All the sites recognised here are damaged, some by the plough, as at Cockey Down, others by woodland, as in Home Copse. In this respect the site at the eastern end of Gilbert's Copse is unusual.

92. This group of sixty-seven sherds includes Oxfordshire and New Forest colour-coats, grey wares and ceramic building material (Timby 2004).

93. Graham and Newman 1993.

94. Wainwright et al. 1971.

95. Rawlings and Fitzpatrick 1996.

96. Ashbee 1966, 27.

97. McOmish et al. 2002, 88.

98. Such a pattern contrasts with more dispersed settlement to the east, in Hampshire, but matches evidence emerging from Salisbury Plain (Graham and Newman 1993).

99. We thank Vanessa Straker and Mark Robinson for their assistance.

100. Bowsher 1987; Rackham 1980.

101. Watson 1982; McOmish et al. 2002, 151. This sequence is also suggested by recent work in the Avon Valley which confirms tillage of slopes, followed by colluviation in the Bronze Age (Graham and Newman 1993, 45–50).

102. Leeds and Shortt 1953.

103. Eagles 1994, 15.

104. Grave XXI.

105. Avent and Evison 1982, 117. Button brooches are later fifth- and early sixth-century AD.

106. Anon. 1984.

107. Eagles 1994; 2001.

108. Eagles 1994, 27.

109. Lucy 2002.

110. Eagles 2001.

111. Specifically, recycled or curated Roman objects here include third-/fourth-century coins (some pierced), pottery, a bronze fibula, a key, a bronze bangle and an iron boss (White 1988).

112. Eagles 1994, 18.

113. Anon. 1969.

114. Anon. 1990.

115. Reynolds 2002.

116. Draper 2002.

117. Salisbury and South Wilts Museum Annual Report 1960–1.

118. For the suggestion that early Anglo-Saxon burials on parish boundaries suggest the limits of early estates see Bonney (1966); for later thoughts see Welch (1985), for example. The Bronze Age barrows on Cockey Down are on the park boundary too, but they are also on the watershed. They do not prove continuous recognition of that boundary.

119. Otherwise Pancet, Panchet, Penchet etc., cf. modern Welsh *pen coed*.

120. Alderbury has been classified as an ancient mother church though there are no visible remains of the Anglo-Saxon period (Royal Commission 1987, 101).

121. Brakspear 1934; Pitt 1999, 26–8.

122. A suggestion first made by Thorn 1989, 37.

123. Pitt 1999, 29.

124. Gover *et al.* 1939, 12–13, 375–7.

125. Bates (1998, 449–52) disputes the 1072 date given by Round (1909) and accepted by Gover *et al.* (1939, 375), arguing for c. 1070 or earlier, so nearer the Conquest.

126. Ekblom (1917) cites Clarendon, with Clarborough and Clarewood, as being derived from personal names such as Clare or Claringa coupled with -dun (down) and the possibility that Clarendon was derived from 'claefren dun' or 'clover hill', although he adduced no examples of any name incorporating the 'f'. He argued further that Clarborough and Clarewood were also 'clover' names, despite the loss of the 'v'. The 'clover-grown' derivation was accepted by Gover *et al.* (1939, 376).

127. The 'dun' element is found more commonly associated with hills further north in Wiltshire (Gelling 1984, 149) such as Blunsdon, Swindon, etc., though note Downton nearby.

128. A recent work denies the 'clover hill' interpretation, proposing in its place a Celtic river-name, as found at Clare (Suffolk) and Clere (Hants) (Gelling and Cole 2000, 171). Clarendon is not adjacent to the River Bourne, however, and there is no other evidence of that river ever otherwise being called the 'Clare', so the mutually reinforcing nature of the British 'end of the wood' and the Saxon 'clover-grown hill' remain favoured here.

129. Grundy 1939; Jonathan Pitt pers. comm.

130. Hooke 1998a, 145–6, also notes that 'leah' is included within those terms used most frequently between AD 400 and 730, though it continued in use after that date. Many people regard 'leah' as a late Saxon place-name element.

131. Rackham 1980.

132. Hooke 1998a, 154–60; 1998b, 27, describes similar landscapes in northern Hampshire where, as at Clarendon, chalk overlain with clay-with-flints shows considerable evidence of late prehistoric and Roman archaeology, 'leah' place-names indicating woodland in the later Anglo-Saxon period, and ghost woods which go unmentioned at Domesday but were by later medieval times mostly royal forest.

133. Draper 2004.

134. 'Ancient woodland' designation emerges from a count of ancient woodland indicators, typically between 18 and 24 AWIS. Home Copse (24), Great Gilbert's (18) and Pitton Copse (17) exemplify the 'ancient woodland' character of much Clarendon woodland. KACAC 1996, 42–3.

135. Harding and Rose 1986; for papers on saproxylic invertebrates and historic land use, see Kirkby and Drake 1993.

136. Gerrard 1998. We thank David Clements for discussions on all these points.

137. Woodland as a territorial marker: a specific frontier between emerging kingdoms has been suggested at Woodstock/Blenheim (Bond and Tiller 1987, 20).

138. Wickham 1994, 155–99.

139. See, for example, Short 2000, 132; Watts (1998) speculates on pre-Domesday traditions of hunting at Wardour, Brook and Ludgershall, all in Wiltshire.

140. Though at this date deer-hunting had not acquired the complexities of ceremony and procedure of the later medieval period (Hooke 1998b).

141. Hooke 1998a, 158–9; 1998b, 21.

142. Hyland 1999.

143. Loveluck 1998; Keith Dobney pers. comm.

144. A gold niello baptismal ring of Ethelwulf (d. AD 858), King Alfred's father, found in 1780 in a cart-rut at Laverstock, just north-west of the park, reminds us of royal historic associations of the landscape beyond the park. Wilson 1964, no. 31; Webster and Backhouse 1991, no. 243; Webster 2003, 91–3; Hinton 2004. Claims by the antiquary Hearne that King Edward the Martyr (d. AD 978) was hunting at Clarendon at the time of his death is a confusion with Corfe. We thank Barbara Yorke for discussing this reference with us.

145. To add to our difficulties, Clarendon was not among 335 places mentioned in the Wiltshire Domesday because the park was part of the royal forest of Panshett (Penchet). These names were used throughout the Middle Ages at least down to 1670 (WSRO 212B/1878). 'Clarendon' was used c. 1070 and came to be used for the forest by 1200 (Pugh and Crittall 1959, 427 and n).

146. Hooke 1998a, 156. Unlike Hooke we show only three 'hagas' in south-east Wiltshire on Figure 19. There are nine mentions in the charters in all: one for Downton (S891); another for Downton, which is reiterated five times (S229, S275, S540, S819, S821); and another for Frustfield, which is reiterated twice (S492, S766). These charters can now be accessed at www.anglo-saxons.net. Though some claim to be earlier, they are probably all tenth-century in date.

147. Bond 1994, 122. Other wooded areas recognised as having forest officials include Savernake, Mendip and Windsor (Short 2000, 133), and these too probably reflect much older arrangements.

148. Domesday information is extracted here from Thorn and Thorn (1979) and the county-by-county Alecto Historical Editions (Hooper and Thorn 1989). Barlow (1970, 236–40) notes that Edward the Confessor and his brother Tostig were at St Peter's Church in Britford in 1065 when the Northumbrians rebelled against Tosti, their earl.

149. Darby and Finn 1967; Darby 1977, 354–5.

150. Other parts in Wiltshire with similar population densities were Savernake, Chute and Melchet, all forest areas (Darby and Finn 1967, 364).

151. Though there were periods when the use of this area for hunting was ill-advised: for example, during disruptions caused by Danish presence in the ninth century and in the early eleventh century when Wilton and perhaps Old Sarum were sacked in 1003, as well as during military events leading up to Cnut's conquest in 1016.

152. Hooke 1998b, 25.

153. At Goltho, Lincs (Beresford 1987), and Sulgrave, Northants (Davison 1977), for example. We should not find it strange that Clarendon goes unmentioned at Domesday. Many castles known to have existed are omitted and parks are seldom mentioned.

154. Fairbrother 1984, 62–7.

155. Rahtz 1979.

Notes to Chapter Three: Clarendon Park 1000–1500: Laying out a Landsacpe

1. Bates 1998, 449–52, prints the charter and discusses the date.

2. Whitelock *et al.* 1961, 165.

3. Wace, chronicler, historian and poet of the Norman invaders, writing c. 1150. See Mayr-Harting and Moore 1985, 30–1, and Steane 1999, 146.

4. Colvin 1963, 84.

5. £50 was not a great deal of money. £100 was spent by the Bishop of Winchester on his Hampshire deer parks in 1332–3 and £20–30 per year for maintenance seems to be a routine sum for most medieval owners (Birrell 1991).

6. Woodstock, in Wychwood Forest, was a park by 1113 (Cantor 1983, 76), the earliest of over thirty parks in Oxfordshire (Bond 1987, 23).

7. The Pipe Roll reference to Clarendon and Woodstock contains a clear reference to a park which could be Clarendon: *'Et In Conduct' vini (et) Frum'ti. (et) Robe Reg' (et) Regine. De Vdestoc ad Clarendon'a.xlvij.s.(et).v.d. (et) obl.n'uo.p' br' R. Et in lib'at' Rog'i de Caustona. (et) c'ductu ej'de' ad Parcu'. (et) de Oxenf' ad Wint ... '* One interpretation of this passage is that Causton was taking the items (i.e. *ejusdem*) to the park, that is to Clarendon, as instructed in the previous passage. We thank Amanda Richardson for discussing this entry with us. See also Steane 2001, 21, 38, 44. Giant-sized 'colonial' landscapes and structures featured elsewhere in the time of William the Conqueror and his sons Rufus (1087–1100) and Henry I (1100–35); the New Forest, the Tower of London, the huge cathedral at Winchester, the Great Hall at Westminster and the prodigious, if unfinished, outer earthwork defences, also at Winchester, are good examples.

8. Paul Everson and David Stocker pers. comm.

9. Richardson 2005, 114. Parks were not static suites of structures but developed organically to meet different monarchs' circumstances. For example, we know with hindsight that the Great European Famine of 1315–22 came to an end: Edward II, with people trampled to death in bread queues in London before 1320, might well have been motivated to extend his deer 'larder on legs' at Clarendon to ensure continuing food supplies. He did not know the famine would end.

10. Cantor and Wilson 1965, 224.

11. Bond and Tiller 1987, 29.

12. According to Colvin (1983) only Westminster was normally referred to as a 'palace', but medieval

documents and literature are full of references. For the development of the use of the term *palace*, see James 2001.

13. Colvin 1963, 82; Grose 1777.

14. Another reason why so many places were associated with King John was that he was never in the same place for more than a month in his seventeen-and-a-half-year reign.

15. Colvin 1963, 242–3; James 1990, 164–5.

16. Colvin 1963, 120; James and Robinson 1988.

17. Bushell 1906, 37–43.

18. See Eyton (1878) for Henry II's itineraries; Richardson (2005, 59–61, Chapter 3) for seasonality. The season for the hunting of fallow bucks was 1 August to 14 September from the thirteenth century; boar and doe hunting appear to have taken place in the winter, terminating on or about 2 February (Candlemas). Before it was recorded in the fifteenth century as being extended to Candlemas, boar hunting occurred in the months September to November. For the use of Clarendon and the functions of government exercised from there, and for royal visits, see James and Robinson 1988, 33ff. Before Richard I's reign chancery issues were not related to places, bedevilling itinerary studies. John's reign shows the great mobility of that monarch, and was probably typical, but in his reign and thereafter instruments are dated on the same day in widely spaced places. From the early years of Edward III's reign, with the monarch campaigning abroad and the administration functioning at home, the link between itineraries and documentary sealings is further fractured.

19. 2nd earl, Henry (1534–1601); 3rd earl William, (1580–1630), 4th earl Philip (William's brother) (1584–1650) (Atkinson 1995, 73). The Pembrokes became involved with Clarendon at the end of the boy-king Edward VI's reign, and secured their hold further in return for demolishing the rabbit warrens under James I.

20. The Walton Ordinances of 1338 established a procedure for continuing financial and other administration when the king was out of the country. The situation was addressed in 1338 as Edward III was about to sail for France at the beginning of what became the Hundred Years' War.

21. Ellis 2000.

22. The royal park at Gillingham was about 307 ha (760 acres) (Cantor and Wilson 1965). Bond (1994) gives comparative sizes of parks, showing Clarendon as a giant. In all, there were seventy royal parks in medieval England (Birrell 1991); Cantor (Cantor and Hatherly, 1979) claims twice this number, but

includes places which were only briefly in royal hands.

23. Cantor and Hatherly 1979.

24. *CLR 1251–60*, 180.

25. Muir and Muir 1987. Because it grows vigorously and quickly, ash could produce a taller canopy suited to deer containment, but the greater longevity of ash and field maple, as contrasted with more usual hedging species such as hawthorn, may indicate they have simply outlasted remnants of other species, which have long since died and decayed. We thank David Clements for these observations.

26. TNA:PRO E317/Wilts.30, 1652.

27. Though this report highlighted faults as one official took office from his predecessor (TNA:PRO C145/31(2); Phillipps 1833, 155).

28. TNA:PRO E317/Wilts.27. The 18-foot (5.4 m) cordon is matched by an 18-foot 'verge' at Marshwood Park, Somerset (Bond 1998, 27).

29. Bond 1987, fig. 21.

30. The excavation (labourers' wages) and fencing (carpenters' wages) of a new deer leap 68 feet (20.4 m) long and 13 feet (3.9 m) wide required twenty-four oaks in 1399–1400, when it also took thirty-eight oaks to make twenty-seven perches of park pale by Pitton Gate (TNA:PRO E101/502/15/41a; /42a; /43).

31. First recorded in 1322 (Gover *et al.* 1939, 375–6).

32. Originally four canons, there were fourteen before the Black Death, during which all but one died. There were twelve canons at the suppression in 1536 (Knowles and Hadcock 1953, 141; Pugh and Crittall 1956, 289). For recent architectural study of Ivychurch see Royal Commission (1987).

33. For the development of links between Clarendon Palace and Ivychurch, see James and Robinson 1988.

34. For discussion, see Liddiard 2000, 56.

35. Thompson 1986.

36. Religious intensity at the palace varied from reign to reign but evidence from elsewhere suggests the royal family attended chapel regularly while in residence (Mertes 1988, 139–60).

37. The Chalk Road today has rich flora on the banks on either side, including an abundance of characteristic chalk grassland species such as rock rose (*Helianthemum nummularium*), kidney vetch (*Anthyllis vulneraria*), lady's bedstraw (*Galium verum*), oxlip (*Primula elatior*), chalk milkwort (*Polygala calcarea*), salad burnet (*Sanguisorba minor*) and quaking grass (*Briza media*). All these were presumably a common sight in the medieval landscape at Clarendon. David Clements pers. comm.

38. The modern track from Fussell's Lodge to Savage's Farm Cottage pond survives as an earthwork in one short stretch, comprising two substantial parallel banks enclosed within a long-established, but secondary, scrub belt.

39. Colvin 1963, 910; Robertson 1877, 278.

40. *CLR 1240–45*, 224; for the king's chambers references see James and Robinson 1988, 12–17.

41. 'Trench' is used here in the sense of a cut path or track through the forest (*Oxford English Dictionary*).

42. Much later, in 1903, a rights of way case at Clarendon argued exactly this point: see Chapters Six and Seven.

43. These 'sleights' had their own hazards, as in 1258 when a woman described as having 'died of a disease of her own making', was killed by a falling branch at Clarendon (Brentnall 1939).

44. *CFR 1327–37*, 224.

45. Bond (1994, 120) notes that beech was especially common at medieval Clarendon, as today.

46. TNA:PRO E317/Wilts.26; .27.

47. *CFR 1327–37*, 475. Coppices named in the medieval period are Cattesgrove (1319), Culverhill Copis (1466), Gylberdis Copice (1477), Grounden Copice (1477), Feyrecokcopice (1477) or a 'Copes called Feyre ake' (1568) and Warnerscopice (1477). These names, in modern forms, mark copses today (Catsgrove, Caveral, Little and Great Gilbert's, Crendle Bottom, Fairoak and Warner's), demonstrating that the coppices were already defined by the fourteenth and fifteenth centuries.

48. Information from CEA Nature Conservancy Council survey of Pitton, Great Gilbert's, Old Park, and Home and Hunt's Copses by Gillian Lewis, 23 June 1981.

49. Birrell 1991, 117.

50. To give an idea of the quantities involved, at nearby Beaulieu Abbey bavins were cropped at 40,000 bundles per acre (Rackham 1986; Landsberg n.d., 43).

51. *CPR 1401–05*, 491.

52. Birrell 1991.

53. Bond 1994, 129.

54. Tyers 1999.

55. Remarkably, if these oaks were c. 120 years old when cut down in 1330, then by analogy, their predecessors might have been planted in the park for Henry I c. 1100.

56. *CPR 1377–81*, 229.

57. *CCR 1242–47*, 168.

58. An alternative explanation is that this was a period of harsher exploitation of forest resources which began in the adverse political circumstances of Henry III in the early 1240s, and especially from 1244 (Maddicott 1984, 33–4; Richardson 2005, 49).

59. Roberts 1995.

60. Rackham 1980. We thank David Clements for this observation. For further detail on Clarendon forest management c. 1200–1650, see Richardson 2005, Chapter 2.

61. A grant surrendered to the Crown in 1423 in exchange for land at Upavon (Pugh and Crittall 1956, 290–3; Brakspear 1934, 433).

62. Identified during recent fieldwork, damaged first by the railway and then by the Alderbury bypass.

63. TNA:PRO E 317/Wilts.30 March 1652.

64. In 1335 'making of a pond' in the park was paid for; *CCR 1333–37*, 425–6.

65. In other words, maiden trees with well-spread canopies above the browse line; whether these trees support saproxylic beetle faunas characteristic of such landscapes is unknown. David Clements pers. comm.

66. Perhaps the ones named in the nineteenth century as 'Monarch' and 'King John' (CEA visitor's account of Clarendon Park).

67. In 1355 one of the perquisites for the Warden of the Forests of Clarendon, Melchet, Grovely and Buckholt was the 'profit of a meadow in Claryndon park called Whitemerssh' (Whitmarsh) (*CPR 1354–8*, 198).

68. David Clements pers. comm.

69. Musty *et al.* 1969, 84. No evidence has been found to substantiate this during recent fieldwork, but much of the southern part of the park is pasture and therefore unavailable to fieldwalkers.

70. TNA:PRO E32/199/10. James and Robinson 1988, 41. There was one isolated coppice called Cattesgrove on the north-west side by 1319.

71. We would expect a thin spread of medieval pottery from the manuring of these fields if they had been arable in the medieval period.

72. The first mention of rabbits on the mainland is in 1235 at the royal park at Guildford, Surrey (Short 2000).

73. TNA:PRO E32/267 mm. 6d, 13; Bond 1994, 146; Richardson 2005, 35–9.

74. *CPR 1396–99*, 551.

75. Lever 1979, 73.

76. Colt-Hoare 1837/44, 129; Cox 1905, 316–7.

77. Bond 1994, 146; Hare 1994, 164.

78. *CPR 1553*, 276–7; Pugh and Crittall 1959, 430; Fryde *et al.* 1986, 477.

79. The earliest English treatise on hunting is a translation by John Gifford of the *Art de Venerie* by Guillaume Twici, the French huntsman of

Edward II. The most comprehensive source, however, is *La Livre de Chasse* by Gaston III, Count de Foix and Béarn, known as Phoebus, who died in 1391. This was translated into English as *The Master of the Game* by Edward, Duke of York, for the later Henry V. Subsequent sources include *The noble arte of venerie or hunting*, attributed to George Turbevile (1576), and Thomas Cockaine's *A Short Treatise on Hunting* (1591). Most illustrations of hunting are late and Continental.

80. Bond 1994, 146.
81. Some round or long barrows, however, might be candidates for reuse or misidentification. There are pillow mounds just outside the park, immediately north of Ranger's Lodge.
82. *CSPD 1660–61*, 286.
83. TNA:PRO E178/4728 now printed in Bettey 2005, 311–12; see also Richardson 2003b, 72 and n.
84. CEA inventory 1925. *CLR 1245–51*, 352. James and Robinson 1988, 18–19.
85. Reproduced by Borenius (1943, 44 and fig. 11) who notes a similar scheme painted at Kennington in 1265; Stothard (c. 1820) reconstructed the contemporary Westminster fireplace, also depicting seasons, from reused fragments, citing Lethaby (1905), 263).
86. BLO, MS Corpus Christi College 285, c. 1280; Henisch 1999, figs. 2–9.
87. Bond 1998, 24; 1994, 128; Cantor 1982, 57.
88. Not 'farmed', because the economic contribution of deer is hidden from us. Venison was gifted, neither bought nor sold for market (Birrell 1991).
89. Bond 1998, 24.
90. See Rackham 1994, 63. However, given Henry III's unbounded enthusiasm for Clarendon it seems unlikely that he did not partake of its central activity, hunting, as well as decorating its buildings.
91. Richardson 2005, 29.
92. Gidney 2004.
93. Cummins (2001, 63) attributes disease in parks to the build-up of parasites because of over-stocking. The mechanics of catching, checking age by dental examination, and transporting fallow deer requires significant manpower and skill, especially in loading and transporting. Anthony Dodds, pers. comm.
94. For fallow deer at Clarendon, see TNA:PRO DL 39/2/20; also Bond 1994, 128; and Richardson 2003b.
95. Cummins 2001, 85.
96. John Lovel, Master of the King's buckhounds in the early fourteenth century, travelled with running-hounds, greyhounds and sometimes a bercelot.

He took twelve bucks in Clarendon Forest in July 1313 (Cummins 2001, 183). Whether a lymer was employed in the hunting of fallow deer is unclear. *The Boke of St Albans*, of the late fifteenth century, says lymers were used, so possibly practices changed over time (Cummins 2001, 86).
97. Cummins 2001, 84.
98. Thiebaux 1967, 265–71.
99. Cummins (2001, 47–67) cites several documentary sources, including Gaston Phoebus, who considered this an English version of the hunt.
100. Five fingers to the end of the barb.
101. One possibility is that the inner park was intended as a deliberately managed shooting ground from which wounded animals could not easily escape. After being chased across country, deer might have been driven inside the pale and slaughtered there. This would also allow viewers from the palace to witness the final moments of the chase and to be close to the kill. If this were so, however, the ditch might be better placed inside the bank and not the other way around. Once more, the inner park seems to be a twelfth-century feature (at the latest) and this seems very early for this type of public display, patronage and formalised ceremony, which is more often associated with the fourteenth century. If the former date were proven then this is a very early example of a designed medieval landscape.
102. Cummins 2001, 66.
103. Birrell 1991.
104. Such statistics are a very rough estimate. Medieval records never tell us how many animals there were in the park. Rackham (1980) calculated that the king took 607 deer a year from all the royal forests and parks c. 1250, and Birrell (1991) considers those to have been peak years – but under Henry III, who was apparently not an active hunter.
105. It might be noted here that huntsmen Richard Luverez and Eudes, the 'velterers', were paid in 1210 for taking a wolf in Clarendon Forest (*alio lupo capto apud Clarendone*).
106. We are grateful to Aleks Pluskowski for discussing this point with us prior to the publication of his book *Wolves and the Wilderness in the Middle Ages* (forthcoming 2006). For the original reference see *Rotuli de liberate ac de misis et praestitis, regnante Johanne*, 144; White 1950, 54; James and Robinson 1988, 32.
107. Louisa Gidney pers. comm.; King and Jackson 1988; *Salisbury Times* 9 September 1938.
108. King and Jackson 1988, 262; Gidney 2004; perhaps by scenting hounds and greyhounds (Cummins 2001, 110–19).

109. Cummins 2001, 212.

110. Gidney 2004; King 1988, 263.

111. Pugh and Crittall 1959, 396; TNA:PRO E32/214/2.

112. James and Robinson 1988, 4, 8; Poole 1954, 88.

113. Mention is made of herons being sent to London from Clarendon forest (Cox 1905, 39).

114. Albarella and Thomas 2002.

115. TNA:PRO E101/352/32 m. 5; also Richardson 2003b, 376; gyrfalcons were probably used to catch the cranes.

116. Cox 1905, 39.

117. Pettigrew 1859.

118. Gidney 2004.

119. Brown 1978.

120. This species may have had a more inland distribution in the past (Baxter 1993b).

121. Baxter 1993a.

122. *Boke of St Albans*, quoted in Cummins 2001, 188.

123. A possible saddle fragment was excavated at the palace site in the 1930s (Crowfoot and Bayley 1988, 258).

124. Dobney 2002, 80.

125. *The Book of Howlett*, fifteenth-century, quoted in Cummins 2001, 189.

126. Both these lodges were provided with new chimneys in 1459 but their locations are unknown. They may have lain within the palace precinct, though as Dale was probably Forester of Melchet, his lodge may not have been within Clarendon Park at all (Richardson 2005, 78).

127. Richardson 2003b.

128. TNA:PRO E101/593/18; /20. Richardson (2005, 70–1) notes that a hall, chambers and a chapel are implied. The walls mentioned in 1342–3 were made of flint with Tisbury stone dressings, and reused timbers at Queen Manor have been dated by dendrochronology to c. 1330 (Tyers 1999).

129. If they are originally from this site at all. Later references to cartloads of materials being brought from the palace site render this interpretation problematic. In 1495–6, for example, the chimneys of Robert Nynges Lodge at Shreeves Wood were mended with 'tylesherdes' from the palace (TNA: PRO E101/460/16). In 1607–8 the wages for repairs at the then Queen Manor included money 'for digging … stone at the King Manor' (Richardson 2004).

130. Possibly references to the queen's apartments at the palace, but a more detailed reading makes that unlikely.

131. Richardson 2005, 70–1.

132. Bond 1987, 46.

133. The organisation of wells and water supply at the palace remains a topic on which virtually nothing is known, beyond the documented wells. Dowsers have proposed well-sites.

134. TNA:PRO E101/502/15; E101/542/20 indicates there is a Winchester Gate, with locks, suggesting a gatehouse and/or lodge for the key-keeper.

135. Roberts 1995.

136. Bond 1994, 150; Colvin 1963, 917.

137. There is also later documentation to support this (Richardson 2003b).

138. Phased by the RCHME as late medieval, early seventeenth-century, and 1700–1750, with an eighteenth-century barn.

139. Miles and Bridge 2004.

140. The 'new lodge at Sharpegoregate' mentioned in 1476–8 (TNA:PRO E101/460/14) could have been something more temporary, only made permanent later.

141. Cummins 2001, 175.

142. A medieval kennel would have included running-hounds (similar to the foxhound), greyhounds (some resembling deerhounds) and alaunts (burlier and more aggressive than greyhounds). The numbers of dogs kept could have been over a hundred if English kennels compared to French royal packs (Cummins 2001, 12–31).

143. Saunders 1986, 224–5. R.C.Clarke and M.Smith pers. comm.

144. Cummins 2001, 211–12.

145. The presence of dog was noted by King and Jackson (1988, 261). These new data come from excavation of spoil heaps in that part of the site (Gidney 2004). Three sizes of animal were identified. The wither height of the largest animals can be estimated at 0.50–0.56 m, and there were at least two smaller dogs, indicating a variety of stature, purpose and possibly age.

146. Cummins 2001, 22, states that the lugubrious lymers were sometimes favoured with accommodation with the huntsman.

147. The forest warden's lodge is thought to have been on the periphery of the palace precinct (James and Robinson 1988, 81).

148. Cat bones were infrequent but the majority came from areas of food preparation (Gidney 2004).

149. *CPR 1553*, 276.

150. *CPR 1391–96*, 410, 683.

151. *CPR 1405–08*, 37, 179.

152. Pugh and Crittall 1959, 430.

153. *CPR 1377–81*, 427–8. A 'pricket' is a buck in its second year.

154. *CPR 1377–81*, 477–8 (1380), the events had occurred before 1360; Goodall 1988, 222–3 and fig. 83. Each

plated arrowhead is a different type, two barbed and one birding bolt.

155. Colt-Hoare 1837/44, 157–8, interpreting Exch R.38 Hen III, 1259.

156. The inner park measures 480 m north to south by between 630 m and 420 m east to west. Harvey (1990, 11–12) mentions a length of paling 660 feet (220 yards; 201 m) long which was moved in 1254 from the top of the park to the bottom, towards the 'lawn'. Harvey evidently saw the latter as being a vast turfed area, but the reference is to grazing land for deer rather than a garden. The length of the upper bank of the inner park between the eastern corner of the southern wall and the eastern corner of the inner park is about this length, but if this paling was moved to the southern bank, it cannot have been sufficient. The southern bank is three times that length.

157. James and Robinson 1988, 76–8. Pales at royal parks at Devizes (Wilts) and Woodstock (Oxon) also had stone walls (Short 2000, 126), as did Moulton Park (Northants), Beckley (Oxon) and Newton Blossomville (Bucks) (Cantor 1982, 75; Cantor and Hatherley 1979).

158. *CLR 1267–72*, 7.

159. A section of this perimeter wall was excavated by John Musty in 1961 and is discussed in James and Robinson 1988, 77–8. A provisional date of the late thirteenth or early fourteenth century was proposed from the finds. Several phases of boundary are likely.

160. The authors remain divided over this map. CMG believes in it, TBJ does not.

161. *Salisbury (and Winchester) Journal*, 23 August 1935.

162. Thus the map must post-date 1241, but it could hardly have been thirteenth-century and would be almost unique in the fourteenth century. The Gough Map of Britain was made c. 1350. For a discussion of medieval maps, see Sekules 2003, 480.

163. Barber and Barker 1989, 193–4.

164. Rymer 1816, I, 65.

165. Gidney 2004.

166. Apple trees were stolen from the park c. 1355 (Richardson 2005, 50).

167. The bittern is only recorded from a late sixteenth-century context in London (Albarella and Thomas 2002).

168. King and Jackson 1988; Gidney 2004.

169. Clarendon is not among the Black Prince's nine studs. Princes Risborough was his principal stud; there was none in Wiltshire or the south-west (Hyland 1999).

170. Dyer 1989, 71.

171. Woolgar 1992, 114.

172. Horse is scarce because most of the faunal assemblage examined comes from high-status kitchen waste. Younger and elderly horses were present, which may indicate breeding or simply kennel food for dogs (Bracegirdle and Serjeantson 1988; King and Jackson 1988; Gidney 2004).

Notes to Chapter Four: Clarendon Palace 1000–1500: Romanesque to Gothic

1. *CLR 1240–45*, 224.

2. *CLR 1245–51*, 291 (1245).

3. Colvin 1963, 1009–1017; Colvin also refers to towers built at Woodstock, presumably for similar purposes to that of the balcony.

4. Higham *et al.* 1982.

5. Liddiard 2000, 67.

6. Johnson 2002, for example.

7. Harvey 1990, 11.

8. James and Robinson 1988, 79 and 241.

9. *CLR 1245–51*, 291; *1251–60*, 61.

10. Pettigrew 1859, 247 citing Liberate Roll 30 July 1250; James and Robinson 1988, 22, 241; Anon. 1962, 247.

11. Colvin 1963; Harvey 1990, 79.

12. Bond 1998, 35.

13. Letter from Ted Gange, Salisbury Natural History Society, to CMG, n.d.; Whitlock 1955, 151.

14. Whitlock (1970; 1955, 151) comments on flora, observing that he visited the 1930s excavations 'almost weekly'; NCC surveys of flora on the estate

since the 1980s have recorded neither *Wahlenbergia undulata* nor *Paris quadrifolia*.

15. *CLR 1240–45*, 223.

16. James and Robinson 1988.

17. Zarnecki *et al.* 1984.

18. Fragments of Romanesque sculpture survive for Clarendon and some, such as the cat's head springer, have resonances with, for example, the beak-head voussoirs from Tortington (Sussex). These have been compared to similar pieces from Reading Abbey, where some of the most extravagant work sponsored by this king survives. The remains of the cloister there have been compared with work at Westminster (Baxter and Harrison 2002, 302–312; Pevsner and Nairn 1965, 353–4; James and Robinson 1988, 243, no. 46). Recycled Caen stone is ubiquitous across the site, and is mixed with Tisbury in the springer of the northern arcade vault of the Great Hall – a good example of later reuse of stone under Henry III (James, Green and Tatton-Brown,

2005). For Norman stonework at Ludgershall see Stocker 2000.

19. Ashurst and James 1988, 252. Tancred Borenius was an expert in art history. It was the documentary references to cycles of wall paintings which originally attracted him to Clarendon.

20. Blair 1993, 6–7 and fig. 2. Although Blair's interpretation of the date of the hall seen today has been revised since 1993 from the 1180s to c. 1230, his argument stands, as there is evidence of structures underlying the present hall which may be interpreted as the previous hall.

21. James and Robinson 1988, 99–103.

22. James and Robinson 1988, 4–8, 81–126, for more detailed discussion.

23. In the absence of any excavation records from that part of the site.

24. *CLR 1240–45*, 60, 223.

25. However, while the interpretation of these features as the remains of the old hall is very plausible, it should be noted that this fireplace is in the west, not the south, wall of an apparently twelfth-century building. Fragments of chimneys were recovered here in recent work, and match standing chimneys dated to Henry III at Windsor (James, Green and Tatton-Brown 2005; Tim Tatton-Brown pers. comm.).

26. TNA:PRO E101/460/1; E364/2.m.D; James and Robinson 1988, 37–8.

27. TNA:PRO E101/502/15.

28. One 'couple' rafters per metre seems reasonable.

29. TNA:PRO E101/502/15.

30. John Musty's attempt to establish an eastern entrance by excavation near this structure in 1961 drew a blank.

31. Crowfoot and Bayley 1988, 258.

32. A word here on the use of these rooms. The Great Hall would have been used for great occasions but for much of the time it was the administrative and judicial centre of the complex; other halls within the precinct would have been for informal family use. The duplication of apartments is also a common theme in great castles, though the number of chapels at Clarendon is exceptional.

33. Tatton-Brown (1996, 63) points out that so-called Chilmark stone was probably quarried in the medieval period from workings to the south-east of Tisbury, though suitable stone could also have come from Teffont Evias, at the west end of the royal forest of Groveley (Simpson 1996, 12; James, Green and Tatton-Brown, 2005).

34. Borenius 1943.

35. Ashurst and James 1988, 234–58.

36. The Clarendon pavements are illustrated in Eames (1980) and displayed in the British Museum. In addition to those previously reported in Eames (1988), a further 400 kg (c. 3,000 sherds) of floor tile were recovered during recent fieldwork (Richardson 2004). During recent fieldwork finds of floor tiles away from the royal apartments were insignificant.

37. This pavement has been compared with another from Cunault, Anjou, in the heartland of the Angevin kings, and now copied in Chichester Cathedral, strengthening understanding of the international links and aspirations of the medieval kings (Eames 1963). Eames (1988, 142) suggests that this may have been one of three circular pavements at the palace.

38. Lewis 1999.

39. Henry III gave orders to tile the queen's rooms, the final payments being made by Michaelmas 1252 (Richardson 2004).

40. Eames 1960; Gutiérrez 2004c.

41. For further discussion, see Eames 1988. Around 138 kg of wasters and material used in building the tile kiln were recovered during recent fieldwork (Gutiérrez 2004b). The kiln is reconstructed at the British Museum. Van Geersdaele and Davison (1975), as well as James and Robinson (1988), discuss the excavation and reconstruction.

42. Cherry 1991 provides an overview of the industry.

43. Marks 1988, 232–3.

44. Fourteen painted grisaille designs survive from Salisbury Cathedral (Marks 1996, 114–15) and they give a good impression of how Clarendon windows might have looked.

45. *CLR 1245–51*, 297, 324.

46. This absence has a parallel in Wolvesey Palace, Winchester, where documentary evidence refers to a complete reglazing of the hall and other chambers in the late fourteenth century. However, no recognisable fragments of this glazing scheme were recovered during the extensive excavations there (Biddle 1990).

47. Brown 1999, 79–110.

48. Biddle 2000.

49. *CLR 1240–45*, 222; *CCR 1242–47*, 185; described and reconstructed in Ellis 2000, 91–6.

50. Despite the Winchester evidence, it remains debated whether the arcade was stone or timber. At Clarendon the pillars were probably of stone, which might have been necessary as the hall was built on previously developed land; on the south side of the hall at least there was deep rubble, the possible residue of an infilled undercroft. However, the rectangular profile of the slot above the corbel is suggestive of

a timber post at the eastern end of the arcade. A further issue is that the corbel is not well aligned to the pier bases ranged down the hall, possibly indicating different pier and roofing arrangements at different dates (Colvin 1983, 138; James and Robinson 1988, 94–5; Stocker 2000, 91ff). We are grateful to Virginia Jansen, David Stocker, and Tim Tatton-Brown for discussion of these points.

51. *CLR 1240–45*, 224 (1244).

52. Prestwich (1988, 259) argues that Edward I did not particularly mourn the loss of his children.

53. Lavallée 1854/1992.

54. All recent finds were from samples from spoil heaps. Although unstratified, many can be assigned to particular buildings. One third of the identified bone fragments come from spoil heaps associated with the North Kitchen. This redeposition of animal bones has accelerated their decay, with enhanced loss from small species and juvenile animals. Nevertheless, the assemblage recovered is certainly more representative of medieval diet than any previous Clarendon collection. The results described here are taken from Gidney (2004).

55. Redon *et al.* 1998, 6.

56. The presence of veal indicates the release of the dam for milking and therefore, indirectly, dairying and its associated products, particularly milk and butter at Clarendon, since cheese was considered low status (Dyer 1989, 63).

57. Pig bones were most abundant in the assemblage available in 1988 'most likely … due to post-excavation selection' (King and Jackson 1988, 262). That deduction now seems vindicated. The sucking pig bones are tiny and only underline the exceptional preservation conditions of the original assemblage, now damaged, though a great deal remains *in situ*.

58. Woolgar 1999, 114.

59. Roe deer were hunted at any season, though the period February–April was generally avoided (Cummins 2001, 87–92).

60. Gidney 2004.

61. This is in complete contrast to cattle and sheep, which were butchered and then brought to the palace.

62. Just as their eggs were, presumably (King and Jackson 1988, 263).

63. One bone was comparable in size to a wild species (Gidney 2004) while another from the 1988 publication was thought to be similar to a Greylag (Bramwell 1988).

64. Among official duties in Clarendon Forest was swan-warding.

65. A 1331 enquiry referred to a search for swans 'lately in the King's manor and forest of Clarendon' (*CPR 1330–34*, 200; WRL CLA; Cox 1905, 38).

66. WRL CLA. By 1400 the exclusive royal right to swans along the Avon appears to have been compromised; a licence to a subject to keep a swannery was issued, suggesting a curtailment of royal rights – but probably not on the river adjacent to Clarendon.

67. Waders are found as commonly in urban as on high-status sites, though they are rarely found on peasant sites (Albarella and Thomas 2002).

68. Bramwell 1988, 263–4.

69. See Albarella and Thomas 2002 for use and consumption of wild birds in medieval England. We might expect wild bird consumption to increase towards the end of the Middle Ages. Albarella and Thomas suggest that meat consumption was no longer a strong marker of status in the fourteenth to the sixteenth centuries and therefore exclusivity was sought by seeking out expensive wild birds which were more difficult to obtain. For further information, see Dyer (1989, 60) and Woolgar (1999; 2001). Taking into account regional availability of game, the archaeology and documentary evidence for Clarendon suggests similar feasting.

70. See Dyer (1989, 58 and generally). James (1990, 84–7) discusses food provision to palaces, including Clarendon, in the time of Henry III.

71. Jacques 2004. The assemblage recovered is too small to give any impression of the significance of fish in the diet but it indicates a good range of species, some of which may have been intended for the royal table, others of which may have been consumed by lesser members of the household. Previously, no identifications were possible from 1930s–1960s excavations, beyond the report of 'numerous vertebrae … about the size of cod' (King 1988, 263).

72. Woolgar 1992, 114–5.

73. Coy 1996.

74. James 1983.

75. Bunyard 1941; Locker 2001.

76. A total of 602 valves were recovered during recent excavation of the palace spoilheaps, mostly from around the North Kitchen (Light 2004). Several valves from spoil heaps could be matched, an important observation since it demonstrates that the archaeological deposits have retained their integrity – in other words, once-intact layers were shovelled together and piled into heaps. These are clearly not Roman food residues.

77. Oystermongers from Southampton supplied the royal household at Ludgershall c. 1450 (Woolgar 1999, 119), and the supply of 'farmed' oysters would be expected for élite consumption.

78. Such notches have been found in shells recovered from, for example, Eynsham Abbey (Light 2003) and Poole (Winder 1983), implying a specific implement for that purpose.

79. The mollusc findings are completely at odds with those previously published by King (1988, 263) who found a predominance of whelk shells (190) compared with oyster valves (90). The new study, in contrast, has yielded 7 whelks and 602 oyster valves. Many of the whelks in that earlier assemblage were also extremely large (up to 12 cm), whereas the whelks in the new group barely reach half that size. Perhaps previous excavators collected the unusual-looking whelks, particularly the large ones, and disregarded the more common oysters. King noted that his results were unusual, and was wary of making economic interpretations, beyond observing that the middens they came from were 'of specialized food remains not typical of general refuse deposits found on other sites'.

80. Woolgar 1992, 114–5.

81. The unusual species may have been imported to the site for their shells, rather than those shells' contents. A single carapace fragment of a large individual is the only evidence for crab (Light 2004). For crab at King's Langley see Neal 1971, 70.

82. Woolgar 1999, 119.

83. *CLR 1240–45*, 270 (1244).

84. Woolgar 1999, 120; Steane 1988, 50; Currie 1994, 101.

85. WRL CLA 1909 Letters relating to Fishery Rights in Clarendon Park.

86. *CLR 1240–45*, 10, 11; *1251–60*, 346.

87. Jacques 2004.

88. Woolgar (1992, 110, 113–4) who confirms, pers. comm., that '*dominus*' refers to de Nevill, although we know that King John came to Clarendon in 1207 to receive part of the regalia which had been pledged as part of the ransom for his brother, Richard I (Cheney 1970, 147; Fryde *et al.* 1986, 37; James and Robinson 1988, 8).

89. *CLR 1260–67*, 69, 181 records only 1261 7 tuns, 1265, 5. *CLR 1267–72*, 57, 108, 147, 197: 1268 (4); 1269 (30); 1270 (40), 1271 (12); this final record is for November 18 1271, just a year before the old king's death on 16 November 1272.

90. Charleston 1988, 194.

91. Trevor-Cox 1947, 18–19.

92. Dyer 1989, 62.

93. Goodall *et al.* 1988; Goodall 1988, 218; Hinton 1988, 200–1.

94. Woolgar 1999, 147.

95. Dyer 1989, 76.

96. Goodall *et al.* 1988, 207.

97. 1,730 sherds (48 kg) of medieval pottery were recovered from Clarendon Palace during recent fieldwork (Gutiérrez 2004a), slightly more than the quantity previously published (Robinson 1988).

98. Laverstock-type wares have been reviewed by Mepham 2000a. More than one source may be represented and the date range is wider than the phase of production established during excavations at the pottery workshop (c. 1230–75). The curious predominance of thirteenth-century material previously reported at Clarendon is therefore probably a fiction (Robinson 1988, 170–1), but chronologies cannot yet be refined for lack of well-dated groups in the region.

99. For medieval Newbury wares see Mepham 2000b; for London-type medieval jugs and Surrey white-wares see Pearce *et al.* 1985; for Verwood see Draper 1993, 296.

100. Gutiérrez 2004a. The Italian jar is a rare find. Only one other example of thirteenth-/fourteenth-century Italian pottery is known in Wessex, from Southampton. For context and imports in Wessex generally, see Gutiérrez 2000. Taken together, these wares present a very different picture to that previously published by Charlton (Borenius and Charlton 1936) and Robinson (1988, 176–7). Rather than being limited to Laverstock products with little apparent international dimension, the palace drew on a wide regional hinterland for its pottery and included a wide range of exotics among its tablewares. The differences between the published assemblage and those recently analysed are due to our improving appreciation of Wessex pottery types and several new publications on imported medieval pottery.

101. Gutiérrez 2000, 178–9.

102. In 1289 there are records of the arrival of goods for her particular use, including pottery 'of strange colours' (Childs 1995).

103. Gutiérrez 2003.

104. Inland finds of Malagan lustrewares are rare but there is a noticeable clustering in and around Southampton (Gerrard *et al.* 1995).

105. Gutiérrez 2000, 143.

106. James, Blunt and King 1988.

107. Goodall *et al.* 1988; Goodall 1988.

108. Such knives were used for food preparation and dining: they were personal multi-purpose tools.

109. Of Dorset. Governor of Corfe Castle in 1304 and of Winchester Castle in 1316–17, though the arms might also have been used by his father or his son (Goodall *et al.* 1988, 204).

110. This object was found north-east of the North

Kitchen in 2003, a location which may suggest a domestic use (Gutiérrez 2004d).

111. Hughes and Lewis 1988, 258–60. The scallop shell was the sign of St James and this looks like a reused souvenir from Santiago de Compostela in Galicia, north-west Spain. The shell is not dated but by the twelfth century Santiago was the third most important pilgrimage after Jerusalem and Rome. This example, typically, has two holes for suspension. For further discussion and references see Spencer (1998, 244–8) where an almost identical example is illustrated. The use of a medieval relic as a palette presumably held symbolic meaning for the painter as personal achievement, as advertisement for the travelled Christian and as devotional aid, but was most likely intended to imbue paint and paintings with magical benefits, just as, for example, liquids dipped with badges might be administered as medicine.

112. Musty *et al.* 2001, 171–2. None was discovered in the extensive excavations at Winchester, for example.

113. Dyer 1989, 55.

114. It is likely that the status of every member of the royal household could be distinguished by their livery (Dyer 1989, 78).

115. Useful comparisons with the Clarendon assemblage are Carisbrooke Castle on the Isle of Wight (Young 2000), Launceston Castle in Cornwall (Saunders forthcoming) and Ludgershall Castle in Wiltshire (Ellis 2000); Clarendon is not unusual.

116. Footprint identified by Leslie Cram, to whom we record our thanks. For pig-prints at differing ages see Brown, Lawrence and Pope (1984, 160) and Lawrence and Brown (1974, fig. 4:41) We can confirm that the tiles were laid out rather than stacked or shelved and that the tilery was part of, or very close to, a farmyard. Probably the tile-making was only a summer occupation.

117. Robinson 1988, 193 and fig. 65; Hare 1991.

118. TNA:PRO E101/459/29–30; /460/1.

119. *CLR 1240–45*, 222 (1244).

120. Musty *et al.* 1969; Musty *et al.* 2001.

121. A section of the Hampshire pipe roll account, referring to the marble columns for Clarendon, was photographed for John Charlton from the Public Record Office in the 1930s and remains among the glass lantern-slide collection. See Borenius and Charlton 1936, 58.

122. Blair (1991, 47–50) provides earlier uses than at Clarendon, including Henry of Blois's Wolvesey Palace in 1141–54 and his hospital of St Cross (1160–70), both in Winchester. After 1182, Blair comments, 'almost every English church of importance included Purbeck marble shafts, bases or string-courses'. This included Salisbury Cathedral after 1220.

123. *CLR 1245–51*, 322; James and Knight 1988.

124. Borenius and Charlton (1936) suggested that the brick kitchen, adjacent to the royal apartments, was created to supply food to Henry VI in his chambers, while he remained incapacitated in a trance-like state for several weeks, and that he therefore did not go into the hall to eat communally. Recent thermoluminescence dating of the bricks promises results (Ian Bailiff, pers. comm., work in progress) and may prove or disprove this theory.

125. TNA:PRO E101/460/10 and see Richardson 2005, 78.

126. Eames 1988, 127–67; James and Robinson 1988, 116, 237.

127. Moore 1991.

128. Royal Commission 1987, 149ff cites this comment by Henry VIII's commissioners at the Dissolution in 1536; Brakspear 1934, 435; see references to brick building at Clarendon after 1450, above.

129. Colvin 1963, 918.

Notes to Chapter Five: Cultivating Change 1500–1800: Property and Parkland

1. James 1990, 165.

2. *LPFD Henry VIII* ix, 467; Nichols 1788, sub 1574, 18–19.

3. Toulmin Smith 1907–10, I, 268–9.

4. In 1553, towards the end of the boy-king Edward VI's reign, William, Earl of Pembroke (created 1551, d. 1570) and his son, Henry, Lord Herbert (d. 1601), had been granted for their lives 'the office of warden and keeper of the Forest and Park of Clarendon'.

5. Nicholas 1955; Pugh and Crittall 1959, 430.

6. Batho 1967, 260–4.

7. Camden 1586 (trans 1695), 119.

8. TNA:PRO E101/542/21, 1603–?7.

9. These estimates provide a detailed perambulation, setting out the park circuit furlong by furlong, with trees required, named sites and costs for timber, carriage, gates, locks and keys (TNA:PRO E101/542/21).

10. E101/542/22.

11. This expenditure on digging at King Manor was 36s 8d, representing, at 8d per man per day, 55 man days of work (TNA:PRO E101/542/22).

12. TNA:PRO E101/542/21; /22. The total cost for the lodges and the rails and pales was £335 18s and 7d (compared with the estimate of £67), to which was

added £73 8d of 'surplusage' for tasks made 'by his majesties commandment', for 234 additional perches for a 'crosse rail', requiring 114 trees.

13. 19 August 1607.

14. Wall 1983, 40.

15. This included over £32 on Ranger's Lodge and £18 on King Manor (for a sawpit, tiles, lime and ladders), and the £33 on the pales. At Whitmarsh Mead the old pale was pulled up and replaced with 180 perches of hedge costing £21 (TNA:PRO E101/542/23).

16. Clarendon 1704/1839, xi, 231.

17. Pugh and Crittall 1959, 431.

18. Some of these 'others' may have numbered among those who desperately claimed compensation from Clarendon Park as unsatisfied creditors of Charles I in 1660 (Pugh and Crittall 1959, 43; *CSPD 1660–61*, 127).

19. Ogle *et al*. 1872, no. 7739.

20. CEA estate map c. 1650. The traditional date for the map is about 1640, possibly made in association with Charles I's war-chest funding project, which may be the case. However, the wealth of detail from parliamentary surveyors c. 1650 provides a more likely date and is the basis for Figure 43.

21. Clarendon was marginal to military strategy during the Civil War.

22. Pugh and Crittall 1956, 294; Hammond 1914–16, 7.

23. Hammond 1914–16, 6; Ravenhill 1872, 125–6.

24. Clay 1985, 154–5.

25. Clay 1985, 154–5.

26. Manning 1993, 30. The Pembrokes were also dedicatees of Shakespeare's folio plays (examples of which were to be found among the Christie-Miller Britwell Library: see Chapter Six n.89, below). William Herbert (1580–1630) was described by Edward Hyde (Clarendon 1704/1839, i, 93) as 'the most universally loved and esteemed of any man of that age' (1628).

27. Kerry 1922, 412; TNA:PRO E317/Wilts.27.

28. McWilliams 1996, 28–9; Clay 1985, 155; Thirsk 1984, 87.

29. Probably George Cooper, brother of Anthony Ashley Cooper. Ashley Cooper, originally a royalist, joined the parliamentary side in 1644 and rose to be a member of Cromwell's Council of State.

30. *CSPD 1658–59*, 23–4.

31. Aylmer 1973a, 131–2; *CSPD 1658–59*, 23. Ashley Cooper recovered from his exclusion with the Restoration and went on to be Chancellor of the Exchequer from 1661, surviving the fall of Clarendon in 1667. He became the first earl of Shaftesbury in 1672.

32. Christie 1871, xlv.

33. *CSPD 1660–61*, 179, 286, when a disappointed would-be commissioner stated that 'Hawles, by backwardness in doing his duty, was nearly guilty of the late king's death; moreover he bought part of the park and opposes its being imparked again'. The 'unlawful' sale refers to anxiety among potential purchasers about the status of Clarendon land, which had been confiscated from the Crown, sold, recovered and resold. They were covering their backs.

34. Worden 1978, 104–5, 111–13.

35. TNA:PRO E320/V4.

36. TNA:PRO E320/V1; /V4; /V12; /V16.

37. Colman 1991, 129.

38. Thirsk 1984, 111; Habbakuk 1978, 211, 219.

39. This income was presumably the rents from the farmers who had embarked on ploughing up the launds and removing some of the coppices.

40. *CSPD 1660–61*, 286.

41. HRO Hervey-Bathurst Collection 193M85/141 dated old-style in HRO to 1660. This grant refers to the royal warrant of 30 August 'last', i.e. 1660.

42. Colt-Hoare was correct in reciting a tradition that Clarendon Park was granted to the duke of Albemarle as one of the rewards for bringing about the Restoration. However, his statement 'All proving that the duke of Albemarle never sold Clarendon Park' is wrong.

43. Cockayne 1982, II *BRA–C*, under Clarendon.

44. Hyde said that in 1660 Charles II gave him £20,000, and that he purchased Clarendon Park from the Duke of Albemarle for £18,000, and 'as there was a mortgage on it from Charles I's time, Charles II cancelled it for £20,000 in 1663' (*CSPD 1660–61*, 275). For the mortgage of Clarendon by Charles I, repayment to Edward Hyde of £20,000, the assignment of Clarendon by Charles II to Albemarle, and Albemarle's sale to Hyde see KACAC 1996, paragraph 1.9; Chettle 1952; Jackson 1884, 350; Harris 1983, 407 and Pepys's *Diary*, where the diarist's informant, Alsopp, the king's brewer, provided misinformation that the estate passed to the earls of Bath, an error which has been often repeated since.

45. HRO 193M85/142; /145.

46. Harris 1983, 407, states that in 1667 Clarendon Park reverted to Albemarle but we have found no evidence for this. He appears to follow Colt-Hoare.

47. In the 1640s Edward Hyde was at the heart of the royalist party. In 1645 he was Chancellor of the Exchequer: 'almost certainly the youngest and certainly the most intellectually formidable [of the king's advisers] was Hyde, a plump, fair, ruddy faced man of 36' – this compared with the diminutive king, aged 49, and his sons Charles and James,

aged 15 and 12 respectively (Hutton 1989, 7; Jones 1862, 297). For over twenty years Edward Hyde remained unswerving in supporting the royalist cause.

48. Hutton 1985, 276.

49. This great London house was built to a design of Roger Pratt in the years 1664–5 (Platt 1994, 39–40, 69ff).

50. Brownley 1985, 84–7; Harris 1983, 374.

51. Craik 1911, ii, 323.

52. Pevsner and Sherwood 1974, 534.

53. Ollard 1987, 347–9.

54. For Hyde's will made 11 December 1674 (he died on 19 December), proved 14 December 1675, see HRO 193M85/148 etc. The demise (i.e. lease) made on 6 March 1675 by the earl of Clarendon (Henry Hyde) to Edward Hales for 99 years at £600 p.a. or for the life of the earl (HRO 193M85/148–70) indicates that the new earl was soon raising money using Clarendon as collateral. For raising money from Clarendon post-1767, see HRO 193M85/146 and Cockayne 1982, BRA-C sub Clarendon. This evidence contradicts the statement by Pepys's editors that 'Clarendon never obtained ownership of the estate which reverted to Albemarle on Clarendon's disgrace' (Latham and Matthews 1972, 61n).

55. Henry Hyde was his father's secretary by 1655. He married in 1660 and was appointed by Queen Catherine as her Lord Chamberlain in 1667, the year of his father's exile.

56. He completed building the magnificent east wing and chapel there in 1677 (Pevsner and Sherwood 1974, 553–5; Harris 1983, 408). Edward Hyde maintained his interest in his son's building activities from afar, enjoining him to plant 'as much as you can', including walnut trees – which the older man hoped to enjoy before he died.

57. Platt 1994, 69; Griffiths 1998, 270. Eventually Henry Hyde sold Cornbury to his brother, Lawrence Hyde, Earl of Rochester. He died intestate in 1711 and his son, also Henry, united the titles of Clarendon and Rochester in 1753. He too encountered financial difficulties and finally sold Cornbury to the duke of Marlborough in 1751.

58. HRO 193M85/146; /147; /148–70 (see n.55 above).

59. Such transactions, as security for loans, assign an estate to trustees. It is likely that by so doing tax was avoided. We are grateful to Hugo Hodge for discussing these property transactions with us.

60. Willan 1937, 593.

61. HRO 193M85/148–151.

62. HRO 193M85/150–160.

63. FRC PROB 11/405/116, 1691.

64. The third earl of Clarendon was Henry's son Edward (1661–1723) 'a childless widower of bad character' (Harris 1983, 407).

65. HRO 193M85/162; /167–8; /177.

66. HRO 193M85/171–4. Sir Benjamin was called 'a wealthy Spanish merchant', having moved to Spain during the Interregnum (NRO XYZ 1157.16). In the first half of the eighteenth century there were various Bathursts in parliament and at court. Peter Bathurst was brother of Allen Bathurst MP, 1st Earl Bathurst (1684–1775), one of twelve Tory peers created in 1712 – but whose career was cut short by the death of Queen Anne in 1714 and the fall of the Tory government; for 1st earl Bathurst see Whitehead 1952, for genealogies see Brayley and Britton 1803. The third brother in parliament was Benjamin Bathurst (?1691–1767, MP for Cirencester 1713–37; Gloucester 1728–1754; and Monmouth 1754/5–1767). They were generally Tories.

67. HRO 193M85/177; Manley 1937, 235.

68. He was defeated standing again for Salisbury in 1747. Peter's only recorded speech opposed clandestine marriages 'with wit' in 1736. A snapshot of his life and achievement, composed by his widow Selina (née Shirley, one of the daughters of Robert, Earl Ferrers), is preserved 'to perpetuate his memory when the living witnesses of his virtue are no more' on a memorial tablet in the porch of Laverstock Church (Everett 1994, 12; monumental inscription, Laverstock Church; Crittall 1962, 26). Unfortunately the parish registers for Laverstock (Bathursts), West Grimstead (Hyde or Ewer), and Alderbury (Bathursts) do not exist for the appropriate periods of the eighteenth and nineteenth centuries.

69. Lainston House was mostly let or had caretaker occupants. We thank John Hervey-Bathurst and Roger Young for this information.

70. Peter Bathurst's daughter Louisa appears with her husband and daughter (Selina) in Gainsborough's portrait of the Byam family dated to 1763–4 (Anon. 1937, 270). This family was small compared to that of his brother Benjamin Bathurst (?1691–1767) of Lydney, Glos. whose two marriages produced a total of thirty-six children.

71. GRO D2525, Box 46, doc. 10.

72. HRO 193M85/177.

73. A fallow buck in its first year is a fawn; in its second a pricket and in its third a sorrel.

74. Atkinson 1995, 68; WSRO 549/8; Richardson 2005, Appendix 8.

75. Nicholas 1955, 221.

76. WSRO 549/8 f23.

77. Rackham 1989, 176–9.

78. Musty 1986. See the grandstand and course at Lodge Park, Gloucestershire.

79. The 1650 survey refers to 'the old holes of the post paddock course being the boundary' (TNA:PRO E317/Wilts.26).

80. TNA:PRO E178/4728; Richardson 2005, 80–81. In 1631 £768 15s 4½d was paid to Philip, Earl of Pembroke 'for paling out a course in the park of Clarendon … ' (CSPD 1661–63, 114). In 1914 there was still a field here called 'Paddock Corse Field'. The evidence for sixteenth- and seventeenth-century paddock courses is reviewed by Taylor (2005). Deer-coursing remained a popular pastime into the nineteenth century.

81. In 1607 the Haybarn required 7,000 tiles and 24 cresting tiles (TNA:PRO E101/542/22).

82. Richardson 2003b.

83. WSRO 212B/302.1.

84. Now Large Gooseneck, Rex's and 69K/69D respectively not mapped for security.

85. Probably a temporary structure erected especially for Elizabeth I's visit; it had disappeared by 1650.

86. TNA:PRO E317/Wilts 27.

87. TNA:PRO E317/Wilts.26; Tyers 1999.

88. TNA:PRO E317/Wilts.27.

89. Tyers and Hibberd, 1993. If this oak does come from the grandstand, it is a fragment of a precursor to the surviving standing of 1543, Queen Elizabeth Hunting Lodge at Chingford in Epping Forest (Essex), but Clarendon has no claim to be the earliest such structure (Taylor 2005).

90. Tyers 1999, 6.

91. Roberts Report, UW Archaeological Consultancy Clarendon Archive.

92. TNA:PRO STAC 2/11, f.31; Manning 1993.

93. Merriman 1885, 25.

94. Hidden 1988, 104.

95. TNA:PRO STAC 8/183/40; Manning 1993.

96. TNA:PRO E317/Wilts.26; .27.

97. Aubrey 1847/1969, 59.

98. These figures may be compared against the 2,000–3,000 at Woodstock in 1577, considered a 'very large number for the size of the enclosure', while at Windsor in 1607 Norden reckoned there were 1,800 fallow deer (including 500 bucks) but parliamentary commissioners mid-century noted many fewer deer there, 953 of various sorts (Bond and Tiller 1987, 25; Roberts 1997, 250–2).

99. TNA:PRO E317/Wilts.27; .28; .29.

100. In contrast to the family bequests these were protected by the caveat 'void if not in my service at my decease' (HRO 193M85/224).

101. TNA:PRO E317/Wilts.27.

102. Recalled in the 1812 fieldname of Stile Field.

103. TNA:PRO E317/Wilts.30.

104. TNA:PRO E317/Wilts.27.

105. Bond 1998, 23.

106. TNA:PRO E317/Wilts.26.

107. TNA:PRO E317/Wilts.27.

108. CSPD 1660–61, 179. At least one commissioner who contributed to this report had purchased part of the park, and so may have exaggerated the reduction. However, the dendrochronology sequence at Clarendon appears to break down completely after about 1650, which is not the case in Oxfordshire, for example, and tends to support the view that the timber resources at Clarendon were devastated (Daniel Miles pers. comm.).

109. Colt-Hoare 1837/44, 145; Latham and Matthews 1972, 203.

110. HRO 193M85/141.

111. Stagg 1989.

112. Roberts 1997, 252.

113. Rackham 1976, 101.

114. HRO 193M85/141. It is possible that the field today called Picket Sainfoin was among the experimentations with crops at this time. Sainfoin, first recorded 1626 (OED), is, as its name indicates, a health-giving forage crop/grass which was growing in Wiltshire by 1651 (Thirsk 1984, 173, 183–4). See Richardson 2005, 82 and fig. 45, for a similar arrangement at Windsor.

115. Gutiérrez 2004a.

116. The stamp is either Thomas Hill of Fisherton Anger or Thomas Hunt of Marlborough (Lewcun 2004).

117. Hyde and Henry Osgood, farmer. Below are listed Thomas Naish, Henry Osgood, Stephen Maten, Joseph Maten, William Borrow, John King (and for 'Kingemaner' and for the 'strats' £3), Henry Hayter, Mrs Ludlow, William Hayter and Robert Freemantle (WSRO G23/1/187, May 1703).

118. They paid the high sum of £25 14s 4d (compared to twelve Allington people who paid only 4s 11¾d: Anon. 1934, 141–2, extracted from the Quarter Sessions rolls. See also Salisbury Journal 15 January 1932).

119. Full references are found in the Bibliography, below, under named testators, from the Family Records Centre (Clerkenwell) and the WSRO, Salisbury Diocese Sub-Dean's Peculiar Records.

120. Aubrey 1847/1969, 59.

121. Ironically, it was John Evelyn, Clarendon's neighbour, who had reported for the Royal Society in 1664 on the destruction of woodland in England. He appealed to landowners to plant trees and claimed success subsequently (Evelyn 1664).

122. TNA:PRO E317/Wilts.27. Fuller's earth is a highly absorbent blue clay which was used in the cloth industry to remove grease from wool.

123. TNA:PRO E317/Wilts.30.

124. WSRO 130/16.

125. Fowler and Needham 1995; Wyatt 1870, 578–90.

126. The correlation between areas mapped as arable and those with seventeenth- and eighteenth-century pottery is perfect with two exceptions: Cockey Down and Hendon. Perhaps these areas were ploughed only towards the end of the eighteenth century or possibly they were not as intensively cultivated as other parts of the park (Gutiérrez 2004a; Lewcun 2004).

127. The granary at Ranger's Lodge is probably eighteenth-century in origin, a contemporary of that at Fussell's Lodge Farm and some of the agricultural buildings at Queen Manor. A hipped and thatched aisled barn, recorded by the RCHME at Dog Kennel as of early eighteenth-century date, has recently been demolished without trace.

128. Field names indicative of dairy cattle in the southern half of the park in 1812 included Cow Pasture, Cow Closes and Cow Ground.

129. Again this correlates with the fieldwalking, which recovered no sherds of seventeenth- or eighteenth-century pottery from New Pond Field, an area to the east of Queen Manor mapped as pasture in the eighteenth century.

130. For listed Wardens of Clarendon Forest from 1066 to 1665, deputies, etc., see Pugh and Crittall 1959, 441–2.

131. TNA:PRO E317/Wilts.26; .27.

132. Nicholas 1955, 11, 74, 113, 199–201, 221. The term 'place' in this context refers to a position rather than a property: the Nicholases did not live at Clarendon. In 1486–7 a Walter Bowbearer had a room at the palace; other bowbearers are mentioned in the 1570s (Richardson 2005, 53).

133. *CPR 1578–80*, 137 no. 176.

134. TNA:PRO 317/Wilts.27; WRL CLA.

135. These incidents are dated 1757–1789 (WSRO B18/; Hunnisett 1981, 2145, 2259, 2410, 2662).

136. From the Prerogative Court of Canterbury wills. Five of these come from the period 1656 to 1691. See Archives in the Bibliography, below, under testators' names (FRC, WSRO Salisbury Diocese Sub-Dean's Peculiar Records and PRFD references).

137. WSRO P/4/1666/1; /1680/4; /1684/6.

138. Hammond 1914–16, 5.

139. FRC PROB 11/354/51, 1677.

140. Christopher and Mary Ewer, who had died more than ten years before. Christopher Ewer described William Hyde as his 'loveing kinsman' and asked to be buried 'near to Mary my dear wife lately deceased'. Hyde called them 'uncle and aunt' (WSRO P/4/1680/4).

141. Ranger's Lodge is probably the 'Keeper's Lodge' built by Edward III in the fourteenth century. At that time the building comprised a hall with two chambers, a garderobe, cellar, pantry, kitchen, larder and stable (Colvin 1963, 917).

142. TNA:PRO E 101/542/22.

143. TNA:PRO E178/4728.

144. TNA:PRO E317/Wilts.27.

145. In 1773 this complex was still known as 'Lodlow' Farm. The current Ranger's building is in part nineteenth-century, and was gutted in the twentieth century, though there are earlier earthworks here representing traces of the pales and outbuildings.

146. TNA:PRO E317/Wilts.27.

147. TNA:PRO E317/Wilts.27.

148. The bricks here are 5.6 cm (2¼ inches) x 5 cm (2 inches). A truss embedded inside the north wall has clasped purlins and one remaining raking queen strut between the tiebeam and the collar. These sections may correspond with the rebuilding of the farmhouse shortly after 1618, when they would have been linked to another house, possibly timber-framed, on the site of the present main range (Wiltshire Buildings Record 1997a).

149. TNA:PRO E101/542/22.

150. TNA:PRO E178/4728.

151. TNA:PRO E317/Wilts.27.

152. Gutiérrez 2004a; Lewcun 2004; Willmott 2004.

153. TNA:PRO E317/Wilts.27.

154. WSRO P/4/1666/1.

155. Verwood bowls, pancheons, crocks, jars and chamber pots were all identified (Gutiérrez 2004a).

156. I. Goodall 2005; A. Goodall 2005.

157. Lewcun 2004.

158. WSRO P/4/1680/4.

159. Lewcun 2004.

160. TNA:PRO E317/Wilts.27.

161. WSRO P/4/1684/6.

162. The largest ashlar blocks are 22½ inches by 66½ inches; these are probably from the palace site and were possibly reused from the previous Queen Manor rebuilt by James I.

163. Wiltshire Buildings Record 1997a.

164. Tyers 1999; NMR date 1634–99.

165. e.g. Tyers 1999, 6–7, table 1, core 7.

166. The key roof feature is the diminished principal, slingbrace roof, in use locally from the seventeenth to the nineteenth centuries. The slingbraces in the

Queen Manor granary are attached to the floor, with a fairly low collar and clasped purlins, which are particular features of east Wiltshire during the sixteenth and seventeenth centuries. A final element which places the granary in the seventeenth century, rather than the eighteenth century, is the straight windbracing, of which only isolated later examples are known (Wiltshire Buildings Record 1997b). At Petersfinger Farmhouse, where the detail on the framing and the gable stacks are visually similar to Queen Manor Farmhouse, there is a convenient datestone in the end gable of building which reads 1683.

167. This would explain the discrepancy in dates between the dendrochronology, which suggests AD 1609–1625 (Tyers 1999), and the architectural evidence.

168. McCann 1996, 3–4.

169. Miles and Bridge 2004.

170. Colt-Hoare 1837/44, 140.

171. The location of a medieval lodge, possibly Palmer's, was examined using geophysical survey.

172. RCHME 50316/1.

173. RCHME 50317/0. Dendrochronology has contributed to dating these buildings: Kennel Farm was typologically thought to be of similar date, 1640–1733, but is now known to be largely 1588, with a reused smoke-blackened beam of earlier date. This led the Commission surveyors to suggest a medieval hallhouse origin for the present structure. Four Cottages, Pitton Lodge and King Manor Cottage were all examined for the purposes of dendrochronology, but were found to be unsuitable, the last two on account of the small scantling of the timbers used, and the former because of a bat-colony in the roof and a description of the roof timbers which, like the other thatched structures, were very slight where early, only later strengthened to bear slate.

174. Lewcun 2004.

175. Dated 1734–99 by the RCHME but it must have been built after 1773, since it does not appear on the map of this date.

176. Mowl and Earnshaw 1985, 71.

177. King Manor and Pitton Lodge are today twice or three times their original size.

178. May 1998; Royal Commission 1993; Royal Commission 1996.

179. Royal Commission 1996.

180. Turle 1998, 22.

181. Tyers 1999; 2001.

182. If this is not the post-1660 main house, then no other candidate suggests itself, all other documented buildings being accounted for. A section of rafters from trees cut in 1653 is to be found today forming a substantial section of the 'motor garage' roof west of the barn and granary of 1765 (see Chapter Five, p. 103) and is reckoned to be in its original position, which makes this an interesting building. Could it be Hyde's coach house? (Miles and Bridge 2004; Daniel Miles, pers. comm.) Brickwork at the rear of this building matches the façade of the Cowper/Hyde house.

183. We thank Frank Green for discussing this with us. At the time of writing it is not clear whether the brick (north) façade and the stone (east) facade are parts of the same seventeenth-century building.

184. Darvill and Gerrard 1994, 124.

185. KACAC 1996, second gazetteer entry. RCHME Listed Buildings File.

186. Ian Tyers pers. comm., who subsequently laid this date aside on the grounds of imperfect statistical probability due to a fragmentary sequence in the seventeenth century. No other dendro dates were helpful in respect of the eighteenth-century sections of the mansion; however, the will of Pierce A'Court of Ivychurch (made 1724, proved May 1725) refers to 'my friend Peter Bathurst of Clarendon Park', which implies that Peter Bathurst was living at Clarendon before 1737 (Brown 1889, 47).

187. WSRO G23/1/187 1703–42 Land Tax assessments for the Liberty of Clarendon Park.

188. Pevsner 1975, 181. Pevsner discusses the 1737 date but considered the appearance of the house to be somewhat earlier, more in the style of John Vanbrugh (1664–1726) or Nicholas Hawksmoor (1661–1736), though it has also been associated with Thomas Archer (1668–1743), who produced some of his best work in the second decade of the century – for example, at Chatsworth (from 1704) and Heythrop (1706–18) (Sherwood and Pevsner 1999, 396–7 and 647). Sir John Summerson compared Clarendon House to Iver Grove, Buckinghamshire, which has many shared motifs but also no known architect (Pevsner 1975, 181). Pevsner (1960, 177) says of Iver Grove 'Built in 1722, and one of the finest houses of Buckinghamshire in the Baroque style of that date'. Those motifs again connect Iver Grove with the work of Hawksmoor, Vanbrugh and another architect, John James. Of these three, it is the last who emerges as the likely author of Clarendon. James had just finished Hawksmoor's west front at Westminster Abbey and in 1736 was advising Francis Price on the new roof of the thirteenth-century cross-wing in the Salisbury Bishop's Palace (Royal Commission 1993, 32a; Georgian Group visit, pers. comm.). More precisely, James was at that time being consulted by Francis Price on carpentry prices

(SCA letter of FP to JJ 'at the Royall Hospitall Greenwich', 1736); we thank Tim Tatton-Brown for a copy of this letter. James's work was certainly familiar to the Bathurst family as Allen, Lord Bathurst (1684–1775) was a subscriber to James's translation of Claude Perrault's *Treatise of the Five Orders of Columns Architecture etc.* of 1708, dedicated to the earl of Pembroke and 'approv'd by, Sir Chr. Wren, J. Vanbrugh and N. Hawksmoor' – of which trio the latter two were also subscribers.

189. See Back Cover.

190. Chubb 1912, 234.

191. 1709, translated by John James in 1712.

192. Rackham 1980.

193. Knyff 1707; the 'Lodge' was perhaps too small to attract his attention.

194. At Stowe 1716–39; Paston Manor 1718; Rousham 1721–9; Chiswick 1725 (Taigel and Williamson 1993).

195. The ages of oak trees in the avenues radiating from the mansion were estimated by eye in the 1980s as about 150 years. Dendrochronological evidence suggests they are in fact considerably older.

196. Trees in the beech and lime avenues were also reckoned by eye, erroneously, to be c. 150 years old. At present only small numbers have been sampled and these results are provisional (Miles and Bridge 2004).

197. RCHME dates the dovecote in the band 1700–90. Significant dendrochronological sequences of over 100 rings were recovered from this structure, but did not date, possibly being from an old, isolated tree in the park, and add to the unresolved complexities of the dendrochronological sequence c. 1650–1750 (Daniel Miles pers. comm).

198. Tyers 2001. This 1765 barn/granary compares well with an example at Countess Farm, Amesbury, with a datestone of 1772. The Clarendon example is built of slow-grown oak, all apparently from the estate and cut down at the same time. It is the first 'new built' (i.e. not made of reused ancient oak) structure found at Clarendon (Slocombe 1989, 27).

199. Lees-Milne 1962; Gerrard and Clements 1994.

200. He dammed a lake in Cirencester Park in 1736.

201. Kingsley 1989.

202. Note Pope's Bottom at Clarendon.

203. Colman and Garrick 1766, Act II, i.

204. Perhaps the site was deliberately 'enhanced' by planting of yew trees, as at Alfred's Hall, Cirencester Park. Scots pines grew at the palace site until their removal about 1998, as did ivy, which may have been planted deliberately to trail over the gable end of the Great Hall.

205. This was also the case in Cirencester Park; there is, for example, no focal point at the Sapperton end of the Broad Ride in Cirencester Park.

206. Pope sketched out a serpentine walk at Cirencester Park in 1724, apparently complete by 1733 (Martin 1984, 90).

207. Mandler 1997.

208. HRO 9M73/G345/69, 73–4, 78, 81, 82–6.

Notes to Chapter Six: A Working Estate 1800–2000: Survival and Revival

1. Peter Bathurst left Clarendon Park and his other estates, including Lainston House at Sparsholt (Hants), to his brother Henry (HRO 193M85/224). From Henry the estate passed to his sister, Selina, and thence to Frederick Hervey, Selina's second son, if he took the name Bathurst (HRO 193M85/224).

2. Wheat was also the leading crop in Wiltshire in 1801 (Prince 1989, 39–41).

3. Other early nineteenth-century Clarendon Marchments include William and John, yeoman, named in a bastardy case by Diana White of St Edmund's, Salisbury in 1814 (WSRO B18/100/10).

4. Mowl and Earnshaw 1985, 138. Similar designs highlighted in Mowl and Earnshaw (1985, 142) include Tawstock Court (Devon), Charnborough Park (Dorset), and Ickenham House (Middlesex).

5. Phillipps's original annotated plan of his excavation is in the Bodleian (BLO Phillipps–Robinson MA b108, f34–7), together with a more finalised version (BLO MS Top. Wilts a.1). Two pencil sketches of the east gable of the Great Hall and the barrel vaulting in the cellar also survive in the Wiltshire Archaeological and Natural History Society Library in Devizes, together with two further unpublished plans with measurements of the Queen's chamber area (WHWANHS Hensley album D6.6). William Hensley was Phillipps's agent and it was probably he who was in charge on site.

6. Cowan 1996, 811: letter dated 13 July 1828.

7. HRO 193M85/181; Cowan 1996. The Penistons were still brick-making there in 1891.

8. Roberts 1997, fig. 91.

9. See Roberts 1997, 95–6 and figs 91 (W[indsor]G[reat] P[ark] brick) and 92 (Teulon Cottages). 'CLARENDON' bricks are found, for example, at Savage's Farm Cottage and at the house immediately outside Pitton Gate.

10. Cowan 1996, x, xii, 832, 1252, 1273.

11. Cowan 1996, 893, 1235, 1273.

12. The intention was to erect this structure in summer 1829, but in August the owner was fidgeting because the conservatory was not finished. It finally arrived in September.

13. Bond 1998, 122.

14. Cowan 1996, 1130, 1156.

15. Cowan 1996, 844; August 1828.

16. For example, when the billiards table was installed his instructions for supporting it on solid piers above the groins of the cellar were ignored. In some cases instructions could not be followed because of the constraints of working within an existing building shell. For example, we now know it was the façade of the seventeenth-century house which was being knocked into when alterations to the fireplace in the north-west bedroom 'cannot well be effected without cutting more into the old wall than I would wish to do' (Cowan 1996, 954).

17. Cowan 1996, 844; August 1828.

18. Cowan 1996, 1332.

19. Tyers 1999, 4.

20. Jones's was supplied with the dimensions of the rooms to be lit: four rooms of 27 x 24 x 14 feet high (8.1 x 7.2 x 4.2 m); entrance hall 20 x 14 feet (6 x 4.2 m); staircase 20 x 20 x 30 feet high (6 x 6 x 9 m); conservatory 27 x 20 feet (8.1 x 6 m).

21. Cowan 1996, 1210, 1252.

22. Cowan 1996, 926.

23. FHHB attended Winchester College and married Louisa Mary, eldest daughter of Walter Smythe of 'Branbridge' (Hants), in 1832 (HRO 193M85/217 and 218; HRO 193M85/232, 233, 235).

24. WHWANHS Press cuttings, vol XVI, 163; TNA: PRO RG/11/2066.

25. Simons 1993, 11 and 12. Both FHHB and his son Lionel Hervey-Bathurst (b. Clarendon 1849, later Paston-Cooper) played county cricket for Hampshire (Wisden 1901 cited in Lyon 1930; Noel 1926, 53–4). FHHB's commitment to the pleasures of cricket is patent. He laid down a cricket pitch south-east of the mansion, which was used until 1980 and is now pasture named 'Cricket Field'.

26. Mandler 1997, 86. Though Hervey-Bathurst did permit skating on the lake for local people.

27. CEA visitor's account, 1880.

28. 'The good keep of the whole place', our observer records, 'reflects great credit on Mr Frisby'. Clarendon's gardeners were successively housed close to the mansion. Robert Frisby, the gardener, appears at 'Private Cottage' in the 1881 census, probably the later Gardener's Cottage (now 1 Estate Cottage) built 1851–61. Frisby is recorded as aged 35, native of Ryhall, Rutland, with his wife Sarah, a native of Scotland (TNA:PRO RG 11/2066). Since Frisby was not present in 1891, his gardening career at Clarendon may have ended with the death of Sir Frederick in 1881. In 1891 a gardener and forester shared a house at 'Clarendon Garden', with another gardener at Piper's (TNA:PRO RG 12/1618).

29. Cowan 1996; HRO 193M85/339.

30. Rackham 1994, 26.

31. 'He would not have done that later' (RCHME 50312/0; Pevsner 1975, 182).

32. Original lattice-glazed iron casement windows were removed in the 1970s. The overall feel of this Victorian lodge is 'Jacobethan', very different from the later (1843) Pugin Gothic gatehouse design at Peper Harow in Surrey, for example, but, in its day, a novelty. A pair of local Jacobethan lodges of the 1830s is also to be found at Charlton Park, Wiltshire (Mowl and Earnshaw 1985, 165).

33. Pevsner 1975, 83. The medieval palace cannot be claimed as a direct inspiration for Pugin's Grange, though the latter did contain a tower, turret with garderobe and a chapel. The Grange's main window also frames a view towards Salisbury Cathedral.

34. FHHB was a patron of the rebuilding of Alderbury Church by the architect and 'arch-fiend' of restoration, S. S. Teulon, in 1857–8. Hervey-Bathurst's £500 secured him fifty seats for Clarendon people (Anon. 2000, 50). For his contribution at West Grimstead c. 1835 see Royal Commission (1987, 85, 87, 101).

35. For example, Kelly 1931; Boodle 1901–2, 140. The FHHB additions are visible in photographs taken in the early twentieth century and those in the Royal Commission collection taken c. 1979, prior to the demolition of these structures.

36. Letter from Railtrack dated June 1996. Plans of railway as it affected Brick Kiln Farm are among the Peniston Papers (WSRO 451/91 and /93).

37. Brick Kiln Farmhouse was 'building' in the 1851 census (TNA:PRO HO107/1846) while the farmer, Thomas Perkins, kept out of the way in Harnham. Ashley Hill Farmhouse and Pitton Lodge share architectural features suggesting major alterations about 1850, and cottages including the Gardener's Cottage, Fair Oak Cottages, Belmont Dairy Farm (about 1848), 1 and 2 Dairy Cottages and Brick Kiln Cottages all appear within a decade of the railway (KACAC 1996). We thank John Steane for discussing railway-funded buildings with us.

38. In 1891 there were five, based at Pitton Lodge, Four Cottages, King Manor, Beech Tree Cottage and the Gate Lodge near Clarendon House (TNA:PRO RG12/1618).

39. The properties were very often sub-let.

40. The switch in occupancy at Beech Tree from farmer to gamekeeper reflects changing priorities over the course of the century but otherwise this sketch of Clarendon activities in the nineteenth century remained unaltered in essence until the 1960s, when four tenants managed blocks of land at Queen Manor/Ranger's, Brick Kiln/Hole Farm, Dog Kennel and Savage's.

41. Brassley 2000, 457. TNA:PRO MAF 68/151; /1861; /4367; /6134).

42. Bettey 1987, 38.

43. TNA:PRO MAF68/436 (1875).

44. Cheesemaking, though not apparent in the census, is recorded locally at Petersfinger Farm, where cheese was made in living memory and where the trapdoor from the cheese dairy to the storage lofts is still to be seen (UW Oral sources R.C.Clarke/TBJ 2002).

45. WSRO G23/1/137/118; /166; /138/101; /145/32; /147/121. Because properties were sub-let, these are not necessarily individuals of whom the Hervey-Bathursts had any knowledge.

46. Ceramic finds from Gutiérrez (2004a), glass from Willmott (2004).

47. For example, from Caveral Coppice in 1858, when there were twenty-six separate sales for faggots (firewood), bringing an income of £88 (HRO 193M85/360).

48. In 1832 a single flittern fetched £1 8s 3d, while another twenty were sold at 5s each.

49. Less £81 9s for cutting, stripping and barking, leaving a profit of £176 11s (HRO 193M85/339).

50. See HRO 193M85/360 (1858), for example.

51. Collins 2000.

52. Clarkson 1974.

53. For example, '5 pairs of Scotch firs for 5s.' (HRO 193M85/339).

54. Kelly 1931. There is no evidence of osiers at the Clarendon withybeds today, though the wetter areas are dominated by sedges and soft rush (*Juncus effusus*). They appear to have been cleared and replanted, perhaps at the turn of the twentieth century judging by the diameters of the oak and ash found there today (David Clements pers. comm.). Given FHHB's interests, one wonders whether the growing of cricket-bat willow was ever attempted.

55. The holdings of Messrs Mussell and Moody, brickmakers, are identified on the 1887 map drawn to accompany the 1889 mortgage (HRO 193M85/190 and /206).

56. *Salisbury Times and South Wiltshire Gazette* 26 January 1894.

57. HRO 193M85/339.

58. HRO 193M85/360 accounts for Clarendon, Lainston, Sparsholt and Little Somborne 1858.

59. FTAHB (1833–1900). Conservative MP for the South Wiltshire constituency 1861–85. Married Ada, daughter of Sir John Sheppey of Ribton, in 1869. Also a cricketer, FTAHB played for Eton against Winchester in the resoundingly successful teams of 1849–50 (Noel 1926).

60. Average rents declined nationally by 17 per cent between 1872 and 1893 (Collins 2000, 143).

61. An extensive estate at Whiteparish (Wilts), with no house, kept mainly for the shooting, was also sold in the 1890s. We thank John Hervey-Bathurst for this information. Clarendon shooting was let (HRO 193M85/378). In 1899, for example, the estate was 'let' to Mr Hartmann.

62. At his death in 1900, FTAHB's personal estate was valued at £80,156, with debts of £20,000 to the Wilts and Dorset Bank, a £7,000 overdraft, loans of £11,000 and a £16,000 mortgage (HRO 193M85/229).

63. On October 21 1891 lots 1–8 were from Petersfinger Cottages to Ashley Hill House; lot 9, opposite Belmont, to 20 by Dog Kennel Farm; lot 15 lay west of Chowringhee (WHWANHS Estate sales catalogues vol. 22, 1; HRO 193M85/378).

64. The sale was to be by auction and a notice to that effect appeared in the *Times* in May 1894 (HRO 193M85/379).

65. According to John Hervey-Bathurst, by this time FTAHB was 'becoming senile, and was very stubborn … They took pictures etc, but not much furniture, and left behind a Jacobean library, bringing with them instead bound copies of the *Illustrated London News* and early editions of Dickens, abandoning most of whatever records/papers there must have been'. We thank John Hervey-Bathurst for this information. No visitors' books etc. survive from the late nineteenth century (WHWAHNS, Press cuttings, volume VII, 261).

66. *Who's Who* 1900, 159; Anon. 1900, 89–90; PRFD will of FTAHB, 1900; Kelly 1915.

67. *Times*, June 1894.

68. HRO 193M85/206. He was a Wiltshire JP in 1906, Chairman of the Shepton Mallet Urban District Council and a member of the Salisbury Infirmary Committee. Married Florence, daughter of C.R.Wainwright of Christon (Somerset).

69. Robert Corbett pers. comm.

70. CEA Clarendon Park, Wilts. The Hervey-Bathurst sale had included a lawn marker and two lots of tennis nets, supports and stop-netting.

71. The trees in these 'high and broad spruce belts planted by a "shooting architect" before World War I', as they were described in the 1930s, were cut down during the Second World War, but still exist as thick boundary lines (CEA G.H. Mills Memoir). The belts are not shown on the 1887/1889 OS insurance maps (HRO 193M85/189; /190).

72. They include, for example, Savage's Farm Cottage, Fussell's Farm Cottage, Best's Cottages and a miniature playhouse with a 1907 datestone embellished with the initials EAG (Ellen Audrey Garton, later Alcock) and RVG (Ronald Verner Garton), two of James Garton's younger children. These brick houses have survived their first century well, and now provide core properties on the modern estate for staff and for letting.

73. Salisbury RDC and Attorney General vs. Mr Garton (WSRO G11/141/1).

74. *Wilts County Mirror and Express*, 16 Jan 1903.

75. Anon. 1903, 85; *Devizes Gazette*, 15 and 22 January 1903; *Wilts County Mirror and Express*, 16 January 1903.

76. Dorling 1906, 57.

77. Hammond 1914–16.

78. Mandler 1997, 124.

79. CEA Sales catalogues 1919–20.

80. When Garton died in 1940 at Lilliput, his bequests included a collection of guns and a library of works on natural history. His interests still included brewing (William Cooper and Co. of East Street, Southampton) and the motor trade (Wessex Motors) (Kelly 1939–40; PRFD will J.W. Garton 1940; Burke's *Landed Gentry*).

81. CEA Sales catalogues 1919–20. 'Game Rearing Appliances' included egg-incubators for 1,660 eggs; 100 movable pheasant pens; two pheasant carriers and five 'Foster-mother[s], with run complete'.

82. CEA Sales catalogues 1919–20.

83. WRL CLA letters relating to fishery rights in Clarendon Park. The 1909 report was originally supported by twelve, and that of 1910 by thirty-three, appendices of documentary evidence, now lost, and addressed Clarendon fishery and swannery rights from the Middle Ages onwards.

84. These rights are not exercised from the estate now though they were recorded in the purchase document of summer 1919 (TNA:PRO E317/Wilts.29). Before his death in 1968 Major Christie-Miller opened an investigation into access to the Avon and reviving these rights (R.C. Clarke, pers. comm.).

85. 13 pots of arum lilies, 14 of spirea, 40 of various ferns, 12 of primulas, 9 of grasses, 4 hydrangea, 26 small pots of geraniums, 9 ivy geraniums, 45 pelargoniums, 36 small pots of carnations, 180 pots of chrysanthemums, 96 of maidenhair fern, 19 of orchids, 12 of primulas, 8 of 'aspidestras', 5 of fuschias, 5 of arums, 4 of large palms, 48 of amarylis, 18 azaleas in pots, 3 cytisus and 5 pots of 'pancratum'.

86. CEA purchase papers, and relating to the subsequent court case which was settled in Mr Christie-Miller's favour in November 1921.

87. Something which did not happen at Temple Newsam and Newstead Abbey, for example.

88. Mandler 1997, 246.

89. The library at Britwell was of old English books and said to be the greatest ever brought together by a private individual. It was assembled largely by William Henry Miller (1789–1848) between 1825 and 1840 and included the Heber collection of black letter ballads. There are catalogues in the BLO dating to 1852 and 1872–3.

90. Hermann 1980.

91. Veronica, Rosemary and Lavender born 1905, 1907 and 1909 respectively.

92. Brooks 1999.

93. This room contained 'THE EXPENSIVE ("The Eureka") FULL-SIZE BILLIARD TABLE by Burroughs and Watts', 12 feet 6 inches x 6 feet 9 inches (outside measurements; 3.75 x 2.02 m) with 'wired electric connections', circular scoring dial, two walnut revolving cue stands and other accoutrements. CEA Clarendon Park, Salisbury inventory 1925, nos. 57–63. This item probably matched that still *in situ*, also with electric scoring and circular dials, at Tyntesfield near Bristol.

94. An Ethophone Wireless Apparatus with valves and earphones and Ethovox Loud Speaker, batteries, etc.

95. CEA G.H. Mills Memoir.

96. James and Robinson 1988.

97. CEA G.H. Mills Memoir.

98. CEA G.H. Mills Memoir; UW Oral sources, Gordon Eastman.

99. For Godolphin School girls until well into the twentieth century, being recalled by those at the school after 1945 – and who also recalled going to the estate to take part in the back-breaking potato harvest (CEA visitor's account, 1880; ex-Godolphin October 2002, pers. comm.).

100. James 1989; Gerrard 2003, 67–8 and fig. 3.8; Anon. 2000, 134.

101. Horses were not included in the early agricultural census returns but in 1925, seventy-five horses were found on the estate; in 1939 there were forty, thirty-four for agriculture, two unbroken and four

others; in 1951 there were seventeen, fourteen used in agriculture and three others. In 1957 there was a total of six (all agricultural). The 'Agricultural' total always included horses used in market gardening and mares used for breeding. Steam machines and motors were among the disputed items in 1919–21.

102. For example, where the 1925 agricultural return notes 180 apple, 17 pear, 7 cherry, 65 plum and 5 'other orchard trees', by 1951 there were only three acres (1.2 ha) of orchard left (TNA:PRO MAF 68/2887; /4367; /6134).

103. TNA:PRO MAF 68/3265; /4367; /5454; 6134. These totals include all the farms in the park.

104. CEA G. H. Mills Memoir. With the decline in coppicing and less interest in timber, it is the shooting and fox-hunting which has guaranteed the survival of woodland as ground cover.

105. The former at Queen Manor and Hole Farm, the latter at Best's Farm, Home Farm and Fussell's Lodge. Numbers of dairy cattle at Clarendon rose from 347 in 1900 to 723 in 1951 (TNA:PRO MAF 68/151; /4367; /6134).

106. CEA Sale catalogue 1952.

107. Nearly 400 of them in the pre-1939 period, but only 81 in 1951 (CEA 1919/1920 sales catalogues). Berkshires were the favoured breed.

108. There were 1,947 in 1925, a substantial increase from the 1,148 recorded in 1866 (TNA:PRO MAF 68). Two galvanised shepherds' caravans remain on the estate today: one between Fussell's and Four Cottages, another near Beech Tree Cottage.

109. These figures are from 1951. They were bred by the Sykes family, expanding from just 2202 birds in 1939 (TNA:PRO MAF 68/3923; /5454; /6134).

110. Searchlights were portable (on the backs of lorries), but concrete remains lie in the hedge across the road north of Tilting Field near Searchlight Field.

111. KACAC 1996, 83–4; Richard Price, pers. comm.; Gordon Eastman pers. comm.; 1942 is found carved on a beech tree at the western extremity of the palace site.

112. Anon 2000, 68–9; Norman Parker, pers. comm. Both Spitfires were built in Salisbury. The gunner of the Dornier, called Grossman, was captured and, later on, sang in Salisbury Cathedral Choir.

113. Michael (1922–1944) was killed while serving with the Coldstream Guards (CEA G. H. Mills Memoir; WSRO 2142/24).

114. In 1968–70 there were 626 acres (253 ha) of grassland, 80 acres (32 ha) of kale for the livestock and 1,000 acres (405 ha) of cereal, mainly spring-sown. For this work there was one foreman, one mechanic and six full-time tractor drivers, as well as casual workers at harvest. Today there are four fewer full-time tractor drivers for two and a half times the area, and higher yielding winter-sown crops, together with improvements in crop protection and management, have increased the average yield from 1.5 tons per acre in 1968–70 to nearer 3.5 tons in 2003. We are grateful to Richard Price for providing information on twentieth-century farming at Clarendon.

115. Best's Farm was closed in 1985; the tenanted Hole Farm dairy was closed in 1990; Queen Manor dairy produced until 1995; Fussell's dairy closed in 2000.

116. The chief bull was imported from Canada in the spring of 1975 and sold in 1978 (CEA Sale Catalogue of Clarendon Poll Herefords, May 1980). Field-name evidence near the mansion to the north, in an area visible to those approaching by car, shows that the Herefords were kept close to the mansion, providing an impressive aesthetic of grand cattle among the oaks of the park.

117. Subsidies are inevitably the greatest influence on crop selection; the Common Agricultural Policy (CAP) introduced set-aside. In 1994 15 per cent of the arable acreage was left fallow; in 2004 that figure is reduced to 5 per cent. In future, much will depend on changing CAP payment regimes, introduced in 2005.

118. CEA visitor's account, 1880. Of the four trees mentioned, three can still be identified today. A sample from a fallen tree from the vicinity of the eighteenth-century park included 290 rings in 1995, taking it back to 1705, and standing trees go back at least as far as 1500 (based on a combination of dendro-drilling and circumference-measuring: Tyers 1999, 9; Miles and Bridge 2004; Daniel Miles, pers. comm.).

119. CEA P. H. Carne, Gerald Johnstone writing on deer for *Countryman* magazine winter 1950/1951; CEA correspondence files (S. V. Christie-Miller) January 1951; NCC Survey 1981; AWMCM lectures 13 June 1990; February 1995.

Notes to Chapter Seven: Valuing the Landscape

1. Toulmin Smith 1907, I, 268–9.
2. Cox 1725, 51; Cartwright 1889, 244.
3. Camden 1600.
4. Defoe 1928 i, 192, 199. We thank John Chandler for discussing the Defoe references with us.
5. Aubrey 1665–93, 971. The reference implies that diggings were already underway at the palace.
6. BLO Gough maps 33; Anon. 1893–5.
7. Stukeley and Herbert were both involved with the Royal Society, Herbert being President in 1689–90. In 1722 Stukeley founded the Society of Roman Knights, with Herbert as patron (Haycock 2002).
8. Stukeley 1724, 2nd edn 1776, 138.
9. Harris was a classicist and an author, MP for Christchurch (1761) and Lord of the Treasury (1763). He is buried in Salisbury Cathedral (Stephen and Lee 1891, 7–8).
10. Warton wrote a three-volume *History of English Poetry* (1778–81), among other books.
11. Sweet 2004, 249–55.
12. Lyttleton 1769–73.
13. HRO 9M73/G515/9. The original letter with Harris's measurements is in BL Add. MSS 18729. There is no plan. Thanks to Rosemary Dunhill for pointing out the original documents.
14. Warton 1778–81, 79; Rinaker 1916, 15; Partridge 1927, *passim*.
15. Britton 1801, 118.
16. Phillipps, MA (Oxon), was 28 when he came to Clarendon but was already a Fellow of the Society of Antiquaries of London (Stephen and Lee 1896, 192–195; Kite 1908).
17. The Protestant Scot David Hume, in his *History of England* (1826, 350–2) chooses the words 'obstinately refused' to characterise Becket's response to Henry II's demands in the Constitutions of Clarendon that secular power in the hands of churchmen should be curbed. In this account Pope Alexander 'abrogated, annulled and rejected' all the Constitutions except six, which he deemed 'less evil', condemning the document 'in the strongest terms'. The Catholic historian Lingard, on the other hand, downplays the historical significance of events at Clarendon in 1164 (Lingard 1855 ii, 66). For later accounts see, for example, *Cameos from English History* (Yonge 1883, 144); *History of England* (Trevelyan 1926, 155); *A Shorter History of England* (Belloc 1934, 136), and many more specialised works. Given his involvement, it is interesting to note that Phillipps was vehemently anti-Catholic. His will stated that no Roman Catholic should ever be allowed to enter his house (Kite 1908).
18. BLO MS Phillipps-Robinson c271 fs 27v–8; BLO MS Top. Wilts a. l. and a working plan of part of the site; WHWANHS Hensley album D6.6.
19. Turner and Parker 1851–9; Pettigrew 1859.
20. Henry Hatcher asserted that a Roman mosaic had been seen in Clarendon Wood (Hatcher 1845). The 'villa' was then discounted by twentieth-century scholars (e.g. Cunnington 1932, 169) but is now proven correct; see Chapter Two. In July 1846 'numerous skeletons' were exhumed when the railway cut through Bronze Age and Saxon cemetery sites at Petersfinger, and further graves were found by a labourer. By 1862 a skull came into the collection of Dr H. P. Blackmore when he excavated more bones, a grave with pottery and other grave goods (Moore and Algar 1968, 103–5). Dr Blackmore and his brother William were involved in the foundation of the museum in Salisbury in 1867 (Conybeare 2003, 49; Darby 2003, 216).
21. The 1844 text includes the following: 'The building of which this fragment formed a part was long a favourite residence of English monarchs, and has been historically connected with many important transactions and distinguished characters. Amongst others Philip, King of Navarre, here rendered the first homage which was paid Edward I as King of France; and John, King of France, with David, King of Scots, spent a portion of their captivity. More especially were here enacted the Constitutions of Clarendon, the first barrier raised against the claims of secular jurisdiction by the See of Rome. The spirit awakened within these walls ceased not until it had vindicated the authority of the laws and accomplished the Reformation of the Church of England'.
22. The confusion of Edward I and Edward III, for example.
23. The 1930s excavators referred to the crag and its plaque as the 'Protestant Fragment'.
24. Though Morgan and Grundy's research in the late 1930s on Wiltshire's medieval forests made its contribution (Morgan 1935, Grundy 1939; Turner 1901 and Cox 1905).
25. Borenius lived locally at Coombe Bissett, and worked at London University 1922–47. His publications included *English Medieval Painting* (with E. W. Tristram 1927), which mentions lost wall paintings at Clarendon (1927), 28–9 and *St Thomas Becket in Art* (1932).

26. Borenius and Charlton 1936, 55.

27. Borenius and Charlton 1936, 66–7.

28. James 1989. See Figure 72. In c. 1985 Borenius's daughter, the late Clarissa Lada-Grodzicka, recalled that he advised Queen Mary on art, and also talked about Clarendon on pre-war television, 'heavily made up in bright yellow'.

29. Mortimer Wheeler gave advice. The work was part-funded by the Society of Antiquaries, who had also sponsored John Charlton's previous excavations at Old Sarum. For Clarendon excavations the Society provided these funds: in 1933, £30; 1934, £30; 1935, £25; 1936, £20; 1937, £30; 1938, £30; 1939, £40 (Society of Antiquaries research fund accounts). We thank Adrian James for this reference. Private donors included Lord Herbert and Miss Edith Olivier (Borenius and Charlton 1936, 65–6 and n. 1).

30. James and Robinson 1988, 72–9.

31. Removal and reassembly of the kiln for British Museum display pioneered reconstruction for exhibition (van Geersdaele and Davison 1975). Plaster of Paris moulds used in lifting the bricks were, until recently, still to be seen discarded on site. The excavation is published in James and Robinson 1988.

32. Colvin 1963.

33. TNA:PRO WORKS/14/1777, memo 23 October 1941.

34. TNA:PRO WORKS/14/1777, memos 26 November and 16 December 1941.

35. TNA:PRO WORKS/14/1777, memo 28 August 1944.

36. Times, December 1952; January 1953. A further thirty-five years were to elapse before publication.

37. For the full record on this site TNA:PRO WORK 14/2533.

38. TNA:PRO WORK 14/1777.

39. TNA:PRO WORK 14/1777.

40. Fasham 1985.

41. Games 2002 and News from Split (BBC Third Programme 3 March 1966). 'We have a lot to do at home before we can match up to the achievement at Split. Think of Clarendon … when visiting Split as an English tourist, and you ought to be thoroughly ashamed … ' We thank Stephen Games for providing this reference for us.

42. Times 1977, Letters on 5, 9, 11 and 27 May.

43. Saunders 1991, 157.

44. Zarnecki et al. 1984, 189–90.

45. A. D. Saunders to TBJ, 23 July 1984; Chairman of English Heritage to AWMCM, 13 September 1984.

46. Tim Tatton-Brown to the Times, 3 and 13 October 1986.

47. James and Robinson 1988.

48. KACAC 1996.

49. KACAC 1998.

50. For a ten-year plan under Countryside Stewardship in 1999. It includes ceasing to cultivate over barrows and other earthworks, enhancing fencing and stock management, reinstating an historic orchard and enhancing access to the palace site from the Clarendon Way footpath.

51. John Ashurst (Ingram Consultancy) drew up specific proposals for palace masonry conservation. Consolidation and clearance at the palace was undertaken as a joint five-year venture between the estate and English Heritage. Masonry conservation materials used included lime putty, hydraulic lime and sand and limestone aggregates, blended into a bedding and tamping mix and a plastering mix.

52. A survey of ramblers and members of the public walking the footpath by the palace during 2000 revealed unanimous support for preserving Clarendon Palace. Almost all those interviewed said they would visit the site if it were open and wished to know more about the palace and its history (Collings 2001, Appendices 14–18).

53. Hebridean and Beulah sheep were introduced in 1999 from the English Nature reserve at Martin Down. Both breeds do well on unimproved vegetation and graze much unwelcome scrub.

54. Through its scoping meetings the estate engages with wider initiatives such as woodland Biodiversity Action Plans, Species Action Plans, etc., and actively encourages species monitoring.

55. For example, Edward Windsor's Crown and Country episode on Salisbury, shown in July 1998. For Easter 2002 a programme on King Arthur was filmed on the western slope atop the fifth-century cemetery at Petersfinger to make the programme's point that Clarendon lay on the boundary between Saxon east and British, so-called 'Arthurian' west country, etc.

56. Marks 1988, 232–3.

57. Other 1980s productions filmed here have been a feature length Only Fools and Horses episode, 'A Royal Flush', broadcast at Christmas 1986, and another episode which included a shoot. Thomas Hardy's The Day After the Fair included scenes at Clarendon, as did Ruth Rendell's Wexford mystery An Unkindness of Ravens.

58. Jones and Cloke (2002, 31–40) propose reasons for this unpopularity, including their lack of individuality, the tendency to plant in rows, the lack of birds and wildflowers, etc. By contrast, the size, texture and varying hues of deciduous trees engages us with place and nature.

59. Serovayskaya 1998.

60. Although, in the shift from written perambulations to maps, some landscape detail is lost. Individually named trees, for example, become homogenised as 'woodland'.

61. Compare, for example, Clarendon with Windsor, an estate which has suffered more deaths of owners than Clarendon but has not been subject to the same duties.

62. Dwyer and Hodge 1996, 28–30.

63. CEA 1919 Sale catalogue. The loss of 3,200 British soldiers to the Boers at Mafeking and the stubborn defence of Ladysmith by Baden-Powell struck chords on the home front.

64. Crittall 1962, 26; Sedgwick 1970, 446–7.

65. This is the 'landscape of polite exclusion', as Williamson (1995, 107) has called it.

66. CEA Sale catalogue and Inventory.

67. Humphrey and Hugh-Jones 1992.

68. Cantor 1982, 66.

69. It is therefore noteworthy that at this time of steeply declining Crown forest assets, it has been suggested that the size of Clarendon Park was increased substantially by Edward II c. 1319 (Richardson 2005, 114 and fig. 73).

70. Young 1987, 87ff, cites Office of Works for structures; Office of the Treasurer of the Chamber, which paid for the 'apparelling'.

71. Thompson 1963, 43.

72. Williamson 1995, 136–7.

73. Carter and Greenway 1983, 60.

74. The forest also figures in both *Sir Gawain and the Green Knight* (late fourteenth-century) and *Morte D'Arthur* (c. 1470) as well as subsequently in works by Spenser and Shakespeare.

75. Saunders 1993, 119.

76. There may also be a yearning here for a development from the dark world of the Romanesque: the small windows, thick defensive walls and mighty tree-trunk columns, a prefiguring of the Gothic with its glorious windows and floods of light, soon to grace both Clarendon Palace at the top of the hill and Salisbury Cathedral below. Abbot Suger's first Gothic programme at St Denis dates to 1138.

77. Saunders 1993, 119.

78. Five formerly gilded lead stars were found during the 1930s excavations, three near the Antioch Chamber and two at the King's Chambers. They were also formerly to be seen decorating the walls of St Stephen's Chapel, Westminster (James and Knight 1988, 224–9; Eames 1965, 65; Borenius 1943, 45–6).

79. Professor Tristram thought the crescents with stars might be a 'badge' of Henry III (Borenius 1943).

However, a mitre of c. 1180–1210 displays crescents like those at Clarendon with scenes of the stoning of St Stephen and the killing of Thomas Becket. Both crescents and stars are found in a BLO manuscript of cats hunting of c. 1210. Perhaps the lead ornamentation represents decoration from the less fully documented Romanesque period, even recalling the Becket incident of 1164 at Clarendon. See also Staniland (1991, 8).

80. As at St Albans Cathedral (mid thirteenth-century), and the Chapel in the Bishop's Palace, Chichester.

81. St Katherine of Alexandria. Her emblem is the spiked wheel of her martyrdom; her image is often depicted with a crown, sword and palm of martyrdom, as in the stained glass of Ludlow church (Speake 1994, 25).

82. There are examples at other palaces (Richardson 2003a).

83. As at Thornhill (Salop) (Speake 1994, 144). Notably, there was a Jesse Tree in another rural residence at Windsor in 1237.

84. Speake 1994, 97–8.

85. Richardson 2003a. It is also possible that the portrayal of Margaret in the king's chamber was not that of her emerging from the dragon, but was of a less common scene from the saint's life, such as her grasping the demon by the hair. A cult and its associations were not always rigorously fixed and could be more fluid than is often suggested (Larson 2002).

86. Borenius 1943.

87. Saunders 1993, 18.

88. Richardson (2005, 33) discusses an increase of poaching in the park in the hungry early fourteenth century.

89. Saunders 1993, 65.

90. Pearsall and Salter 1973, 76–118.

91. Comfort 1913, 174.

92. In England they came later to signify Lancaster and York, combined as Tudor, as their repeated appearance in the loyalty-décor of early Tudor bishops of Lincoln at their Lyddington Palace demonstrates.

93. Harvey 1990, 11.

94. Biddle 2000.

95. Vale 1982, 45.

96. Vale 1982, 170.

97. Vale 1982, 49. In 1384–5 Richard II's books included 'Vne Romance de Roy Arthure', 'Queste del Saint Graal' 'Mort Artu', 'Roman de la Rose' and 'Vn Romance de Perciull et Gawyn'; perhaps all these books were purchased by Edward III or The Black Prince (Scattergood 1983, 33).

98. Short 2000, 149.

99. See Miles and Bridge 2004, which includes oaks estimated to be 500+ years old.

100. Taigel and Williamson 1993, 83.

101. Tsouvalis 2000.

102. Richardson 2003a, 151.

103. Antioch, in the Eastern Mediterranean, was captured by the crusaders in 1098 and destroyed by the Mamluks in 1268 (Foss 1985).

104. Thiebaux 1967, 273; recalled in the nineteenth- and twentieth-century stags' heads in hunting lodges.

105. Thiebaux 1967, 274.

106. Deer symbolism focuses on red deer. Cummins 2001, 68–83.

107. Short 2000, 148.

108. Cummins 2001, 55.

109. Note the three sizes of dog found at Clarendon (Gidney 2004).

110. Thiebaux 1974, 136.

111. Eames 1988; Robinson 1988; Gutiérrez 2004c; Richardson 2004.

112. For another medieval context, see Stocker and Stocker 1996.

113. James and Robinson 1988, 14, 16

114. Possibly the Virgin Mary, or St Mary Magdalene, depicted in medieval art with flowing hair and a pot

115. The location of All Saints chapel is unidentified.

116. His attribute is a ring he gave to a pilgrim who asked for alms, as shown at Plymtree (Tasker 1993, 125–7). Henry III restored the Confessor's shrine at Westminster, named his eldest son Edward as a tribute to pre-Conquest Englishness, and had himself buried in the Confessor's own coffin, which he had recovered during work on the national saint's shrine. The shrine was said to have miraculous properties. Evidence of pious practice can be seen at Clarendon in the building of a penthouse for the poor (1245–68), shown on Figure 31.

117. Since the room was known by this name by 1237 we may assume the paintings were already there, although it is noteworthy that in the same year Henry III ordered silver hasps and a key for his 'great book of Romances', likely to have been the Alexander story (James and Robinson 1988, 25).

118. The retable of c. 1260 of Christ in Glory is at Westminster Abbey.

119. For the development of the cult of Edward the Confessor, see Binski 1995, 52; Binski 1999.

120. Binski 1999.

121. Binski 1999.

Notes to Chapter Eight: Time and Landscape

1. In this analysis we are influenced by the *Annales* school of historiography (Knapp 1992). *Annales* scholars stress the importance of debating the processes that have shaped a landscape at different scales of time. Braudel identified three time frames: *longue durée* (here geographical time); *moyenne durée* (here social time); and the specific *événement* (here individual time). Several other studies have taken a similar route to the analysis of regions, most notably Barker (1995) in the Biferno Valley in Italy, and Astill and Davies (1997) in Brittany, while a recent medieval case study can be found in Bintliff (2004). Barker, for example, uses the *Annales* structure to ask which disciplines work best at which scales, whether political events have any impact on landscape and settlement, and how external influences have an impact.

2. i.e., an 'extra parochial place' under the Sub-Dean of Salisbury's court.

3. FRC PROB 11/148/14 Hele.

4. John Aubrey, writing in 1685, recorded that 'they say' Becket was curate at 'Winterbourn' and used to 'goe along this path up to the chapel at Clarendon Parke to say mass'. The path was noteworthy because whether the common field of Winterbourne 'be sown or lies fallow' the path is seen, and it is 'wonderful'. Aubrey's servant, riding in winter, noted that the path even showed up in the snow, which Aubrey explained as being 'caused by a warm subterraneous steame from a long crack in the earth, which may cause snow to dissolve sooner there than elsewhere' as different shades of white appear on damask (Aubrey 1969 edition, 37). Aubrey's account is also corroborated by two twentieth-century sightings in different seasons (Bray 1949, 7–8; *Salisbury Times* 13 September 1963). This is perhaps one of the earliest recorded examples of a cropmark in archaeology.

5. He would certainly be pleased with the recent wave of interest in the archaeological and historical past, which has brought film crews to the palace for film-clips of the location of Becket's quarrel with Henry II of 1164. The first crew filmed amidst the jungle-shrouded ruins for Simon Schama's *History of Britain* (1999, BBC 2). At a

later stage of site-restoration the topic filmed related to the civil wars of Stephen and Matilda and the coming of Henry II in 1154 (Nigel Spivey's *English Royalty* (2002) Channel 4).

6. A statement that there has been no diminution in woodland hectarages over a long period fails to take into account removal of medieval vegetation in the period 1945–1970 and its replacement with conifers and beech stands for timber.

7. James and Robinson 1988, 199–200, plate LVIII.

8. One candidate might be William Hyde, who died at Clarendon in 1691. Other artefacts susceptible to this kind of 'biographical' approach vary from the seal of the second master of St Anthony of Vienne (d. 1254), which encloses Our Lady and Child (Goodall 1988, 206–7) to the game cart used by the Christie-Millers at Clarendon in the 1920s and 30s and recently sold at auction (CEA pictures of Clarendon game cart).

9. The practice of breaking then burying artefacts in order to 'kill' them is one familiar to prehistorians, and it has been suggested that some medieval pilgrim badges were deliberately mutilated in order to take them out of circulation. But this object was not damaged and we do not know for certain how it was buried.

Bibliography

....

Archives

Bodleian Library, Oxford (BLO)
MS Corpus Christi College MS 285 occupations of the months, c. 1280
MS Gough maps 33
MS Phillipps–Robinson b108 for Phillipps excavation in 1821
MS Phillipps–Robinson c271 for Phillipps excavation plans in 1821
MS Top. Wilts. Stukeley
MS. Top. Wilts. a. 1 ground plan of King John's Palace, Clarendon Park, drawn by William Hensley, c.1821

Borthwick Institute of Historical Research, York

Archbishop's Register of Wills

Volume 17 f.108 will of John Lee, yeoman

Bourne Valley History Society Archive, Winterbourne Gunner

35/27 BV02167

File note: the myth of St Thomas a Beckett and his association with the Winterbournes.

British Library, London (BL)
Add MSS 18729, James Harris autograph papers 1768–9, letter to Lord Lyttleton

Clarendon Estate Archive (CEA)
Estate map of c. 1650
Estate maps c. 1713 and c. 1812
Visitor's account of Clarendon Park (anon. 1880)
Clarendon Park, Wilts. Catalogue of a portion of the …

furnish of the mansion. By direction of Major J W Garton, who has sold the estate. 6–8 August 1919
Sale catalogues: 17 September 1919 (Farming Stock, Home Dairy); 19 September (Savages Farm, Horses and Pigs); 29 September 1919 (Rangers Lodge Farm, Farming Stock); 26 February 1920 (Rangers Lodge Farm); 22 July 1920 (Timber Plant, Piper's Barn). Live and dead stock sold by instructions of Major Garton
Purchase papers 1919
Court papers 1919–21
Clarendon Park, Salisbury. Inventory and valuation of furniture etc. for insurance purposes by Ralph Pay and Taylor, February 1925, bound typescript
Letters home from evacuees, 16 February and 6 June 1941
P. H. Carne, Gerald Johnstone writing on deer for *Countryman* magazine winter 1950/1951
Sale catalogue of Ayrshire Cattle the property of Messrs SVCM (Farms) Ltd, 29 September 1952
Sale catalogue of Clarendon Poll Herefords, May 1980
Nature Conservancy Council surveys of Pitton, Great Gilberts, Old Park, Home and Hunts Coppices, 23 June 1981, by Gillian Lewis
Text relating to Clarendon, Tasmania
AWMCM lecture text, June 1990
AWMCM lecture text, June 1992
AWMCM lecture text, February 1995
G. H. Mills memoir of Michael Christie-Miller, dated December 1992
Historic sites on Clarendon Plantation, Port Royal Island, Beaufort County, South Carolina, unpublished typescript by Sarah Fick, March 1998
Pictures of Clarendon game cart, 2003

239

Correspondence files

Family Records Centre, Clerkenwell (FRC)

Clarendon/Claringdon/Clarington Park wills

PROB 11
/136/113 Soame: will of Michael Sid[d]enham, gent., 1620
/148/14 Hele: will of John Fussell, yeoman, 1626
/164/83 Russell: will of John Stallen[d]ge the elder, 1633
/259/370 will of Anne Pile, Parish of St Martin, Salisbury, 1656
/325/168 will of Margaret Dunch, widow, 1667
/354/51 will of Katherine Ludlow, Spinster, 1677
/356/10 will of John Alford, 1676
/405/116 will of William Hyde, 1691

Gloucestershire Record Office, Gloucester (GRO)
D2525, Bathurst family settlements. Box 46, D16F4 doc. 10 trust declarations for the mortgage of Clarendon, eighteenth-century

Hampshire Record Office, Winchester (HRO)

Harris Papers

9M73/G515/9 Lord Lyttleton to James Harris, 11 January 1770

Hervey-Bathurst Collection

Documents relating to Clarendon Estate: 193M85
/141 grant of Clarendon Park to Duke of Albemarle, 22 March 1661 (old style 1660)
/142 indenture of grant and covenant to lead the uses of assignment of Clarendon Park from the Duke of Albemarle to the Earl of Clarendon, 22 April 1664
/145 quitclaim by Duke of Albemarle of Clarendon Park to the Earl of Clarendon, 20 April 1665
/146 lease of Clarendon Park for a year by Earl of Clarendon, 1 November 1670
/147 release, 2 November 1670 (last record of First Earl)
/148–170 leases, concords, mortgages etc on Clarendon and it sale by Second Earl, 1675–1707
/171–4 purchase by Lady Bathurst, 1707
/175 counterpart lease by Peter Bathurst (1), 1746
/176 surrender of lands at Clarendon to Peter Bathurst (2), 1755
/177 schedule of deeds relating to Clarendon Park, 6 April 1773
/181 sale particulars of Clarendon Park tithes, 27 January 1813
/189 and 190 estate maps prepared to support mortgage agreement, 1887, 1889
/206 mortgage by Sir F.T.A. Hervey-Bathurst

/212 articles upon the marriage of Peter Bathurst and Elizabeth Evelyn, 1750
/217, 218 marriage settlement, Sir F.H. Hervey-Bathurst and Louisa Smythe, 1831
/224 original will of Peter Bathurst, 13 June 1796
/229 Papers relating to the division of the estates in Sir Frederick Hutchinson Hervey-Bathurst's will, c. 1880.
/232 Commission of Frederick Hutchinson Hervey-Bathurst as a captain in the Wiltshire Yeomanry, 20 September 1833
/233 Appointment of Sir Frederick Hutchinson Hervey-Bathurst as Sheriff of Wiltshire, 1 January 1837
/235 Commission of Sir Frederick Hutchinson Hervey-Bathurst as a Lieutenant Colonel in the Wiltshire Yeomanry, 4 May 1867
/339 rental and account of estates for the Clarendon, Lainston and Sparsholt and Little Somborne, 1832
/360 rental and account of estates for the Clarendon, Lainston and Sparsholt and Little Somborne, 1858
/378 consents relating to proposed sale of property, 1892
/379 sale plan of estate for proposed sale by Daniel Smith, Son and Oakley, 1894

Malmesbury Collection

Peter Bathurst correspondence during Seven Years War re Salisbury candidature etc.
9M73/G345/69; 73–4; 78; 81–6; 1761–2

National Monuments Record (NMR)
Aerial photographs of Clarendon

Northamptonshire Record Office, Northampton (NRO)
XYZ 1157.16 indenture for manor of Paulerspury

Probate Registry Family Division/Principal Probate Registry, London (PRFD)
Will of Sir F.H. Hervey-Bathurst, 1881
Will of F.R.G. Hervey-Bathurst, 1881
Will of S. Christie-Miller 1889
Will of Sir F.T.A. Hervey-Bathurst 1900
Will of Ada Hervey-Bathurst 1914
Will of S.R. Christie-Miller 1931
Will of J.W. Garton 1940
Will of S.V. Christie-Miller 1968

Royal Commission on Historical Monuments (England), Swindon (RCHME)
Listed Buildings Files for Clarendon Estate
Plans 50312 Southampton/Pugin Lodge; 50316/1 Bests Farm; 50317/0 King Manor etc.

Salisbury Cathedral Archive, Salisbury
Letter of Francis Price to John James, 1736

Society of Antiquaries of London
Correspondence files
Research fund accounts

The National Archives: Public Record Office, Kew
(TNA:PRO)

Chancery: C

/145/31(2) survey 1272

Duchy of Lancaster: DL

/39/2/20 1488 Duchy of Lancaster and Justices of the Forest South of Trent: Forest Records

Exchequer: E32

/199/10 Justice of the Forest 1262–3
/214/2 Swanimote 1331–2
/267 Justice of the Forest Records 1355

Exchequer Accounts various: E101

/351/24, m.1. 1285–6 Falconry and Hunting Roll. Expenses of king's foxhunters
/352/14 1288–9 wages of John Foucard
/352/32 1289 expenses of Henry III's trumpeter, cranes' heads brought
/459/29–30 1354 building accounts
/460/1 1354–9 building accounts
/460/10 1448–9 building accounts
/460/14 1477 building accounts
/460/16 1482–97 building accounts
/502/15/41a; /42a; /43 accounts various temp. Henry IV 1399–1400
/542/20 accounts various 1461–71
/542/21 accounts various 1603–7
/542/22 accounts various 1607–8
/542/23 accounts various 1607–8
/593/18; /20 accounts various 1341–4

Special Commissions: E178

/4728 survey of Clarendon Park 1618

Parliamentary Surveys: E317

/Wilts.26/13570 survey of Clarendon Park 1651 entitled 'Survey of Clarindon Parke … divided into five partes … heretofore belonging to the late King, Queene and prince'
/Wilts.27 parliamentary survey of Clarendon Park, May 1650
/Wilts.29 survey of the Park 'A Supplimentall Survey of Clarindon Parke, Wilts', 10 December 1650

/Wilts.30 survey of the part of the park called 'Hunt's Division' lying in the parishes of New Sarum and Alderbury, March 1652
/Wilts.32 survey of a parcel of ground in the park, January 1657

Particulars of sale of estates of Charles I: E320

/V1; /V4; /V12; /V16

Exchequer Pipe Office: Foreign Accounts: E364

/2.m.D Bartholomew de Bradden for works 1356–60

Housing and Local Government: HLG

/103/119 country houses abandoned or demolished 1939/1952

Home Office Census: HO107

/1164/4 the Liberty of Clarendon Park, 1841
/1846 Clarendon Park extra parochial, 1851

Ministry of Agriculture Fisheries and Food: MAF

/32 Agricultural Census and Farm Survey, 1941
/33/194 Clarendon Park

Agricultural Returns Parish Surveys: Wiltshire, Clarendon Park: MAF68

/73 (1866) Arable; /74 (1866) Livestock; /151 (1867); /436 (1875); /1861 (1900); /2887 (1918); /3265 (1925); /3923 (1939); /4367 (1951); /4589 (1957); /5454 (1975); /6134 (1988)

Ministry of Public Building and Works: WORK

/14/1777 Clarendon Palace, 1942–60
/14/2533 Fussells Lodge Long Barrow, 1957–62

Registrar General Census: RG

/9/1313 Parish of Clarendon, 1861
/10/1947 Liberty of Clarendon Park, 1871
/11/2066 Liberty of Clarendon Park, 1881
/12/1618 Liberty of Clarendon Park, 1891

Star Chamber: STAC

/2/11 Margaret Yorke of Laverstock case, temp. Henry VIII.
/8/183/40 Pembroke vs Moggeridge poachers, temp. James I.

University of Winchester, Archaeological Consultancy Clarendon Archive (UW)

Charlton notebooks and plans of 1930s excavations
Dendrochronology reports
Fieldwork records
Photographic archive
Roberts report on Queen Manor Farmhouse

Spoilheap excavation records
Copy of visitors' book from Stocks Bridge Cottage, Coombe Bissett

Oral sources

R. C. Clarke, 2002, taped interview
Gordon Eastman, 1996, taped interview

Wiltshire Heritage, Wiltshire Archaeological and Natural History Society Headquarters, Devizes Museum (WHWANHS)

Estate sale catalogues etc. volume 22. Sale particulars and maps of Clarendon, October 1891
Hensley Album D6.6 Clarendon excavation drawings, 1821

Press cuttings volumes

VII 1844 Henry Hatcher's account of the medieval palace 1894 sale advertisement from *Times*
IX 1903 Devizes newspaper account of rights of way case
XVI 1860 volunteer review report

Wiltshire Reference Library, Trowbridge (WRL)
CLA Letters to J. W. Garton relating to fishery rights in Clarendon Park 1909

Wiltshire and Swindon Record Office, Trowbridge (WSRO)
G11/141/1 Papers in the case of the Attorney General and Salisbury and Wilton RDC versus Mr Garton concerning footpaths in Clarendon Park (two boxes including photographs)

Miscellaneous estate documents: 130

/16 1655–1792 File of deeds of lands in Alderbury, Clarendon Park etc.

Wiltshire deeds: 212B

/1878 10 October 1670 21 Year Lease of Great and Small Tithes of Clarendon Park
/302.1 Serial no. 1 1679 lease of Haybarn, belonging to Queen's Manor Lodge
/302.1 Serial no. 2 lease of park and lands enclosed called Claringdon
/549/8 Sir George Penruddocke's ranger's book 1572–5

Alderbury Parish Council: 2142

/24 Alderbury Roll of Honour note book 1939–45

Land Tax Assessments. G23/1

/137/106; /118; /166; /138/101; /145/32; 147/121; /187 1703–42 for the Liberty of Clarendon Park

Land Tax Returns

A1/345/113 Clarendon Park 1825–70

Peniston Papers

451/91; /93 railway land purchase papers and plans: Clarendon

Salisbury and Amesbury County Division. B18

/100/4 Justices' Minute Books. Bastardy Order, 1792
/100/10 Justices' Minute Books. Bastardy Order, 1813
/100/13 Justices' Minute Books. Bastardy Order, 1818
/100/23 Justices' Minute Books. Bastardy Order, 1823

Salisbury Diocese Sub-Dean's Peculiar Records, Trowbridge; Probate Records P/4

/1666/1 inventory etc. of Henry Hayter of Clarendon
/1680/4 will etc. of Christopher Ewer of Clarendon
/1684/6 will etc. of John Bristol or Bristow of Clarendon

Published primary sources

Andrews' and Dury's Map of Wiltshire, 1773 (1952) ed. E. Crittall, Wiltshire Archaeology and Natural History Society Records Branch v. 8, Wiltshire Archaeology and Natural History Society, Devizes.

Calendar of Close Rolls, Henry III vol. 5 1242–47 (1916).

Calendar of Close Rolls, Edward III vol. 3 1333–37 (1898).

Calendar of Close Rolls, Edward III vol. 4 1337–39 (1900).

Calendar of Close Rolls, Edward III vol. 5 1339–41 (1901).

Calendar of Fine Rolls, Edward III vol. 4 1327–37 (1913).

Calendar of Liberate Rolls, Henry III vol. 1 1226–40 (1917).

Calendar of Liberate Rolls, Henry III vol. 2 1240–45 (1931).

Calendar of Liberate Rolls, Henry III vol. 3 1245–51 (1937).

Calendar of Liberate Rolls, Henry III vol. 4 1251–60 (1959).

Calendar of Liberate Rolls, Henry III vol. 5 1260–67 (1961).

Calendar of Liberate Rolls, Henry III vol. 6 1267–72 (1964).

Calendar of Patent Rolls, Edward III vol. 2 1330–34 (1893).

Calendar of Patent Rolls, Edward III vol. 3 1334–38 (1895).

Calendar of Patent Rolls, Edward III vol. 10 1354–58 (1909).

Calendar of Patent Rolls, Richard II vol. 1 1377–81 (1895).

Calendar of Patent Rolls, Richard II vol. 5 1391–96 (1905).

Calendar of Patent Rolls, Richard II vol. 6 1396–99 (1909).

Calendar of Patent Rolls, Henry IV vol. 2 1401–05 (1903–09).

Calendar of Patent Rolls, Henry IV vol. 3 1405–08 (1907).

Calendar of Patent Rolls, Edward VI vol. 4 1550–53 (1923–9).

Calendar of Patent Rolls, Edward VI vol. 5 1553 (1923–9).

Calendar of Patent Rolls, Elizabeth vol. 8 1578–80 (1986).

Calendar of State Papers Domestic, Commonwealth vol. 12 1658–59 (1875–86).

Calendar of State Papers Domestic, vol. 1 Charles II 1660–61 (1860).

Calendar of State Papers Domestic, vol. 2 Charles II 1661–63 (1861).

Calendar of State Papers Domestic, vol. 3 Charles II 1663–64 (1865).

Letters and papers, foreign and domestic, of the reign of Henry VIII: preserved in the Public Record Office, the British Museum, and elsewhere in England. Arranged and catalogued by J. S. Brewer (1862–1910) eds J. S. Brewer and J. Gairdner, Longman, Green, Longman and Roberts, London.

Rotuli de liberate ac de misis et praestitis, regnante Johanne (1844) ed. T. D. Hardy, Record Commission.

Secondary sources

Albarella, U. and Thomas, R. (2002) 'They dined on crane: bird consumption, wild fowling and status in medieval England', *Acta Zoologica Cracoviensia* **45**, 23–38.

Allen, D. F. (1978) 'The origins of coinage in Britain: a reappraisal', in *Problems of the Iron Age in Southern Britain*, ed. S. Frere, Institute of Archaeology Occasional Paper 11, University of London, London, 242.

Anon. (1846) 'Proceedings of the Central Committee', *Archaeological Journal* **2**, 86.

Anon. (1893–5) 'Clarendon Palace', *Wiltshire Notes and Queries* **1**, 206–11.

Anon. (1900) 'Wilts obituary. Lt.-Col. Sir Frederick Thomas Arthur Harvey-Bathurst', *Wiltshire Archaeological Magazine* **31**, 89–90.

Anon. (1903) 'Wiltshire books etc', *Wiltshire Archaeological Magazine* **33**, 77, 85.

Anon. (1934) 'Wiltshire books, pamphlets and articles', *Wiltshire Archaeological Magazine* **46**, 141–2.

Anon. (1937) 'Notes. The Byam family by Gainsborough', *Wiltshire Archaeological Magazine* **47**, 270.

Anon. (1952) 'Annual General Meeting and excursions', *Wiltshire Archaeological Magazine* **54**, 222–3.

Anon. (1962) 'Clarendon Palace', *Wiltshire Archaeological Magazine* **58**, 247.

Anon. (1969) 'Laverstock and Ford (SU 157293) Saxon settlement', *Wiltshire Archaeological Magazine* **64**, 128.

Anon. (1973) 'Clarendon Park (SU 17263080)', *Wiltshire Archaeological Magazine* **68**, 129, 132–3.

Anon. (1984) 'Early medieval finds', *Wiltshire Archaeological Magazine* **79**, 257.

Anon. (1990) 'Excavations and fieldwork in Wiltshire, 1988', *Wiltshire Archaeological Magazine* **83**, 222.

Anon. (2000) *Alderbury and Whaddon: A Millennium Mosaic*, Alderbury and Whaddon Historical Research Group, Alderbury.

Arnold, J. J., Green, M., Lewis, B. and Bradley, R. (1988) 'The Mesolithic of Cranborne Chase', *Proceedings of the Dorset Natural History and Archaeological Society* **110**, 117–26.

Ashbee, P. (1958) 'The Fussells Lodge long barrow', *Antiquity* **32**, 106–11.

Ashbee, P. (1966) 'The Fussells Lodge long barrow excavations', *Archaeologia* **100**, 1–80.

Ashbee, P. (1984) *The Earthen Long Barrow in Britain*, 2nd edition, Geo Books, Norwich.

Ashbee, P. and Simpson, D. D. A. (1969) 'Timber mortuary houses and earthen long barrows again', *Antiquity* **43**, 43–5.

Ashurst, J. and James, T. B. (1988) 'Stonework and plasterwork', in *Clarendon Palace. The History and Archaeology of a Medieval Palace and Hunting Lodge near Salisbury, Wiltshire*, T. B. James and A. M. Robinson, Reports of the Research Committee of the Society of Antiquaries of London XLV, Society of Antiquaries and Thames and Hudson, London, 234–58.

Astill, G. and Davies, W. (1997) *A Breton Landscape*, UCL Press, London.

Atkinson, R.F. (1995) *The Manors and Hundred of Alderbury: Lords, Lands and Livery*, Richard F. Atkinson, Alderbury.

Aubrey, J. (1847; 1969) *Aubrey's Natural History of Wiltshire: A Reprint of The Natural History of Wiltshire*. Originally published in 1847 by Wiltshire Topographical Society, ed. J. Britton. Reprint of 1969 introduced by K.G. Ponting, David and Charles, Newton Abbot.

Aubrey, J. eds J. Fowles and R. Legg (1982; compiled 1665–93) *Monumenta Britannica. Volume 2: Part 3 and Index*, Dorset Publishing Co, Sherborne.

Avent, R. and Evison, V.I. (1982) 'Anglo-Saxon button brooches', *Archaeologia* **107**, 77–124.

Aylmer, G.E. (1973a) *The State's Servants. Civil Service of the English Republic 1649–1660*, Routledge and Kegan Paul, London.

Aylmer, G.E. (1973b) *The Struggle for the Constitution*, Blandford Press, London.

Barber, R. and Barker, J. (1989) *Tournaments: Jousts, Chivalry and Pageants in the Middle Ages*, Boydell Press, Woodbridge.

Barlow, F. (1970) *Edward the Confessor*, University of California Press, Berkeley.

Barker, G. (1995) *A Mediterranean Valley. Landscape Archaeology and Annales History in the Biferno Valley*, Leicester University Press, London.

Barrett, J., Bradley, R. and Green, M. (1991) *Landscape, Monuments and Society: The Prehistory of Cranborne Chase*, Cambridge University Press, Cambridge.

Bates, D. ed. (1998) *Regesta Regum Anglo-Normannorum: The Acta of William I 1066–1087*, Clarendon Press, Oxford.

Batho, G. (1967) 'The decline of the Chamber system, 1509–54', in *The Agrarian History of England and Wales. Volume IV 1500–1640*, ed. J. Thirsk, Cambridge University Press, London, 260–4.

Baxter, I.L. (1993a) 'An eagle, *Haliaeetus albicilla* (L) skull from Roman Leicester, England, with some speculations concerning the palaeoecology of the Soar valley', *Circaea* **10** (1), 31–7.

Baxter, I.L. (1993b) 'Eagles in Anglo-Saxon and Norse poems', *Circaea* **10** (2), 78–81.

Baxter, R. and Harrison, S. (2002) 'The decoration of the cloister at Reading Abbey', in *Windsor. Medieval Archaeology, Art and Architecture of the Thames Valley*, eds L. Keen and E. Scarff, British Archaeological Association Conference Transactions 25, Maney, Leeds, 302–12.

Belloc, H. (1934) *A Shorter History of England*, G.G. Harrap, London.

Beresford, G. (1987) *Goltho. The Development of an Early Medieval Manor, c. 850–1150*, HBMCE, London.

Bettey, J.H. (1987) *Rural Life in Wessex 1500–1900*, Alan Sutton, Stroud.

Bettey, J. ed. (2005) *Wiltshire Farming in the Seventeenth Century*, Wiltshire Records Series vol. 57, Wiltshire Record Society, Trowbridge.

Biddle, M. (1990) *Object and Economy in Medieval Winchester*, Oxford University Press, Oxford.

Biddle, M. (2000) *King Arthur's Round Table: An Archaeological Investigation*, Boydell Press, Woodbridge.

Binski, P. (1995) *Westminster Abbey and the Plantagenets. Kingship and the Representation of Power, 1200–1400*, Yale University Press, New Haven and London.

Binski, P. (1999) 'Hierarchies and orders in English royal images of power', in *Orders and Hierarchies in Late Medieval and Renaissance Europe*, ed. J. Denton, Macmillan, London, 74–93.

Bintliff, J. (2004) 'Time, structure and agency: the annales, emergent complexity and archaeology', in *A Companion to Archaeology*, ed. J. Bintliff, Blackwell, Oxford, 174–94.

Birrell, J. (1991) 'Deer and deer farming in medieval England', *Agricultural History Review* **39**, 112–26.

Blair, J. (1991) 'Purbeck marble', in *English Medieval Industries. Craftsmen, Techniques, Products*, eds J. Blair and N. Ramsey, Hambledon Press, London, 41–56.

Blair, J. (1993) 'Hall and chamber: English domestic planning 1000–1250', in *Manorial Domestic Buildings in England and Northern France*, eds G. Meirion-Jones and M. Jones, Occasional Papers from The Society of Antiquaries of London, Society of Antiquaries, London, 1–21.

Bond, J. (1987) 'Woodstock Park in the Middle Ages', in *Blenheim: Landscape for a Palace*, eds J. Bond and K. Tiller, Alan Sutton and OUDCE, Gloucester and Oxford, 22–54.

Bond, J. (1994) 'Forests, chases, warrens and parks in medieval Wessex', in *The Medieval Landscape of Wessex*, eds M. Aston and C. Lewis, Oxbow Monograph 46, Oxbow Books, Oxford, 115–55.

Bond, J. (1998) *Somerset Parks and Gardens. A Landscape History*, Somerset Books, Tiverton.

Bond, J. and Tiller, K. eds (1987) *Blenheim: Landscape for a Palace*, Alan Sutton and OUDCE, Gloucester and Oxford.

Bonney, D. (1966) 'Pagan Saxon burials and boundaries in Wiltshire', *Wiltshire Archaeology and Natural History Society Magazine* **61**, 25–30.

Boodle, R.W. (1901–2) *Wiltshire, Volume II. A–D*, Devizes.

Borenius, T. (1932) *St Thomas Becket in Art*, Methuen and Co, London.

Borenius, T. (1943) 'The cycle of images in the palaces and castles of Henry III', *Journal of Warburg and Courtauld Institutes* **6**, 40–50.

Borenius, T. and Charlton, J. (1936) 'Clarendon Palace: an interim report', *Antiquaries Journal* **16**, 55–84.

Borenius, T. and Tristram E.W. (1927) *English Medieval Painting*, The Pegasus Press, Paris.

Bowden, M., MacKay, D. and Topping, P. eds (1989) *From Cornwall to Caithness*, British Archaeological Reports British Series 209, Oxford.

Bowsher, P. (1987) *Wiltshire Inventory of Ancient Woodland (Provisional)*, unpublished report, Nature Conservancy Council.

Bracegirdle, M. A. L. and Serjeantson, D. (1988) 'Appendix II: animal remains from the ditch beneath the salsary and the kiln', in *Clarendon Palace. The History and Archaeology of a Medieval Palace and Hunting Lodge near Salisbury, Wiltshire*, T. B. James and A. M. Robinson, Reports of the Research Committee of the Society of Antiquaries of London XLV, Society of Antiquaries and Thames and Hudson, London, 165–7.

Brakspear, H. (1934) 'Ivychurch Priory', *Wiltshire Archaeological Magazine* **46**, 433–40.

Bramwell, D. (1988) 'Bird bones', in *Clarendon Palace. The History and Archaeology of a Medieval Palace and Hunting Lodge near Salisbury, Wiltshire*, T. B. James and A. M. Robinson, Reports of the Research Committee of the Society of Antiquaries of London XLV, Society of Antiquaries and Thames and Hudson, London, 233–4.

Brassley, P. (2000) 'Farming systems', in *The Agrarian History of England and Wales. Volume VII 1850–1914*, ed. E. J. T. Collins, Cambridge University Press, Cambridge, 453–94.

Braudel, F. (1972) *The Mediterranean and the Mediterranean World in the Age of Philip II*, Collins, London.

Bray, C. H. (1949) *The Three Winterbournes* I, No. 4, Easter 1949.

Brayley, E. W. and Britton, J. C. (1801–15) *The Beauties of England and Wales*, Vernor and Hood, London.

Brentnall, H. C. (1939) 'Savernake Forest in the Middle Ages', *Wiltshire Archaeological Magazine* **48**, 371–86.

Britton, J. (1801) *The Beauties of Wiltshire*. Volume I, printed by J. D. Dewick for Vernor and Hood, London.

Brooks, A. (1999) 'Building Jerusalem: transfer-printed finewares and the creation of British identity', in *The Familiar Past? Archaeologies of Later Historical Britain*, eds S. Tarlow and S. West, Routledge, London, 51–65.

Brown, F. (1889) *Abstracts of Somersetshire Wills, etc.*, privately printed for F. A. Crisp, London.

Brown, L. (1978) *British Birds of Prey*, Collins, London.

Brown, R.W., Lawrence, M. J. and Pope, J. (1984) *Animals of Britain and Europe and Their Tracks, Trails and Signs*, Country Life, Feltham.

Brown, S. (1999) *Sumptuous and Richly Adorn'd. The Decoration of Salisbury Cathedral*, The Stationery Office, London.

Brownley, M.W. (1985) *Clarendon and the Rhetoric of Historical Form*, University of Pennsylvania Press, Philadelphia.

Bunyard, B. D. M. (1941) *The Brokage Book for Southampton 1439–40*, Southampton Record Society 40, Southampton.

Bushell, W. D. (1906) *Elias de Derham. Rector of Harrow and Architect of Salisbury Cathedral*, Harrow Octocentenary Tracts 12, Macmillan and Bowes, Cambridge.

Camden, W. (1586; 1600; 1607) *Britannia*, ed. Richard Gough (1806) vol. I, Nichols, London; edition of 1695 reprinted 1971 with an introduction by S. Piggott; 1722 with addition of corrections left by Edmund Gibson for the press, London.

Cantor, L. ed. (1982) *The English Medieval Landscape*, Croom Helm, London.

Cantor, L. (1983) *The Medieval Parks of England: A Gazetteer*, Department of Education, Loughborough University of Technology, Loughborough.

Cantor, L. M. and Hatherley, J. (1979) 'The medieval parks of England', *Geography* **64**, 71–85.

Cantor, L. M. and Wilson, J. D. (1965) 'The medieval deer-parks of Dorset', *Proceedings of the Dorset Natural History and Archaeological Society* **87**, 223–33.

Carter, F. E. L. and Greenway, D. E. eds (1983) *Dialogus de Scaccario: The Course of the Exchequer and Constitutio Domus Regis: The Establishment of the Royal Household*, trans. Charles Johnson, revised Carter and Greenway, Clarendon Press, Oxford.

Cartwright, J. T. ed. (1889) *The Travels Through England of Dr Richard Pococke*, Publications new series 42, Camden Society, London.

Case, H. (1995) 'Some Wiltshire Beakers and their contexts', *Wiltshire Archaeological Magazine* **88**, 1–17.

Catt, J. A. (1978) 'The contribution of loess soils in lowland Britain', in *The Effect of Man on the Landscape: The Lowland Zone*, eds S. Limbrey and J. G. Evans, CBA Research Report 21, Council for British Archaeology, London, 12–20.

Charleston, R. J. (1988) 'Vessel glass', in *Clarendon Palace. The History and Archaeology of a Medieval Palace and Hunting Lodge near Salisbury, Wiltshire*, T. B. James and A. M. Robinson, Reports of the Research Committee of the Society of Antiquaries of London XLV, Society of Antiquaries and Thames and Hudson, London, 193–7.

Cheney, C. R. (1970) *Handbook of Dates for Students of English History*, Royal Historical Society, London.

Cherry, J. (1991) 'Pottery and tile', in *English Medieval Industries. Craftsmen, Techniques, Products*, eds J. Blair and N. Ramsey, Hambledon Press, London, 189–209.

Chettle, H. F. (1952) 'Dinton and Little Clarendon', *Wiltshire Archaeological Magazine* **54**, 403.

Childs, W. (1995) 'Documentary evidence for the import of Spanish pottery to England in the later Middle Ages (thirteenth to early sixteenth centuries)', in *Spanish Medieval Ceramics in Spain and the British Isles*, eds C. M. Gerrard, A. Gutiérrez and A. Vince, British Archaeological Reports International Series 610, Oxford, 25–31.

Christie, W. D. (1871) *A Life of Anthony Ashley-Cooper: First Earl of Shaftesbury 1621–1683*, Macmillan, London.

Chubb, T. (1912) 'A descriptive catalogue of the printed maps of Wiltshire from 1576 to the publication of the 25 in. Ordnance Survey', *Wiltshire Archaeological Magazine* 37, 211–326.

Clarendon, Edward, Earl of (1704; reprint 1839) *The History of the Rebellion and Civil Wars in England*, 7 vols, Oxford University Press, Oxford.

Clark, A. J. and Nichols, J. F. (1960) 'Romano-British farms south of the Hogsback', *Surrey Archaeological Collections* **57**, 42–72.

Clarkson, L. A. (1974) 'The English bark trade, 1660–1830', *Agricultural History Review* **22**, 136–52.

Clay, C. (1985) 'Landlords and Estate Management in England' in *The Agrarian History of England Volume 5 ii 1640–1750: Agrarian Change*, ed. Joan Thirsk, Cambridge University Press, Cambridge, 119–251.

Cleal, R. and Allen, M. J. (1994) 'Investigation of tree-damaged barrows on King Barrow Ridge, Amesbury', *Wiltshire Archaeological Magazine* **87**, 54–84.

Cockayne, G. E. C. (1982) *The Complete Peerage of England, Scotland, Ireland, Great Britain, and the United Kingdom, Extant, Extinct or Dormant*, 13 vols, Alan Sutton, Gloucester.

Collings, M. (2001) *Presentation, Interpretation and Accessibility: Public Archaeology and Clarendon Palace*, unpublished BA dissertation, King Alfred's College, Winchester.

Collins, E. J. T. (2000) 'Rural and agricultural change', in *The Agrarian History of England and Wales. Volume VII 1850–1914*, ed. E. J. T. Collins, Cambridge University Press, Cambridge, 72–223.

Colman, G. and Garrick, D. (1766) *The Clandestine Marriage: A Comedy*, London.

Colman, P. (1991) 'The Wiltshire Sheriffs of Charles I; to whom the loyalty?', *Wiltshire Archaeological and Natural History Society* **84**, 127–30.

Colt-Hoare, R. (1837/44) *The History of Modern Wiltshire. Hundred of Alderbury*, Nichols, London.

Colvin, H. M. ed. (1963) *The History of the King's Works. II The Middle Ages*, HMSO, London.

Colvin, H. (1983) 'The 'court style' in medieval English architecture: a review', in *English Court Culture in the Later Middle Ages*, V. J. Scattergood and J. W. Sherborne, Duckworth, London, 129–40.

Comfort, W. W. trans. (1913) *Arthurian Romances by Chrétien de Troyes*, J. M. Dent, London.

Conybeare, C. (2003) 'Museums in Wiltshire: the experience of Devizes', in *Wiltshire Archaeological and Natural History Society. The First 150 Years*, ed. J. H. Thomas, Wiltshire Archaeological and Natural History Society, Devizes, 45–64.

Corney, M. (1989) 'Multiple ditch systems and late Iron Age settlement in central Wessex', in *From Cornwall to Caithness*, eds M. Bowden, D. MacKay and P. Topping, British Archaeological Reports British Series 209, Oxford, 111–28.

Corney, M. (2001) 'The Romano-British nucleated settlements of Wiltshire', in *Roman Wiltshire and After. Papers in Honour of Ken Annable*, ed. P. Ellis, Wiltshire Archaeological and Natural History Society, Devizes, 5–38.

Cowan, M. ed. (1996) *The Letters of John Peniston, a Salisbury Architect, Catholic and Yeomanry Officer, 1823–1830*, Wiltshire Records Series vol. 50, Wiltshire Record Society, Trowbridge.

Cox, J. C. (1905) *The Royal Forests of England*, Methuen, London.

Cox, T. (1725) *Complete History of Wiltshire*, Devizes.

Coy, J. (1996) 'Medieval records versus excavations results – examples from Southern England', *Archaeofauna* **5**, 59–132.

Craik, H. (1911) *The Life of Edward, Earl of Clarendon, Lord High Chancellor of England*, with portraits of EH Nat Port Gall, and Ann Hyde by Sir Peter Lely, Smith, Elder and co., London.

Crittall E. ed. (1962) *Victoria History of the Counties of England. A History of Wiltshire*, vol. VI, Institute of Historical Research and Oxford University Press, London.

Crowfoot, E. and Bayley, J. (1988) 'Textiles: metal thread', in *Clarendon Palace. The History and Archaeology of a Medieval Palace and Hunting Lodge near Salisbury, Wiltshire*, T. B. James and A. M. Robinson, Reports of the Research Committee of the Society of Antiquaries of London XLV, Society of Antiquaries and Thames and Hudson, London, 258.

Cummins, J. (2001) *The Hound and the Hawk. The Art of Medieval Hunting*, Phoenix Press, London.

Cunliffe, B. (2003) 'Roman Danebury', *Current Archaeology* **188**, 344–51.

Cunliffe, B. and Poole, C. (2000a) *Suddern Farm, Middle Wallop, Hants, 1991 and 1996*, The Danebury

Environs Programme. The Prehistory of a Wessex Landscape. English Heritage and Oxford University Committee for Archaeology 49, Institute of Archaeology, Oxford.

Cunliffe, B. and Poole, C. (2000b) *Nettlebank Copse, Wherwell, Hants 1993*, The Danebury Environs Programme. The Prehistory of a Wessex Landscape. English Heritage and Oxford University Committee for Archaeology 49, Institute of Archaeology, Oxford.

Cunnington, M.E. (1925) 'Figsbury Rings. An account of the excavations in 1924', *Wiltshire Archaeological Magazine* **43**, 48–58.

Cunnington, M.E. (1932) 'Romano-British Wiltshire', *Wiltshire Archaeological Magazine* **45**, 166–216.

Currie, C.K. (1994) 'Earthworks at Compton Bassett, with a note on Wiltshire fishponds', *Wiltshire Archaeological Magazine* **87**, 101.

Darby, H.C. (1977) *Domesday England*, Cambridge University Press, Cambridge.

Darby, H. and Welldon Finn, R. eds (1967) *The Domesday Geography of South-West England*, Cambridge University Press, Cambridge.

Darby, M. (2003) 'WANHS and natural history', in *Wiltshire Archaeological and Natural History Society. The First 150 Years*, ed. J.H.Thomas, Wiltshire Archaeological and Natural History Society, Devizes, 210–28.

Darvill, T.C. and Gerrard, C.M. (1994) *Cirencester: Town and Landscape*, Cotswold Archaeological Trust, Cirencester.

Davies, N. (2000) *The Isles: A History*, Papermac, London.

Davison, B.K. (1977) 'Excavations at Sulgrave, Northamptonshire, 1960–76: an interim report', *Archaeological Journal* **134**, 105–14.

Defoe, D.C. (1725; 1928 edn; reprint 1959) *A Tour Through England and Wales*, 2 vols, ed. G.D.H.Cole, J.M.Dent, London.

Dobney, K. (2002) 'Flying a kite at the end of the Ice Age: The possible significance of raptor remains from proto- and early Neolithic sites in the Near East', in *Archaeozoology of the Near East* V, eds H.Buitenhuis, A.M.Choyke, M.Mashkour and A.H.Al-Shiyab, Arc-Publicaties 62, Groningen, 74–8.

Dorling, E.E. (1906) *Wilts and Dorset at the Opening of the Twentieth Century. Contemporary Biographies*, ed. W.T.Pike, Pike's New Century Series No 16, W.T.Pike and Co, Brighton.

Draper, J. (1993) 'Medieval pottery', in *Excavations at the Old Methodist Chapel and Greyhound Yard, Dorchester, 1981–1984*, P.J.Woodward, S.M.Davies and A.H.Graham, Dorset Natural History and Archaeology Society Monograph 12, Dorset Natural History and Archaeological Society, Dorchester.

Draper, S. (2002) 'Old English *wic* and *walh*. Britons and Saxons in post-Roman Wiltshire', *Landscape History* **24**, 29–43.

Draper, S. (2004) *Landscape, Settlement and Society: Wiltshire in the First Millennium* AD, unpublished PhD thesis, University of Durham.

Dwyer, J. and Hodge, I. (1996) *Countryside in Trust*, J.Wiley and Sons, Chichester.

Dyer, C. (1989) *Standards of Living in the Later Middle Ages. Social Change 1200–1520*, Cambridge University Press, Cambridge.

Eagles, B. (1994) 'The archaeological evidence for settlement in the fifth to seventh centuries AD', in *The Medieval Landscape of Wessex*, eds M.Aston and C.Lewis, Oxbow Monograph 46, Oxbow Books, Oxford, 13–32.

Eagles, B. (2001) 'Anglo-Saxon presence and culture in Wiltshire c. AD 450 – c.675', in *Roman Wiltshire and after. Papers in Honour of Ken Annable*, ed. P.Ellis, Wiltshire Archaeological and Natural History Society, Devizes, 199–233.

Eames, E. (1963) 'A thirteenth-century tiled pavement from the King's Chapel, Clarendon Palace', *Journal of the British Archaeological Association* 3rd series **26**, 40–50.

Eames, E. (1965) 'The royal apartments at Clarendon Palace in the reign of Henry III' *Journal of the British Archaeological Association* 3rd series **28**, 57–85.

Eames, E. (1980) *Catalogue of Medieval Lead Glazed Earthenware Tiles in the Department of Medieval and Later Antiquities, British Museum*, 2 vols, British Museum, London.

Eames, E. (1988) 'The tile kiln and the floor tiles', in *Clarendon Palace. The History and Archaeology of a Medieval Palace and Hunting Lodge near Salisbury, Wiltshire*, T.B.James and A.M.Robinson, Reports of the Research Committee of the Society of Antiquaries of London XLV, Society of Antiquaries and Thames and Hudson, London, 127–67.

Ekblom, E. (1917) *The Place-Names of Wiltshire*, Appelbergs boktryckeri, Uppsala.

Ellis, P. ed. (2000) *Ludgershall Castle. A Report on the Excavations by Peter Addyman 1964–72*, Wiltshire Archaeological and Natural History Society Monograph Series 2, English Heritage and WANHS, Devizes.

Esmonde Cleary, S. (2000) 'Putting the dead in their place: burial location in Roman Britain', in *Burial, Society and Context in the Roman World*, eds J.Pearce, M.Millett and M.Struck, Oxbow Books, Oxford, 127–42.

Evans, J.G., Limbrey, S., Máté, I. and Mount, R. (1993) 'An environmental history of the Upper Kennet Valley, Wiltshire for the last 10,000 years', *Proceedings of the Prehistoric Society* **59**, 139–95.

Evelyn, J. (1664) *Sylva: Or a Discourse of Forest Trees, and* the Propagation of Timber in His Majesty's Dominions, Royal Society, London.

Everett, N. (1994) *The Tory View of Landscape*, The Paul Mellon Centre and Yale University Press, New Haven and London.

Eyton, R.W. (1878) *Court Household and Itinerary of Henry II*, Taylor and Co., London.

Fairbrother, J.R. (1984) *Faccombe Netherton*, British Museum Occasional Paper 74, British Museum, London.

Fasham, P. (1985) 'A bell barrow in Clarendon Park', *Wiltshire Archaeological Magazine* 79, 92–100.

Fitz Nigel (Fitz Neal), R. (1950) *Dialogus de Scaccario*, ed. C. Johnson, Nelson, London.

Foss, C. (1985) 'Antioch', in *Dictionary of the Middle Ages*, vol. 5, ed. J. F. Strayer, Charles Scribner's Sons, New York, 325–6.

Foster, A. (2001) 'Romano-British burials in Wiltshire', in *Roman Wiltshire and After. Papers in Honour of Ken Annable*, ed. P. Ellis, Wiltshire Archaeological and Natural History Society, Devizes, 165–77.

Fowler, M.J.F. and Needham, H.J. (1995) 'Gun-flint industries in the Salisbury region', *Wiltshire Archaeological Magazine* 88, 137–41.

Fowler, P.J. (2000) *Landscape Plotted and Pieced. Landscape History and Local Archaeology in Fyfield and Overton, Wiltshire*, Society of Antiquaries, London.

Fowler, P.J. and Blackwell, I. (1998) *The Land of Lettice Sweetapple. An English Countryside Explored*, Tempus, Stroud.

Fretwell, K. (1995) 'Lodge Park, Gloucestershire', *Garden History* 23.2, 133–44.

Fryde, E.B., Greenaway, D.E., Porter, S. and Roy, I. eds (1986) *Handbook of British Chronology*, Royal Historical Society, London.

Fulford, M.G. (1975) *New Forest Roman pottery*, British Archaeological Reports British Series 17, Oxford.

Games, S. (2002) *Pevsner on Art and Architecture*, Methuen, London.

Gelling, M. (1984) *Place-Names in the Landscape*, J.M. Dent, London.

Gelling, M. and Cole, A. (2000) *The Landscape of Place-Names*, Shaun Tyas, Stamford.

Gerrard, C.M. (1998) 'Looking for history under the branches', *British Archaeology* 34, 6–7.

Gerrard, C.M. (2003) *Medieval Archaeology: Understanding Traditions and Contemporary Approaches*, Routledge, London.

Gerrard, C.M. and Clements, D. (1994) *Cirencester Park, Cirencester, Gloucestershire. History, Archaeology, Ecology*, English Heritage Survey Grant for Presentation, 2 vols, unpublished typescript.

Gerrard, C.M., Gutiérrez, A., Hurst, J.G. and Vince, A.G. (1995) 'A guide to Spanish medieval pottery', in *Spanish Medieval Ceramics in Spain and the British Isles*, eds C.M. Gerrard, A. Gutiérrez and A. Vince, British Archaeological Reports International Series 610, Oxford, 281–96.

Gidney, L. (2004) *Clarendon Palace: Animal Bones from the Spoil Heaps*, unpublished typescript report.

Gingell, C. (1984) *The Marlborough Downs: A Later Bronze Age Landscape and its Origins*. Wiltshire Archaeological and Natural History Society Monograph 1, Wiltshire Archaeological and Natural History Society, Devizes.

Goodall, A. (2005) *Objects of Copper and Lead Alloy from Clarendon Park*, unpublished typescript report.

Goodall, A., Hinton, D.A. and James, T.B. (1988) 'Copper-alloy objects', in *Clarendon Palace. The History and Archaeology of a Medieval Palace and Hunting Lodge near Salisbury, Wiltshire*, T.B. James and A.M. Robinson, Reports of the Research Committee of the Society of Antiquaries of London XLV, Society of Antiquaries and Thames and Hudson, London, 201–7.

Goodall, I. (1988) 'Iron objects', in *Clarendon Palace. The History and Archaeology of a Medieval Palace and Hunting Lodge near Salisbury, Wiltshire*, T.B. James and A.M. Robinson, Reports of the Research Committee of the Society of Antiquaries of London XLV, Society of Antiquaries and Thames and Hudson, London, 208–23.

Goodall, I. (2005) *The Iron Objects from Clarendon Park*, unpublished typescript report.

Gover, J.E.B., Mawer, A. and Stenton, F.M. (1939) *The Place-Names of Wiltshire*, English Place-Name Society vol. 16, 375–6.

Graham, A. and Newman, C. (1993) 'Recent excavations of Iron Age and Romano-British enclosures in the Avon Valley, Wilts.', *Wiltshire Archaeological Magazine* 86, 45–50.

Green, M. (2000) *A Landscape Revealed: 10,000 Years on a Chalkland Farm*, Tempus, Stroud.

Griffiths, A. (1998) *The Print in Stuart England 1603–1689*, British Museum Press, London.

Grose, F. (1777) *The Antiquities of England and Wales. Volume V*, published for S. Hooper, London.

Grundy, G.B. (1939) 'The ancient woodlands of Wiltshire', *Wiltshire Archaeological Magazine* 48, 530–98.

Guido, M. and Smith, I.F. (1982) 'Figsbury Rings: a reconsideration of the inner enclosure', *Wiltshire Archaeological Magazine* 76, 21–5.

Gutiérrez, A. (2000) *Mediterranean Pottery in Wessex Households (Twelfth to Seventeenth Centuries)*, British Archaeological Reports British Series 306, John and Erica Hedges, Oxford.

Gutiérrez, A. (2003) 'The Spanish jar', in *Aelfric's Abbey. Excavations at Eynsham Abbey, Oxfordshire 1989–92*, A. Hardy, A. Dodd and G.D. Keevill, Thames Valley

Landscapes vol. 15, Oxford Archaeological Unit, Oxford, 199–200.

Gutiérrez, A. (2004a) *Medieval and Later Pottery from Recent Fieldwork at Clarendon*, unpublished typescript report.

Gutiérrez, A. (2004b) *Kiln Material from Recent Fieldwork at Clarendon*, unpublished typescript report.

Gutiérrez, A. (2004c) *Roof Tile from Recent Fieldwork at Clarendon*, unpublished typescript report.

Gutiérrez, A. (2004d) *Bone Objects from Recent Fieldwork at Clarendon*, unpublished typescript report.

Habbakuk, J. (1978) 'The land-settlement and restoration of Charles II', *Transactions of the Royal Historical Society*, Fifth Series **28**, 201–22.

Hadfield, M. (1988) *The English Landscape Garden*, Shire Publications, Aylesbury.

Hammond, J. J. (1914–16) 'Clarendon Park', *Wiltshire Notes and Queries* **8**, March 1914.

Harding, A. F. and Lee, G. E. (1987) *Henge Monuments and Related Sites of Great Britain. Air Photographic Evidence and Catalogue*, British Archaeological Reports British Series 175, Oxford.

Harding, D. W., Blake, I. M. and Reynolds, P. J. (1993) *An Iron Age Settlement in Dorset: Excavation and Reconstruction*, University of Edinburgh, Edinburgh.

Harding, P. A. and Bridgland, D. R. (1998) 'Pleistocene deposits and Palaeolithic implements at Godolphin School, Milford Hill, Salisbury', *Wiltshire Archaeological Magazine* **91**, 1–10.

Harding, P. T. and Rose, F. (1986) *Pasture-woodlands in Lowland Britain: A Review of their Importance for Wildlife Conservation*, Institute of Terrestrial Ecology, Abbots Ripton.

Hare, J. (1991) 'The growth of the roof-tile industry in late medieval Wessex', *Medieval Archaeology* **35**, 86–103.

Hare, J. (1994) 'Agriculture and rural settlement in the chalklands of Wiltshire and Hampshire from c. 1200–c. 1500', in *The Medieval Landscape of Wessex*, eds M. Aston and C. Lewis, Oxbow Monograph 46, Oxbow Books, Oxford, 159–79.

Harris, R. W. (1983) *Clarendon and the English Revolution*, Chatto and Windus, London.

Harvey, J. (1990) *Medieval Gardens*, Batsford, London.

Hatcher, H. (1845) 'Proceedings of the Committee', *Archaeological Journal* **2**, 86.

Haycock, D. B. (2002) *William Stukeley. Science, Religion and Archaeology in Eighteenth-Century England*, Boydell Press, Woodbridge.

Henisch, B. A. (1999) *The Medieval Calendar Year*, Pennsylvania State University Press, Pennsylvania.

Hermann, F. (1980) *Sotheby's*, Chatto and Windus, London.

Hidden, N. (1988) 'A riotous affray in Salisbury in 1610', *Wiltshire Archaeological Magazine* **82**, 99–114.

Higham, R. A., Allan, J. P., Blaylock, S. R. (1982) 'Excavations at Okehampton Castle, Devon: part 2: the bailey', *Proceedings of the Devon Archaeological Society* **40**, 19–151.

Hinton, D. A. (1988) 'Silver-gilt objects', in *Clarendon Palace. The History and Archaeology of a Medieval Palace and Hunting Lodge near Salisbury, Wiltshire*, T. B. James and A. M. Robinson, Reports of the Research Committee of the Society of Antiquaries of London XLV, Society of Antiquaries and Thames and Hudson, London, 200–1.

Hinton, D. A. (2004) *Gold and Gilt, Pots and Pins: Possessions and People in Medieval Britain*, Oxford University Press, Oxford.

Hooke, D. (1998a) *The Landscape of Anglo-Saxon England*, Leicester University Press, London.

Hooke, D. (1998b) 'Medieval forests and parks in southern and central England', in *European Woods and Forests. Studies in Cultural History*, ed. C. Watkins, CAB International, Wallingford, 19–32.

Hooper, N. and Thorn, F. eds (1989) *The Wiltshire Domesday*, Alecto Historical Editions, London.

Hughes, H. and Lewis, P. (1988) 'Paint palettes', in *Clarendon Palace. The History and Archaeology of a Medieval Palace and Hunting Lodge near Salisbury, Wiltshire*, T. B. James and A. M. Robinson, Reports of the Research Committee of the Society of Antiquaries of London XLV, Society of Antiquaries and Thames and Hudson, London, 258–60.

Hume, D. (1826) *The History of England*, W. Pickering, London.

Humphrey, C. and Hugh-Jones, S. ed. (1992) *Barter, Exchange and Value. An Anthropological Approach*, Cambridge University Press, Cambridge.

Hunnisett, R. F. (1981) *Wiltshire Coroners Bills 1752–96*, Wiltshire Records Series vol. 36 for 1980, Wiltshire Records Society, Devizes.

Hutton, R. (1985) *The Restoration: A Political and Religious History of England and Wales, 1658–1667*, Clarendon Press, Oxford.

Hutton, R. (1989) *Charles II*, Clarendon Press, Oxford.

Hyland, A. (1999) *The Horse in the Middle Ages*, Stroud, Sutton.

Jackson, J. E. (1884) 'Notes on the border of Wilts and Hants', *Wiltshire Archaeological Magazine* **21**, 330–54.

Jacques, D. (2004) *Fish Remains from Clarendon Palace*, unpublished typescript report.

James, T. B. (1983) *Southampton Sources 1086–1900*, Southampton Records Series **24**, Southampton University Press, Southampton.

James, T. B. (1989) 'Visitors to Coombe Bissett and Clarendon Palace, 1930–1939', *Hatcher Review* **28**, 407–15.

James, T. B. (1990) *The Palaces of Medieval England*, Seaby, London.

James, T. B. (2001) 'Le palais Anglais: le terme *palatium* et sa signification dans l'Angleterre médiévale (1000–1600)', in *Aux Marches du Palais: qu'est-ce-qu'un palais médiéval? Données historiques et archéologiques*, ed. A. Renoux, Universitie du Maine, Le Mans, 135–43.

James, T. B., Blunt C. E. and King, A. (1988) 'Coins, jettons and coronation medallion', in *Clarendon Palace. The History and Archaeology of a Medieval Palace and Hunting Lodge near Salisbury, Wiltshire*, T. B. James and A. M. Robinson, Reports of the Research Committee of the Society of Antiquaries of London XLV, Society of Antiquaries and Thames and Hudson, London, 197–200.

James, T. B., Green, G. and Tatton-Brown, T. (2005) *Clarendon Palace: Stonework from Site and Spoil*, draft unpublished typescript report.

James, T. B. and Knight, B. (1988) 'Lead and lead-alloy objects', in *Clarendon Palace. The History and Archaeology of a Medieval Palace and Hunting Lodge near Salisbury, Wiltshire*, T. B. James and A. M. Robinson, Reports of the Research Committee of the Society of Antiquaries of London XLV, Society of Antiquaries and Thames and Hudson, London, 224–9.

James, T. B. and Robinson, A. M. (1988) *Clarendon Palace. The History and Archaeology of a Medieval Palace and Hunting Lodge near Salisbury, Wiltshire*, Reports of the Research Committee of the Society of Antiquaries of London XLV, Society of Antiquaries and Thames and Hudson, London.

Johnson, M. (2002) *Behind the Castle Gate. From Medieval to Renaissance*, Routledge, London and New York.

Jones, O. and Cloke, P. (2002) *Tree Cultures. The Place of Trees and Trees in their Place*, Berg, Oxford.

Jones, W. H. (1862) 'The Wiltshire possessions of the Abbess of Shaftesbury', *Wiltshire Archaeological Magazine* 7, 278–301.

Kelly (1915; 1931) *Directories, Wiltshire*, Kelly's Directory, London.

Kelly (1939–40) *Directory, Southampton*, Kelly's Directory, London.

Kerry, Earl of (1922) 'Kings Bowood Park [No I]', *Wiltshire Archaeological Magazine* **41**, 407–23.

King, A., incorporating reports by the late J. Wilfrid Jackson and Don Bramwell (1988) 'Animal bones and shells', in *Clarendon Palace. The History and Archaeology of a Medieval Palace and Hunting Lodge near Salisbury, Wiltshire*, T. B. James and A. M. Robinson, Reports of the Research Committee of the Society of Antiquaries of London XLV, Society of Antiquaries and Thames and Hudson, London, 260–4.

King Alfred's College Archaeological Consultancy (KACAC) (1996) *Clarendon Park, Salisbury Wiltshire. Archaeology, History and Ecology*, English Heritage Survey Grant for Presentation, 2 vols, unpublished typescript, King Alfred's College, Winchester.

King Alfred's College Archaeological Consultancy (KACAC) (1998) *Clarendon Park, Salisbury Wiltshire. Historic Landscape Management Plan*, unpublished typescript, King Alfred's College, Winchester.

Kingsley, N. (1989) *The Country Houses of Gloucestershire, Volume 1, 1500–1660*, N. Kingsley, Cheltenham.

Kinnes, I. A (1992) *Non-Megalithic Long Barrows and Allied Structures in the British Neolithic*, British Museum Occasional Papers 52, Department of Prehistoric and Romano-British Antiquities, London.

Kirkby, K. J. and Drake, C. M. (eds) *Dead Wood Matters: The Ecology and Conservation of Saproxylic Invertebrates in Britain*, English Nature Science Series 7, English Nature, Peterborough.

Kite, E. (1908) 'Wiltshire topography [1659–1843] with some notes on the late Sir Thomas Phillipps, and his historical collections for the county', *Wiltshire Notes and Queries* **6** (December 1908), 144–161.

Knapp, B. ed. (1992) *Archaeology, Annales, and Ethnohistory*, New Directions in Archaeology, Cambridge University Press, Cambridge.

Knowles, D. and Hadcock, N. (1953) *Medieval Religious Houses. England and Wales*, Longmans, London.

Knyff, L. (1707) *Britannia Illustrata*, D. Mortier, London.

Landsberg, S. (n.d., c. 1995) *The Medieval Garden*, British Museum Press, London.

Larson, W. R. (2002) 'The role of patronage and audience in the cults of Sts Margaret and Marina of Antioch', in *Gender and Holiness. Men, Women and Saints in Late Medieval Europe*, eds S. J. E. Riches and S. Salih, Routledge, London, 23–35.

Latham, R. and Matthews, W. eds (1972) *The Diary of Samuel Pepys: A New and Complete Transcription*, G. Bell and Sons, London.

Lavallée, J. ed. (1854; facsimile 1992) *La Chasse de Gaston Phébus, Comte de Foix*, Lacour, Nîmes.

Lawrence, M. J. and Brown, R. W. (1974) *Mammals of Britain, Their Tracks, Trails and Signs*, Blandford, London.

Leeds, E. T. and Shortt, H. (1953) *Anglo-Saxon Cemetery at Petersfinger, near Salisbury Wilts*, South Wilts and Blackmore Museum, Salisbury.

Lees-Milne, J. (1962) *Earls of Creation*, H. Hamilton, London.

Lethaby, W. E. (1905) 'English primitives. The painted chamber and the early masters of the Westminster School', *Burlington Magazine* **VII**, 257–69.

Lever, C. (1979) *The Naturalised Animals of the British Isles*, Granada, St Albans.

Lewcun, M. (2004) *Clarendon – The Clay Tobacco Pipes*, unpublished typescript report.

Lewis, C. (1994) 'Patterns and processes in the medieval settlement of Wiltshire', in *The Medieval Landscape of Wessex*, eds M. Aston and C. Lewis, Oxbow Monograph 46, Oxbow Books, Oxford, 171–93.

Lewis, J. M. (1999) *The Medieval Tiles of Wales*, National Museum of Wales, Cardiff.

Liddiard, R. (2000) *Landscapes of Lordship. Norman Castles and the Countryside in Medieval Norfolk, 1066–1200*, British Archaeological Reports British Series 309, Oxford.

Light, J. (2003) 'The oyster shells and other molluscs', in *Aelfric's Abbey. Excavations at Eynsham Abbey, Oxfordshire 1989–92*, A. Hardy, A. Dodd and G. D. Keevill, Thames Valley Landscapes vol. 15, Oxford Archaeological Unit, Oxford, 1427–32.

Light, J. (2004) *Clarendon Palace. Analysis of Marine Molluscs from Spoil Heaps and Areas Excavated 2002–2003*, unpublished typescript report.

Lingard, J. (1855) *History of England*, vol. II, Charles Dolman, London.

Locker, A. (2001) *The Role of Stored Fish in England 900–1750 AD: The Evidence from Historical and Archaeological Data*, Chatham Publishing, Sofia.

Lovell, J., Hamilton-Dyer, S., Loader, E. and McKinley, J. (1999) 'Further investigations of an Iron Age and Romano-British farmstead on Cockey Down, near Salisbury', *Wiltshire Archaeological Magazine* **92**, 33–8.

Loveluck, C. (1998) 'A high-status Anglo-Saxon settlement at Flixborough, Lincolnshire', *Antiquity* **72**, 146–61.

Lucy, S. (2002) 'Burial practice in early medieval Eastern England: constructing local identities, deconstructing ethnicity', in *Burial in Early Medieval England and Wales*, eds S. Lucy and A. Reynolds, Society for Medieval Archaeology Monograph 17, Maney, Leeds, 72–87.

Lyne, M. A. B. and Jefferies, R. S. (1979) *The Alice Holt/Farnham Roman Pottery Industry*, CBA Research Report 30, Council for British Archaeology, London.

Lyon, W. R. (1930) *The Elevens of Great Schools*, Spottiswoode Ballantyne and Co, Eton.

Lyttleton, G. (1769–73) *The History of the Life of King Henry the Second, and of the Age in Which He Lived*, 6 vols, printed for J. Dodsley, London.

Maddicott, J. R. (1984) *Simon de Montfort*, Cambridge University Press, Cambridge.

Mandler, P. (1997) *The Fall and Rise of the Stately Home*, Yale University Press, London.

Manley, F. H. (1937) 'A list of the representatives in Parliament from 1295–1832 for the county and burroughs of Wiltshire as given in the Parliamentary Return of 1872', *Wiltshire Archaeological Magazine* **47**, 177–264.

Manning, R. B. (1993) *Hunters and Poachers. A Social and Cultural History of Unlawful Hunting in England 1485–1640*, Clarendon Press, Oxford.

Marks, R. (1988) 'The window glass', in *Clarendon Palace. The History and Archaeology of a Medieval Palace and Hunting Lodge near Salisbury, Wiltshire*, T. B. James and A. M. Robinson, Reports of the Research Committee of the Society of Antiquaries of London XLV, Society of Antiquaries and Thames and Hudson, London, 229–33.

Marks, R. (1996) 'The thirteenth-century glazing of Salisbury Cathedral', in *Medieval Art and Architecture at Salisbury Cathedral*, eds L. Keen and T. Cocke, The British Archaeological Association Conference Transactions 17, Maney, Leeds, 106–20.

Martin, P. (1984) *Pursuing Innocent Pleasures. The Gardening World of Alexander Pope*, Archon Books, Hamden (Conn).

May, M. R. (1998) *Winchester Houses and People: A Study Based on Probate Inventory Evidence*, unpublished PhD thesis, University of Southampton.

Mayr-Harting, H. M. and Moore, R. I. (1985) *Studies in Medieval History Presented to R. H. C. Davis*, Hambledon, London.

McCann, J. (1996) 'The influence of rodents on the design and construction of farm buildings in Britain to the mid-nineteenth century', *Journal of the Historic Farm Buildings Group* **10**, 1–28.

McOmish, D., Field, D. and Brown, G. (2002) *The Field Archaeology of the Salisbury Plain Training Area*, English Heritage, Swindon.

McWilliams, J. (1996) *From Medieval Deer Park to Post-Medieval Estate*, unpublished BA dissertation, King Alfred's College, Winchester.

Mepham, L. (2000a) 'The pottery', in 'Excavations at Ivy Street and Brown Street, Salisbury', ed. M. Rawlings, *Wiltshire Archaeological Magazine* **93**, 20–62.

Mepham, L. (2000b) 'Medieval pottery', in *Archaeological Investigations on the A34 Newbury Bypass, Berkshire/Hampshire, 1991–7: Technical Reports*, M. Allen, P. Andrews, P. S. Bellamy, N. Cooke, J. Ede, R. Gale, S. E. James, E. Loader, R. I. McPhail, L. Mepham, F. Raymond, R. S. Smith and S. F. Wyles, Trust for Wessex Archaeology, Salisbury, 52–66.

Merriman, R. W. (1885) 'Extracts from the records of the Wiltshire Quarter Sessions', *Wiltshire Archaeological Magazine* **22**, 24.

Mertes, K. (1988) *The English Noble Household, 1250–1600. Family, Sexuality and Social Relations in Past Times*, Basil Blackwell, Oxford.

Miles, D. and Bridge, M. (2004) *Interim Dendrochronology Report*, unpublished typescript report.

Moore, C. N. and Algar, D. J. (1968) 'Saxon 'grass-tempered ware' and Mesolithic finds from Petersfinger, Laverstock', *Wiltshire Archaeological Magazine* **63**, 103–5.

Moore, N.J. (1991) 'Brick', in *English Medieval Industries. Craftsmen, Techniques, Products*, eds J. Blair and N. Ramsey, Hambledon Press, London, 211–36.

Morgan, F.W. (1935) 'Woodland in Wiltshire at the time of Domesday Book', *Wiltshire Archaeological Magazine* **47**, 25–33.

Mowl, T. and Earnshaw, B. (1985) *Trumpet at a Distant Gate: The Lodge as Prelude to the Country House*, Waterstone, London.

Muir, R. and Muir, N. (1987) *Hedgerows: Their History and Wildlife*, Michael Joseph, London.

Musty, J.W.G. (1961–3) 'Excavations and fieldwork in Wiltshire, 1961; Clarendon Park (SU/182302)', *Wiltshire Archaeological Magazine* **58**, 247.

Musty, J.W.G. (1986) 'Deer coursing at Clarendon Palace and Hampton Court', *Antiquaries Journal* **66**, 131–2.

Musty, J., Algar, D.J. and Ewence, P.F. (1969) 'The medieval pottery kilns at Laverstock, near Salisbury, Wiltshire', *Archaeologia* **102**, 83–150.

Musty, J., Algar, D., Gerrard, C.M. and Hadley, J. (2001) 'Pottery, tile and brick', in *Salisbury and South Wiltshire Museum. Medieval Catalogue Part 3*, ed. P. Saunders, Salisbury and South Wiltshire Museum, Salisbury, 132–212.

Neal, D.S. (1971) 'Excavations at the palace and priory of King's Langley', *Hertfordshire Archaeology* **3**, 31–72.

Neil, B. (1993) *The Possession of Delia Sutherland*, Bloomsbury, London.

Nicholas, D. (1955) *Mr Secretary Nicholas (1593–1669). His Life and Letters*, Bodley Head, London.

Nichols, J. (1788) *The Progresses and Public Processions of Queen Elizabeth*. Volume I, printed by and for the editor, Printer to the Society of Antiquaries of London, London.

Noel, E.B. (1926) *Winchester College Cricket*, Williams and Norgate, London.

Ogle, O. and Bliss, W.A. with Coxe, H.O. (1872) *Calendar of the Clarendon State Papers Preserved in the Bodleian Library. Volume I to January 1649*, Clarendon Press, Oxford.

Ollard, R.L. (1987) *Clarendon and His Friends*, Hamish Hamilton, London.

Palmer, R. (1984) *Danebury: An Iron Age Hillfort in Hampshire. An Air Photographic Interpretation of its Environs*, Supplementary series 6, Royal Commission on Historical Monuments (England), London.

Partridge, E. (1927) *The Three Wartons*, Scholartis Press, London.

Pearce, J. (2000) 'Burial, society and context in the provincial Roman world', in *Burial, Society and Context in the Roman World*, eds J. Pearce, M. Millett and M. Struck, Oxbow Books, Oxford, 1–12.

Pearce, J.E., Vince A.G. and Jenner, M.A. (1985) *A Dated Type-Series of London Medieval Pottery, Part 2: London-Type Ware*, London and Middlesex Archaeological Society Special Paper 6, London and Middlesex Archaeological Society, London.

Pearsall, D. and Salter, E. (1973) *Landscapes and Seasons of the Medieval World*, Paul Elek, London.

Pettigrew, T.J. (1859) 'On the ancient royal palace of Clarendon', *Journal of the British Archaeological Association* **15**, 246–90.

Pevsner, N. (1960) *The Buildings of England. Buckinghamshire*, Penguin, Harmondsworth.

Pevsner, N., revised by B. Cherry (1975) *The Buildings of England. Wiltshire*, Penguin, Harmondsworth.

Pevsner, N. and Nairn, I. (1965) *The Buildings of England. Sussex*, Penguin, Harmondsworth.

Pevsner, N. and Sherwood, J. (1974) *The Buildings of England. Oxfordshire*, Penguin, Harmondsworth.

Phillipps, T. (1833) 'Survey of the manor and forest of Clarendon, Wiltshire in 1272', *Archaeologia* **25**, 1–10.

Piggott, S. (1945–7) 'An early Bronze Age vessel from Ashley Hill near Salisbury', *Wiltshire Archaeological Magazine* **51**, 384–5.

Pitt, J.M.A. (1999) *Wiltshire Minster Parochiae and West Saxon Ecclesiastical Organisation*, unpublished PhD thesis, University of Southampton.

Platt, C. (1994) *The Great Rebuildings of Tudor and Stuart England. Revolutions in Architectural Taste*, UCL Press, London.

Pluskowski, A. (forthcoming) *Wolves and the Wilderness in the Middle Ages*, Boydell Press, Woodbridge.

Pollard, J. and Reynolds, A. (2002) *Avebury: The Biography of a Landscape*, Tempus, Stroud.

Poole, A.L. (1954) *From Domesday to Magna Carta*, Oxford History of England, Oxford.

Prestwich, M. (1988) *Edward I*, Methuen, London.

Prince, H.C. (1989) 'The changing rural landscape, 1750–1850', in *The Agrarian History of England and Wales. Volume VI 1750–1850*, ed. G.E. Mingay, Cambridge University Press, Cambridge, 7–83.

Pugh, R.B. and Crittall, E. eds (1956) *Victoria History of the Counties of England. A History of Wiltshire*, vol. III, Institute of Historical Research and Oxford University Press, London.

Pugh R.B. and Crittall E. eds (1957) *Victoria History of the Counties of England. A History of Wiltshire*, vol. I, Institute of Historical Research and Oxford University Press, London.

Pugh R.B. and Crittall E. eds (1959) *Victoria History of the Counties of England. A History of Wiltshire*, vol. IV, Institute of Historical Research and Oxford University Press, London.

Rackham, O. (1976) *Trees and Woodland in the British Landscape*, Dent and Sons, London.

Rackham, O. (1980) *Ancient Woodland: Its History, Vegetation and Uses in England*, Arnold, London.

Rackham, O. (1986) *The History of the Countryside*, Dent, London.

Rackham, O. (1989) *The Last Forest. The Story of Hatfield Forest*, J. M. Dent/Phoenix Press, London.

Rackham, O. (1994) *The Illustrated History of the Countryside*, Weidenfeld and Nicolson, London.

Rahtz, P. A. (1979) *The Saxon and Medieval Palaces at Cheddar*, British Archaeological Reports British Series 65, Oxford.

Ravenhill, W. W. (1872) 'Records of the Rising in the West AD 1655', *Wiltshire Archaeological Magazine* 13, 119–88, 252–74.

Rawlings, N. and Fitzpatrick, A. P. (1996) 'Prehistoric sites and a Romano-British settlement at Butterfield Down, Amesbury', *Wiltshire Archaeological Magazine* 89, 1–43.

Redon, O., Sabban, F. and Serventi, S. (1998) *The Medieval Kitchen: Recipes from France and Italy*, University of Chicago Press, London.

Reynolds, A. (2002) 'Burials, boundaries and charters in Anglo-Saxon England: a reassessment', in *Burial in Early Medieval England and Wales*, eds S. Lucy and A. Reynolds, Society for Medieval Archaeology Monograph 17, Maney, Leeds, 171–94.

Richardson, A. (2003a) 'Gender and space in English royal palaces c. 1160 – c. 1547: a study in access analysis and imagery', *Medieval Archaeology* 47, 131–66.

Richardson, A. (2003b) *The Medieval Palace, Park and Forest of Clarendon, Wiltshire, c. 1130–c. 1650*, unpublished PhD thesis, University of Southampton.

Richardson, A. (2004) *Clarendon. Report on the Medieval Floor Tiles Found at the Palace Site and Elsewhere in the Medieval Deerpark*, unpublished typescript report.

Richardson, A. (2005) *The Forest, Park and Palace of Clarendon, c. 1200–c. 1650. Reconstructing an Actual, Conceptual and Documented Wiltshire Landscape*, British Archaeological Reports British Series 387, Oxford.

Rinaker, C. (1916) *Thomas Warton: A Biographical and Critical Study*, University of Illinois Studies in Language and Literature, University of Illinois, Urbana.

Roberts, E. (1995) 'Edward III's lodge at Odiham, Hampshire', *Medieval Archaeology* 39, 91–106.

Roberts, J. (1997) *Royal Landscape. The Gardens and Parks of Windsor*, Yale University Press/Hawthornden Trust, New Haven and London.

Robertson, J. C. (1877) *Materials for the History of Thomas Becket, Archbishop of Canterbury*. Volume 3, Rerum Britannicarum Medii Aevi Scriptores, Longmans, London.

Robinson, A. M. (1988) 'Pottery and roof tiles', in *Clarendon Palace. The History and Archaeology of a Medieval Palace and Hunting Lodge near Salisbury, Wiltshire*, T. B. James and A. M. Robinson, Reports of the Research Committee of the Society of Antiquaries of London XLV, Society of Antiquaries and Thames and Hudson, London, 169–93.

Round, J. H. (1909) *Feudal England*, S. Sonnenschein, London.

Royal Commission on the Historical Monuments of England (1987) *Churches of South-East Wiltshire*, HMSO, London.

Royal Commission on the Historical Monuments of England (1993) *The Houses of Salisbury Close*, HMSO, London.

Royal Commission on the Historical Mouments of England (1996) *Emergency Report on Interior Discoveries in Clarendon Mansion House, June 1996*, unpublished typescript by B. V. Jones.

Rutherfurd, E. (1987) *Sarum*, Century Hutchinson, London.

Rymer, T. ed. (1816) *Foedera*, Record Commission, London.

Salisbury & South Wilts Museum Annual Report 1960–1, Bennett Brothers (Journal Newspapers) Ltd, Salisbury.

Salzman, L. F. (1952; 2nd edn 1967) *Building in England Down to 1540. A Documentary History*, Clarendon Press, Oxford.

Saunders, A. (forthcoming) *Launceston Castle*, Society for Medieval Archaeology Monograph, Maney, Leeds.

Saunders, C. (1993) *The Forest of Medieval Romance. Avernus, Broceliande, Arden*, D. S. Brewer, Cambridge.

Saunders, P. (1986) 'A medieval horse pendant from Clarendon Park', *Wiltshire Archaeological Magazine* 80, 224–5.

Saunders, P. (1991) 'Review', *Wiltshire Archaeological Magazine* 84, 155–7.

Scattergood, V. J. (1983) 'Literary culture at the court of Richard II', in *English Court Culture in the Later Middle Ages*, V. J. Scattergood and J. W. Sherborne, Duckworth, London, 29–44.

Scott, R. (2004) *Prehistoric Flint from Clarendon Park*, unpublished typescript report.

Sedgwick, R. (1970) *The History of Parliament: The House of Commons 1715–1754*, vol. I, HMSO, London.

Sekules, V. (2003) 'Art and society', in *A Companion to Britain in the Later Middle Ages*, ed. S. H. Rigby, Blackwell Publishers Ltd, Oxford, 472–96.

Sellar, W. C. and Yeatman, R. J. (1930) *1066 And All That*, Methuen.

Serovayskaya, V. (1998) 'Royal forests in England and their income in the budget of the feudal economy from the mid twelfth to the early thirteenth centuries', in *European Woods and Forests. Studies in Cultural History*, ed. C. Watkins, CAB International, Wallingford, 33–7.

Sherwood, J. and Pevsner, N. (1999) *Oxfordshire*, Penguin, London.

Short, B. (2000) 'Forests and wood-pasture in lowland England', in *The English Rural Landscape*, ed. J. Thirsk, Oxford University Press, Oxford, 122–49.

Sidney, P. ed. Skeltkowicz, V. (1987) *The Countess of Pembroke's Arcadia (New Arcadia)*, Clarendon Press, Oxford.

Simons, J. (1993) *A History of Cricket in Hampshire, 1760–1914*, Hampshire Paper 4, Hampshire County Council, Winchester.

Simpson, D. D. A. (1968) 'Timber mortuary houses and earthen long barrows', *Antiquity* **42**, 142–4.

Simpson, G. (1996) 'Documentary and dendrochronological evidence for the building of Salisbury Cathedral', in *Medieval Art and Architecture at Salisbury Cathedral*, eds L. Keen and T. Cocke, The British Archaeological Association Conference Transactions 17, Maney, Leeds, 10–20.

Slocombe, P. M. (1989) *Wiltshire Farm Buildings 1500–1900*, Devizes Books Press for the Wiltshire Buildings Record, Devizes.

Speake, J. (1994) *Dictionary of Symbols in Christian Art*, Dent, London.

Spencer, B. (1998) *Pilgrim Souvenirs and Secular Badges*, Medieval Finds from Excavations in London: 7, The Stationery Office, London.

Stagg, D. J. (1989) 'Silvicultural inclosure in the New Forest to 1780', *Hampshire Field Club and Archaeological Society* **45**, 133–46.

Staniland, K. (1991) *Medieval Craftsmen: Embroiderers*, British Museum Press, London.

Steane, J. M. (1988) 'The royal fishponds of medieval England', in *Medieval Fish, Fisheries and Fishponds in England*, ed. M. Aston, British Archaeological Reports British Series 182 (i), Oxford, 39–68.

Steane, J. M. (1999) *The Archaeology of the Medieval English Monarchy*, Routledge, London.

Steane J. M. (2001) *The Archaeology of Power: England and Northern Europe AD 800–1600*, Tempus, Stroud.

Stephen, L. and Lee, S. (1891–96) *Dictionary of National Biography*, Smith, Elder and Co., London.

Stocker, D. (2000) 'The Great Tower and Henry III's Great Hall', in *Ludgershall Castle. A Report on the Excavations by Peter Addyman 1964–72*, ed. P. Ellis, Wiltshire Archaeological and Natural History Society Monograph Series 2, English Heritage and WANHS, Devizes, 83–96.

Stocker, D. and Stocker, M. (1996) 'Sacred profanity: the theology of rabbit breeding and the symbolic landscape of the warren', *World Archaeology* **28(2)**, 265–72.

Stukeley, W. (1724; 2nd edn 1776) *Itinerarium Curiosum. The Second Edition with Large Additions*, Baker and Leigh, London.

Sweet, R. (2004) *Antiquaries. The Discovery of the Past in Eighteenth-Century Britain*, Hambledon, London.

Taigel, A. and Williamson, T. (1993) *Parks and Gardens*, Batsford, London.

Tasker, E. G. (1993) *Encyclopedia of Medieval Church Art*, Batsford, London.

Tatton-Brown, T. (1996) 'The archaeology of the spire of Salisbury Cathedral', in *Medieval Art and Architecture at Salisbury Cathedral*, eds L. Keen and T. Cocke, The British Archaeological Association Conference Transactions 17, Maney, Leeds, 59–67.

Taylor, C. C. (2000) 'Medieval ornamental landscapes', *Landscapes* **1.1**, 38–55.

Taylor, C. C. (2005) 'Ravensdale Park, Derbyshire, and medieval deer coursing', *Landscape History* **26**, 37–58.

Thiebaux, M. (1967) 'The medieval chase', *Speculum* **42**, 260–74.

Thiebaux, T. (1974) *The Stag of Love. The Chase in Medieval Literature*, Cornell University Press, Ithaca and London.

Thirsk, J. (1984) *The Rural Economy of England*, Hambledon Press, London.

Thomas, K. (1983) *Man and the Natural World: Changing Attitudes in England 1500–1800*, Allen Lane, London.

Thompson, F. M. L. (1963) *English Landed Society in the Nineteenth Century*, Routledge, London.

Thompson, M. W. (1986) 'Associated monasteries and castles in the Middle Ages: A tentative list', *Archaeological Journal* **143**, 305–23.

Thorn, C. and Thorn, F. (1979) *Domesday Book. Wiltshire*, Phillimore, Chichester.

Thorn, F. (1989) 'Hundreds and wapentakes', in *The Wiltshire Domesday*, eds N. Hooper and F. Thorn, Alecto Historical Editions, London, 31–48.

Thorpe, I. J. (1984) 'Ritual, power and ideology: a reconstruction of Earlier Neolithic rituals in Wessex', in *Neolithic Studies: A Review of some Current Research*, eds R. Bradley and J. Gardiner, British Archaeological Reports British Series 133, Oxford, 41–60.

Thorpe, I. J. (1996) *The Origins of Agriculture in Europe*, Routledge, London.

Thurley, S. (1993) *The Royal Palaces of Tudor England: Architecture and Court Life, 1460–1547*, Yale University Press, New Haven.

Timby, J. (2004) *Clarendon Palace. Prehistoric and Roman Pottery Report*, unpublished typescript.

Tingle, M. (1991) *The Vale of the White Horse Survey: The Study of a Changing Landscape in the Clay Lowlands of Southern England from Prehistory to the Present*, Tempus Reparatum, Oxford.

Toulmin Smith, L. ed. (1907–10) *The Itinerary of John Leland In or About the Years 1535–43*, George Bell, London.

Trevelyan, G.M. (1926) *History of England*, Longman, London.

Trevor-Cox, H.B. (1947) 'Further notes on the manor of East Winterslow', *Wiltshire Archaeological Magazine* **51**, 18–23.

Trott, M. (1989) *Archaeological Excavation on the Route of the Cockey Down to Petersfinger Main Pipeline, near Salisbury, Wiltshire, Archaeological Excavations 1989*, unpublished client report, Wessex Archaeology.

Trott, M. (1991) 'Archaeological excavation on the route of the Cockey Down to Petersfinger main pipeline, near Salisbury, Wiltshire', *Wiltshire Archaeological Magazine* **84**, 117–19.

Tsouvalis, J. (2000) 'Socialised nature: England's royal and plantation forests', in *Cultural Turns/Geographical Turns: Perspectives on Cultural Geography*, eds I. Cook, D. Crouch, S. Naylor and J.R. Ryan, Prentice Hall, Harlow, 288–312.

Turle, R.C. (1998) *Clarendon Standing Buildings: An Evaluation of Standing Building Values and Management at Clarendon Park, Wiltshire*, unpublished MSc dissertation, Oxford Brookes University School of Planning and University of Oxford Department for Continuing Education.

Turner, G.J. ed. (1901) *Select Pleas of the Forest*, Publications of the Selden Society 13, Selden Society, London.

Turner, T.H. and Parker, J.H. (1851–9) *Some Account of English Domestic Architecture in England, vols I–III*, J.H. Parker, Oxford.

Tyers, I. (1999) *Tree-Ring Analysis of Three Buildings from the Clarendon Estate, Wiltshire*, unpublished ARCUS Project Report 429, June 1999.

Tyers, I. (2001) *Tree-Ring Analysis of Further Buildings on the Clarendon Estate, Wiltshire*, unpublished ARCUS Project Report 429a, August 2001.

Tyers, I. and Hibberd, H. (1993) 'List 53 – tree-ring dates from Museum of London Archaeology Service', *Vernacular Architecture* **23**, 50–54.

Vale, J. (1982) *Edward III and Chivalry. Chivalric Society and its Context 1270–1350*, Boydell Press, Woodbridge.

van Geersdaele, P.C. and Davison, S. (1975) 'The thirteenth-century tile-kiln from Clarendon Palace – its removal and reconstruction for exhibition', *Studies in Conservation* **20**, 158–68.

Wainwright, G., Donaldson, P., Longworth, I.H. and Swan, V. (1971) 'The excavation of prehistoric and Romano-British settlements near Durrington Walls, Wiltshire, 1970', *Wiltshire Archaeological Magazine* **66**, 78–128.

Wall, A.D. (1983) *Two Elizabethan Women: Correspondence of Joan and Maria Thynne 1575–1611*, Wiltshire Records Series vol. 38, Wiltshire Record Society, Devizes.

Warton, T. (1778–81) *The History of English Poetry from the Close of the Eleventh to the Commencement of the Eighteenth Century*, Ward, Lock and Tyler, London.

Watson, P.V. (1982) 'Man's impact on the chalklands: some new pollen evidence', in *Archaeological Aspects of Woodland Ecology*, eds M. Bell and S. Limbrey, British Archaeological Reports S146, Oxford, 75–92.

Watts, K. (1998) 'Some Wiltshire deer parks', *Wiltshire Archaeological Magazine* **91**, 90–102.

Webster, L. (2003) '*Aedeficia Nova*: treasures of Alfred's reign', in *Alfred the Great*, ed. T. Reuter, Ashgate, Aldershot, 79–103.

Webster, L. and Backhouse, J. eds (1991) *The Making of England, Anglo-Saxon Art and Culture AD 600–900*, British Museum Press, London.

Welch, M. (1985) 'Rural settlement patterns in the early and middle Anglo-Saxon periods', *Landscape History* **7**, 13–25.

Wessex Archaeology (1993) *The Southern Rivers Palaeolithic Project. Report no. 1, 1991–1992. The Upper Thames Valley, the Kennet Valley and the Solent Drainage System*, Wessex Archaeology, Salisbury.

Williams, H. (1997) 'Ancient landscapes and the dead: the reuse of prehistoric and Roman monuments as early Anglo-Saxon burial sites', *Medieval Archaeology* **41**, 1–31.

White, G.H. (1950) 'The Constitutio Domus Regis and the king's sport', *Antiquaries Journal* **30**, 52–128.

White, R.H. (1988) *Roman and Celtic Objects from Anglo-Saxon Graves. A Catalogue and Interpretation of their Use*, British Archaeological Reports British Series 191, Oxford.

Whitehead, P. (1952) *Cirencester Park: Historical Portraits and Family Possessions*, Woodchester.

Whitelock, D. ed. (1961) *The Anglo-Saxon Chronicle: A Revised Translation*, Eyre and Spottiswode, London.

Whitlock, R. (1955) *Salisbury Plain*, Robert Hale, London.

Whitlock, R. (1970) 'Clarendon: the vanished palace', *The Field*, 19 November.

Whittle, A. (1994) 'Excavations at Milbarrow Neolithic Chambered Tomb, Winterbourne Monkton, North Wiltshire', *Wiltshire Archaeological Magazine* **87**, 1–53.

Who's Who 1900 (1900) Adam and Charles Black, London.

Wickham, C. (1994) *Land and Power: Studies in Italian and European Social History, 400–1200*, British School at Rome, London.

Willan, T.S. (1937) 'Salisbury and the navigation of the Avon', *Wiltshire Archaeological Magazine* **47**, 592–4.

Williamson, T. (1995) *Polite Landscapes. Gardens and Society in Eighteenth-Century England*, Alan Sutton, Baltimore.

Willmott, H. 2004. *Clarendon: Report on Glass from Recent Work*, unpublished typescript.

Wilson, D. M. (1964) *Catalogue of Anglo-Saxon Ornamental Metalwork 700–1100 in the British Museum*, British Museum Press, London.

Wiltshire Buildings Record (1997a) *Queen Manor Farmhouse. Clarendon Park*, unpublished typescript by P. M. Slocombe.

Wiltshire Buildings Record (1997b) *Queen Manor Granary. Clarendon Park*, unpublished typescript by P. M. Slocombe.

Winder, J. M. (1983) 'The oysters', in *Excavations in Christchurch 1969–1980*, ed. K. S. Jarvis, Dorset Natural History and Archaeology Society Monograph Series 5, Dorset Natural History and Archaeology Society, Dorchester, 194–200.

Woolgar, C. M. ed. (1992) *Household Accounts from Medieval England (Part 1)*, Records of Social and Economic History, New Series 17, Oxford University Press for The British Academy, Oxford.

Woolgar, C. M. (1999) *The Great Household in Late Medieval England*, Yale University Press, New Haven and London.

Woolgar, C. M. (2001) 'Fast and feast: conspicuous consumption and the diet of the nobility in the fifteenth century', in *Revolution and Consumption in Late Medieval England*, ed. M. Hicks, Boydell Press, Woodbridge, 7–25.

Worden, B. (1978) *A Voyce from the Watchtower, 5. 1660–1662*, Camden 4th Series, 21.

Wyatt, J. (1870) 'Manufacture of gun-flints', in *Flint Chips, a Guide to Pre-Historic Archaeology as Illustrated by the Collection in the Blackmore Museum*, E. T. Stevens, Bell and Daldy, London, 578–90.

Yonge, C. M. (1883) *Cameos from English History*, Macmillan, London.

Young, A. (1987) *Tudor and Jacobean Tournaments*, George Phillips, London.

Young, C. J. (2000) *Excavations at Carisbrooke Castle, 1921–1996*, Wessex Archaeology Report 18, Salisbury.

Young, C. R. (1979) *The Royal Forests of Medieval England*, Leicester University Press, Leicester.

Zarnecki, G. *et al.* (1984) *English Romanesque Art, 1066–1200*, Arts Council of Great Britain in association with Weidenfeld and Nicolson, London.

Newspapers

Devizes Gazette
Salisbury Times and South Wiltshire Gazette
Salisbury (and Winchester) Journal

The Times
Wilts County Mirror and Express

Film, television and radio

An Unkindness of Ravens (ITV 1990)
Arthur (March 2002) BBC Religious Broadcasting, director Jean Paul Bragard.
Barry Lyndon (1975) director Stanley Kubrick.
Crown and Country (1998), Meridian, director Edward Windsor.

English Royalty (2002) Channel 4, Nigel Spivey.
History of Britain (2000) BBC 2, Simon Schama.
News from Split (March 1966) Nikolaus Pevsner, BBC Third Programme.
Only Fools and Horses (Christmas 1986) BBC 1.
The Day After the Fair (BBC 1987).

Index

Entries in bold refer to the Figures